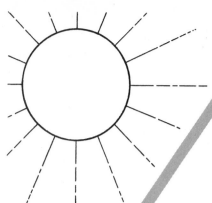

# Handbook of Vacation House Planning and Building

MORTIMER P. REED

PRENTICE-HALL INC., *Englewood Cliffs, New Jersey 07632*

*Library of Congress Cataloging in Publication Data*

REED, MORTIMER P
    Handbook of vacation house planning and building.

    Includes index.
    1. Summer homes—Design and construction.
I. Title.
TH4835.R43      690'.8'7     78-13549
ISBN 0-13-382770-4

© 1979 by Prentice-Hall, Inc., Englewood Cliffs, N.J. 07632

All rights reserved. No part of this book
may be reproduced in any form or
by any means without permission in writing
from the publisher.

Printed in the United States of America
10  9  8  7  6  5  4  3  2  1

Editorial/production supervision and
interior design by Virginia Huebner
Page layout by Jayne Conte
Cover and jacket design by Edsal Enterprise
Manufacturing buyer: Cathie Lenard

PRENTICE-HALL INTERNATIONAL, INC., *London*
PRENTICE-HALL OF AUSTRALIA PTY. LIMITED, *Sydney*
PRENTICE-HALL OF CANADA, LTD., *Toronto*
PRENTICE-HALL OF INDIA PRIVATE LIMITED, *New Delhi*
PRENTICE-HALL OF JAPAN, INC., *Tokyo*
PRENTICE-HALL OF SOUTHEAST ASIA PTE. LTD., *Singapore*
WHITEHALL BOOKS LIMITED, *Wellington, New Zealand*

*To Merry and Jerry, for whom I designed my
first vacation house. They liked it so
well they gave me my own key—
which didn't fit the lock.*

# Contents

## 15. *Trimming and Cabinetry*

## 16. *Protecting and Decorating Surfaces* 332

## 17. *Building Decks and Finishing the Site* 343

# Preface

This book assumes only one thing: that you would like to own a vacation house. It discusses the types of structures that might meet your needs. It tells how to determine what you can get for your vacation dollar. It guides you toward selecting a good site and a good floor plan. It gives you basic how-to information to build the house yourself, if you have the talent to use the necessary tools. It suggests how to coordinate your efforts with contractors if you want to do only part of the work yourself. It outlines the procedures to follow if you want to have the entire house built for you. It covers what to do before you build, while you build, and after you build.

Perhaps most important, the principles and procedures in the book will carry you from today's desire for a vacation house to tomorrow's enjoyment of it, and help you avoid the mistakes and headaches of less well-informed vacationers.

Those in the building industry who contributed to this book are too many to list. I am grateful to the dozens of local builders and building material suppliers who provided background data and verified facts. Contributors of photographs are credited with the individual illustrations, but special thanks go to the staffs of American Plywood Association and California Redwood Association for their efforts in making a good selection available. Equal thanks also go to Commercial Trades Institute for granting permission to use data, tables, and forms from their course in *Building Construction* which I wrote.

*Atlanta, Georgia*

MORTIMER P. REED

# Getting Yourself

# Organized

Building a vacation house is an emotional experience. It begins with the excitement of planning. Excitement turns into anticipation as the dream begins to take the shape of reality. In the end anticipation gives way to the pleasure of having your own home away from home.

Or it should. Yet because so much emotion and effort are involved, people often go at a vacation house project in the wrong way. And sometimes the final emotion is disappointment or sheer exhaustion.

This book gives you a practical method of organizing a vacation house project, from planning to moving in, to assure the most satisfying results possible—and without interfering with the emotional side of the experience.

By picking up this handbook, you showed your interest in having your own vacation house. The question is: what other steps have you taken? You probably fit into one of the following pictures:

- You have done nothing else yet; you are just toying with the idea of a vacation house.
- You want a vacation house, but don't know how to estimate how much it will cost you.
- You have picked out an area of the country where you want to build, but haven't looked for a site.
- You have already picked out or perhaps bought a site.

Only enough land was cleared to build this A-frame design and its access road. Because of heavy shade, glass areas are large. Flood lights at the roof peak illuminate the deck and parking area. *Photographer: Kelly Severns. Courtesy American Plywood Association.*

• You have seen plans for a vacation house you like, but don't yet have a site.

• You have already picked out a site and plan, but haven't selected a contractor.

• You are ready to build the house yourself—or at least do part of the work—and are looking for how-to help with construction procedures that you can clearly understand.

The fewer steps you have taken, the more useful this book can be to you, for the correct first step is one that many people bypass. That step is to analyze your desires and needs, to be analytical instead of emotional. You should look for the answers to three basic questions:

1. What do I want to build?
2. How much can I afford to spend?
3. Where do I want to build?

Begin by defining your dream. What does a vacation mean to the father of a family? What does it hold for the mother, for each child, and for any other relatives who will take vacations with you? What does each want from a vacation? What should a vacation house have—and not have—to satisfy these desires?

Part of the answer to the ideal vacation house lies in the word *vacation* itself. It comes from the Latin *vacatio,* which means *freedom from duty.* A vacation should bring a change of pace. If possible it should bring a change of place, too. But most of all it should permit a break in the day-to-day routine that everyone follows the rest of the year. Freedom from duty gives you the chance to do the things of which fond memories are made. The ideal vacation house is specifically planned for this leisure time, and not as a principal residence.

So analyze those desires. Get everyone in the family involved. Make a game of it. Perhaps you have played the game in which someone says a word and everyone else writes down the first thought that comes to mind. The thoughts written down are often quite varied, because each person relates his or her thinking to personal experiences.

There is one big advantage to planning as a family. When actual construction begins, everyone will be eager to pitch in and help with the work. But there is a possible disadvantage, too. If plans fall through, everyone is disappointed. Yet if your plans are solidly laid, the chances of their falling through are slight.

So start out by making a list. Figure 1-1 shows the type of list to make

**Figure 1-1.** On a blank sheet of lined paper list questions that must be resolved. Leave space for all members of the family to write in their choices. Post the list in a prominent place, such as the refrigerator door, where everyone can see it and add thoughts as they occur.

| | DAD | MOTHER | SUSAN | JACK | M.J. | AUNT MAE | CONSENSUS |
|---|---|---|---|---|---|---|---|
| *PREFERRED AREA* | | | | | | | |
| *Region* | | | | | | | |
| *State* | | | | | | | |
| *Specific Place* | | | | | | | |
| *Distance from Home* | | | | | | | |
| *SEASON OF USE* | | | | | | | |
| *Summer* | | | | | | | |
| *Winter* | | | | | | | |
| *All Year* | | | | | | | |
| *AMOUNT OF USE* | | | | | | | |
| *Weekend* | | | | | | | |
| *No. Weeks* | | | | | | | |
| *No. Months* | | | | | | | |
| *Season* | | | | | | | |
| *USAGE BY* | | | | | | | |
| *Family* | | | | | | | |
| *Guests and Relatives* | | | | | | | |
| *ACTIVITIES* | | | | | | | |
| | | | | | | | |
| | | | | | | | |
| *WHAT NOT TO DO* | | | | | | | |
| | | | | | | | |

and some of the questions that require thought in answering. Good planning isn't something you can do after dinner one evening. It's a process you keep going in the back of your mind and, as new thoughts occur to you, write them in. You can dream of the ideal vacation, but you achieve it only by relating those dreamt-of experiences to the pattern of your family life.

## LAYING THE GROUNDWORK

Obviously, the first point of agreement must be on where to spend your vacations. A cabin atop a mountain may be a great place for father to unwind. But if children don't have anyone to play with during the best days of summer, Father may not find the peace he is looking for.

On the other hand a house at the seashore may be the children's ideal, but Mother may not agree. Sand tracked into the house increases the time spent on housekeeping, and blowing sand adds to maintenance costs. You may have to compromise, weighing advantages against drawbacks, to find a location that has something for everyone.

Next, estimate how often you will use a vacation house, and how long at any one time. Your answers here will help you determine how far from your year-round home your vacation house can be. The shorter the distance, the more you will use it. A retreat used for a few days at a time—such as on weekends in summer and long weekends the rest of the year—should be within 150 miles, or roughly a three-hour drive. A retreat used less often, but for a week or more at a time, can be farther away, but should not be more than 400 miles, or roughly a day's drive. If you plan to use the retreat for a whole season, distance is not as important as a difference in region and climate. If you plan to do much of your own construction, build close by. The ratio of round-trip driving time to chunks of time available for building must be as low as possible.

How many people will be using the house at any one time? You should plan for your family first, of course. But the size and number of rooms you will need often depends on whether your guests are your child's friend for a weekend or a family of relatives for a week.

What will you do when you get there? A vacation house used primarily as a base for outdoor activities can be small, economical, and simply furnished. A vacation house that is more like a home away from home, and occupied most of the day, should have a few more comforts and a little more space. In any case, plan a comfortable place to sit and good light for every member of the family. It does rain some days, remember.

Think through what happens when you indulge in your favorite vacation activity. Even though this activity takes place outdoors, what indoor space do you need? What equipment or clothing must be stored, such as fishing tackle and hip boots? Where do you dry wet clothing, such as swim suits and hiking boots?

Where do you cull and wash the wild berries you've picked? Where do you skin rabbits or clean fish? Where do you oil ski boots?

These may seem to be minor questions, but they all relate to convenience. And in a vacation house, convenience is often more important than comfort. Convenience saves everyone time that they can spend as they like. There is no convenience if someone has to clean up someone else's mess on a vacation.

Which brings up the final question: what *don't* you want to do? Mother, for example, won't want to spend all day in the kitchen. There are some duties she can't be free of, but with careful planning she can reduce the time spent on meal preparation and housekeeping to a minimum.

Here's an example of good planning. A young couple wanted to build a vacation house on a small lake in New Hampshire. Their site had a gentle slope to the water, with a fine tree-framed view. The owner liked traditional architecture, and pressed hard for traditional double-hung windows with sixteen panes of glass in each window; this was the type of window he grew up with. After many hours of discussion with his architect, he grudgingly agreed to large, fixed, single-paned windows, each with a ventilating sash above and below. Today he understands why. He can look at the beautiful view without any little muntins in the way. Even more important, each window has only four corners that must be cleaned instead of sixty-four.

That is convenience that saves time.

As you make out your lists, think ahead to your needs five, ten, and twenty years from now. A child's interests at age five are quite different at ten and fifteen. A parent's interests at thirty-five are certainly a lot different at fifty-five. You can't predict authoritatively what things will be like many years ahead, but it's worth thinking about. Might you use a vacation house some day as a permanent home for retirement? The minor inconveniences you put up with in your forties can become major drawbacks in your sixties.

The lists you and your family make are extremely important as a guide when you take the next three steps in building a vacation house: developing a budget, selecting a site, and finding a plan that meets all your requirements.

## WHAT CAN YOU SPEND?

Money is a difficult subject to approach because there are so many variables. You can narrow the variables considerably by laying out a budget.

First determine how much ready cash you have available to put toward a vacation house. You must have enough to buy the site. Otherwise you will have trouble financing any construction. Then calculate how much you can pay per month, exclusive of utility bills and the cost of maintenance and repairs.

Here is a list of the items that should be included in most budgets. List them at the left of a sheet of paper. Then, as you proceed with your investigation, enter your estimate of costs in another column. In a third column keep a record of actual construction costs.

Raw land
Improvements to the land (grading, clearing, temporary access road)
Surveyor's fee (for a land survey)
Legal fees (title search, deed)
Real estate fees (site search)
Building materials
Tool rental
Casual labor (people you pay by the hour, week, or job to help you)
Contracted labor (contractors hired to do certain parts of the construction or all of it, including materials provided by the contractors)
Utility connections (fees or charges for extension of existing utility lines)
A well (drilling and piping to the house)
A septic system
A power generator (when electricity is not available near the site)
Appliances
Furnishings
Site finishing (landscaping, access road, walkways, outdoor living areas not part of construction)
Insurance (builder's, homeowner's)

Leave a few blank lines for other costs that may be peculiar to your site and house alone. They should be minor.

## WHAT CAN YOU GET FOR YOUR MONEY?

You can acquire a vacation house in two basic ways: you can buy it or build it. Either way you have additional choices. You can buy an existing house already built on its site. You can buy a factory-built home and set it up on your own site. You can buy a precut house and assemble it yourself on your site. Or you can build a new home yourself.

### An Existing House

This is the simplest and least time-consuming way to have a vacation retreat. Buying an existing house is not the least expensive way, but it has some important advantages. You know exactly what the final cost is, for example. By studying the finished house carefully you can see how good its quality is. You can see the views and surroundings in actuality, without having to visualize them. The existing house is ready for vacationing much sooner than one you build yourself. So if time is more of a problem than money, this may be the best route to take.

The points covered in Chapters 2 and 3 can serve as a guide to purchasing procedures and for judging how well the house will suit you.

You can find existing vacation houses in several ways. Watch the advertisements in local and area newspapers for leads to homes for sale by owners. When you talk to owners, always ask why they want to sell. The very reason they want to sell may be the reason you should not buy.

The safest way to buy is through local real estate agents who know the particular vacation area, know the owners in many instances, and know the market. You may pay a little more, because the owner will add at least part of the agent's fee into the selling price, but you have more assurance that you are paying a fair price.

Check the features of each house under consideration against your own list of the features you want, as recommended in this chapter. Check the site for good points and problems as outlined in Chapter 2. Compare the features inherent in a good vacation house (see Chapter 3) with the features of each house you look at. If the house meets these standards, you can buy yourself a good vacation house.

## Land

The cost of the site is included in the cost of an existing house. Under all other circumstances you must buy the site separately. There is no fixed ratio between the cost of vacation land and the cost of a vacation house. In isolated areas, the land may be as little as 5% of the combined cost of land and house. At a beach resort the land may be as much as 50% of the combined cost. In the cost of land, remember, you include all costs of preparing the site for building.

Real estate agents can help you estimate land costs, but you can usually get a better idea by talking with some of the insurance agents who insure vacation houses in the community. Ask each what percentage of the total selling price he did *not* insure in the last five contracts he wrote for new vacation houses. Suppose that the average selling price was $25,000, and the average insurance coverage was $20,000. The $5,000 difference is the value of the improved land, which is seldom insured. Therefore land value in this case is 20% of the total sale price. Based on your budget for a total vacation house package, you can estimate what you should pay for a site.

## A Factory-Built House

The terms used to describe various kinds of factory-built housing are confusing and have changed as the product itself has changed. But the two general categories have remained the same: the home that is manufactured with floors, walls, and roof already assembled at the factory, and the home with its structural components finished in the factory for final assembly on site.

The first completely assembled homes, built in the late 1940s and early 1950s, were usually called *trailers* and sometimes dubbed *house cars.* They were about 8 feet wide and 30 to 40 feet long. Outside they were sheathed in metal, and inside they were lined with plywood. They contained sparse furnishings and minimum bath and kitchen facilities. They were designed for mobility, and were

Tones of wood shingles and redwood siding blend with the sand of this exposed dune site. Tongue-like deck is accessible from interconnected living, sleeping, and service units of the house. *Architect: Edward Collins. Photographer: Lisanti. Courtesy California Redwood Association.*

towed from place to place. The wheels were rarely removed. A few of these units still exist in fishing camps and at construction sites.

Today's product, properly called a *mobile home,* is 12 or 14 feet in nominal width and 50 to 70 feet long. It may have a metal exterior, or it may be finished with wood siding and a shingle roof. The interior has carpet on the floor, acoustical tiles on the ceiling, and wood or gypsum panels on the walls. Each home comes completely furnished, with all appliances, furniture, and draperies. It is towed from factory to site by special truck. After it is positioned, the wheels and towing hitch may be removed.

At the site the mobile home is jacked onto supports. These supports are usually stacks of concrete blocks placed beneath the steel I-beam undercarriage at specified intervals. The home is then anchored both to the supports and the ground with strapping and anchor bolts to hold it firmly during high winds.

Each home comes with built-in connections for electric power, water, waste, and the fuel you intend to use for heating and cooking. Local utility companies complete the connections.

Mobile homes have several advantages. Costs are reasonable. They range from about $10 to $15 per square foot of interior space, furnished. This price also includes the work of setting up and leveling the home on your site. As owner, you must prepare the area of the site where you want to place the home, as well as the access to it. You pay the costs of a well and septic tank, and piping to the connections at the home. If public water and sewer lines are available, you may have to pay a small connection charge.

Mobile homes are ready almost immediately for occupancy. It takes only one day of good weather to set up a home and connect utilities.

Financing is fairly simple. You can finance a mobile home through the dealer, or you can arrange your own financing through some banks and savings and loan institutions. Mobile homes are financed like automobiles—so much as a down payment and so much a month. The minimum down payment is seldom over 20% of the sale price, and monthly payments can be spread over at least five years.

Mobile homes require little maintenance. Exterior and interior materials are prefinished. The major items of care are periodic washing, tightening of trim and anchor straps, and removal of debris from the roof. Interior surfaces require the same care as the surfaces in an ordinary house. Most other maintenance steps are standard procedure for any home—lubricating door and window parts, caulking joints, inspecting fuel and water lines, and cleaning exhaust fans and furnace parts.

One important maintenance step, however, is peculiar to mobile homes—checking its level. As the ground thaws in spring and freezes in winter, the home's supports will rise or fall slightly. Mobile homes must be kept level at all times, or maintenance problems can be severe and expensive. Each manufacturer provides a homeowner's manual that tells how to level a home, what other maintenance is required, and when to do the work.

Mobile homes do have some disadvantages as vacation homes. First, make sure that local ordinances do not prevent you from placing a mobile home on your site. In some areas they are allowed only in mobile home parks.

Second, before you buy either a site or mobile home, look over the site with your dealer. Mobile homes move easily along highways, but they are awkward to move into position on a sloping or heavily wooded site. The cost of clearing and grading for access to the selected location could quickly eat up any savings in the cost of the home itself.

Third, few mobile homes are designed specifically for vacation housing. You can get rustic exteriors that blend into vacation sites. But the interior layout is still that of a standard mobile home—with comparatively small glass areas, cramped traffic patterns, and conventional interior materials.

*Temporary Quarters.* If you intend to build your own vacation house, a mobile home makes an excellent temporary home on the site. It affords you the opportunity to see the site at all seasons and gives you added time to make decisions on the details of the house you build. It gives you a place to live in comfort while construction is under way. With good planning you can sink a well, install a septic tank, and bring in power lines for your mobile vacation home, then simply transfer these connections to your permanent home when it is finished.

A used mobile home can serve temporarily as well as a new one. But used mobile homes in good condition are hard to find, especially in vacation areas.

This is a disadvantage when you are trying to buy, but a big advantage when you are ready to sell. You should have little trouble selling a temporary home.

## A Sectional Home

In the 1960s manufacturers of mobile homes began to build what they call *double-wides*. A double-wide is a pair of mobile units, each 12 or 14 feet wide and from 48 to 65 feet long, designed to fit together on a site to form a complete house. When set up, a double-wide looks like a house, with a peaked roof, overhangs, and walls with 2 × 4 studs like stick-built houses.

The two sections are transported from factory to site either on their own wheels like a mobile home or on flatbed trucks. At the site they may rest on supports like a mobile home, but this method is not recommended. A standard foundation is much better, and many double-wides have full basements under them. The units are lifted or slid onto the foundation and securely fastened together at the floor, end walls, and roof. Usually all plumbing is in one of the two sections, and connections are easily made to water, waste, and power lines. Set-up time is at most two days of good weather.

In the late 1960s, as demand for vacation housing grew, manufacturers began to produce homes designed specifically for leisure use. By now called *modular houses* or *sectionalized housing,* many of the houses have a modified A-frame design with a high-peaked, steeply-pitched roof and a second floor. Each house has a living room, kitchen, dining space in either kitchen or living room, one full bath, and two, three, or four bedrooms. Manufacturers offer special optional features such as decks. Exteriors are rustic. Interiors are like those in standard homes, but with rustic touches.

Costs for sectional homes are higher than for mobile homes—on the order of $12 to $20 per square foot. This cost is still less than for a site-built home erected by a contractor. But factory-built homes are not as large as their nominal sizes. A home described as 24' by 60', for example, has overall dimensions of approximately 23' 4" by 57' 4". State laws specify maximum widths that can be hauled on highways, and manufacturers stay on the safe side of the maximums. The hitch (towing device) is included in overall length, which reduces usable length by 2 1/2 to 4 feet.

In general the advantages and disadvantages of mobile homes also apply to sectionalized housing. Local ordinances seldom exclude the latter, however.

## A Prefab House

More than forty years ago a few companies began producing housing components. The idea was that a company, because of its volume of purchases, could buy materials more economically than the individual builder. By standardizing parts and assembly procedures, the companies used less skilled labor at lower cost and at the same time produced structural components for houses that were uniform in size and consistent in quality.

In order to sell their products, these companies drew floor plans that used the components they produced. Soon all the structural elements of a house—

floors, walls, roof, partitions—were built in factories and shipped to building sites for assembly. Thus was prefabricated housing born.

Today three kinds of packages of prefabricated components are available for assembly at the site. The simplest and least expensive is the shell. A shell includes only the components for a weathertight house—floors, walls, roof, structural partitions, windows, and exterior doors—and nothing more. You provide the foundation, plumbing, heating, wiring, and all interior finish materials. The shell comes in large sections and is erected by the contractor from whom you buy the package. You finish it.

A more complete package is the rough-finished prefab. In addition to the shell of the house, this package includes plumbing, heating, and wiring already in place. You provide the foundation and interior finish materials, and complete the interior. The contractor who erects the house connects piping, wiring, and ducts between the components.

With the most comprehensive package you get a complete home. Everything is finished, inside and out.

The final price of a prefabricated home is the sum of the manufactured package, the cost of erection by the contractor, the cost of the materials you must furnish, and the cost of shipping the package. If your site is a long way from the nearest factory, the shipping cost may be high enough to make other ways of getting your vacation house more attractive economically.

### A Precut House

Manufacturers of precut houses do not provide complete structural components. Instead, they send you all the individual pieces of material needed for the shell of a vacation house, which are then assembled on the site. The packages vary with the manufacturer. You may receive framing members for floor, walls, and roof cut to length, or sections of these elements ready for assembly. Windows and doors arrive in their frames. The manufacturer usually provides all special fasteners and any tools for use with these fasteners. He also provides drawings and detailed instructions for assembly.

Like prefabricated packages, precut packages are available for erection either by you as owner or by a contractor-dealer.

## COMPARING YOUR CHOICES

The various methods of construction of a vacation house, rated in general order of personal skill required, are

> building your own house from scratch (requiring the most skill)
> the precut house you assemble yourself
> the prefabricated shell
> the contractor-assembled precut house
> the rough-finished prefab
> the finished prefab

All angles are right angles in this rectangular house. Because glass areas are so large, part of the open deck could be made into a screened porch on sites where insects are more common than vacationers. *Photographer: Alan Hicks. Courtesy American Plywood Association.*

the mobile or sectionalized home
an existing house (least skill required).

Rated on the basis of on-site construction time required by you as owner, the methods rank in about the same order, with the self-built house taking the most time.

The rating in general order of total cost, assuming that each house contains about the same square footage of space, is

building your own house (lowest cost)
the precut house you assemble yourself
a mobile home
the prefabricated shell
a sectionalized home
the contractor-assembled precut house
the rough-finished prefab
the finished prefab
an existing house (highest cost)

Since transportation and local labor are important but highly variable costs, these ratings can be only rough guides. The only sure comparison is one you make yourself.

As you weigh the facts you gather first hand, look also at the intangible aspects. In these days when more and more of our freedoms and prerogatives are being squeezed, building a vacation house yourself to your own standards and to fit your own desires presents one of the remaining opportunities for a family to say: "We did it ourselves," and be proud of it.

# Selecting
# a Good Site

When you build a new house in your home town, it is best to select the site first, and then find a floor plan that fits both the site and your family's needs. Site is important, but it is secondary to the comfort and livability of the house itself.

With a vacation house you *must* select the site first. It is of primary importance, and the house itself is secondary. When you take a vacation, where you go is more important than where you stay.

There is another advantage to finding the site first. It's almost always easier and less expensive to adapt a house to a site than to adjust a piece of land to fit a house. This is particularly true in popular vacation communities where land is scarce and sites are small. In isolated areas where sites are larger, you can usually find some spot on the land to put a house. This may not always be the ideal spot, however. So as a general rule, look for a good site first.

Start looking for land as soon as practicable. Real estate experts suggest that you buy as much land as you can afford. Land continues to appreciate in value from the moment you take ownership. Later, if local laws permit it, you can resell pieces to friends or buyers you like, and control your choice of immediate neighbors.

Experts also advise buying land with the smallest down payment and the longest terms possible. As soon as you buy, the appreciation in land value accrues to you, and you pay off this increase in equity with inflated dollars. A low down payment also leaves you with more cash to put toward the house itself.

## HOW TO LOOK FOR A SITE

You can discover potential sites in four ways. You can work with national real estate firms. You can work with a local real estate agent. You can watch the ads or advertise your needs in local newspapers. Or you can do your own looking. The best method for you depends partly on the size of the geographical area to be searched, and also on the type of property you are looking for.

### National Real Estate Firms

If you have only a general idea of where you want to settle, start your search by contacting a national real estate firm with agents throughout the country. There are two long-established firms of this type:

*Strout Realty, Inc.,* Plaza Towers, Springfield, Missouri 65804. Telephone number is (417) 887-0100.

*United Farm Agency,* 612 West 47th Street, Kansas City, Missouri 64112. Toll-free telephone number is (800) 821-2599 except in Missouri, where it is (800) 392-7790.

Suppose that you know only that you want to be on a lake in northern Wisconsin, or in the mountains of Utah, or along the Carolina, Maine, or Oregon coast. Write these agencies, or give them a call. Each firm puts out a free catalog with more than 250 pages listing available real estate—shore property, farm land, ranches, and mountain property, both with and without homes on it. Details of the property and the asking price are included, often with a photograph. Not all available real estate is listed, of course, but enough is to give you an idea of the cost of land in various communities.

In each catalog is a return card. On the card you indicate what you are looking for, the general area, the price range, and how large a down payment you can make. Be honest. You aren't going to get a bargain by understating what you are willing to pay. More likely you won't see anything you like in a lower price range, and you waste everyone's time.

The information you send in goes to the company's affiliated agents in towns in the area you specify. These agents then mail to you information on land in the area that appears to meet your requirements. In this way you can narrow the possibilities until you have three or four good ones. Then take a trip to visit each site, working with the agent, until you find the land you want. You can profitably invest long weekends or even entire vacations in your search for the right area and the right bit of land.

A third national firm, *Century 21 Real Estate Corporation,* 18872 MacArthur Boulevard, Irvine, California 92715, operates a bit differently. Through affiliated real estate agencies it maintains a client referral network. You contact the Century 21 affiliate in your home town, specify what you are looking for, and the agency in turn refers your request to affiliates in your area of search. The affiliates receiving the referral then work directly with you. If there is no affiliated agency near you, write the home office for the address of the nearest regional office. That office will then handle the referral.

## Local Real Estate Agents

In every vacation area are real estate agents more than willing to help you find the ideal site. Be sure the agent you select is reputable. He is if he is a member of NAREB (National Association of Real Estate Boards) or the local real estate board.

The agent will show you first the sites for which he has the listing. He gets the full commission on such sales, paid by the seller of the land. If nothing suits your fancy, he will then show you what other agents have available. He gets only part of the commission here.

A good agent knows what sites are available in his community and, often, in the entire county. He frequently knows about land that will be available in the near future but is not yet listed—the type of site you could not find in any other way.

He will work hard to satisfy you. Give him time to relate your desires to the sites available—no less than a month. But if you aren't satisfied with his efforts by that time, try another agency. It is never good practice to work with more than one agency in a community at one time. If you do change agents, be honest enough to tell the first agent so that he doesn't devote any more time to you. Also tell the second agent what you have done, and what sites you have seen. In this way you save both your time and his.

You can also hire an agent to conduct a search for you on a fee basis. Ask him how much he charges before you tell him to proceed.

## Local Advertising

If you want a lot of action, place an ad in the local newspaper nearest your site area, stating clearly what you are seeking. The response is likely to be heavy, much of it from real estate agents suggesting that you use their services. But you are also likely to hear from landowners who prefer to sell direct rather than through an agent.

There are two dangers inherent in advertising for a site. First, there is no way you can cut off the flow of mail once it starts, and it can continue long after you have found the site you want. Second, unless you have a good idea of land values, plans for development in the community, and local history, you could easily make a bad purchase. You could pay more than necessary, or buy land on a country road scheduled for widening into a highway in a few years, or buy land subject to flooding or erosion. A real estate agent makes it his business to know about past, present, and future problems with sites, and will steer you away from them.

It often pays to subscribe to the local newspaper in the area in which you are interested. You may find a good site offered in the want ads. More important, you keep up with happenings in the community that might affect your decision to settle there or to buy a certain site.

## Conducting Your Own Search

If you and your family are in complete agreement on exactly where you want to build—say on a particular lake or in one valley or along one road—it is practical to look for a site yourself. You have confined the area of search, and can see what is available with a minimum of time and effort.

As you study an area, list the locations of potential sites. Make your descriptions as complete as possible. For example:

1. West shore of Duck Lake, on Cumberland Road, 6/10 of a mile north of its intersection with Bradley Road.

2. About 2.5 miles west of Highway 28 on the south side of Burnt Tree Road across from the David Dalton farm.

If there are no signs on the site that identify a source of further information—either an owner or real estate firm—then head for the county courthouse. Bring your descriptions with you.

Go to the county tax assessor's office. Even the smallest county has a tax assessor, and he keeps the records of ownership of all property in the county. He will probably have a map of the county, divided first into districts and then into land lots. The map shows all roads. That's why the name of the road and its distance from another road are important in your description. The tax assessor can find the David Dalton farm on the map, and he can tell you who owns the land across from it.

Next, gather all available information on land contours, building permits, zoning, and local building ordinances. In some thinly populated counties you may find nothing. There are no aerial photographs or maps in the files. Building permits are not required or, if required, are free. There is no zoning and there are no local restrictions, except for approval of your water supply and sewage disposal system by the county Department of Public Health. Any information that is available will be concentrated in the county assessor's office.

In more populous counties with a higher tax base, there may be a county engineer. He may have large maps, called *topographical maps,* that show land contours, locations of utility lines, and sometimes property lines (Fig. 2-1). Topographical maps also show easements. An *easement* is a legal right to the use of land that is entirely separate from ownership of that land. Often a telephone company has an easement for lines on poles across private property or for cables buried below the surface. You own and maintain the strip of land with an easement, but the law does not allow you to use it yourself.

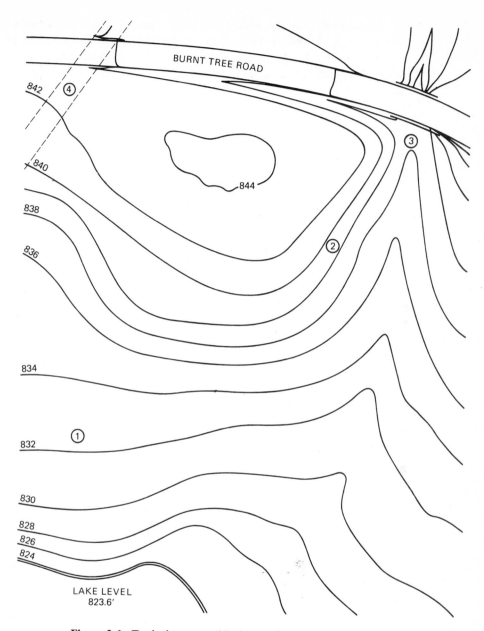

**Figure 2-1.** Typical topographical map shows contour lines at two-foot intervals. Lines far apart (1) indicate a gentle slope. Lines close together (2) indicate a steeper slope. Sharp turns in contour lines (3) mark points of drainage; the points aim upstream. Easements (4) are shown as dotted lines.

If you find a topographical map, take time to study the contours of the prospective site. *Contour lines* show the height of land above sea level and are usually drawn at two-foot intervals of height. When contour lines are far apart, land slopes gently. The closer together the lines are, the steeper the slope. Contour lines that come to a point indicate where water is likely to drain. The points aim upstream.

From the county engineer (or the building inspector in still more populous counties) get copies of any zoning laws and local building ordinances. One important ordinance establishes setbacks. A *setback* is the minimum distance you can build from a road, a lake shore, and side property lines. A front setback is usually measured in feet from the front property line, not the center or edge of the road. Side setbacks may be measured in feet or as a percentage of the total width of the property.

After studying all this information, you may find that some sites don't meet your requirements. Cross these sites off your list. Then find out which of the remaining sites are available. Many of the best sites don't have a "For Sale" sign, but can still be bought.

You can learn if a site is for sale in two ways. One is to call a real estate agent and have him conduct an investigation for you—for a fee, of course. The other is to talk to the owner yourself; you will have gotten his name from the tax assessor.

When you ask if his land is for sale, the owner may give you an immediate "no." If so, leave your name and address in case he changes his mind after thinking about it awhile. If he gives you any other answer—"yes," "maybe," or "perhaps part of the land"—get his permission to "walk" the site. Call him after you have done so, and tell him of your interest or lack of it. If you are interested, you thus give him time to adjust to the idea of selling, and to establish a price as a basis for negotiation.

## WHEN TO LOOK

To judge a site fully, you should study it at all seasons. The best time to start is in late fall, after leaves have fallen but before snow covers the ground. The next best season is early spring before foliage is out and after a major thaw or heavy rain. Early in your search you want to study a site at its worst. You're looking for what is wrong with it, not what's good about it. Happiness with a site's good points comes later, after wise selection.

## WHAT TO LOOK FOR

In your preliminary planning, you paid attention to some of the considerations for a good site: distance from home, distance from other people, and building restrictions. When you walk the site, you look at other factors: accessibility, drainage, soil conditions, availability of utilities, weather, flora and fauna, surroundings, and contours. Look critically, before you become emotionally attached to any one site.

## Accessibility

You are looking for the answers to three questions here:

1. Can I get to the property directly from a public road? If you have to drive across someone else's property to get to yours, even with full permission, cross that site off your list. Even if you can arrange to buy an access strip for a driveway, forget it. The legal complications aren't worth the trouble, no matter how beautiful the site is otherwise.

2. Can I easily reach the best location on the site for the house? Figure out not only how you would get into the site, but where to turn around to get out of it. As you walk the route you visualize for your access road, look for low spots that will be muddy in bad weather. Look for ridges and humps that would catch the chassis of your car and damage exhaust and brake fluid systems. Study the steepness of slopes. You won't be building a highway, but you must be able to negotiate grades in all weather. And so must the trucks that deliver building materials, or components for precut or prefabricated homes, or a mobile or modular home. Flat-bed trucks and mobile homes are awkward to maneuver into position on a sloping or heavily wooded site. An access road wide enough for a materials truck may be nowhere near adequate for delivering a home half again as wide and twice as long.

3. Can I put in a road economically? You can bridge a ditch, a stream, or a marsh. You can blast through rock ledges and cut into a hillside to reduce grade. You can fell big trees that are in the way. But all these operations are expensive, and add little to the value and enjoyment of the site.

Are all three answers positive? Great! You're off to a fine start toward finding a good site. Next, study the land itself.

## Drainage

The main reason for looking at a site when it is wet is to see what happens to rainwater or melting snow. Does it sink quickly into the ground, settle in pools, or run off the surface? What path does it take when it runs off? The ideal location for a vacation house is on a knoll or rise from which water drains in all directions. Next best is on land that slopes gently. Flat land or land at the bottom of a slope make the poorest sites.

Not everyone can live or wants to live on a hilltop. If your site isn't the highest, what happens to water that drains off adjacent property? Walk around the property line looking for the path such drainage takes. One sign is tall grass—taller than surrounding grass because it receives more moisture. Another is dense underbrush in low spots on the site. A third is bare spots where topsoil has washed away and subsoil has eroded. These signs of runoff won't be omens of a major problem as long as the runoff bypasses your access road, walks, outdoor living areas, and the location of the house itself.

If a site is below road level, make especially sure that runoff from the road drains past your land rather than onto it.

### Soil Conditions

If drainage is satisfactory, take a look at the soil. You can learn a lot about soil conditions by studying the surface. Loose, sandy topsoil lets water sink in and dissipate harmlessly. Heavy clay topsoil absorbs little water and forces it to run off. Thick underbrush is a sign that the soil holds moisture. Bare spots along a slope often indicate a rock ledge just below the surface. Big trees have big roots below the surface that could be in your way. Big rocks or boulders on the surface bespeak more rocks and boulders under the surface. All these are clues to the quality of soil for building purposes.

Bring a sharp spade with you when you visit each site. At the most likely spot for your vacation house, dig down about 12 inches. In many vacation areas topsoil isn't more than 6 inches deep, and you can reach subsoil with a few minutes' effort. Subsoil (Fig. 2-2) may vary widely from spot to spot on the same site, but you can usually tell whether you would be building on rock, gravel, clay, loam, or sand. The best soil for building drains well, is free of large rocks, and

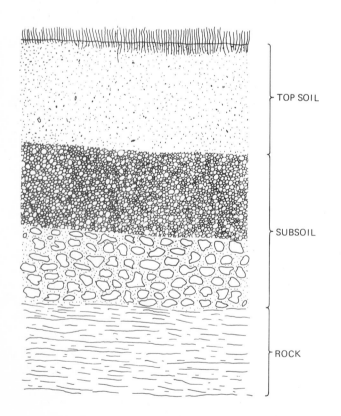

TOP SOIL

SUBSOIL

ROCK

**Figure 2-2.** On any site the depth of topsoil may vary from a few inches to several feet. Topsoil absorbs water. The subsoil below is more dense, and may lie in several layers, or strata. Depth of subsoil varies greatly. Still farther down is solid rock.

has good bearing qualities—that is, it will support the weight of your house easily. If you have any doubt about soil conditions, send in core samples for professional analysis. See Chapter 5 under the heading "Testing the Soil" for details on procedures.

## Utilities

You must have a source of water on the site. You will need power for lighting and fuel for cooking and perhaps heating. And you will need a sewage disposal system. The next step is to find out how far away from the proposed location for the house the present utility lines lie.

*Water.* You can't live without water. A flow of 15 gallons per day is minimum for vacation living, and you need a lot more to fight a fire. Some vacation communities have central water systems to which you can attach your pipes for a connection fee. Sometimes you can draw water from a lake or stream. Your costs are for piping, a pump, and filters. More often you will have to sink a well. Your costs are for sinking the well and for piping, a pump, and filters. If flow is limited, add the cost of a storage tank or cistern.

How much a well will cost you depends to a great extent on the water table. A *water table* is the point below the land's surface where soil is soaked with water. That point may be a few feet or a few hundred feet down. A low water table increases the cost of sinking a well. On the other hand, a high water table may cause problems in building a foundation, and also interfere with proper operation of a septic system. A water table 15 to 30 feet below the surface is ideal.

You probably can't determine the water table while you are at the site. The best sources of information are the local Department of Public Health and owners of neighboring property. From the health department you can find out what sources of natural water are approved, as well as the approximate depth of the water table at the site. Officials also know about how deep a well must be, the likely flow, and the average cost per foot to sink a well. They can recommend the best locations for a well and septic system. Follow their suggestions, because they must approve both your water and sewage disposal systems.

*Sewer.* Two of the biggest problems on a vacation site are disposal of sewage and garbage. Few areas have central sewer systems and garbage pickup. But environmental standards increasingly limit what you can do on your own. In parts of the country where soil is heavy and does not absorb readily, ordinances often specify the minimum lot size on which you can install a septic system. The Department of Public Health can advise you on this subject, and also tell you about local restrictions on burying garbage and burning refuse.

*Power.* Electric power is available today near all but the most remote sites. Most power companies will extend their lines a fixed number of feet at their own expense. You pay for any further extension beyond that point. At the site, then, pace off the distance to the nearest existing power line and make a note of the distance.

If electricity isn't available, you will either have to do without or buy and install a gasoline-powered generator. Good generators are readily available and provide reliable power. But they are an extra expense that you must consider when you compare sites.

*Fuel.* Few vacation areas have natural gas for cooking and heating. Most vacationers use either electricity or bottled gas. Each type of fuel has its advantages, assuming that costs are about the same for each in the area. Electricity is always available for use. Bottled gas is a fuel you have to monitor, even though delivery service of replacement bottles is quite reliable. On the other hand, when a storm knocks out a power line and weather is at its worst, you can still heat (and eat) with your bottled gas system. Or with a fireplace.

### Weather

Every inch of a site is affected by weather. You can't control it, but by understanding how weather functions you can make it work for you. Study first the direction of air movement over the site. You want to catch the breeze but avoid the wind.

In hilly country the wind blows downhill during the night and uphill during the day, usually at a speed greater than the prevailing breeze on level land. Winds pass completely over a house tucked behind a rounded hill, but blow down onto a house hidden behind a cliff. Valleys have less breeze than slopes, but offer more protection against strong winds. Narrow valleys or draws between hills have more summer breeze than broad valleys. Still air is usually more humid and oppressive than moving air. Because warm air rises and cool air tends to settle in low spots like water, valleys are warmer than surrounding slopes during the day, but cooler at night.

Along the coast the breeze generally comes off the sea during the day and off the shore at night. There is less variation in air movement along the water than inland, but fog may occur frequently over some sheltered bays and coves.

Normally you want to let the sun's light into a vacation house but keep out the sun's heat. Therefore the relationship between existing shade trees and the final location of your house is very important. But even with good shade, the lay of the land can have a decided bearing on temperature. A site that slopes downward toward the north receives less sunlight than other slopes throughout the year, and therefore has cooler temperatures all year. A slope to the south may be as much as 10° warmer, and spring comes earlier and fall stays later because of it. A slope to the east warms quickly from the morning sun, but begins to cool earlier than a south or west slope. A slope to the west stays cooler longer in the morning, but remains warmer from the afternoon sun later in the day.

Even sites on small bodies of water are affected differently by weather. On the sheltered side of a lake air temperatures are more constant and a little warmer than on the other side of the same lake. But water temperatures are a little cooler on the sheltered side.

Rain falls indiscriminately on all parts of all sites, with one exception. Rainfall is often a little heavier on the west side of a mountain ridge than on the east side. On the other hand the east side often has more clouds and early morning fog.

On a large piece of land, say of five acres or more, there are probably several good spots to build, each with its own little variations in climate. So as you compare sites, and building spots on any one site, keep in mind the assets that weather can bring you. But don't let a nice breeze overrule the more important considerations of good drainage, good soil for building, good shade from trees, and pleasant views.

### Flora and Fauna

There is one disadvantage to shopping for sites in cold weather. It is hard to visualize them in full summer verdure. A beautifully framed view through trees in the winter may be completely screened by those same trees in summer. Conversely, bare branches that don't even slow strong winter winds may provide protective shade in summer.

The trees you save should give you pleasant shade, but not block out light needed in the house. They should permit air movement for ventilation and cooling, but block out damaging winds.

Study also the wild growth closer to the ground. Check especially for poisonous plants, such as sumac and poison ivy, that you may have to remove. Look also for bushes that provide a privacy screen, and flowering shrubs that add color and beauty during the vacation season. Of course this same ground cover and shrubbery probably provides a home for insects, rodents, and reptiles. But no site is completely free of such creatures. You should merely find out what you have to live with.

If you want to spend your vacations close to nature, leave the site as undisturbed as possible. After all, the birds and squirrels and rabbits and raccoons, and perhaps even some deer or bear, made their homes there first. You can protect your house against intrusion, yet still live in harmony with the forest denizens.

### Surroundings

In the excitement of finding the ideal site, it is easy to forget to look just beyond it—on the other side of the hill, across the lake, or around the bend. The other homes within sight may be of good quality and well kept up. Are the homes just out of view in equally good condition? And during the time you are vacationing, will the prevailing breeze bring you the smell of pine boughs or a pulp mill, open water or stagnant marshes, new-mown fields or a hog farm? You are about to make a major investment, and taking an extra hour or two to look all around you can pay big dividends.

### Special Features to Look For and Avoid

Most of the discussion so far applies to all sites. Certain sites, however, require further study.

If you are searching for a site on water, for example, how constant is the water line? Unless water level is controlled by a dam or streams that can handle an overflow, lakeshore property may suffer from spring flooding. If the level is controlled by man, find out whether the lake is drained in the fall. Your lake may look ugly during times of low water. On the other hand such times are excellent for repairing docks and piers.

In the spring look for signs of high water from melting snow. Look also for springs and creeks that are dry most of the year but can cause water problems annually. Once a year is too often. A creek bed may appear dry, but if it had water in it at one time, it can have water in it again.

At the shore of large lakes, seek signs of erosion. High winds sometimes have a tidal effect and wash away the sand, gravel, and rock at the water's edge. You can control this damage with rock walls and jetties, but it is an added expense that you can avoid by choosing wisely.

Seashore property is even more subject to erosion from wind and tide. Look for sites where the sand is solidly anchored by dune grass. The very fact that you find grass is a good indication that the shore is holding its own against wind and waves. Vacation houses near beaches often require extra bracing to withstand high winds, as well as exterior materials that don't deteriorate under blasts of sand and the effects of salt spray.

Mountain property is sometimes difficult to evaluate. Any sloping site is subject to erosion and to runoff of water from above. Climb as far as you can above a potential site, looking for signs of watersheds, trees with exposed roots, and loose boulders. Look below the site for the same clues. Find out what the maximum depth of snow has been, and estimate how much of your house would be covered at that depth. Above all, check soil samples carefully. You must have rock or firm soil into which to anchor a mountainside home.

## PICTURING A HOUSE ON THE SITE

As you walk a site, you automatically see what views you have. Find the best place to take advantage of those views. When you find it, picture how the house will look there. Study the contours of the land around you. You want to take maximum advantage of every slope, every tree, every natural feature of the site. With all the negatives safely put to rest, you can now begin to dream again.

Think a little about the house you plan to build here. You don't have to have a specific house in mind, but you should think in terms of what type of house will best fit the site. How will the contours of the house blend with the contours of the land?

If you want your house to virtually disappear into its site, such as a cabin in the woods, match the contours of the house with the contours of the land and

Scarcely visible on its sloping site is this vacation house with trees puncturing the two-level deck and dappling it with shade. Clear grade redwood and cinnamon heartwood stripe the exterior walls. *Photographer: Ernest Braun. Courtesy California Redwood Association.*

use exterior materials like those found on the site, such as wood and stone. But don't overlook the beauty of contrast. On sites with uneven contours, houses with long horizontal lines often look best. Similarly, on nearly level sites, houses with vertical lines stand out. Contrast between house and site can bring extra beauty to both. The Grand Tetons of Wyoming are beautiful because of their sharp, rugged contours. But the valleys among the mountains are just as beautiful. It is the contrast between the two that brings beauty to both.

On most vacation sites you scarcely have to consider the size and style of other houses nearby; they won't be close enough to affect the appearance of your house. On smaller sites, however, your house must relate to the houses next door.

You shouldn't build a two-story house between two one-story contemporary houses, for example. If you have a one-story house in mind, pick a site that is among other one-story houses of similar size and style. This may not seem important now, but if the day comes when you want to sell your vacation house, it will sell more quickly and at a better price if it fits into its neighborhood.

Like a sentry on a parapet, this two-level vacation house with vertical siding and a cedar shingle roof stands guard on a bluff overlooking the sea. Up-slope breeze and trees that block the setting sun keep the house comfortable all day. *Photographer: Jim Ball. Courtesy Red Cedar Shingle and Handsplit Shake Bureau.*

| SITE IS ON | 1 CUMBER-LAND ROAD | 2 BURNT TREE RD. | 3 HWY. 28 | 4 (UNNAMED LANE OFF 28) | 5 DUCK LAKE RD. | 6 PEAKS PIKE | 7 SHORELINE DRIVE | 8 LOON LANE | 9 BOX FARM ROAD | 10 ROCKY FACE RD. |
|---|---|---|---|---|---|---|---|---|---|---|
| DRAINAGE | 5 | 5 | 4 | 3 | 4 | 5 | 2 | 5 | 1 | 5 |
| SOIL CONDITION | 4 | 4 | 5 | 5 | 5 | 1 | 4 | 3 | 5 | 2 |
| ACCESS | 5 | 4 | 5 | 2 | 5 | 3 | 5 | 5 | 5 | 1 |
| WATER SOURCE | 3 | 4 | 5 | 3 | 5 | 3 | 5 | 5 | 5 | 3 |
| POWER SOURCE | 5 | 2 | 5 | 1 | 4 | 5 | 5 | 3 | 5 | 5 |
| CONTOURS | 4 | 5 | 5 | 5 | 5 | 3 | 2 | 5 | 5 | 3 |
| SURROUNDINGS | 4 | 5 | 3 | 4 | 5 | 5 | 3 | 5 | 5 | 5 |
| VIEW | 5 | 5 | 3 | 5 | 5 | 5 | 4 | 5 | 5 | 5 |
| WEATHER | 5 | 5 | 3 | 5 | 5 | 3 | 5 | 4 | 5 | 2 |
| SHADE | 5 | 3 | 2 | 5 | 4 | 1 | 5 | 4 | 4 | 5 |
| TOTALS | 45 | 42 | 40 | X | 47 | X | 40 | 44 | X | X |
| SITE PREPARATION | $500 | $800 | $500 | | $800 | | $1200 | $500 | | |

**Figure 2-3.** One good way to compare sites is to rate them on the factors important to you. In the point system used here, excellent conditions rate 5, unacceptable conditions rate 1. No site you consider should have a 1 rating for any factor.

# MAKING THE FINAL SITE SELECTION

One of the most difficult but pleasant tasks you face is deciding on a site. After you have seen the tenth or eleventh site, you won't remember much detail about the first two or three unless you keep a written record of the details. When you go site-seeing, take along pencil and paper and note the salient facts about view, contours, soil conditions, drainage, distance to utilities, access, and surroundings. Then rate each factor on each site. Be practical, not emotional. And be as honest as you can.

Figure 2-3 shows a typical way of rating sites. List at the left the factors that are important to you in site selection, and across the top the locations of the sites you visited. Use a scale of points from 5 to 1, meaning

5—Excellent. Meets all our requirements.
4—Very good. With small cost for improvements, meets all requirements.
3—Fair. Will take some cost and effort to correct site faults.
2—Poor. Flaws will be expensive to correct.
1—Not acceptable.

Fill in your chart. If any site has a rating of 1 anywhere in its column, cross it off immediately. There are better sites available. For all other sites, add up the points.

If you have narrowed down prospective sites carefully, there should be little difference in point totals. The best overall site has the highest point total. To make sure, you have one more calculation to make, and that is to estimate the cost of site preparation. Talk to a local contractor who does grading. If one isn't listed in the local telephone book, ask the county engineer or tax assessor for names of people who do that type of work. Explain to the contractor what you are doing, and point out that you are only in the site selection stage. (It is advisable to contract site preparation work anyway, rather than attempt to do it yourself, since such work requires equipment that you won't have and probably can't rent.) Tell the contractor that all you want at this time is a rough estimate, not a firm bid.

Suppose you have budgeted $5,000 for land ready to build on. The contractor estimates $500 as the preparation cost for sites 1, 3, and 8 on your list (Fig. 2-3), $800 for sites 2 and 5, and $1,200 for site 7. You know then that you can afford to pay up to $4,500 for sites 1, 3, and 8, $4,500 for sites 2 and 5, and only $3,800 for site 7.

The final step is acquiring the land. If you have been thorough in your research and have an accurate estimate of costs for site preparation, the selling price will be close to what you are willing to pay. If the selling price is either much higher or much lower than expected, recheck your figures and walk the sites again. Either the owner's asking price is out of line, or you have made a mistake somewhere.

# THE DEED

To acquire a site for a vacation house, you and the owner must first come to an agreement on a price. Then hire a local lawyer to make absolutely certain that the present owner's title to that land is clear. *Title* is the right of ownership. The lawyer will search the title—that is, check all available records—to assure that

- The owner is legally competent to transfer title.
- There are no lawsuits outstanding against the present owner.
- All taxes and special assessments have been paid.
- Any mineral rights are protected. If oil or gold is found under the land, for example, you benefit from the discovery and not someone else.
- Any easements granted in previous years are shown in the deed.

A *deed* is a contract that transfers title from one owner to the next. The county clerk records the deed at the courthouse, and you keep a copy as proof that you have title to the land.

For the title search and preparation of a deed, your lawyer will charge you a fee. Ask in advance what this fee will be. It may range from as low as $25 to as high as several hundred dollars. If the land has changed hands recently, and the title has been searched within the past twenty years, the fee should be minimal. But if the land has been in one family for several generations, or the title search discloses a problem, the lawyer may charge more. His fee is based primarily on his time.

Usually a title is clear. But make sure *before* you sign a deed. When a title isn't clear, you may have all kinds of trouble. The lawyer's fee is a small price to pay for insurance that, from a legal standpoint, you have a clear title to the land on which you want to build.

# VACATION COMMUNITIES

In this discussion of sites, there has been no mention of planned vacation communities. Throughout the country, developers have bought up huge tracts of land to attract people who want vacation property. The developers put in a water system and paved roads. They have tight security, with a gatehouse and guards to protect property owners. They divide the land into lots and help you select exactly the site you want. A vacation community has quite a few advantages.

But there is one major disadvantage. Most developers—if not all of them—will not permit you to build your house yourself. A committee approves all plans and contractors. The committee will turn down your plans for a do-it-yourself vacation house unless you can prove conclusively that you have the knowledge, experience, and money to build a house that meets all their standards.

# Selecting A Good
# Floor Plan

It is logical to select a site before you begin to look at floor plans for a vacation house. Yet you can't fully judge a site without having some idea of the house you want to build and how it will fit the site.

So go ahead and look at floor plans if you want to. That's part of the fun of dreaming. Just don't become emotionally attached to one plan until you know that it works well for you and is appropriate for your site. There are a lot of questions to answer before you know which floor plan is right for you. The first is: what will the house cost? At this point a rough estimate is sufficient. For a more detailed approach to cost estimating, see Chapter 19.

## ESTIMATING THE COST

The cost of a vacation house itself, excluding the land, may range anywhere from $20 to $40 per square foot when built by a contractor. Included in this cost are materials, labor, the contractor's overhead, and his profit. By building a house yourself, you cut the costs of the work you do yourself about in half. You should estimate your costs for materials at a little more than a contractor's, because you are likely to have more waste, and you don't have another job on which to use any leftover materials.

You can't eliminate all costs for labor, overhead, and profit, because you probably won't do all the work yourself. Like clearing the site, excavating often takes special equipment, and finishing a concrete floor slab is difficult for most amateurs. So is installation of plumbing, heating, and electrical systems. For the work you don't do, you have the full cost of materials, labor, overhead, and profit.

For purposes of making a preliminary estimate, let's assume that you have $25,000 to spend on a vacation house. You estimate $5,000 for the land and site preparation. You estimate another $6,000 for the cost of work done by others. That leaves you $14,000 for the materials to build the rest of the house yourself. If materials are about half the cost of a house, you then divide the estimated cost per square foot by 2. Based on the initial range of $20 to $40, the cost per square foot of the work you do is $10 to $20.

By dividing the new cost per square foot into the money available, you arrive at the maximum square footage of house you can afford. In the example, the $6,000 budgeted for contractors represents 150 to 300 square feet (calculated at full cost). The $14,000 for your work, calculated at half cost, represents 700 to 1400 square feet. Therefore the maximum size of house you can afford ranges from 850 up to 1,700 square feet.

With simple construction and good but inexpensive materials, your cost per square foot will be at the lower end of the range, and the square footage per building dollar at the upper end of the range. The opposite will be true if the house has such features as fancy paneling, ceramic tile floors, and two full bathrooms.

If you find that your desires exceed your budget, consider building a small vacation house now and adding to it later. Most plan books contain plans and sketches for one or two add-on houses. Two good examples are shown in the next chapter. The important point is to decide on the sizes of the rooms you need; then build as many of these rooms as you can afford. This solution is far better and less expensive than building undersized rooms with the hope of re-modeling later. It conforms with the recommendation to look at your future needs. You will put up with a little inconvenience when you are young enough to accept it, and then reach your ultimate goal of the ideal vacation house when you need its comforts the most.

## FITTING THE SITE

With the maximum size house estimated, the next step is to recheck whether the site itself limits the overall dimensions of any house to be built on it. At the county courthouse you asked whether there were any ordinances governing set-backs. In most rural areas there are none, whereas on beach and lake sites setbacks are common.

Let's say you found a waterfront site that is 60 feet wide and 220 feet long from shore to road. The setback ordinance says that you cannot build a house within 10 feet of side property lines or closer than 75 feet from the shore. In addition, you cannot build a house within 50 feet, or a garage within 30 feet, of the property line at the road. The property line lies at the edge of the right-of-way, not at the edge of the road.

These setback restrictions limit you to a space 40 feet wide and 95 feet deep on which to build the house itself (Fig. 3-1). Setbacks are usually measured to the foundation line, not the eave line. Therefore the house can be no more than 40 feet wide, and should have major living areas within this dimension, all with a view toward the lake.

Even when setbacks don't restrict house size, other elements may. Trees, for example. Boulders or rock ledges for another. Steep contours for a third. As you walk a site for the final time before buying it, mark down the locations of good trees and measure the distances between them. Measure on the level,

**Figure 3-1.** Building ordinances often require setbacks. Those shown here are typical. Note that all setbacks are measured from property lines. Although this lot is 60′ by 220′, a house can be built only in the shaded area that measures 40′ by 95′.

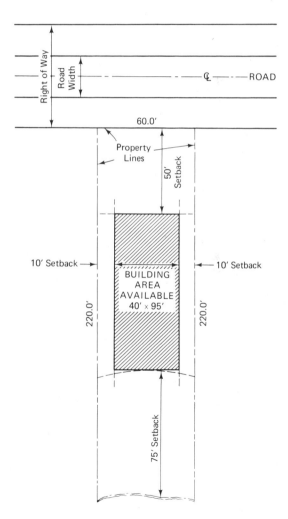

not on any slope. Draw circles with a radius of no less than ten feet around each tree you want to save. By allowing this clearance, you won't cut any major roots during excavation, you allow for roof overhangs, and allow the trees to grow naturally.

## Measuring Slopes

On a rugged site with steep slopes and little level land on which to build, it's not easy to determine the amount of building space available. You don't have a reference point for establishing level. A survey is the only sure way to gauge a slope, and you should have one made before you begin construction. But you can approximate the slope with a pole or board at least 16 feet long, lengths of strong fishing line, a stake, nail, hammer, knife, and a carpenter's level.

The job takes three people. One stands at the approximate location of the entrance door. Drive a stake at that point (Fig. 3-2) and pound a nail part way into the top of the stake. Then attach lengths of fish line to the pole at regular intervals, say every two feet. You'll have to guess at the lengths of string to use, as you will see shortly.

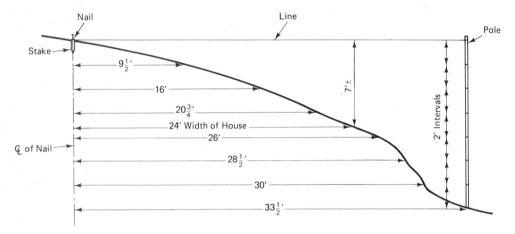

**Figure 3-2.** To draw the contour of a slope, use a wood pole and fish lines as described in the text. You measure the distance from stake to pole with lengths of fish line, then mark the lengths to scale on a sheet of graph paper at 2-foot intervals of vertical height. By connecting the points, you have a sectional view of the slope.

Now start slowly down the hill with the pole, walking at right angles to the front wall of the future house, while the person at the stake has the lowest fish line in hand. When the line looks about level, stop. Have a third person place the carpenter's level on the taut line, while you move the pole slightly up or down hill until the line is actually level. When the fish line is level from pole to stake, cut it at the nail. Continue this process with each line until you have leveled and cut all lines.  Make sure at each stop that you hold the pole vertically, using the level to make sure.

When you finish, you will have seven lengths of line attached to the pole. Let's say that the lengths, from bottom to top, are 9 1/2 ', 16 ', 20 3/4 ', 26 ', 28 1/2 ', 30 ', and 33 1/2 '.  These are the distances from the stake to contour lines at two-foot intervals.  You can now draw a profile of the slope (Fig. 3-2).

Suppose you want to build a house that is 24 feet from front to back.  Using the profile of the slope, you now know that floor level at the rear will be about seven feet higher above ground than floor level at the front.  Rear rooms will be among the tree branches, and the view may be gorgeous, but you will have to build some heavy structure to support the house.  You may want to move the house up the slope where it isn't quite so steep, or else select a narrower house.

## Orientation

As you begin to look at floor plans, keep in mind the way you want rooms to face and how you want each room to relate to other rooms.

The relationship of rooms to the points of the compass—their *orientation*— is extremely important to full use and enjoyment of any house.  To face rooms in the best orientation, you must consider the view, the direction of prevailing breezes in summer and cold blasts in winter, and the amount of shade on the site for protection from the rising, noonday, and setting sun.

The prevailing summer breeze in most land areas of the country blows from the southwest.  Remember that along the shore, however, the breeze during the day comes off the water, whichever direction it is, and off the shore at night.  In hilly country the breeze comes up the slope, which is usually the direction of the best view.

If you intend to heat primarily with a fireplace, the direction of prevailing winter wind is important; usually it is from the northwest.  For a fireplace to function properly, the wind should blow smoothly over the top of the chimney. The chimney of a one-story house is roughly 15 feet above ground level.  Tall trees on the upwind side cause a downflow of air into the chimney that disturbs proper draft in flues (Fig. 3-3, top).  Tall trees on the downwind side (Fig. 3-3, center) force the wind to flow well above chimney level, which limits the amount of draft.  If your site is covered with trees, there isn't much you can do.  A chimney in a forest will work, but it won't draw well, and it is likely to smoke until the fire in the fireplace is hot.  When possible, then, locate the house so its chimney is exposed to smooth air flow (Fig. 3-3, bottom).

From April to August the sun peeks into north windows early and late in the day, but at a low angle and without much heat (Fig. 3-4).  The summer sun is high at noon and doesn't penetrate far into rooms with a south exposure.  West windows let in the most heat, and east windows the next most.

During the rest of the year sun doesn't touch north windows and brings little heat into east windows.  But the low winter sun shines all the way across south rooms, warming them pleasantly.  West windows let in some heat even in winter.

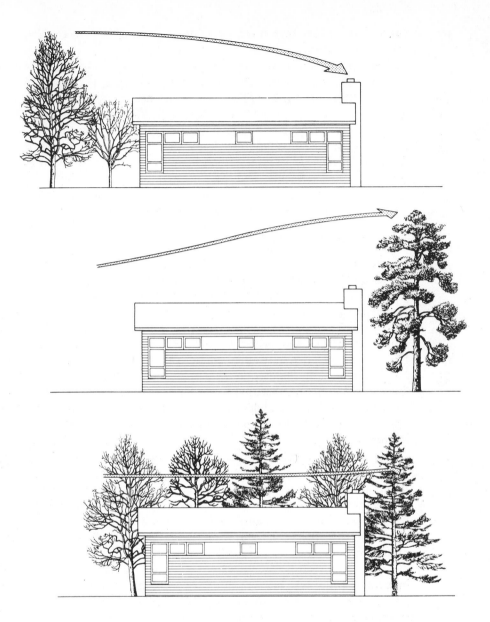

**Figure 3-3.** A grove of trees either upwind (top) or downwind (center) from a chimney upsets efficient operation of a fireplace. Air should be free to move smoothly (bottom) with nothing to interrupt its normal flow.

Trees on the east and west sides of a house help to control summer sun without blocking winter sunlight. And you can use roof overhangs to shade windows that trees don't protect. But neither trees nor overhangs stop reflected heat and glare.

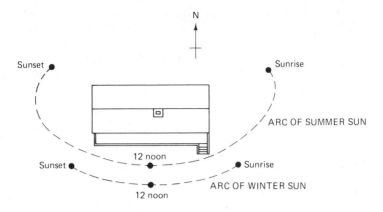

**Figure 3-4.** In summer the sun rises in the northeast and sets in the northwest. The arc of summer sun is long. In winter the sun rises in the southeast and sets in the southwest, and the arc is much shorter. Arcs shown are for northern vacation areas. In the south the summer arc is shorter and the winter arc longer.

If you buy shore property, reflection off the water must be controlled. It brings some heat and a lot of glare at certain hours—the first hour or two after sunrise and the last hour or two before sunset. Reflection of the sun off sand is strong not just in early morning and early evening hours, but throughout the day, regardless of the angle of the sun.

To reduce reflected heat and glare you need some sort of screen. A low wall or fence may do the job, or low planting. Or you can cover the inside surfaces of window glass with a special film that comes in sheets. You cut the sheets to fit individual window panes. From inside the house the view out is unaffected, or at most, a tinge darker. From outside the windows look like mirrors, and the view in is obscured.

### View

Many people think of a view in terms of distance. They walk over a site on a mountainside, find an opening through the trees that permits an unobstructed view for 20 miles, and exclaim "Oh, what a marvelous view!"

At first glance it *is* a beautiful view. Even at second and third glance. But when you live with the same long view day after day, it becomes like a calendar picture. You seldom look at it again unless you see smoke rising at a distance and wonder what is burning.

A static view where nothing moves and little changes soon becomes no view at all. That's why you don't notice it often unless something *is* moving, like that column of smoke from a fire.

A good view has movement—of water, of animals or birds, of branches, of clouds, of people. It has foreground and background. It has a frame to give it scale. Scale is important as a reference point. A photograph of the Grand

Canyon or a giant redwood tree means little unless it has a human figure or animal to give it scale. A good view has changing light. A tree lighted from behind or the side is much more interesting than when seen in full, flat sunlight. Again, contrast between sun and shadow creates interest.

So as you think about which rooms will have views, keep in mind that all of them can have a view if you provide the frame.

With the relationship between house and site at least partially settled in your mind, you can now seriously study individual floor plans.

## SPACE PLANNING

Many people who wouldn't think of designing their own home believe they can design their own vacation house. But it isn't easy. The same principles of good planning that go into the design of a year-round house apply also to a vacation house. Yet these principles must be applied in much less space.

Now more questions beg for answers. How do you intend to use each space you place under roof? Will these spaces be individual rooms or areas in one large room? Which rooms will be used the most, and at what time of day? Which rooms should have the best view? What is their best orientation? How should rooms relate to each other and to the outdoors?

Let's look at spaces one by one. Start with the kitchen.

### The Kitchen

The kitchen area of a vacation house should be compact. Every step saved in preparing meals and cleaning up can be better taken on a trail or along the shore. The kitchen should be open, with only enough wall space for counters, cabinets, and appliances. Mother should not be visually isolated from the rest of the family while she is working there. The kitchen should be out of any traffic patterns through the house, but easily accessible from other rooms.

The kitchen should have a view. This doesn't have to be the best view from the house, but it should provide a glimpse of nature not possible from the kitchen window back home. If there are small children in the family, the kitchen should be like the control tower at an airport—with a clear view of all areas where those children are likely to be playing.

The best orientation for a kitchen is east or north. Kitchen appliances generate heat, so place this room on the cool side of the house. There should be an exterior door nearby, especially if you plan to eat outdoors often on a deck, porch, or patio. Since you probably won't buy food more than once or twice a week, access to the parking area isn't too important. Access to cold drinks and snacks is. Family members should be able to reach the refrigerator without tracking leaves or sand through the house.

Compared to the same room in a year-round house, the kitchen of a vacation house needs fewer cabinets, but fully as much counter space. You need good working light. You need less storage space for dishes, glassware, and utensils,

Though small in area, this kitchen seems as big as all outdoors. Glass to countertop height lets in good working light, and extends beyond ceiling height to afford a view upward to trees and sky. A diagonal beam supports roof structure. Casements provide ventilation, so that the view through fixed glass is totally unobstructed, even by any corner support. *Architect: Donald McDonald, A.I.A. Photographer: Charles Pearson. Courtesy American Plywood Association.*

but more storage space for canned and packaged foods. You can usually get by with smaller appliances (do you really need an oven?).

### Dining Space

Dining space should have the best location in the house, because mealtime is the highlight of indoor activity nearly every day of vacation. It is the time the entire family is together, regardless of individual interests during the rest of the day. The dining area should have an excellent view—the best, since everyone has time while eating to look at it. It should have good light. The dining table is the center of many indoor activities on rainy days. Orientation to view is therefore more important than orientation to the compass.

Dining space may be part of the living area, part of the kitchen, or a separate room. But wherever you prefer to eat, there should be no more than four steps between the dining table and the serving counter in the kitchen.

Huge panes of glass afford diners a view outward, upward, and downward. Note how the walls and ceiling of dark-stained, horizontally-grooved plywood provide a frame for the view. *Architect: Donald McDonald, A.I.A. Photographer: Charles Pearson. Courtesy American Plywood Association.*

### Sleeping Space

Bedrooms, bunkrooms, or sleeping space in one big room should take full advantage of the evening breeze. Bedrooms should be on the cool side of the house, sheltered from the low-angle rays of the sun, which rises very early in summer. View isn't important, but there is something luxurious about being able to wake up and watch your local world outside without having to get out of bed until you're ready.

Bedrooms in a summer home are basically storage areas—for tired bodies at the end of the day, for a wide variety of vacation clothing, and for the trappings of leisure interests. Each bedroom needs hanging space for jeans, slacks, jackets, and heavy shirts; drawer space for flat clothing; and shelves for books, magazines, games, and just plain "stuff." Closet space should be ventilated; this is especially important in areas where humidity is high.

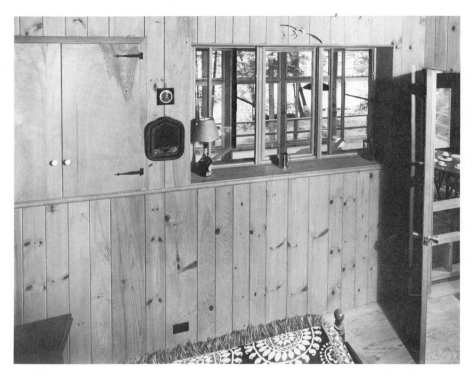

Even though both bedrooms of this house are on the side away from the lake, they have a view of it across the living area and deck. Split-level plan and shed roof permit it. Windows in one bedroom open above living room bookshelves, and in the other above kitchen cabinets. The remaining wall area in both bedrooms is devoted to storage. High window sills provide privacy. *Photographer: Eric M. Sanford. Designer: M. P. Reed.*

Each bedroom should offer privacy. There are times when family members want to be alone, and they need a place where they can be undisturbed. Rooms can be small, however. They aren't activity centers. It is better to put the space you save into the bathroom.

### The Bathroom

A complete bathroom will fit into a space five feet by seven feet. But this isn't large enough for most vacation homes, especially those on water.

Of all bathroom fixtures, the tub takes up the most space. Do you need one? Plans for leisure houses often have only a shower stall. This may be enough, but you can't easily soak muscles tired from hiking or joints stiff from water-skiing in a shower stall.

If the shower will be used frequently to wash off beach sand or for taking off wet swim suits and clothing, consider a compartmented bath (Fig. 3-5). In one compartment, which has an outside door, place the shower stall, a lavatory or wash basin for wringing excess water out of wet suits, and a drying rack. In the other compartment place the toilet and a second countertop lavatory. Build storage space for towels and supplies between the two compartments, with doors opening to both.

You save a little money if all plumbing is concentrated in one wall. But assembling the plumbing system in confined space is often difficult. It's better to place bathrooms where they are most convenient, rather than to mess up a good plan to save a few dollars.

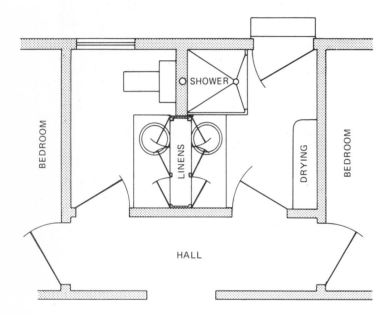

**Figure 3-5.** This bathroom, compartmented for maximum utility, is almost twice the size of a minimum bathroom. Swimmers enter directly from outdoors, and can shower, dress, and hang suits to dry without entering the rest of the house. The toilet is in the second compartment. Linens are stored in cabinets opening to both compartments above twin lavatories.

## Living Space

In a year-round house the living room is the second most important room in the house, after the kitchen. In a vacation house it is among the least important, unless you plan to spend little time outdoors.

On nice days the living room gets less use than either the kitchen or dining room. After dark it is used less than bedrooms. Only when the weather is too wet, cold, or windy does the living room earn its keep during vacations. It should have large windows, not so much to let in the view as to provide good light on cloudy or rainy days. In a vacation house used mostly in warm weather, a north, south, or east orientation is preferable to west. In a vacation house used throughout the year, a south or east orientation is best. Ideally there should be some provision for controlling the effects of wind and sun throughout the year.

Climate is well under control in this house in the deep south. Broad overhang shields glass from rain and direct sun and partially shades the deck. Yet light reflected off undersides of roof planks through upper glass keeps interior rooms bright and cheerful. Construction is post-and-beam. *Architect: Piet A. Kessels, A.I.A. Courtesy Southern Forest Products Association.*

### Decks and Porches

A well-planned outdoor living area is an extension of indoor living space. Properly located and designed, a deck provides a place to sit outdoors that catches every vagrant breeze, sits above any invasion by crawling or slithering creatures at ground level, and gives you a king-of-the-hill view of the world around you.

A deck should extend around at least two walls of the house so that you have a choice of basking in the sun or sitting in the shade. It should be wide enough and close to the kitchen for outdoor meals. And it should improve the appearance and increase the apparent size of a small house.

Many floor plans for vacation houses include decks. Few show porches. Yet in much of the country the insect population makes a deck impractical. Any outdoor living area must be screened to be useful at all.

Seldom can you simply enclose and screen a deck into a porch. A deck doesn't block light from rooms; a porch does. If the porch is large enough to be an extension of the living area, the fact that it shuts light out of the living room isn't too important. But it should not keep light out of the kitchen.

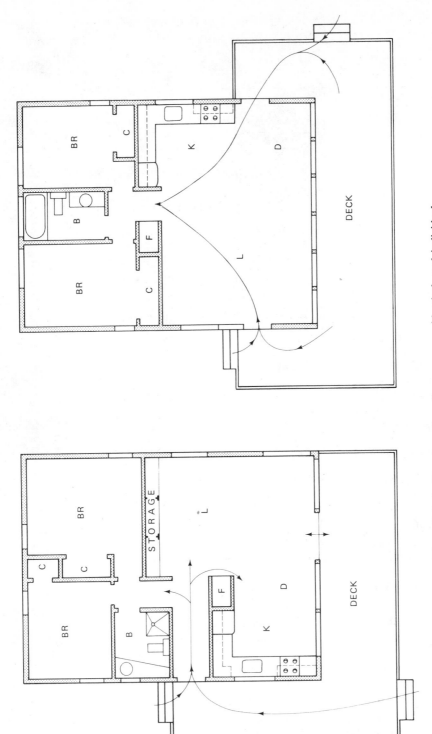

**Figure 3-6.** In these two plans floor areas are identical, and individual room sizes are only slightly different. The plan at left has more hallway, but because of it every room is directly accessible from outdoors and any other room. In the plan at right the main living area becomes a hallway to the bathroom and bedrooms.

Ideally, a porch should lie at a corner of the house where it catches breeze from two directions, is sunlit part of the day but not all of it, and has a view in three directions. And it should be reasonably close to the kitchen for hot-weather dining.

### Storage Space

In addition to the usual indoor storage space, the plan for a good vacation house has bulk space, accessible from outdoors, for storage of equipment used outdoors. Look again at the list you made in Chapter 1 of the items you will need to store. There must be a place for such awkwardly shaped items as luggage, deck furniture, water skis, snow skis, small boats and canoes, oars, and out-board motors.

You may also need some work space with storage for tools. Unlike the situation in the city, you can't call a plumber if your water system springs a leak or a pump breaks down. You must make temporary repairs yourself.

### Traffic Patterns

As you pore over floor plans, study carefully the relationship of each room to the others. Put yourself in each space and figure out what path you would take to get to other rooms and to the outdoors.

In the informal atmosphere of a vacation house, traffic is less crucial than in a year-round house where you need to achieve a balance between busy and quiet areas, open and private areas. But traffic patterns are still important. Every member of the family should be able to walk from the outdoors to the bathroom and kitchen without tracking up much floor. No traffic pattern should cross a room diagonally. Compare the two plans in Fig. 3-6. The two houses are about the same size, and the rooms are also close to the same size. Yet one plan has a simple traffic pattern that crosses no rooms, while the other splits the living area and reduces its usefulness. The difference lies in the hallway.

Some people think that halls are a waste of money. If you are going to spend $15 a square foot for space, they say, why not put it into living space instead of hallway? True, you don't want to waste money on halls. But a living room that must double as a hall is a greater waste. A well-placed hallway directs traffic and leaves other spaces free for their intended use.

# EXTERIOR APPEARANCE

An attractive exterior combines four elements: good use of materials, good scale, good fenestration, and interesting roof lines.

### Materials

Use exterior materials that are as maintenance-free as possible. You can't avoid spending a little of your time on repairs and upkeep, but you don't want to spend all of it that way.

At seashore sites avoid paints and metals. They seldom stand up well under the continuous effects of sand and salt air. Wood, stained or left natural to weather, and masonry products such as stucco are more durable.

On inland sites you have the same range of materials to choose from as you have at home. Materials with a factory-applied finish are generally more durable than materials you finish yourself. But natural materials, such as those found around the site, look better than most manmade materials. Wood and stone blend well anywhere.

From the standpoint of design you are always safe with a single exterior material. Never combine more than two exterior materials. If you use two, the materials should be different in three ways:

- In quantity. One should dominate while the other serves as an accent.
- In texture. If one is smooth, the other should be rougher. Glass counts as a smooth material.
- In tone. One should count as a dark, the other as a light.

### Scale

*Scale* is a ratio or proportion. A house that has awkward proportions is termed *out of scale.* Good scale is difficult to define because it embodies several ratios—the width of a house to its height, window areas to solid walls, and light surfaces to dark, for example. In an attractive house the ratios are never 1 to 1, but closer to 2 to 1 or 3 to 1.

Even if you select a house with good scale, be sure it is also in scale with its site. A house with a high roof peak, such as an A-frame, looks comfortable among tall trees. The same house may look out of place on a flat shore site. Similarly, a low house with a flat roof appears squashed to the ground under tall trees, but seems an integral part of a more level landscape.

### Fenestration

The French word for window is *fenêtre. Fenestration* is the arrangement of windows. In leisure houses large expanses of glass are common and desirable to let in light and view. Even in bedrooms windows should be as large as privacy permits. But for best appearance outside, windows should be grouped together. Avoid plans with small windows placed at random that make the house look like a fort ready to fend off the next Indian attack.

### Roof Lines

A roof serves two basic purposes. It provides protection from the weather, and it improves the exterior appearance of the house, particularly if the house is small.

Most vacation houses have sloping roofs. In general, the snowier the climate the steeper the roof pitch. But you find steep pitches everywhere. Many roofs, whether pitched or flat, have broad overhangs. Overhangs not only protect windows from summer sun while letting in winter sun, they also direct rain water away from the foundation of the house and let you keep windows open during rains. And they throw attractive shadow patterns on walls.

Incidentally, when the eaves of a roof drop below ceiling level, as in an A-frame or a 1 1/2-story house, use the square footage at floor levels for estimating costs. To see how much actual living space you have, however, you must measure the square footage at a point about five feet above floor level (Fig. 3-7). Unless the roof pitch is very steep, the space under sloping ceilings up to the five-foot level isn't usable for much except storage.

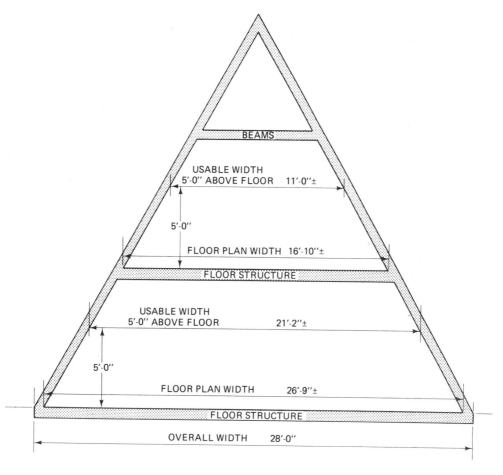

**Figure 3-7.** The popular A-frame is economical and straightforward to build. This section through a two-story house shows the relationship between width at floor level as shown in plans, and the actual usable width when you are standing.

# WAYS TO GET PLANS

All the points discussed in this chapter are elements of the ideal plan for a vacation house. But don't be disappointed if you don't find it. You have to decide what features you must have in your house, those that you would like but could forgo if you can't find them, and those that aren't important to you at all. Some compromise is inevitable.

Where do you go to find the right set of plans? You have a number of choices, some good and some not as good.

## Drawing the Plans Yourself

By drawing the plans yourself and building from them, you put the maximum into your project. Unfortunately you aren't likely to get maximum results, and perhaps not even what you started out to achieve.

Designing an attractive and fully functional house—even a simple, rectangular vacation house—is not a simple undertaking. It requires a knowledge of planning principles, spatial relationships, structural mechanics, architectural design, and scale. Unless you are trained to think like an architect, you are bound to overlook some important facet of design. And regret it. You'll do far better to work from plans that have been professionally designed.

## Hiring an Architect

You can usually spot houses designed by architects. They have a certain flair and excitement about them that ordinary houses don't have. An architect can take your list of desires and translate it into a vacation house that would surpass your dreams.

But unless you are in excellent financial shape, hiring an architect usually isn't the best answer either. Few architects are interested in designing houses except for themselves and close friends, and their fees are likely to be more than you want to pay. Fees are usually 10% to 15% of the cost of construction. Furthermore, you won't often find architects in sparsely populated areas. Part of an architect's fee covers his expenses in supervising construction. If you and your architect live in one place, and you are building in another, he can provide only limited supervision. Yet the very ideas that make a house exciting can often be achieved only with close supervision.

On the other hand, if you insist on doing your own designing, hire an architect as a consultant to keep you from serious errors. Many architects will accept you as a client on a consulting basis for an hourly fee.

## Buying Plans

Most publishers of magazines in the shelter field also publish books of plans for vacation houses. You can buy the books wherever the magazines are sold.

The homes are planned by well-known architects and designers, and they contain the elements of good design you are searching for. Most of the designs have stood the test of time; they have been built and lived in. The plan books are illustrated with photographs reproduced from the magazines' pages. There are designs to fit almost every type of site, orientation, family size, and wallet. Plans are available through the magazine publisher at reasonable cost.

Some architects and qualified designers make a business of designing houses exclusively, and they publish their designs in plan books. Generally the quality is good, and the designs more closely suit the popular taste of the plan-buying public than those shown in magazines. When you buy plans of this type, you are getting professional design for far less than the cost of an architect. Supervision is not included, of course. Exteriors that accompany the plans in the books are almost always shown in sketch form. This does not mean that the houses haven't been built, but that the architects don't have the ready source of photographs that magazines have. Plans are available from the architect; costs of plan packages are comparable with those for plans sold through magazines.

Another good source of vacation house plans is the associations of manufacturers and processors of building materials, mostly wood. The houses in their plan books are also designed by architects, and they are presented either photographically or in drawings. Naturally the drawings, specifications, and materials lists that comprise a package promote the use of the association's products.

A number of mail-order houses make a business of selling plans for houses, including vacation houses. These firms frequently advertise in shelter magazines; they publish their own plan books. All too often, however, the plans are not designed by professionals. They sometimes contain planning faults, such as poor traffic circulation, that are unpleasant to live with. The renderings of exteriors are not always accurate in scale; they tend to make a house look larger or prettier than you could ever build it. The working drawings such firms provide, however, are generally accurate and as complete as you need for doing your own work.

At the end of this chapter is a brief list of sources for good vacation house plans. There are many others, but the author has had personal experience with the sources listed and recommends any one of them. In all plan books the floor plans are drawn to scale and show all room sizes, overall dimensions, and total square footage. These are the facts you need in order to make a choice.

## Using Home Manufacturers' Plans

All manufacturers of mobile, modular, prefabricated, and precut homes produce literature showing their products. Simple floor plans drawn to scale show room arrangements and sizes and are usually accompanied by an exterior drawing or photograph. Manufacturers of prefabricated and precut houses send you several sets of working drawings as part of the total package of materials that you buy from them; there is no extra charge.

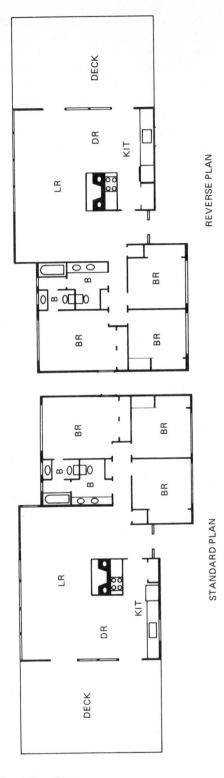

STANDARD PLAN

REVERSE PLAN

**Figure 3-8.** Plans for some vacation houses are available in reverse. Sometimes a reverse plan will match the orientation of your site when a standard plan won't. These two plans are identical in size and function, but the orientation of the deck, dining area, and bedrooms is reversed.

# ORDERING PLANS

As you look at plans, you may find one that you like in every respect but one: it doesn't suit your site. In this case check the plan book to see if reverse plans are available.

A reverse plan has the identical room arrangement to the plan as presented in the book, but the plan is flipped over on its short axis. It's as if you were looking at the plan through the page behind it. Compare the plans in Fig. 3-8. At the left is the standard floor plan for a leisure house as it appears in a book. At the right is the same plan reversed. Suppose you have a site where the rear of the house—the side with the view—faces north. In the standard plan the kitchen, dining area, and deck would all be on the west, exposed to the hot afternoon sun. In the reverse plan the kitchen and dining area would be on the cooler east side, and the deck would be shaded during the heat of the day. Yet all rooms have essentially the same views in both plans.

The prices of sets of working drawings vary, but you can usually buy four sets for under $75. Four sets is a standard package; prints get dog-eared, dirty, and torn apart rather quickly on the job, and you will need all four sets before you are through.

If you aren't certain of your choice by looking at a plan book, and you would like to study the drawings more thoroughly to make sure, order a single set of prints. The cost of one set is about one third the cost of a package. If you later decide to go ahead, however, most sellers of plans will provide the extra three sets of prints, charging only for the remainder of the set-of-four price.

# SOURCES OF VACATION HOUSE PLANS

*American Plywood Association,* 1119 A Street, Tacoma, Washington, 98401.

*W. D. Farmer, Residence Designer, Inc.,* 2007 Montreal Road, Tucker, Georgia, 30359.

*Home Planners, Inc.,* 16310 Grand River Avenue, Detroit, Michigan, 48227.

*Western Wood Products Association,* 1500 Yeon Building, Portland, Oregon, 97204.

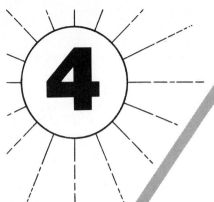

# Working with Contractors

Unless you are experienced in all phases of construction or supremely confident of your ability to master building specialties, you are likely to deal with contractors. As early as possible in your planning for your vacation house, decide what work you can do yourself and what work you will have others do. The worst mistake you can make is to start some phase of construction, find out you can't complete the work yourself, and hire a contractor to finish it. If he accepts the job at all, you are likely to pay dearly. A contractor doesn't want to jeopardize his reputation by completing work someone else starts.

Working with contractors takes long-range planning, superb coordination of effort, and close communication. This teamwork is difficult when you and your contractor are several hundred miles apart. But it can be done, and is done all the time. How well you and your contractor work together depends on your selection of him and cooperation with him.

## SELECTING A CONTRACTOR

Start your hunt for a good contractor by talking with local materials suppliers from whom contractors buy. Ask for the names of their good customers. Since each supplier hopes to have you too, as a customer, he will give you only the names of men with good reputations. Ask how promptly each man play his bills. A contractor who pays promptly is generally reliable. Prompt payment is also a clue to good workmanship. It means the contractor's clients are paying him without delay also, and therefore his work receives their approval readily.

Then talk to the contractor himself. Find out where he banks and the names and addresses of previous customers for whom he has done similar work. Visit these jobs, calling first to explain your purpose. Most owners are flattered that you want to see their home, and they will give you a top-to-bottom tour of the house. Ask what they think are the contractor's strong points, but also ask about weak points. After all, a contractor isn't going to give you the names of people who weren't satisfied.

Judge for yourself the quality of workmanship. If you are satisfied that the work is good, that the contractor knows how to do the work you want done, and you were compatible when you talked, then take one last step: talk with officials of his local bank. They can give you a good picture of financial stability and may confirm local reputation.

This process takes time, especially if you have three or four small contractors in different trades to check out, but it is time well spent. Once in awhile you may go wrong. When this occurs, however, the cause is usually poor communication between owner and contractor, rather than poor workmanship.

Approach each interview initially with a negative attitude. Dig for bad points, not good points. Then evaluate the negatives. If they aren't enough to knock a contractor out of the running, put him on your list of possibilities. Once he is on the list, look for good points and select the man with the greatest number of plusses over minuses.

## CONTRACTING THE ENTIRE JOB

Even if you do none of the work on your house, you must be closely involved and available to resolve questions. Most questions should be settled before you sign a contract, but some situations are bound to occur during construction that require your decision. For the most part, however, your contractor will be working on his own.

If you plan to have someone do all the work, start your search for that man at the earliest possible moment. In fact, go over the site with him before you buy it. His costs include site preparation, excavation and foundation work, and installation of any well or septic system. Sure, he and his crews may not do all this work themselves, but your contractor shoulders the responsibility for the work of the subcontractors he chooses. After walking the site with you, he may have some suggestions that can save you money before you are fully committed to the site.

Ask the contractor to go over the plans for the house you have tentatively selected. He isn't qualified to give you an architectural critique, but he can spot items of construction that will cost more than you estimated. If you are sold on a particular plan, you will probably go ahead anyway, but at least you both know what lies ahead, and you won't be caught by surprise.

## Specifications

Go over specifications carefully. Look for three types of situations. One is where the specifications that come with the plans call for one thing, the contractor prefers another, and you have no preference. Suppose that the plans show a concrete block foundation, and your contractor prefers poured concrete. As long as his method brings the desired result, and doesn't increase costs without also increasing the value to you, amend the specifications. He will do a better job, probably a faster job, and work more willingly if he builds in the way in which he is most familiar. He will also estimate his costs more accurately.

Of course, if you have a definite preference—the second situation—stick to your guns. If you want a wood shingle roof and he suggests asphalt, or vice versa, don't back down. Appearance is a factor here, and the designer of the house had appearance in mind when he wrote the specifications. A contractor who argues with you at length on such a point is not the right contractor for you.

Sometimes specifications aren't specific—the third situation—which seems contradictory. They seldom specify color, for example. You do. Before the contractor buys such materials as roofing, paneling, tile, plumbingware, light fixtures, and hardware, you have to make some decisions. The best way is to go with your contractor to his supplier, see what is in stock or can be ordered, and make decisions then. On some items that aren't installed until near the end of construction, the contractor quotes an allowance, and you make the selection later. Lighting fixtures are an example. The contractor allows you, say, $100 for light fixtures. If you go over that limit, he charges you the difference in his final billing. If you are under the limit, he gives you a credit for the difference in his final billing.

One frequent stumbling block between owner and contractor is the term "or equal" in specifications. The specifications writer lists a product by brand name, then follows with "or equal." In effect he is saying, "I know this specific product will work here, because I have used it before and know what it does. But there are others just as good that I haven't used."

Whenever you see "or equal," and the specified product isn't carried locally, find out from your contractor or supplier what "equals" are available. Carefully check out every substitute. If one is satisfactory, amend the specifications by listing the substitute by name along with any specific data, such as model number. If you can't find a satisfactory substitute, strike out "or equal" and either order the item yourself for delivery to the site (or to the contractor), or ask the local merchant to order it. Never leave selection of substitute materials to chance. What your contractor thinks is equal may not be equal at all in your judgment.

On the other hand, if the contractor suggests a substitute that he has used successfully, rely on his good judgment.

## Quotations

After studying the site, working drawings, and specifications, the contractor submits a quotation, or bid. The quotation states a firm price for the work to be done. It states the scope of the work—that is, what work is included, what work is excluded, and on what documents the bid is based. Quotations from contractors covering the entire house are usually quite simple because the work is all-inclusive. They agree to do all work required by your working drawings and specifications as amended. In contrast, the bid of a subcontractor who completes only one aspect of the job must be more detailed. You must both know what work he is to do, and what work you are to do. More on this subject later in this chapter.

Any special conditions or provisos should be clearly stated in the quotation. There may be none. In some cases, however, the contractor may base his estimate on being able to start work by a certain date, or to delay starting until a certain date. Or you may want the work completed by a certain date. These special conditions must be in writing.

Get more than one quotation if possible, so that you can compare prices and terms. To do so, you need a set of working drawings and specifications for every contractor you ask to bid. He returns all documents with his bid, and you give all but one set to the general contractor you select. You keep the other set. If you contract the work yourself, each subcontractor you hire needs a complete set.

Because all contractors are quoting on the same house and working from the same documents, you might expect that all quotations would be within a few dollars of each other. This rarely happens, and it is the reason for securing more than one bid. Sometimes a contractor will shave his profit a little because he needs the work to keep his crews busy. Conversely, a contractor may bid high because he doesn't need or want the work, and he feels he deserves extra profit for taking on the job.

When all quotations name about the same price, and you verify that all the contractors are quoting on the same basis, you are usually safe in awarding the work to the low bidder. When any bid is much lower than the others, try to find out why. The contractor may have made an error or overlooked something. If so, he is likely to discover this during the course of the job. He may then have to cut corners just to break even, and you won't get the quality of work you expect.

If all quotations come in higher than you expect or can afford, talk to each contractor separately. Level with him. Tell him you can't afford that much, and ask his suggestions for ways to reduce the cost. He can often come up with ideas for changes that bring costs into line, but not for exactly the same house you had in mind. You must then decide whether to build a lesser house or find some way to raise a little more money.

## The Contract

A quotation is not a legal document. A contract is. It formalizes the agreement between you and a contractor that is based on his quotation. It should include

1. A copy of working drawings, with any changes you have agreed upon clearly indicated on drawings and in a separate listing.

2. A copy of specifications upon which you have agreed. Any handwritten changes, additions, or deletions should each be initialled by both of you.

3. A list of allowances. This list is usually incorporated in specifications.

4. Terms of payment. The method of billing varies, but normally it is related to stages of completion rather than fixed dates. A contractor may bill 20% of the total price at five different times—after completion of the foundation, structural framework, mechanical installation, and finishing, and finally upon acceptance. Or he may bill three or four times in equal or varying percentages.

5. A firm total price, or carefully stipulated terms if the price is not firm.

*Types of Contracts.* A contract may be one of three types: fixed-price, cost-plus, or cost-plus with a fixed maximum.

A *fixed-price* contract is the most common type covering new construction. The contractor agrees to build for so many dollars—the firm total price stated in the contract. You pay no more and no less. You know in advance what your vacation house will cost, which is a help if you need to arrange financing. If actual cost is less, the contractor makes a greater profit. If costs run higher than expected, the contractor makes less profit. A reputable contractor absorbs the loss; others may cut quality to maintain their profit margin. This is one reason for investigating a contractor thoroughly before you hire him.

Avoid making changes after construction is in progress under a fixed-price contract. Changes are possible, but they open the door to legal complications. Make your decisions before you sign a contract, not afterward.

Under a *cost-plus* contract you pay the cost of all materials the contractor buys for the job, plus the labor of his crews, plus a fixed percentage of the total cost of materials and labor. This percentage covers the contractor's overhead and profit, and is usually around 15%. It applies to all materials, even those you supply.

A cost-plus contract is most commonly used between you as a builder-owner and subcontractors you hire to do some of the work. A few variables now enter the picture—the speed at which you complete your part of the work, and the quality of work you do. These variables won't greatly affect a subcontractor's materials costs, but delays could easily increase his labor costs. Under a cost-plus contract, he is protected against potential losses over which he has no control.

The main disadvantage to you of a cost-plus contract is that you can't calculate total costs in advance. Your contractor will bill you only for what he earns. But to keep his earnings in line you must meet your scheduled deadlines, maintain close communications, and follow good construction practices.

Under a *cost-plus contract with a fixed maximum* you again pay the cost of materials, labor, and a percentage. But the contract also states a maximum price. This fixed price will be high enough to allow the contractor a fair profit under almost any circumstances. But at least you know the most you may have to pay him. If you meet all your obligations, and the contractor's actual billing is below the fixed price, you get the saving. Under a straight fixed-price contract, the contractor gets the saving. The cost-plus contract with a fixed maximum is fair to both parties.

Before you sign any contract, ask your lawyer to check it over for you. Most contracts for small construction jobs such as vacation houses are written on a standard agreement form. If your contractor has a standard form he prefers, by all means use it. To have your lawyer draw up a contract is not wise. It increases your costs for one thing. It also increases the contractor's costs, because he has to have his lawyer check it out. More important, it gets your relationship off to a bad start, creating a climate rife with caution and suspicion. If you can't trust your contractor to use a standard form with which he is familiar, you don't want him as a contractor—and he probably doesn't want you as a client, either.

In many lightly populated areas, small contractors are not used to working under contracts. A handshake and verbal agreement is their bond, and they keep their word. But work up a contract anyway, using a standard form preferably bought in his community. A contract should never be an adversary document that smacks of mutual distrust. It should be a friendly agreement that sets down the foundation for mutual respect and understanding.

## ACTING AS YOUR OWN CONTRACTOR

When you contract any part of a job, you are in effect acting as a general contractor, and individual tradesmen serve as subcontractors. There is nothing wrong with this, but be aware of the added responsibilities you thereby undertake.

How simple or complex your job is depends on what work you subcontract. Hiring someone to clear the site and excavate for the foundation, for example, is fairly simple. The work is a complete stage of construction within itself. It has a definite start and end. No other work goes on before or during this stage. You and your subcontractor agree on a price, draw up a contract that spells out the scope of the work, and sign it. You let him know when he can start, and he lets you know when he is finished. You inspect his work, approve it, and pay his bill. Neat.

Excavating is usually covered under a fixed-price contract. In any case be sure the contract clearly states the scope of the work—not only what is included but what is not included. Under scope the contract might say that the subcontractor shall be responsible for all clearing and grading necessary for a gravel access road 12 feet wide from the main road to the house, including a turnaround.

You can build this simple rectangular vacation house in three stages. Stage 1 (top exterior and plan) is a 24-foot square with four full-sized rooms. Stage 2 adds two bedrooms, and simple cabinets convert the original bedroom into a semiprivate bunkroom. Stage 3 adds bulk storage space and an enlarged living area that may be a glassed-in family room or the screened porch shown in the bottom plan and exterior. *Courtesy Home Planners, Inc.*

He shall provide a temporary gravel access road. He shall remove from the property cut trees, branches, and excess earth. He shall pile topsoil at one side of the site. You will provide protection for the pile against weather. The contractor shall clear within six feet of foundation lines. You do the staking, and establish the lines to which he works. He excavates for the foundation, including trenches for footings. You do the final hand-leveling and cleaning up. He digs all trenches for water lines, drain lines, and a disposal field for a septic system. The septic system shall be installed by others.

More complicated is subcontracting the installation of mechanical systems while you yourself handle the structural framing and finishing. You must not only coordinate your work with your subcontractors, but also their work with

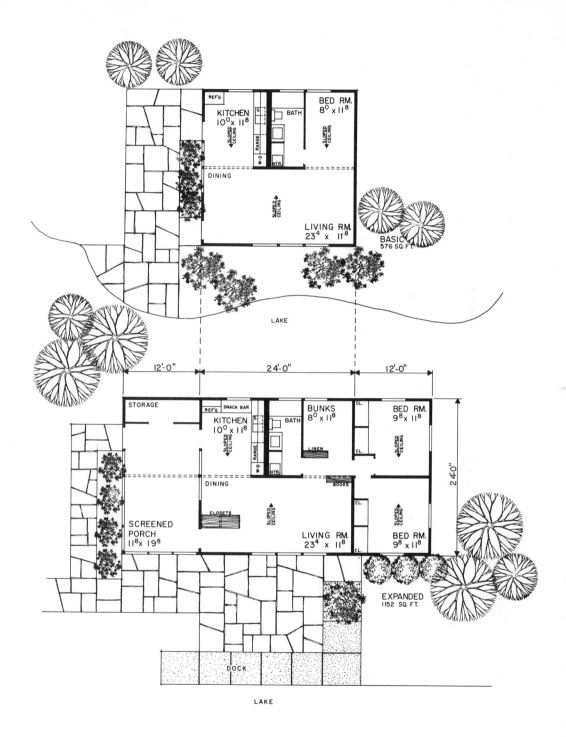

BASIC
576 SQ. FT.

LAKE

12'-0"  24'-0"  12'-0"

STORAGE  SNACK BAR  BUNKS
8⁰ x 11⁸  BED RM.
9⁸ x 11⁸

REF'G  KITCHEN
10⁰ x 11⁸  BATH

LINEN

DINING  BOOKS

SCREENED
PORCH
11⁸ x 19⁸  CLOSETS  LIVING RM.
23⁴ x 11⁸  BED RM.
9⁸ x 11⁸

EXPANDED
1152 SQ. FT.

DOCK

LAKE

24'-0"

each other. A subcontractor's costs are preponderantly labor, and labor cost is based on time. Few contractors will agree to anything but a cost-plus contract under such circumstances, because they can't gauge their time when that time depends on you. To control your costs, you must schedule all work to reduce their time to a minimum.

Unlike excavating, plumbing work, for example, goes on intermittently during the entire period of construction. Drain lines and perhaps water lines are often stubbed in to just below first floor level during foundation work. Rough plumbing and the bathtub are installed after structural work is finished but before interior finishing. Finish plumbing takes place after interior finishing but before decorating. Electrical and heating work also progress in several separate stages.

Although construction now goes on all year long, even in northern parts of the country, it is still a somewhat seasonal business. When a subcontractor isn't busy, he is happy to have small jobs like yours to keep his crews together. But when he is busy, he puts his crews on the bigger, better-paying jobs first, and works on yours when he gets around to it.

How can you avoid delays by subcontractors? You can't, to be honest. But you can minimize the problem by starting construction in late summer and

The cluster concept of vacation housing gives you the opportunity to assemble your own design out of well-planned square units. There are three designs for living units, three for sleeping units, and a smaller garage unit. Clusters may be built simultaneously or in stages, and you arrange and connect them to suit the shape and slope of your site. *Courtesy Home Planners, Inc.*

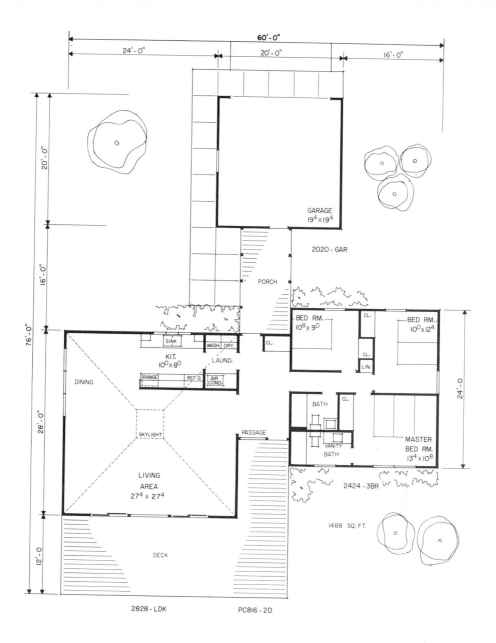

enclosing the house before winter weather sets in. Then subcontractors can work more at a time of their choosing than at one of yours.

Communication is the key to success with subcontractors. Call or talk to each man whenever you visit the site, and keep them fully aware of the job's progress. Give them as much advance notice on each phase as possible, and allow them a little more time than they ask for to complete each phase. If you have a close working relationship with your subcontractors, they will take it upon themselves to check the job on their own when they are nearby, and will keep you advised of their progress.

Select your subcontractors as early in construction as possible. Give them a tentative schedule for your part of the work, and let them tell you at what stages they want to begin their work. Go over specifications carefully so there are no causes for later argument. Go over the working drawings, and note the places where you have to leave room or make cuts for their work.

Ask each mechanical contractor to make a drawing showing where he intends to run his pipes, ducts, or wiring. Include a copy of the drawing in the contract. A rough sketch is adequate as long as it provides you with critical dimensions and pinpoints places where you have special work to do. Then, shortly before you are ready for a subcontractor to bring in his crew, ask him to inspect the work with you to make sure all is ready. Again, the best surprise is no surprise for either of you.

## PAYING YOUR BILLS

Every bill should specifically list the work performed as stated in the contract. If you are paying under a cost-plus contract, a copy of each supplier's bill and each man's time record should be attached. Check each bill item by item. If you have any doubt about an item, question the contractor in a friendly way. Mistakes can be made, and a good contractor is just as anxious to have the bill correct as you are.

To illustrate the point, some years ago an owner noted on a contractor's bill that the labor cost was higher than he had expected. He called the contractor, who replied: "Yes, I know it's up a little. I gave Bill a raise because he is doing good work and I want to keep him with me. But if you don't think I should charge you for his raise, refigure his time at the original rate." The owner was amazed. "Ernie," he retorted, "if Bill is worth the pay increase to you, he's certainly worth it to me. The bill stands approved."

The next day the owner made a point to congratulate Bill on his raise. Bill didn't slow his pace, but beamed at the recognition. When the house was completed and the owner totaled the labor cost for the entire job, he found that Bill's productivity had more than made up for the raise. The cost was below the original estimate.

When you inspect work before paying a bill, do so with a set of plans and specifications in hand. Just as a subcontractor inspects your work to see what problems it might cause him, check his work for problems it might cause you. When you spot something you don't like or understand, question it. If the contractor can't give you a logical reason for what he has done, get him to correct it. Only after correction should you make payment.

But, except for final payment, don't delay payment when work is satisfactory. Your contractor has spent money on your house and has bills to pay, too. By failing to pay promptly, you increase his costs, lose his respect, and won't get as good a result as you should.

No more than 90% of a total contract should be billed or paid prior to final billing upon acceptance. You must withhold final payment until any flaws you find in a final inspection are corrected. Check everything with extreme care. Make a list of corrections you think should be made, and go over each one with the contractor. As each item is disposed of or corrected, cross it off the list. Then send in the final payment along with a letter of satisfaction. Once you pay the final bill, your contractor is no longer legally obligated to make any corrections.

# MECHANICAL SYSTEMS

Beginning with the next chapter, the remainder of this book details the procedures for installing foundations, structural systems, and finishing materials. Instructions are not included for installing a heat distribution system, a fuel supply system, hot and cold water supply system, drainage system, or electrical system. Each of these subjects is worthy of its own book, and several excellent texts on mechanical systems have been written for do-it-yourselfers. If you plan to do your own mechanical work and need a good reference, these provide the basic information you need:

- Heating: *Comfort Heating* by Langley (Reston Publishing Company).
- Plumbing: *Basic Plumbing* by Philbin (Reston)
- Electrical: *Electrical Wiring: Principles and Practices* by Herrick (Prentice-Hall), or *An Introduction to Electrical Wiring* by Doyle (Reston).

Even if you subcontract all mechanical work, you have some decisions to make. And you need at least a rudimentary knowledge of the various systems and how they fit into your structural systems.

## Heating

Details of a heating system are rarely shown in working drawings, although a recommended location for the furnace or boiler is usually indicated. Your subcontractor will make a drawing of the system he plans to install, giving locations of equipment, distribution ducts or piping, and heat outlets, as well as the size of duct or pipe in each run.

Specifications and materials lists say nothing about the heating equipment needed. The size of a furnace or boiler—that is, its heat output expressed in Btus (British thermal units)—is based on heat loss calculations. These calculations are rather complex, but any competent heating contractor is qualified to make them. To do so, he needs to know what interior and exterior materials you intend to use, what types and sizes of windows, and the rated value of insulation you plan to install in walls, ceilings, and floors. He can glean all other information he needs from the drawings.

*Central Heating.* You can heat your vacation house with a central system or with individual space heaters. A central system does a better job of heating, but space heaters are less expensive to install and cost less to operate. For houses not occupied year around, a warm-air system is more practical than a hot-water system. A warm-air system won't freeze, and it provides quick heat to take away the early morning chill in a cold cabin. You must operate a hot-water system on low heat all winter, or else drain all lines to prevent damage from freeze-ups.

The furnace can go almost anywhere. If you haven't bought a furnace in the past twenty years, you will be amazed how much they have shrunk in size. Some are no bigger than a file cabinet, and there are types designed for installation on the floor, in the floor, under the floor, above the ceiling, or in a closet.

Warm-air furnaces operate in one of three ways. A *horizontal-flow* furnace hangs from floor joists in a basement or crawl space, or rests on braced ceiling joists in an attic. A blower pulls fresh air into one end of the furnace and pushes heated air horizontally out the other end into a plenum (a large mixing duct) and then into risers (vertical distribution ducts), which carry the heat to each room.

A *downflow* furnace rests at first-floor level. Heat is blown downward through a distribution system of ducts below joists, and cooled air returns through ducts in attic space. An *upflow* furnace may be placed on the first floor or in a basement. Heat flows upward into a plenum, then travels to rooms through ducts either below first-floor joists or above ceiling joists. Cold air returns at or below floor level.

All three types of furnaces are triggered by a standard wall thermostat. The best place for the thermostat is on a partition in the main living space. It should be mounted 5 feet above the floor at a point where it is within easy reach for resetting, but out of any traffic pattern. It should be away from drafts and out of reach of the sun. It should not be placed where it will be affected by heat from a fireplace, lamp, or any heating appliance.

Registers—the devices at the ends of ducts that diffuse the flow of heat into a room—function best in outside walls beneath or beside windows, or in the floor beneath windows. Be sure the openings won't be covered by draperies at any time. Grilles that let cooled air into return ducts belong on interior partitions either just above the floor or just below the ceiling.

*Space Heating.* Space heaters do not require a duct system; they can heat only one or at most two rooms. One of the oldest types of space heaters is the Franklin stove. Designed by Benjamin Franklin, it is still in steady use today— improved, of course. It burns almost any solid fuel and requires a smoke pipe and chimney. Heat doesn't circulate but radiates, and rooms are likely to be hot near the stove and cool in the corners.

Circulating heaters heat partly by radiation, but also have a small blower that distributes heated air around a room. Circulating heaters are smaller than stoves and are available for use with wood, coal, coke, charcoal, gas, oil, or kerosene as fuel.

Floor heaters operate on gas or oil, and may heat one or two rooms. The heater fits in a framed opening in the floor, and is covered by a large grille at floor level. Heated air is blown upward through baffles that distribute it through-out the room. Fuel connections and the smoke pipe run under the floor to foundation walls. Cost of installation is low and installation is quite simple.

Stoves, circulating heaters, and floor heaters all take up floor space near the center of a room. Wall heaters do not. They fit between studs and may be fueled by gas, oil, or electricity. They project slightly into one room; they can be adapted to heat the room behind the partition, too. Gas- and oil-fired types must be vented—either outward if they are set in an exterior wall, or upward through the roof if they are set in a partition.

An ordinary fireplace heats only one room, but some manufactured fireplaces are designed to heat more than one room. Details of these units and of fireplace construction are discussed in Chapter 11.

If your source of electricity is reliable, and power lines are likely to withstand storms, consider an electric radiant heating system. The most popular system consists of radiant baseboard units, sized to the air space to be heated, and placed in or against walls beneath windows. Baseboard units are more expensive than other space heaters, but they provide quick, clean, and noiseless heat. The best systems have a thermostat in each room for individual control of temperature.

What fuel should you use for heating? There are four considerations. First is availability of the fuel. Second is availability of local delivery and repair services. Another is safety. Still another is fuel cost.

A small furnace running for twenty-four hours in cold weather uses very roughly a million Btus. To produce a million Btus, you burn up about 1/25 of a ton of coal, 7 1/4 gallons of oil, 165 kilowatt-hours of electricity, or 10,000 cubic feet (ten therms) of gas. Different gases have different heat values, so the term *therm* was created to allow for these differences. By checking local prices for each fuel, you can quickly compare the economics of one fuel against another.


## Plumbing

You may work with only one or with several subcontractors before your entire plumbing system is installed. The plumbing contractor who installs water and drain lines and plumbingware may be the same man who drills wells and lays out septic systems. More likely, however, you will work with three separate plumbing specialists.

*Water Supply System.* If your site is served by a municipal water system, your plumbing subcontractor takes care of hooking onto the existing line. He also makes the necessary connections to a fresh-water lake or to a well. A professional well-digger sinks the well.

The limitations on well location are quite stringent. A well must be located outside the house in all states except Alaska. It must lie at least 10' away in horizontal distance from your property lines and from any sewer line with permanent water-tight joints. It must be at least 50' away from other sewer lines, a dry well, or septic tank. Except in rare instances it must be at least 100' away from chemically poisoned soil, or from any part of the disposal field in conjunction with a septic tank.

When the source of water lies less than 22' below ground level, the well-driller drills a shallow well and installs a shallow-well jet or piston pump. Any

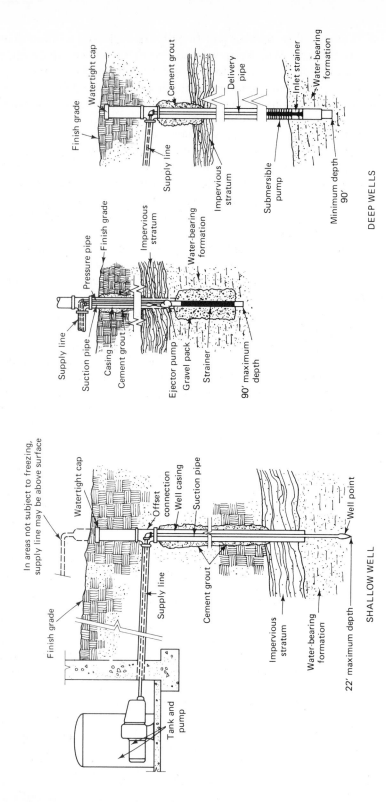

**Figure 4-1.** The water pump is never placed more than 22′ above the lowest level in a well. With a shallow well (left) the pump connects to the end of the supply line and rests on a concrete slab in the basement or crawl space of the house. In deep wells (less than 90′, center, and more than 90′, right) the pump fits inside the well casing. The supply line from well to house must lie below the frost line.

SHALLOW WELL

DEEP WELLS

well more than 22' deep is called a deep well (Fig. 4-1). With wells less than 90' deep you need a deep-well ejector pump, and with still deeper wells you need a submersible pump.

The well-driller selects the most likely spot for a well and proceeds to drill. When he hits water, he measures the flow and takes samples for approval by the state health department. A minimum flow of 5 gallons per minute and state approval are necessary before he can proceed with construction of the well.

You need a pump with enough capacity to meet your need for water, but that capacity must not exceed the flow. You also need a pressure tank for water storage. Standard tank size is 42 gallons, large enough so that the pump doesn't start operating until you have used about 8 gallons of water. If you have no fire department nearby, consider a larger storage tank. The fire chief who serves your area can offer valuable suggestions.

*Sewer System.* Although alternatives exist, a septic system is the best and most economical way of meeting sewage disposal requirements when you are not served by a municipal sewer system. A septic system consists of a sewer line from the house, a septic tank, an effluent sewer, a distribution box, and an absorption field (Fig. 4-2).

Waste flows from the house through the house sewer, which is made of clay tile with tight joints, to the septic tank. A septic tank is nothing more than a watertight container, usually a rectangular box of concrete. Cylindrical tanks are made of steel, plastic, or vitrified (glazed by heat) clay. Minimum tank capacity

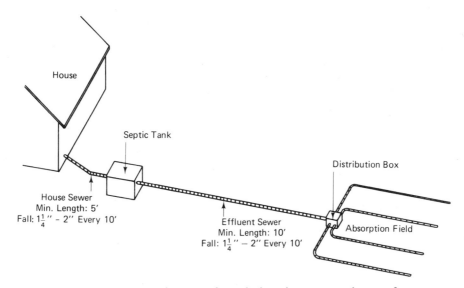

**Figure 4-2.** Here are the parts of a typical septic system, and some of the restrictions on length and slope of sewer lines. Piping in the absorption field may be laid out in a variety of ways that depend on the slope of the land and the area available.

is based on the number of bedrooms in the house. You need a 750-gallon tank to serve one or two bedrooms, a 900-gallon tank for three bedrooms, and a 1,000-gallon tank for a four-bedroom house. The tank must be located at least 5′ from the foundation, 10′ from property lines and any water lines, and 50′ from a well.

As soon as waste reaches the septic tank, bacterial action begins. Heavier parts of the waste sink to the bottom as sludge (Fig. 4-3). Grease and lighter particles float to the top as scum. As the tank fills, the liquid effluent flows from the tank down the effluent sewer to the distribution box. By now the organic material in the waste has largely decomposed.

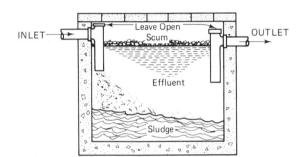

**Figure 4-3.** After a few years of use, sludge fills about one fourth of a septic tank, and scum is about an inch thick. Yet liquid flows out with no restriction. Note in this section through a septic tank that the outlet pipe is slightly lower than the inlet pipe to permit this flow. The tank's top is removable to permit periodic cleaning.

The distribution box is a smaller concrete box with one inlet for the effluent sewer and holes in the other sides for outlet pipes to the absorption field. The sole purpose of the distribution box is to disperse the effluent as equally as possible into all pipe lines in the absorption field. These pipes are usually perforated, and joints are loose to allow the waste to seep into the soil.

The size and configuration of an absorption field depends on the type of soil and contours. You make a percolation test, called a *perc test* for short, to determine how absorptive the soil is. Ask local health officials whether a perc test is required; they may already have ample data on hand. If you need to make a test, follow these steps:

1. With a post-hole auger drill half a dozen holes in the area of the absorption field. Make the holes 6″ to 12″ in diameter and 24″ deep.

2. If the auger compacts the soil, roughen the sides and bottom of the holes. Remove loose soil, then add about 2″ of sand or gravel so the bottom of the hole won't wash out when you pour in water.

3. Add 12″ of water and let it stand overnight. Refill if the water has drained away by morning.

4. Mark a line on the side of the hole 6″ above the bottom, and add water to that point. Then measure the drop in water level every 30 minutes for the next 4 hours.

5. Record the amount of drop in the final 30 minutes. Then refer to Fig. 4-4 to determine the area of absorption field needed per bedroom. If you intend to install an automatic washer, garbage disposal unit, or both, double the areas shown in the chart.

6. If all the water seeps out of the hole in less than 30 minutes, add another 6″ of water and measure the drop every 10 minutes for 1 hour. Use the drop in the final 10 minutes and the chart to determine the area of the absorption field.

| AMOUNT OF DROP IN 30 MINUTES (in inches) | AMOUNT OF DROP IN 10 MINUTES (in inches) | TRENCH BOTTOM REQUIRED PER BEDROOM (in square feet) |
|---|---|---|
| − | 6 | 85 |
| − | 5 | 100 |
| − | 3-3/4 | 115 |
| 6 | 2 | 125 |
| 3 | 1 | 165 |
| 2 | − | 190 |
| 1 | − | 250 |
| $\frac{1}{2}$ | − | 330 |

**Figure 4-4.** By measuring the drop in water level during step 5 (left column) or step 6 (center column) of the percolation test, you determine the square feet of trench bottom required in the absorption field. If the amount of drop falls between the figures in the chart, use the larger square footage. If the drop is 4 1/2″ in 30 minutes, for example, allow 165 square feet of trench bottom per bedroom.

Limitations on the location of an absorption field are as stringent as they are on wells. The water table in that area must be at least 4′ below ground level, and any rock ledge or hard clay must be at least 6′ below the ground. The absorption field must be at least 5′ from property lines and any foundation, 10′ from water lines, and 100′ from a well.

Note that the chart (Fig. 4-4) refers to the amount of trench bottom. Trenches may vary in width from 12″ up to 36″. If the chart shows that you need 190 square feet of bottom, you can meet these requirements with, for example: four trenches 12″ wide and 48′ long, three trenches 24″ wide and 32′ long, or three trenches 36″ wide and only 21′ long. These choices and others depend on the space you have available for an absorption field.

Space between trenches varies with the width of the bottom. Trenches 12″ wide must be at least 6′ apart, 24″ trenches 7′ apart, and 36″ trenches 8′ apart. In the three examples given, then, you need areas of 22′ by 48′, 20′ by 32′, and 25′ by 21′ respectively.

The contractor who installs the septic tank lays out the septic system. A house sewer can be as short as 5′, but 50′ is much better. It must be 18″ below grade at the foundation wall and slope downward 1 1/4" to 2" every 10', with no bend of more than 22 1/2°. The inlet at the septic tank should be at least 2 1/2' below grade in cold climates. The distribution box may be anywhere from 10' to 50' from the septic tank, with the effluent sewer sloped at the same angle as the house sewer. The box should be at least 18" below ground level, and trenches for the absorption field at least 18" deep.

If you plan to design your own septic system, make a drawing of the proposed layout and secure approval from the Department of Public Health before you begin trenching. Show all distances, sizes of tank and box, and slopes. Better still, leave the layout to the experienced contractor who installs the system.

The contractor who plumbs hot water lines, cold water lines, and drain lines in the house will make a drawing of the piping system he plans to install. There won't be much detail, and you may find it difficult to read, but it will indicate where your work and his interlock. He will determine the sizes of piping required and the materials to use, and it is his responsibility to meet all code requirements. You select the plumbingware, however.

*Plumbingware.* The variety of plumbing fixtures available where you build your vacation house may be limited. If local merchants don't stock a complete line, it may be worthwhile to special-order. So that you know what is made, here are general specifications for plumbingware.

*Bathtubs.* Bathtubs are made of vitreous china, enameled steel, or plastic, in descending order of quality and price. Most tubs are rectangular. Standard length is 60" measured from flange to flange, although 54" and 66" rectangular tubs are also made. Widths vary from 28 1/2" up to 32", with 30 1/2" as the standard, measured from flange to rim. Height above floor at the rim varies from 14" to 16". Square tubs have 48" sides and a 12" rim.

The bathtub goes into place as soon as you finish framing around it. A recessed tub is framed on three sides. A corner tub is framed on only two sides. Because of the close relationship between tub dimensions and framing, you must know early in construction the dimensions of the tub you buy. Enter these dimensions and the bathtub material in the specifications that you and your plumbing contractor agree on. Also indicate whether you need a right-hand or left-hand tub. A left-hand tub drains to the left and a right-hand tub drains to the right as you step into it.

*Shower Stalls.* If you plan to take showers in the bathtub, you must provide blocking in the plumbing wall for the showerhead, and for a shower rod or a frame for doors that slide on the outer rim of the tub.

Separate shower stalls of plastic or metal come predrilled for a showerhead, hot and cold water faucets, and a drain. They come in one piece, with lugs on the back that you attach to studs. The three walls are 6' to 7' high, and vary in width from 28" to 36". Some types have a folding or hinged door. Others require a shower curtain. The curtain rod runs above the top of the shower stall, and you must block for it.

*Water Closets.* Water closets are generally designated by flushing action. Of the five types, the washdown type is the simplest in operation and the least expensive, but is rather noisy. More expensive but quiet and efficient in its use of water is the siphon-vortex type.

Widths of tanks vary from 20″ to 22″, and bowls project 25″ to 31″ from the wall behind them. If bathroom space is limited, be sure that the water closet you order fits with at least 2″ clearance on both sides and 21″ in front.

Water closets are made either in one piece, with the bowl and tank formed together out of vitreous china, or in two pieces, with the tank resting on the back of the bowl. Two-piece units cost less. Tanks may be plastic; bowls are always vitreous china. You set the bowl on a gasket called a *closet ring* that fits over flooring of resilient tile or roll goods and around the drain. You bolt the bowl to the floor through the closet ring. With a ceramic tile floor you set the water closet first, then tile up to it.

*Lavatories.* Lavatories come in a wide assortment. They are made of vitreous china, enameled steel, stainless steel, or plastic. They stand on legs, hang from the wall, or fit into a countertop. Although the bowl itself is usually oval, the outer shape may be square, rectangular, round, or semicircular, as well as oval. Overall dimensions range from 12″ by 12″ to 20″ by 36″.

Most lavatories either hang from the wall or fit into a countertop. Manufacturer's instructions that come with the wall-hung type tell at what height above the floor to place blocking. They also give the sizes and locations of plumbing connections. With counter types, plumbing connections lie within the hole cut for the lavatory.

Countertop lavatories are of three types. One type is shaped out of plastic that forms a countertop as well. Another type is self-rimming—that is, it has a rim or lip that fits over the countertop. The third type fits flush with the countertop, and you seal the joint with a metal rim set in caulking.

*Sinks.* Almost all sinks today are made for countertop installation. They may have one, two, or three compartments, and two, one, or no drainboards. The compartments may have the same or different depths. Sinks come in various sizes, but 32″ wide by 21″ from front to back is almost a standard. The plumber works from center lines, so size isn't too important to him. But it is to you when you have to cut the hole in your countertop. Work the sink dimensions into the specifications for your plumbing contractor to follow.

When you select a sink, keep one more point in mind. The sink is one item in a vacation house that should be as much as possible like the one at home. Dishwashing goes more quickly with an established routine. To have to follow one routine at home and another away from home slows the work and cuts into free time.

*Water Heaters.* Gas and electric water heaters range in capacity from 17 up to 80 gallons for residential use. You probably won't use a lot of hot water on vacation, and a 30-gallon heater is usually adequate for a family of four.

If you buy a gas water heater, be sure it has the proper orifice for the type of gas you intend to burn for fuel. The orifices are interchangeable in size, but not in operation.

Most floor plans show a location for the water heater. It does not take up so much floor space, however, that you can't put it somewhere else if a new location takes less piping, and therefore brings hot water more quickly to the places you need it. It should be located close to the sink or bathtub, depending on what you wash the most on vacation.

## Electrical System

Your electrical contractor will make all the necessary calculations to determine the electrical load you are likely to put on power lines. He will determine the size of entrance panel required, and the size and routing of all electrical circuits needed to meet codes. So that he can make an electrical layout, you must tell him what appliances, both fixed and portable, you intend to use and where you will use them. His electrical layout should be part of your contract with him.

*Light Fixtures.* Your contractor will probably give you an allowance for light fixtures in the contract. The allowance is merely a method of accounting; you pay the total cost of fixtures anyway. But before you agree on a figure, visualize where you need light and how much.

Light is measured in footcandles. A *footcandle* is the amount of light a candle throws on a square foot of curved wall one foot away. A 75-watt bulb provides 30 footcandles of light from 3 ' away and 20 footcandles from 6 ' away.

Lighting experts recommend at least 10 footcandles for such activities as playing games, watching television, or just conversing. You need 20 to 30 footcandles for knitting, cleaning, or distinguishing dark colors. You need 30 to 50 footcandles for all kitchen activities, reading, shaving, or applying cosmetics. You need 50 to 70 footcandles for making repairs, writing postcards, or sewing. For fine handicraft you need 70 to 100 footcandles.

Footcandle figures are a guide to the amount of general and specific lighting, as well as direct and indirect lighting in each room. Most rooms need only enough general light so that you can find your way around.

*Indoor Lighting.* The main living and dining areas need a general light level of 10 footcandles, provided by direct light from a ceiling fixture or indirect light from lamps that reflect off ceilings. These rooms also require specific light—for reading, eating, playing games, and for rainy-day hobbies and pastimes. Work out a furniture arrangement to determine where you need overhead lighting and where you need outlets for lamps.

Bedrooms used primarily for sleeping need only enough general light to alleviate the dark. One small lamp on a chest is normally adequate. Add good bedlights if you are addicted to reading in bed. An overhead light is not a good solution. If you want more light, install a fixture in the closet ceiling, where it illuminates clothing but doesn't fill a bedroom with light.

Concentrate most of your light in the bathroom and kitchen. A small bathroom can be adequately lighted by a pair of tubular lights flanking the mirror above the lavatory. Pick the pink rather than blue or cold white tubes; you'll look healthier. Tubes provide good general light, plus shadowless light for shaving and applying makeup. If you want additional light, consider an overhead fixture that is a combination light, ventilator, and small radiant heater all rolled into one.

General light is helpful in the kitchen, but specific light is much more important. By all means have a light over the range; many range hoods have a bright light in them. Provide a light over the sink, but set it close to the wall so that the head of someone at the sink doesn't cast a shadow. Fit fluorescent tubes on the undersides of tall overhead cabinets above work counters. Or provide extra outlets for plug-in tubes now on the market.

For hallways, about the best, and certainly the most inexpensive, lighting is small night lights plugged into outlets near the end of the hallway and every 8′ to 10′ between. They use little power, don't interfere with the movement of people or furniture, and clearly outline a path at night.

For interior stairways the best lighting is a pair of recessed fixtures controlled by a three-way switch. Set the fixtures in the ceiling no more than a foot or two from the vertical planes of the top and bottom risers. This combination concentrates light on the edges of treads where you need it most.

*Outdoor Lighting.* For protection against unexpected and perhaps unwanted visitors, place a pair of flood lights at each corner of the house. Wire them so you can switch them on from the living room, kitchen, and your bed. Look into low-voltage wiring systems for this purpose. Any good electrical contractor can advise you.

If you plan to be outdoors much after dark, consider planting low-standing, low-voltage lights along walkways and at the tops, bottoms, and landings of all outside stairways.

Working drawings show the designer's suggested locations for lights. Their symbol is ─○─ . The symbol for electrical outlets is ⊖ . Their locations are governed by building codes. Check the locations in the drawings against your actual needs, and then make sure any changes you want to make are acceptable to your contractor and are included in both drawings and specifications. Rely on your subcontractor to keep you from violating any electrical code. If an inspector finds a violation, he can delay any further work on the house until the violation is corrected.

Nearly everything you have read so far is background information important to the construction process. But if you are about ready to go to work, turn the page and let's get on with the job.

# 5

# Preparing To Build

You don't get your vacation house project under way with a hammer in hand. After the working drawings you ordered arrive, you have eleven preparatory steps to take before you start actual construction. You must

1.  Learn how to read the drawings.
2.  Develop a plot plan.
3.  Dig test holes to check soil conditions.
4.  Lay out a work schedule and the sequence of construction.
5.  Review your estimate of cost.
6.  Meet with subcontractors.
7.  Arrange any financing.
8.  Get a building permit.
9.  Arrange for temporary utilities at the site.
10.  Clear the site.
11.  Order the first materials.

# A SET OF WORKING DRAWINGS

The contents of the package you order from a plan service will vary with the firm. Regardless of the source of plans, however, the package for even the simplest vacation house should include

- A foundation or basement plan.
- A plan of each floor level.
- A section through a typical exterior wall.
- An elevation of every exterior wall.

Among the drawings for more expensive and complex houses you are also likely to find

- Framing plans.
- Details of cabinets and built-ins.
- Schedules of doors, windows, and interior surface materials.

The seven items listed above make up what is commonly called a set of working drawings. The better plan sources also provide two important documents— a set of specifications and a materials list. You will save yourself a lot of time and possibly avoid some costly errors if you know where among these papers to find the specific information you need as you are building.

## Foundation Plan

A *foundation plan* is a horizontal slice through the foundation wall at a point about 12″ above the top of the footings (Fig. 5-1). This drawing shows what you would see if you looked down from ground level at the house under construction, plus the general structure of the floor that rests on the foundation.

## First Floor Plan

Each floor plan shows what you would see if you looked down while standing on the subflooring—exterior walls, partitions, bathroom fixtures, kitchen cabinets, and built-ins (Fig. 5-2). Door openings appear as gaps in walls because the tops of doors are above eye level. Window openings appear as sections through windows at eye level. Floor plans also show door swings, steps up and down (arrows indicate up or down from the floor level depicted), locations of electrical outlets and switches, general positions of light fixtures, and the points through which major sections are taken.

## Sections

A *section* shows what you would see if you sliced through a wall, special feature, or an entire house along a certain line. On the floor plan in Fig. 5-2, for example, there are two arrows with an *A* at each tip. If you cut along the line

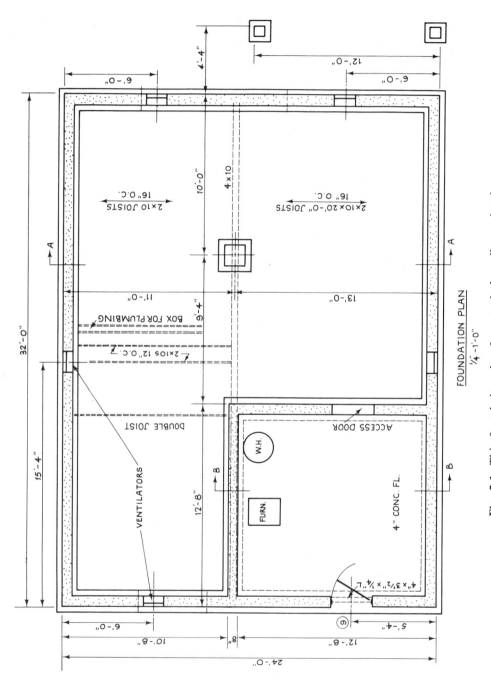

**Fig. 5-1.** This foundation plan for a typical small vacation house has a partial basement for a furnace, water heater, and general storage.

FOUNDATION PLAN
1/4"-1'-0"

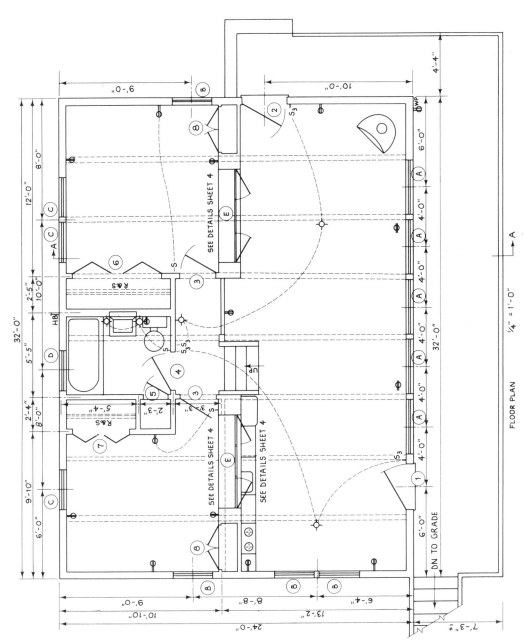

**Fig. 5-2.** Of all drawings the first floor plan is the most complex. Straight dashed lines indicate positions of roof beams. Curved dashed lines show which lights and electrical outlets are operated by switches. Doors are hinged at closed ends. Steps go up from the living level to the sleeping level, and go down from deck level. Note that most dimensions are taken to center lines, shown as dot-dash lines.

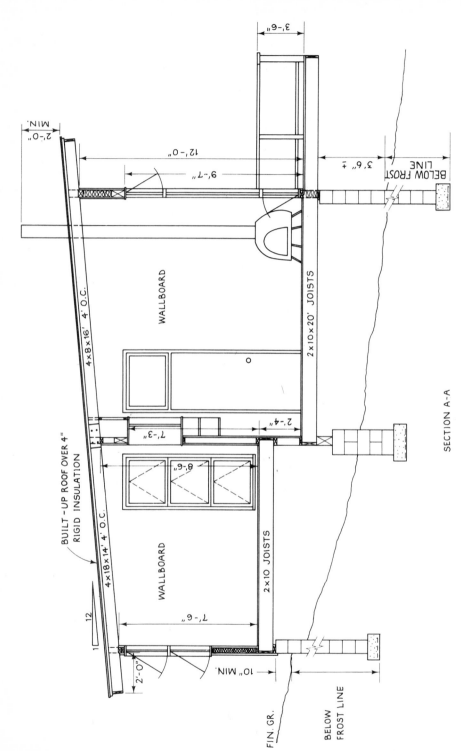

**Fig. 5-3.** A section through the house helps to explain floor plans. This section is taken along line *A-A* in Fig. 5-2.

SECTION A-A

between the arrows, you would see exactly what is shown in Section *A–A* (Fig. 5-3). This section shows the foundation wall and the structure of the floor, wall, and roof at this point. It indicates what materials are used. It also shows how the interior of the vacation house looks—the only drawing that does. You look at sections for information that is not clear or shown on other drawings. Take the roof pitch for example. This slope is shown as a triangle just above the roof line. You'll find more information on roof pitches in Chapter 10.

### Elevations

An *elevation* shows one side of a house (Fig. 5-4). Of all drawings elevations are the simplest, because they are pictorial rather than informative. They show materials as they actually are, and not in symbols. A house in elevation looks very much like it will in its constructed form, except that the roof may appear higher because you see more of it in an elevation than in normal perspective. The only new information on elevations is vertical heights—to the tops of windows, to eaves, and between different levels in the house.

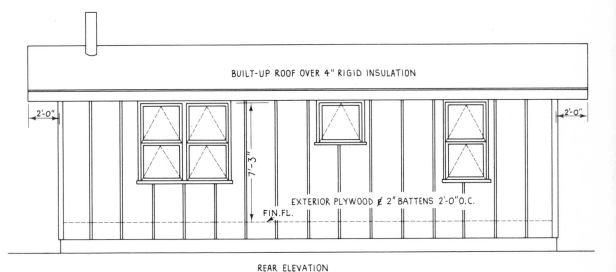

REAR ELEVATION

**Fig. 5-4.** Elevations indicate exterior materials, roof overhangs, and key vertical dimensions.

### Framing Plans

The only drawings that show details of structural framing systems are *framing drawings.* A professional builder doesn't need framing drawings, but they are a big help to do-it-yourselfers. A floor framing plan shows the locations of joists so that you can see the structural pattern. A wall framing plan shows stud locations, usually in the front wall only. A roof framing plan shows rafter locations. Although framing drawings are to scale, they are seldom dimensioned.

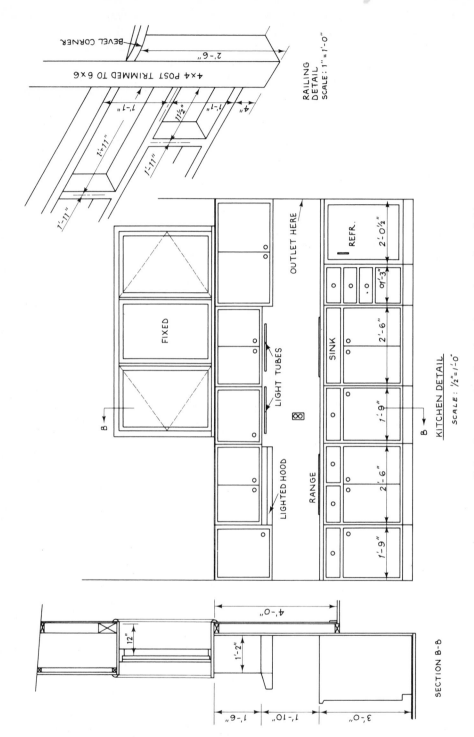

**Fig. 5-5.** Detail drawings may be elevations (center), sections (left), or isometrics (right). They are usually drawn at larger scale than other drawings.

## Details

A *detail* is a close-up drawing that shows a feature or special construction at much larger scale than the main drawings. A detail may be a plan view, an elevation, a section, or an isometric (Fig. 5-5). Because vacation houses are usually simple in design and construction, you won't find many details. There may be elevations and sectional details of kitchen cabinets, or an isometric showing how various pieces fit together (Fig. 5-5, right). An *isometric* is a three-dimensional drawing similar to a perspective, but with lines running parallel instead of converging.

## Schedules

A *schedule* is nothing more than a list that compiles in one place information that may appear in various places on several drawings. The most common schedules are of windows (Fig. 5-6), doors, and interior materials. They are complete specifications, telling you how many you need, what size they are, and what to order.

| WINDOW SCHEDULE | | | |
|---|---|---|---|
| MARK | QTY. | ROUGH OPENING | REMARKS |
| A | 5 | 9'-2⅛" x 3'-8½" | ANDERSEN #1822P or EQUAL, DOUBLE-GLAZED |
| B | 3 | 6'-11⅛" x 2'-8⅛" | "      #22213       "       D.G. |
| C | 3 | 4'-8⅛" x 2'-8⅛" | "      #22212       "       D.G. |
| D | 1 | 2'-5⅛" x 2'-8⅛" | "      #22211       "       D.G. |
| E | 2 | 6'-2½" x 3'-0⅛" | "      #1W3N30       "       SINGLE GLAZED |

**Fig. 5-6.** This schedule gives complete information about windows. Letters in the first column refer to the window designation on floor plans. A rough opening is the size of hole in the wall structure required to accept the slightly smaller window frame.

## Specifications

Specifications are written, not drawn. The standard *specification form* is a typed, multipage document with blanks in it that you fill in as you decide what materials you intend to use to finish the house. Figure 5-7 shows a typical page from a specification form. You use the specification form as a record of agreement between you and your contractor or subcontractors.

## Materials List

The *materials list* is a summary of all the major building materials that are required to build the house shown in the drawings. The list may be on one of the sheets in a set of drawings, or it may be a separate document several pages in length (Fig. 5-8).

**Fig. 5-7.** One type of specification is written in narrative form. A more common type for small houses is a blank form on which you write the specific materials to be used during construction, such as the one shown here.

---

☒ Proposed Construction

**DESCRIPTION OF MATERIALS**

No. _____

☐ Under Construction

Property address _____ City _____ State _____

Mortgagor or Sponsor _____ _____
                               (Name)                            (Address)

Contractor or Builder _____ _____
                               (Name)                            (Address)

**1. EXCAVATION:**
Bearing soil, type ___ Silty Clay – 2500 p.s.i ___

**2. FOUNDATIONS:**
Footings: concrete mix _____ ; strength psi ___3000___ Reinforcing ___2 #4 cont.___
Foundation wall: material ___ Conc. block ___ Reinforcing ___ HORIZ @ 16" O.C VERT.___
Interior foundation wall: material ___n.a.___ Party foundation wall ___n.a.___
Columns: material and sizes ___4" ⌀ steel___ Piers: material and reinforcing ___ Conc. block ___
Girders: material and sizes ___W8 x 24___ Sills: material ___wd.___
Basement entrance areaway ___n.a.___ Window areaways ___n.a.___
Waterproofing ___membrane sheets___ Footing drains ___4"⌀ Clay drain tile___
Termite protection ___Soil POISION___
Basementless space: ground cover ___n.a.___ ; insualtion ___n.a.___ ; foundation vents ___n.a.___
Special foundations ___n.a.___
Additional information: _____

**3. CHIMNEYS:**
Material ___Brick___ Prefabricated (*make and size*) ___na.___
Flue lining: material ___Clay tile___ Heater flue size ___n.a.___ Fireplace flue size ___8" x 12"___
Vents (*material and size*): gas or oil heater ___n.a.___ ; water heater ___n.a.___
Additional information: _____

**4. FIREPLACES:.**
Type: ☒ solid fuel; ☐ gas-burning; ☐ circulator (*make and size*) _____ Ash dump and clean out ___Yes___
Fireplace: facing ___Stone___ ; lining ___Fire Brick___ ; hearth ___Stone___ ; mantel ___Wood___
Additional information: _____

**5. EXTERIOR WALLS:**
Wood frame: wood grade, and species _____ ☐ Corner bracing. Building paper or felt _____
   Sheathing ___Plywood___ ; thickness ___1/2"___ ; width _____ ; ☒ solid; ☐ spaced _____ " o, c; ☐ diagonal: _____
   Siding ___n.a.___ ; grade _____ ; type _____ ; size _____ ; exposure _____ "; fastening _____
   Shingles ___n.a___ ; grade _____ ; type _____ ; size _____ ; exposure _____ "; fastening _____
   Stucco ___n.a___ ; thickness _____ "; Lath _____ ; weight _____ lb
   Masonry veneer ___brick___ Sills ___brick___ Lintels ___Steel angles___ Base flashing ___Yes___
Masonry: ☐ solid ☐ faced ☐ stuccoed: total wall thickness _____ "; facing thickness _____ " ; facing material _____
             Backup material _____ ; thickness _____ ", bonding _____
   Door sills _____ Window sills _____ Lintels _____ Base flashing _____
   Interior surfaces: dampproofing, _____ coats of _____ ; furring _____
Additional information: _____
Exterior painting: material ___Latex___ ; number of coats _____
Gable wall construction: ☒ same as main walls; ☐ other construction _____

**6. FLOOR FRAMING:**
Joists: wood, grade, and species ___#2 SYP___ ; other _____ ; bridging ___#2 SYP___ ; anchors _____
Concrete slab: ☒ basement floor; ☐ first floor; ☐ ground supported; ☐ self-supporting; mix _____ ; thickness ___4"___
   reinforcing ___6x6 10/10 WWF___ ; insualtion ___n.a___ ; membrane _____
Fill under slab: material ___Stone___ ; thickness ___4"___ ". Additional information: _____

**7. SUBFLOORING:** (*Describe underflooring for special floors under item 21.*)
Material: grade and species ___3/4" C·D Plywood___ ; size ___4'x8'___ ; type _____
Laid: ☒ first floor; ☐ second floor; ☐ attic _____ sq.ft.; ☐ diagonal; ☐ right angles. Additional information: _____

**8. FINISH FLOORING:** (*Wood only. Describe other finish flooring under item 21.*)

| LOCATION | ROOMS | GRADE | SPECIES | THICKNESS | WIDTH | BLDG. PAPER | FINISH |
|---|---|---|---|---|---|---|---|
| First floor | all axcent bath | #1 | OAK | 25/32 | — | YES | Stain |
| Second floor ___n.a___ | | | | | | | |
| Attic floor ___n.a___ sq. ft | | | | | | | |

Additional information: _____

**Fig. 5-8.** A page from a materials list gives structural steel requirements and part of the lumber requirements.

| | |
|---|---|
| 1 | 7"–15.3# "I" beam 20'-9" long |
| 1 | 7"–15.3# "I" beam 27'-5" long |
| 5 | 4" steel pipe columns 7'-3" long with plates |
| 1 | complete gas vent |
| 2900 | lin. ft No. 4 reinforcing rods |
| 2300 | sq. ft 6" × 6" × 10/10 gauge reinforcing mesh |
| 7 | galvanized steel areaways 36" diameter 24" high |
| 45 | 1/2" anchor bolts 10" long |
| 270 | lin. ft eave and rake flashing |
| 2 | 10'-0" gable louvers |

**CARPENTERS' LUMBER**

First floor joists and headers

| | |
|---|---|
| 30 | pcs 2 × 10 × 12 ft long |
| 49 | pcs 2 × 10 × 14 ft long |
| 23 | pcs 2 × 10 × 16 ft long |

Sills

| | |
|---|---|
| 6 | pcs 2 × 6 × 12 ft long |
| 8 | pcs 2 × 6 × 14 ft long |
| 2 | pcs 2 × 6 × 16 ft long |

| | |
|---|---|
| 195 | lin. ft 1" × 3"–cross bridging |

House ceiling joists

| | |
|---|---|
| 7 | pcs 2 × 6 × 12 ft long |
| 62 | pcs 2 × 6 × 14 ft long |
| 21 | pcs 2 × 6 × 16 ft long |

Garage ceiling joists

| | |
|---|---|
| 1 | pc 2 × 8 × 12 ft long |
| 19 | pcs 2 × 8 × 22 ft long |

| | |
|---|---|
| 11 | pcs 1 × 6 × 12 ft long–collar beams |
| 1 | pc 2 × 6 × 18 ft long–wood beams |
| 1 | 4 × 4 × 8 ft long–wood post |
| 404 | lin. ft 2 × 4–cornice nailing blocks |

Window and door headers and sill framing

| | |
|---|---|
| 46 | lin. ft 2" × 4" |
| 114 | lin. ft 2" × 12" |
| 36 | lin. ft 2" × 14" |

Basement stairs

| | |
|---|---|
| 3 | 2 × 12 × 14'-0" long-stringer |
| 12 | 2 × 10 × 3'-6" long–treads |
| 1 | landing tread 3'-4" long |
| 2 | 2" diam × 12'-0" long–hand rail |
| 1 | 2 × 4 × 8'-0" long–railing post |

Outside wall and partition studs

| | |
|---|---|
| 370 | pcs 2 × 4 × 8-0 ft long |
| 12 | pcs 2 × 8 × 8-0 ft long |

Head and sole plates

| | |
|---|---|
| 1110 | lin. ft 2 × 4 |
| 3 | pcs 2 × 8 × 12 ft long |

Gable end studs

| | |
|---|---|
| 5 | pcs 2 × 4 × 10 ft long |
| 2 | pcs 2 × 4 × 12 ft long |
| 6 | pcs 2 × 4 × 8 ft long |

The materials list from a plan source is not and cannot be complete. It won't include such items as fasteners, sealants, paints and stains, hardware, flashing, or any parts or equipment for plumbing, heating, and electrical systems. It does list all structural materials, however, and they constitute the bulk of your materials costs.

Accurate estimating of materials takes a lot of experience. Unless you have that experience, use the materials list as your guide. The quantities shown are generally quite accurate, and are based on what you need to buy, not what you will actually use. The materials list, for example, may call for 26 rafters 2″ × 10″ × 24′ 0″. The actual rafter length required may be only 22′ 8″. But because you can't buy lumber exactly 22′ 8″ long, the estimator lists the shortest length from which you can cut the rafters you need; the rest is scrap.

## READING THE PRINTS

In order to build from working drawings, commonly called *prints,* you must be able to "read" or interpret them. This isn't difficult, because all working drawings are prepared according to time-tested standards. You can read drawings if you understand scale, the methods of dimensioning, types of lines, and architectural symbols.

### Scale

The scale of a drawing appears in one of two places. You'll find it in the title block in one corner of each sheet of prints, when all drawings on that sheet are drawn at the same scale. Or else the scale is shown under each drawing or group of drawings on a sheet that has drawings of more than one scale.

Foundation and floor plans are usually drawn at a scale of 1/4″ = 1′ 0″. This means that a vacation house 30′ by 24′ in actual outside dimensions will appear on a floor plan as a rectangle 7 1/2″ by 6″. Elevations are also drawn at 1/4″ scale. Sections, on the other hand, are usually drawn at a scale of 1/2″ or 3/4″ to the foot. Details may be at 3/4″, 1 1/2″, or 3″ to the foot, and on rare occasions are drawn full size. Figure 5-9 may help you to understand scale.

### Dimensioning

As you study dimensioning, look again at Figs. 5-1 and 5-2. Note that overall dimensions—the maximum exterior dimensions—extend from the outside structural edge of one wall to the outside structural edge of the opposite wall. On a foundation the outside structural edge is the outside surface of the poured concrete or concrete block wall. On the first floor plan of a frame house, the outside structural edge is the outside face of wall studs. These dimensions should agree, because the faces of studs line up with the foundation wall, as shown at left in Fig. 5-10. If the exterior wall is brick veneer, however, the overall dimensions on the foundation plan will be greater than on the first floor plan.

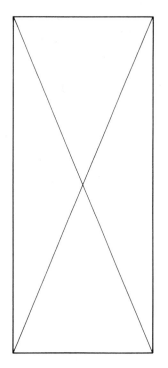

**Fig. 5-9.** The plan view of a standard 2 × 4 stud looks like this when drawn (from left to right) at full size, at 3″ scale, at 3/4″ scale, and at 1/4″ scale.

**Fig. 5-10.** Sections through a stud wall and a brick veneer wall show the points from which overall dimensions are measured.

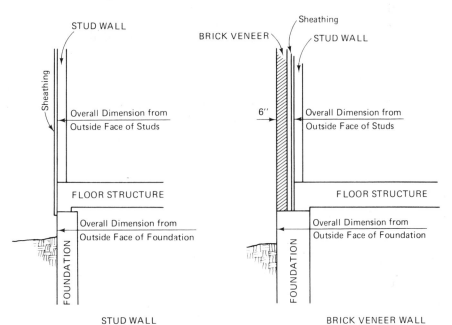

STUD WALL

BRICK VENEER WALL

The reason: brick veneer is not structural, and overall dimensions again run from face of stud to face of stud. The studs are set in from the edge of the foundation, however, as shown in Fig. 5-10, right.

Most interior dimensions are measured to center lines instead of surfaces. This is a logical method that has an advantage for you. The center of a wall, pier, or column is the center of support of the weight above it, and the location of that center is what counts. The advantage to you is that, if drawings show a 1/2"-thick material on a partition, and you want to use 1/4"-thick material, you don't have to recalculate all dimensions.

A pair of arrowheads denotes the beginning and end of a dimension (A in Fig. 5-11). Usually dimensional figures appear right next to a dimension line (B). If there isn't room, however, the draftsman omits the dimension line and places the dimension between arrowheads (C). When space is very limited, he connects a dimension to its location with an arrow (D).

Now is a good time to warn you never to measure on a print with a ruler or architect's scale. Although most original drawings are very accurate, prints of those originals may shrink or grow slightly in the printing process. Therefore always go by the written dimensions on the print. They are carefully checked. A dimensioning error is possible, however, so always add up all dimensions in a series to make sure they agree with overall dimensions *before* you start construction.

**Fig. 5-11.** Here are the four common ways of showing dimensions. The points of arrowheads mark the beginning and end of the dimension.

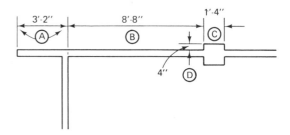

## Types of Lines

On your set of prints you will find four types of lines: solid, dashed, dotdash, and broken lines. Each type has its own meaning.

*Solid Lines.* A solid line ———— indicates an edge that you can see. Examples in Fig. 5-1 are the inside and outside edges of the foundation wall.

*Dashed Lines.* A dashed line ----- indicates an edge that you cannot see. It is either hidden by some other part of the house, or it lies above the point of view. In Fig. 5-1, for example, the inside edge of the footing below the foundation wall is hidden by the concrete basement floor. The outside edge shows as a solid line because no floor covers it. Similarly, a steel angle above the basement door lies above the point of view, and it is also shown dotted.

*Dot-Dash Lines.* A dot-dash line ——— · ——— · ——— · ——— indicates a center line and is used for no other purpose. In Fig. 5-1 dot-dash lines locate the center of the door opening in the foundation wall and the center of the supporting block pier. In Fig. 5-2 dot-dash lines locate the centers of interior partitions. Drawings don't usually locate the centers of interior doors unless position is critical—that is, you must build to the dimension shown or the door won't open properly.

*Broken Lines.* Broken or long dash lines ——— ——— ——— are imaginary lines. You won't find broken lines often in a set of prints, but they are common in drawings of land, such as site plans and surveys. Property lines are shown as broken lines. They are there all right, but you can't see them.

*Slash Lines.* A pair of diagonal lines that interrupt other lines indicate that the construction between the slash lines is the same as outside the lines. The distance between the slash lines may be dimensioned, or it may be indefinite. A typical example is the foundation wall in Fig. 5-3. The frost line varies. Therefore the height of the wall, which is uniform in construction from top to bottom, is broken by slash lines. Your site conditions determine the actual height of that wall.

### Symbols

Architects and designers use many symbols on drawings to save time and space. In Fig. 5-12 are the most common symbols for materials that you find on plans. Note that stud walls are shown as two solid lines with nothing between them. To determine where to place studs, you look at a framing drawing, or figure out the proper locations yourself. This isn't hard to do, and you'll find instructions in Chapter 9.

**Fig. 5-12.** These architectural symbols identify types of common building materials shown in plans and horizontal sections. In elevations and vertical sections they are usually shown as they actually appear to the eye.

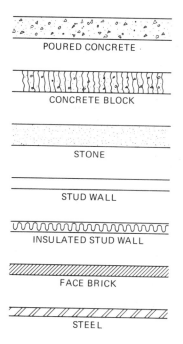

POURED CONCRETE

CONCRETE BLOCK

STONE

STUD WALL

INSULATED STUD WALL

FACE BRICK

STEEL

In sections and details, wood is indicated in one of two ways. Structural members—studs, joists, rafters, etc.—are shown with an X in them, as at (A) in Fig. 5-13. Finished wood and trim pieces, such as window casings and moldings, are drawn with grain lines in them (B in Fig. 5-13). If you find a space without lines, such as (C), this is actually a space. There is nothing there.

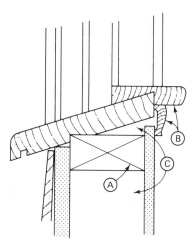

**Fig. 5-13.** Structural members (A) have an X in them. Finished pieces (B) are shown with wood graining. Air spaces (C) are left blank. This is a section through a sill for a double-hung window.

Especially on plans and sections you will find a variety of other symbols not related to the structure, but nevertheless very important to you during construction. These symbols depict nonstructural materials, such as insulation and parts of your plumbing, heating, and electrical systems. Look for them on subcontractors' sketches. The most common symbols are identified in Fig. 5-14.

### Notes

Drawings often have notes that explain what may not be clear in the drawing itself. If your prints don't include a framing drawing, you will find notes on the foundation plan describing the first-floor structure and any special conditions that you must allow for in the foundation. Look once more at Fig. 5-1. One note tells you what size floor joists to use and standard spacing from center to center. Two other notes point to special conditions where joist spacing is not standard. The notes warn you to look at the first floor plan to see why spacing varies here, and to act accordingly.

## MAKING A PLOT PLAN

After you become familiar with the drawings and are sure that the rooms are the sizes you want, that relationships between the rooms are good, and that all rooms have the best possible orientation, the next step is to develop a plot plan.

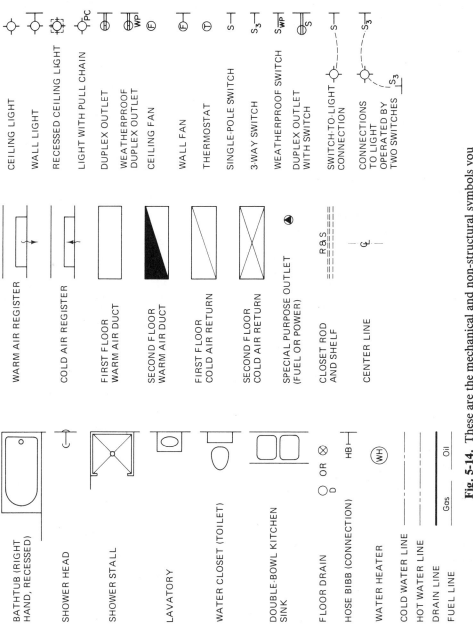

**Fig. 5-14.** These are the mechanical and non-structural symbols you are most likely to see on the working drawings you build from, and on the layouts drawn by your plumbing, heating, and electrical subcontractors.

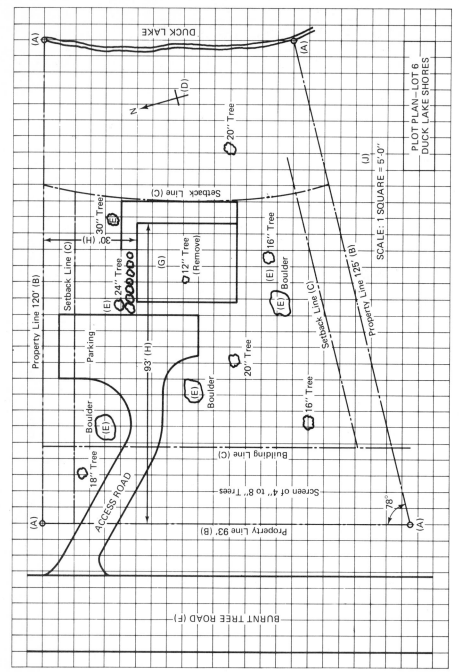

**Fig. 5-15.** A typical plot plan must show property lines, setback lines if any, the location of your buildings, and the access road. The drawing must be either drawn to scale or dimensioned. The other information shown here is optional for your own use.

A *plot plan* is a drawing of your site with all buildings you plan to build located on it (Fig. 5-15). It locates the corners of the property and property lines. It shows the street or road past the site, or the nearest point of access. It also locates any setback lines, as discussed in Chapter 2.

Where do you get this information? You'll find most of it on a *survey,* a drawing of the specific piece of land you own. When you buy the site, ask the owner for a copy of his survey. If he doesn't have one, hire a surveyor to make one for you. Surveyors are listed in the yellow pages of the local telephone directory. If none is listed, ask the county engineer or tax assessor to recommend one. Most full-time surveyors live near large cities, but there is at least one licensed surveyor in every county.

A surveyor marks the corners of your site with metal rods, and records their locations on the survey. You may never use your survey after construction, especially if your site is a large tract in a sparsely settled area. But if you are building among other homes in a resort community, a survey is excellent insurance against future legal problems.

With the survey in hand, you can draw the plot plan yourself. A sheet of graph paper makes a good working background. Use the largest scale possible. First locate the corners of the property (A in Fig. 5-15), and then draw in the property lines (B) and setback lines (C). Add compass points (D).

While you were taking your last look at the site before you bought it, remember that you noted the locations of any obstructions that could cause you building problems—creeks and water runoffs, boulders and ledges, and large healthy trees. Show all these obstructions on your plot plan (E). Also locate and name the street or road (F).

Next, at the same scale as the plot plan, draw the outline of your vacation house on another sheet of graph paper. Cut out this outline and lay it over the plot plan. Move the outline around, always staying within setback lines, until you find a location that suits you—one that seems to give you the views and privacy you want and also fits comfortably on the contours. Then lift off the outline and draw the shape of the house (G in Fig. 5-15) on the plot plan.

If you have difficulty visualizing how your house will look, go back to the site and stake it out. Bring with you a dozen wood stakes, a compass, an ax or hammer, a sharp knife, a 100-foot steel tape, and nylon cord. You'll need a stake—a 1 × 2 about 24″ long with one end sharpened to a point—at each corner of the house and along property and setback lines close to the house. Bring enough cord to go around the perimeter of the house twice. If your house is 32′ by 24′, for example, its perimeter is 112′ and you will need about 225′ of cord.

At the site, first calculate about where you think one front corner of the house should be, and then drive a stake (A in Fig. 5-16) lightly into the ground at that point. Next, if you are close to a property line or have setback restrictions to contend with, find the surveyor's rods at the corners. Stretch the nylon cord between the rods. Then drive two wood stakes into the ground along this line. Now measure off the setback distance from the property line, and drive stakes 1 and 2 along the setback line. Stake 1 should lie forward of a line across the front

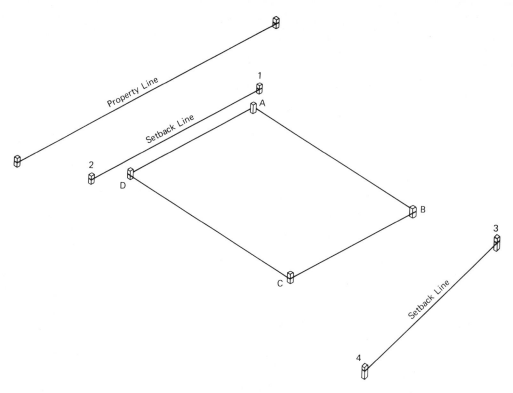

**Fig. 5-16.** To stake out the preliminary location of your house, first find the property lines, then the setback lines, then set stakes at the corners of the foundation.

of the house. Stake 2 should be a distance from stake A equal to the length of the side wall of your house plus 10´. Stretch cord between stakes 1 and 2. Then locate the opposite setback line with stakes 3 and 4 in a similar manner.

As long as stake A is within the legal building limits on the site, you can now stake out the rest of the house. Using your steel tape to measure distance and your compass to make corners as square as possible, work across the front of the house, up one side, across the back, and down the other side, setting a stake (lettered stakes in Fig. 5-16) at each corner. If you measure accurately, you will end up back at stake A. Now stretch the cord from stake to stake, wrapping it at least twice to prevent slippage. When you have finished, you will have the outline of your house on its site.

As you look at the size of the house outlined with cord, you won't believe that you can live in anything that small. This is an optical illusion—the first of many you will have as construction continues. Don't worry about it. Concentrate instead on what you actually see as you walk inside the cord.

Do you have pretty views from the sides of the house that have the most and largest windows? Are any neighbors screened from view? Will trees provide summer shade without blocking out daylight? Are any of the fine trees you want to save inside the cord line? Are there any obstructions inside the cord that will add to building costs? Will the area staked off drain well? Can you reach the spot with an access road wide enough for delivery trucks?

Unless all answers to these questions are satisfactory, pull up the lettered stakes and start over again. When you have the house properly located, drive the lettered stakes firmly into the ground until only about 9″ of each is exposed. With your steel tape, measure the distances from stakes A and B to property lines. Then remove the other stakes and cords, go home, and complete the plot plan.

After you have recorded the key distances (H in Fig. 5-15), add the scale (J) and a title block in the lower right hand corner of the plot plan drawing. Now run off five copies and file the original in a safe place. Never fold an original drawing. If it is small, lay it flat inside a protective envelope in a drawer. If it is too large to lie flat, roll it and store it in a mailing tube.

## TESTING THE SOIL

If you followed the recommendation in Chapter 2, you dug beneath the topsoil on your site to look at the subsoil. Now that you have staked out the approximate location of your house, dig half a dozen test holes, one near each of the four corners of the house and one or two near the center. Dig as deeply as you will have to excavate for footings. If you plan a basement, go down at least 7′. If you plan to build on piers or pilings, go below the frost line (2′ to 6′). If you plan to build on a concrete slab, go down 1 1/2′ to 4′.

The best digging tool is a *post-hole auger,* a two-bladed spade that you twist into the ground like a screwdriver. It digs a hole about 6″ in diameter. When you have reached the desired depth, raise the auger, remove the soil sample, and study it.

Break each sample apart with your hands and feel it. The best soils are firm and dry and don't crumble easily. A combination of sand and gravel also makes a good subsoil for building. Footings must rest on firm soil. If you find fine sand or soft clay, which are poor building soils, try a test hole at some other point on the site. You can overcome poor bearing soil with wider footings to spread the load, deeper foundations that reach better soil, or additional supporting piers or pilings. But all these solutions run up the cost. If you run into a rock ledge, hope that it is only a small shelf. If it extends across the site, you have made a bad site selection that can't be used economically.

A little dampness in the soil is normal, especially in the spring. But if the soil is wet, or the test hole fills with water, talk to the county engineer or your excavating contractor. He is probably familiar with this local condition and can recommend the best solution to your site problem.

Once you are satisfied that you have picked a good site and staked out a good location on that site, order additional sets of prints of your vacation house. You will need at least one set for yourself, a set for each contractor you hire, and one to file when you apply for a building permit.

# LAYING OUT A WORK SCHEDULE

Of all preparatory work, laying out a schedule for construction is the most difficult. Much of schedule-making is a combination of guesswork and an understanding of the conditions that affect a schedule.

First, of course, is the number of hours you can devote to building and when this time occurs. Once you become toughened to the pace, you can do about 25% more work in a 15-hour weekend than you can in five 3-hour evenings. The main reason is that you don't have to recall what you were doing when you quit the previous time. Work flows more evenly in longer stretches, and is usually less tiring.

Second, how much help can you expect from family and friends? Many tasks are hard and slow when done alone, and some are impossible without help. Even a ten-year-old is as good as an adult when the job requires someone to fetch, find, hold, or mark.

Third, how much will weather slow you down? The ground must be dry when you place footings and slabs. The air must be dry when you are doing masonry work. The air must be warm when you are installing materials affected by temperature, such as concrete, mortar, asphalt shingles, and paint. As soon as the house is under cover, of course, you can work inside unaffected by weather.

Fourth, will you have good working light? There is roughly half an hour less evening daylight on June 1 and August 1 than on July 1, about 1 1/4 hours less on May 1 and September 1, and two hours less on October 1. You don't need strong light to lay concrete blocks or nail studs, but you do need good light for finishing concrete, fitting trim, and for measuring and marking throughout construction.

With so many variables to consider, do you really need to make a schedule? The answer is "yes," for three reasons. First, your subcontractors must know when you will need them so they can schedule their work. Suppose you tell your plumbing contractor that you will be ready for him the third week in June, but you aren't ready for him until the first week in July. If all his other work is on schedule, his crew will have to sit around in June with little to do, and then will be busy on other jobs in July. A delay can cost you time and money.

Second, you must schedule so that you can order materials and have them on site when you need them. Most materials in a vacation house are stock items, but occasionally a supplier is temporarily out of an item. When you are delayed because you don't have the materials, you can seldom make up the time lost.

Third, any well-organized person—and you must be well-organized to be your own contractor—wants to know what he must do and the order in which he must do it. With a schedule you never arrive at a project with a "Let's see, what do I do today;" attitude. You know what comes next, and you save time and energy by knowing.

To set up a schedule, follow the order of construction in this book. This sequence is fairly standard until you have the house enclosed. After that you have some flexibility. In Chapter 19 you will find estimates of the time required to complete various phases of construction; you must adjust these estimates to your own knowledge and talents.

Plan to concentrate most of your time and effort on structural work. With it out of the way, you have more opportunity to work when the spirit moves you.

## ESTIMATING YOUR COSTS

If you plan to borrow money to pay for your vacation house, you must develop a reasonably accurate estimate of its cost. Even if you don't borrow, you will probably want to know what the house will cost you.

By using the cost-per-square-foot method discussed in Chapter 3, you can arrive at a rough estimate of total cost. To develop a more accurate estimate for a house you build yourself, begin in the business community nearest to your site.

The local building materials supplier is your best source of help. Using the materials list and a set of prints, he will estimate the cost of all building materials he sells. He can advise you where to rent tools and equipment, and the people at the rental firm will help you estimate the time and rental costs to complete various jobs. The building materials dealer can also direct you to people who can help you on a part-time basis.

With estimates for materials, equipment rental, occasional labor, and the work of subcontractors in hand, you have the basis for an accurate cost estimate. But allow for unexpected problems. Most professional builders figure their costs accurately for materials and labor and then add a small amount for contingencies. The contingency factor covers such events as a heavy rain that damages work already in place; theft; breakage; and damage to raw materials from various causes. It is calculated as a percentage of the total cost of materials and labor. On a job where you do much of the work yourself, the correct percentage is a guess, depending mostly on how careful and well-organized you are, and to some extent on luck. You won't be far off, however, if you add 5% to the cost of materials, rentals, and part-time labor. The bottom line figure is your total cost estimate.

### Insurance

You can't cover all contingencies with insurance, but you can cover some of them. To avoid suits for personal injury on a vacation site, you can extend the liability coverage in your existing homeowner's policy. You should take out a standard builder's risk policy at nominal cost that covers you against damage by fire, wind, and vandalism. Most insurance companies, however, will not insure against water damage or theft. Insurance premiums are included in the 5% contingency figure recommended above.

## BORROWING MONEY

Don't expect to be able to borrow money as a construction loan to build a vacation house yourself. Neither the Federal Housing Administration (FHA) nor Veterans Administration (VA) will finance you. Most banks are not willing to risk lending you the money either; they have not had good experience with construction loans for recreational housing.

The door to financial help isn't completely closed, however; you may still be able to arrange a personal loan. The first places to look are the banks where you have a savings account and where you have your checking account. But don't stop there. It often pays to shop around, not only in your home community but in the community where you will be vacationing. You want to borrow wherever you can get the lowest rate of interest and the best terms. These vary widely.

Most lending institutions will consider lending you up to $10,000 if you have collateral in stocks, savings, or other assets to secure the loan. Some people prefer to take out a loan even though they have enough money for construction in a savings account. The bank may pay 5 1/2% interest on the savings and charge 7 1/2% interest on the loan. Therefore you are paying, in effect, only 2% interest. This may seem like an avoidable expense, but sometimes there are tax advantages to keeping a savings account intact and securing a loan. Many people, too, find it difficult to build up a savings account again, and they consider loan payments as a form of forced saving.

## GETTING A BUILDING PERMIT

In many communities you need a building permit before you can legally begin construction of any kind. The cost of a permit varies, but is usually a fee based on the square footage of the house. The amount is nominal.

To secure a permit, go to the courthouse in the county where you plan to build. Usually the man to see is the building inspector or county engineer. In sparsely populated counties he may be the tax assessor, and issuing permits is only one of many duties. Bring with you your plot plan, a set of working drawings and specifications, and your estimate of costs excluding land and site improvements.

Unless he is very busy, the building inspector will review the information you bring him while you wait at the counter, and he will fill out and issue the permit at that time. You then nail the permit to a tree, pole, or post at the site where it is clearly visible. The permit is your authorization to proceed with construction. The next step is to arrange for power, water, and sewer at the site.

## ARRANGING FOR TEMPORARY UTILITIES

From the very start of construction you need water and electricity—water for drinking, mixing concrete, and cleaning up, and electricity to operate power tools. At many vacation sites neither water nor power lines are close enough to do you much good during construction.

### Water

If your source of water is to be a well, have it drilled before you start work on the house. Installing a well is not do-it-yourself work; you can spend your time more profitably on actual construction. Ask your contractor to run a supply line from the well to a point close to its entry into the house.

If you are building on a site with a natural water source—a spring, stream, or lake—ask the official who signs your building permit where to get information on regulations governing use of existing water sources. Or contact the Department of Natural Resources at the state capital.

After your water system is installed and operating, make sure your contractor calls the state Department of Health or Human Resources Department to have the water tested and approved for drinking.

If you are building in a resort area that has a community water line running past your site, ask the water company to install a temporary connection from their main to your point of need.

At the end of your water supply line, where the pipe sticks out of the ground, screw on a tee that has female threads at all three openings. Then install faucets in the other two openings. With this arrangement you have one faucet for drinking water or filling a bucket, and you can attach a hose to the other one.

### Electricity

If the local power company has a line close to your site, it will install a temporary pole near your staked-out area, extend a line to the pole, and install a meter and weatherproof power outlet. For this service they will charge a small installation fee and a monthly usage fee.

In isolated areas you will need a portable, gasoline-powered generator to provide electrical power. You can rent one from firms that rent tools, or you may be able to rent one from your local power company.

If you must provide your own power for the finished vacation house, discuss your problem with distributors of power generators in the community. You won't need as large a generator during construction as you will when you occupy the house. Therefore you may be able to rent the smaller equipment used, and then apply the rental charge to the cost of larger new equipment.

### Sewage

What you use for temporary toilet facilities depends largely on where you build. If you have neighbors close by, perhaps you can arrange to use their facilities until you have your own in place and operable. In some communities you can rent chemical toilets, but this is a rather expensive solution for the little use you would give them. If you are working at an isolated site, and expect to be living there on weekends during construction, build a small privy where it won't contaminate the water supply. Use the regulations for locating sewer systems, as outlined in Chapter 4, as a guide to location.

Few states have any special requirements for temporary toilet facilities on individual sites. You can find out about local regulations and practices from the state's Human Resources or Health Department.

# CLEARING THE SITE

The final step before you begin actual construction is to clear your site. Clear only the areas that need to be free of obstructions; leave the rest as natural as possible. Work from your plot plan. Start by staking out the access road. Make the cleared space wide enough for supply trucks and grading and excavating equipment. Then clear the area inside your cord lines and at least three feet outside the cord all the way around the house.

With an ax, hand saw, and spade, first remove all underbrush in the areas you marked off. With a power-operated hand saw, cut down all small trees that are in the way. Use a chain saw to cut large trees. Cut the trunks into logs for fuel. Dig up all the stumps, rocks, and boulders that you can pry loose. Collect all the debris you can carry or drag, and stack it for hauling away.

Although it will cost you a little money, you can save yourself days of aching muscles and sore hands if you hire a man to come in with a bulldozer or front-end loader to complete the job. A bulldozer can dig up stumps, knock down large trees, and break up boulders. A front-end loader can do everything a bulldozer can do, though not as efficiently, and it can also pick up the debris and load it into a truck for disposal.

If you intend to leave most of the site in its natural state, you have completed the clearing job after debris is hauled away and cut logs are stacked to one side. But if you intend to have a lawn, you will need to have a grader strip off the topsoil and carefully pile it out of the way at one side of the site. Cover the pile with a tarpaulin or sheet of polyethylene to prevent it from washing away until you are ready to spread it back into place when construction is completed.

## Your Access Road

When you plan an access road, you must consider the width of the road, the terrain it must traverse, the obstructions it must avoid, and its connection with the main right-of-way.

Start at the main road. If it is a state or U.S. highway, talk to the highway maintenance supervisor at the district office of the Department of Highways. He will tell you what you must do to prevent interruption of drainage beside the highway. If the road is maintained by the county, see the county road commissioner or highway engineer. The cost of maintaining existing drainage is yours.

Sometimes you can pave the bottom of a shallow ditch and drive through it to get to your access road. A better and more common solution is to lay a pipe of corrugated metal or concrete and fill above it for the driveway. With deeper ditches you will probably also have to provide stone or concrete headwalls on either side of the driveway to prevent washing. The cognizant official can guide you on the size, length, and type of pipe to use, and the design of the headwall.

Once the access road reaches your own property, it must be at least 9 ' wide on level straightaways and 10 ' wide on grades and curves. Better widths are 10 ' and 12′ respectively. A wider road gives you more surface to drive on, and it wears less on the edges. It allows for some erosion while leaving an area wide enough to drive on. It allows good clearance from obstructions on both sides, and it makes turns a lot easier to negotiate.

The minimum inside radius of any turn is 18′ for a car and 28′ for most delivery trucks. If you plan to buy a precut or prefabricated house, ask the dealer or manufacturer about any special requirements for his delivery trucks.

Most American-made cars can climb an 8% grade in high gear at low speeds. An 8% grade has a vertical rise of 1′ for every 12 1/2′ of road length. The maximum practical grade, except for cars with 4-wheel drive, is a 12 1/2% grade, or a rise of 1′ in every 8′ of length. If space permits, it is better to cross a steep grade than to meet it head on.

When cost is a factor, lay out your road as straight as possible. A road that meanders may be pretty, but it is also pretty expensive. Add bends only to negotiate a grade or to skirt large trees, rock outcroppings, and water runoffs. The less dirt you have to move with a bulldozer or grader, the lower the cost of the road. And it usually costs less to curve around a hill than to cut through it.

If your site is heavily wooded, you may want your access road to look as much like a trail as possible. Chances are, however, that such a road will soon be full of holes, ruts, and pools of water after a rain. You can overcome these problems by digging shallow (3″ to 4″) drainage ditches on both sides of the road over flat land, and on the uphill side where the land rolls. Ditches reduce washing of the roadbed itself.

For a still better road, dig a roadbed to a depth of about 6″. Fill this bed with 2″ to 3″ stones, then cover the stones with a slightly crowned layer of gravel (Fig. 5-17). Traffic will pack down the stones into a usable surface. The roadbed will settle some, but should hold up well during the construction period. Later on you may need to add another layer of gravel and fill chuckholes and soft spots for a good year-around road.

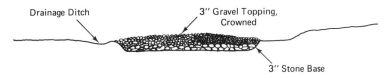

Drainage Ditch    3″ Gravel Topping, Crowned

3″ Stone Base

**Fig. 5-17.** A good temporary access road, shown here in section, has a base of 3″ stone, topped by 3″ of gravel. The gravel should be crowned to help rainwater and melting snow run off into drainage ditches on each side.

## TOOLS YOU WILL NEED

To complete the work in site preparation that you are likely to do yourself, as discussed in this chapter, you will need, as a minimum, the following tools and equipment:

100 ′ steel tape
knife
ax
directional compass
nylon cord
post-hole auger
spade
hand saw or limb saw
power hand saw
chain saw

# Building

# a Foundation

Every building needs a foundation. The foundation must be strong enough to support the weight of the building itself, called the *dead load,* and other loads placed on it or in it. These other loads are the *live load,* which is the total weight of all downward loads such as furniture, people, and snow; and the *wind load,* which is usually a sideways or upward load. Most building codes specify what minimum live loads and wind loads the structural parts of a building must be able to carry. Any plans you buy are designed to meet these minimum loads.

## TYPES OF FOUNDATIONS

You can build three types of foundations under a house. If you want a basement, you build a standard foundation wall. If you build over a crawl space, you can build a foundation wall, support the house on piers or pilings, or use a combination of the two. If you build on a concrete slab, you can support the slab on a foundation wall or pour a floating slab that rests directly on the ground.

Working drawings show one type of foundation. If you decide to use a different type, draw a new foundation plan, and have it checked professionally before you build.

## A Foundation Wall

A foundation wall is built of masonry or concrete (Fig. 6-1). Concrete block is the material commonly used in foundations for vacation houses. The wall rests on a footing made of poured concrete reinforced with steel. The standard depth of a footing is the same dimension as the thickness of the foundation wall. The standard width of a footing is twice the thickness of the wall. With a wall of 8″ concrete block then, the footing has a vertical dimension of 8″ and a horizontal dimension of 16″. The wall is centered over the footing.

A footing must rest on firm soil at least 6″ below the *frost line*—the maximum depth to which the ground freezes in winter. Find out where the local frost line is by asking your building materials dealer, a local builder, or an excavating contractor. If you don't place footings below the frost line, the ground may heave in the spring with enough force to crack the foundation wall.

On firm soil an 8″ by 16″ footing is adequate. When soil is not firm, you can dig deeper until you reach firm soil; pour a wider footing (called a spread footing); or increase the amount of steel reinforcement.

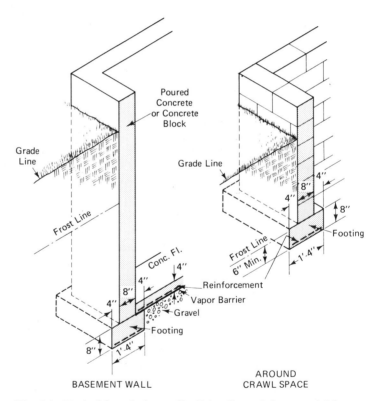

**Fig. 6-1.** Typical foundation walls. Regardless of the material from which they are built, all foundation walls must rest on reinforced concrete footings.

## Piers

A *pier* is a vertical support for floor structure. A standard pier is made of concrete block, brick, stones, poured concrete, or wood posts treated to resist rot (Fig. 6-2). Each pier rests on its own reinforced concrete footing, usually 24″ square and 8″ in depth.

**Fig. 6-2.** Houses not supported on foundation walls may rest on piers of concrete blocks or poured concrete, on short wood posts, or on long wood pilings. Only pilings do not require a footing.

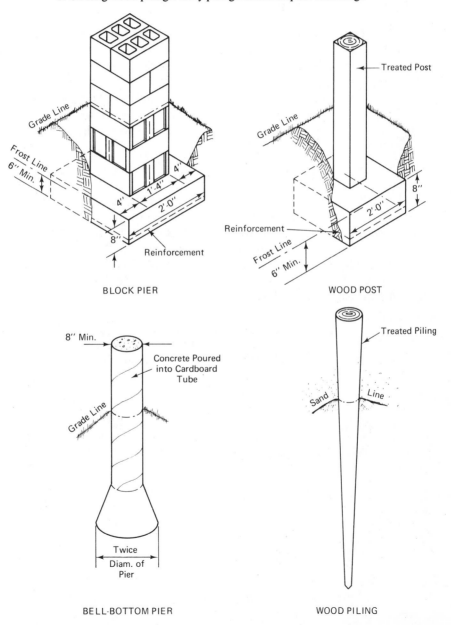

A bell-bottom pier has no seperate footing. Useful when soil is very firm, the bell-bottom pier has a flared base of poured concrete that acts as a footing.

You may use piers as interior supports in crawl space, with a foundation wall forming the exterior support. Or you may support the entire house on piers, one at each corner and others spaced no more than 12 ' apart in any direction. A more common spacing is every 8 '.

On sandy sites, where digging for footings is not practical, wood pilings are often used for foundations. Each piling must be driven into the sand mechanically, work that requires specialized equipment.

### Concrete Slabs

The edges of most concrete slabs rest on foundation walls that are L-shaped at the top (Fig. 6-3). The remainder of the slab rests on a gravel base. Under the entire slab you must have a vapor barrier to prevent moisture in the ground from working its way through the slab. And you must insulate at the edge.

A variation of the standard slab is a slab with a thick edge that serves as a footing. Variously called a *floating slab, turned-down slab,* or *thickened-edge slab,* it is a practical foundation only on sites where the soil does not freeze and is not very firm.

### Comparing Foundations

Pier foundations are the least expensive to build and require the least digging for footings. You must be careful to have the tops of all piers at exactly the same level, however. They make an adequate foundation if you intend to vacation primarily in warm weather. Air flows freely under the house, and floors are likely to be cold and drafty in winter even if you insulate them well. Furthermore, plumbing is difficult to insulate, and you must take extra precautions to prevent frozen and burst pipes.

**Fig. 6-3.** Concrete slab floors usually rest on a foundation wall at the edges and a gravel base elsewhere. A thickened-edge slab may be used only under limited conditions of soil and climate.

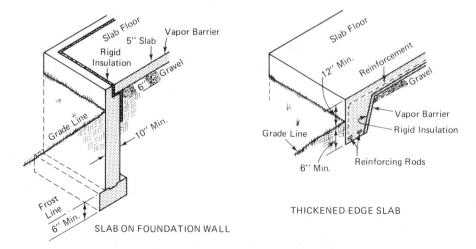

SLAB ON FOUNDATION WALL

THICKENED-EDGE SLAB

A low foundation wall around crawl space, with piers for interior supports, is more expensive than an all-pier foundation but less expensive than a basement. Unless you need a full basement for storage, a crawl space is the best answer for most vacation homes. It is warmer and dryer than a pier foundation, and is easier to build and more comfortable to live on than a concrete slab. If your site slopes, you may be able to combine a low foundation wall with a partial basement for storage, a furnace, and water heater. The foundation in Fig. 5-1 is a typical example.

## SIZE OF EXCAVATION

Although a standard footing is only 16″ wide, you need a wider trench in order to place that footing. You need enough working space to build and set forms, to lay concrete blocks, and to install any drain tiles. If you don't have to dig any deeper than 3′ below ground level, a trench 6′ wide is adequate, because the sides of the trench can be close to vertical. For deeper excavations the sides should have at least a 2-to-1 slope—that is, one extra foot of trench width for every two feet of wall height (Fig. 6-4).

**Fig. 6-4.** Excavations less than 36″ deep may have vertical sides (right). All others should be sloped (below) to prevent cave-ins.

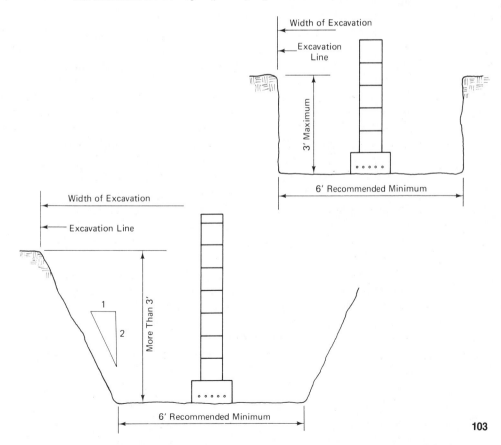

It is possible to dig a trench just wide enough for a footing, pour the footing with the trench serving as a form, and build a low wall on top of it. This saves some digging. But you will waste more time cleaning away fallen dirt and trying to work in tight quarters than you will save in trenching. Dig a wider trench to do the job well.

Exterior piers require a hole 24″ square and 6″ deeper than the frost line. The outside edges of structural floor members rest on the outside edges of piers. Therefore the outside edges of footings lie 4″ outside the foundation line of the house. Center piers should lie under the centers of structural members. Thus the edges of footings for center piers lie approximately 12″ from these center lines.

After you determine the size of excavation you need, draw a rough excavation plan to guide you in the work at the site. Then go back to the site and stake out the exact locations of the foundation and the excavation.

## POSITIONING THE HOUSE

The first step at the site is to see if any obstructions lie between the foundation line and the excavation line. If you find that some trees must be removed, you may want to adjust the location of the house to avoid them.

Earlier you rough-staked the location of the house and left the stakes in place. The next step is to complete the finish staking, mark the excavation line, and erect batter boards.

Many times during construction you will follow the principle of the Pythagorean theorem. The early Greek mathematician Pythagoras discovered that the square of the hypotenuse of a right triangle is equal to the sum of the squares of the other two sides. In building, the most commonly used triangle is the 3-4-5 right triangle or its first multiple, the 6-8-10 triangle. In this triangle the hypotenuse is 10′ long and the other two sides are 6′ and 8′ long (Fig. 6-5). Thus the square of the hypotenuse ($10 \times 10 = 100$) is equal to the sum of the squares of the other two sides, or $(8 \times 8) + (6 \times 6) = 64 + 36 = 100$. You must follow the principle in this theorem to assure that you get the corners of your house square.

Begin with the stake at the most important corner of the house—usually one of two on the view side. From this stake (A in Fig. 6-6 and also in Fig. 5-16), measure 6′ along the cord at the front of the house. Drive in a small stake, E. Then from stake A measure along the side line of the house for a distance of 8′ and scribe an arc in the dirt. Now from stake E measure 10′ and scribe another arc. Where the two arcs meet, drive another small stake, F. The line from A to E will be at right angles to the line from A to F.

To make your measurements as accurate as possible, drive a ten-penny nail into the head of each stake exactly on the foundation line. Then do all your measuring and aligning from the nail head. This system works better than measuring from the edges of stakes.

To verify the location of stake B, which marks the other front corner of the house, use your steel tape to measure off the front dimension of the house as shown on the plans. The tape must pass directly over the nail in the top of stake E. Repeat this process to check the location of stake D, passing directly over stake F.

Follow the right angle procedures to locate stake C. If you have been accurate in your work—and you must be—the lengths of lines AB and CD will be equal, the lengths of lines AD and BC will be equal, and all corners will be right angles. As a final check, measure the distances from A to C and from B to D. These diagonals should also be equal in length.

Staking out a house doesn't take a lot of time, and it isn't as complicated as it sounds. It does take two people to do the job right, however, so bring help with you.

If your house has a wing, as in Fig. 6-6, find the dimensions for AG and AH on the foundation plan. Mark points G and H with stakes. Next, working from stake D, use the same procedures to locate stakes I and J. Then on the plans find the dimension for GK. Measure off this distance from stake G, passing directly over stake I, and drive in stake K. Repeat to locate stake L.

Note that you measure from stake A, rather than from stake G, to find point H. Wherever possible, make all measurements from one starting point to reduce the chances of cumulative error. Suppose that you are off 1/4″ in your measurements. If you find point B by measuring from point A, you are off just 1/4″.

**Fig. 6-5.** This diagram illustrates the Pythagorean theorem, which states that the square of the hypotenuse of a right triangle is equal to the sum of the squares of the other two sides.

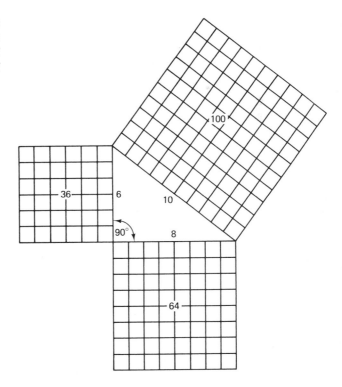

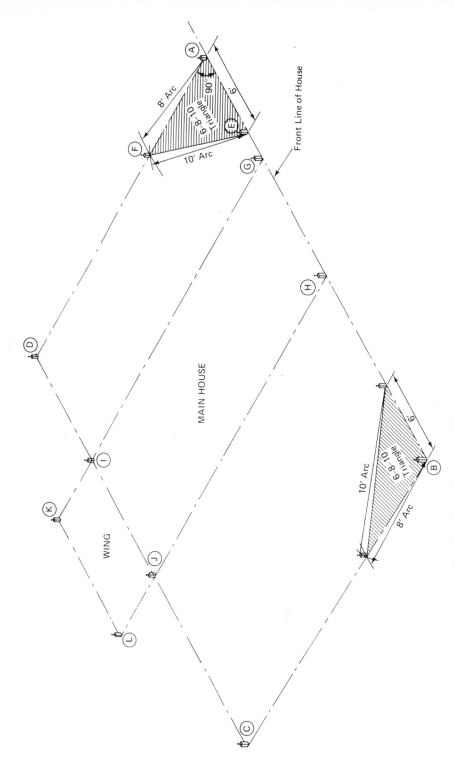

**Fig. 6-6.** To stake out a building, begin at the most important corner (A). Use a steel tape to locate corner B, and a tape and the Pythagorean theorem to locate C and D. Stakes alphabetically from G through K are needed to stake out a wing.

But if you find point B by measuring AE, then EG, then GH, and finally HB, and are off 1/4″ in each measurement, you have a cumulative error of 1″. That is not acceptable.

With the house accurately located, stake out the corners of the excavation. In most cases the overall dimensions for the excavation will be at least 6′ longer than the overall dimensions of the house. Pinpoint accuracy is not as important in staking an excavation as it is in staking a foundation, but since you know how to use the Pythagorean theorem, why not do it right?

## ESTABLISHING FOUNDATION HEIGHT

You can determine from the frost line how deep to go with your footings for the foundation wall. But how do you decide how high the foundation should be? This depends mostly on the type of foundation you build.

The top of any foundation wall or pier should be at least 8″ above *finished grade*—ground level when all construction and earthmoving is completed. On elevations in working drawings you often see a line marked "Fin. Gr." This finished grade may be anywhere from 4″ to 12″ above the grade (ground level) of the site when you bought it. You need to add topsoil around the foundation wall so that water drains away from the wall, never toward it.

With normal platform floor framing, covered in detail in Chapter 8, the underside of a wood floor structure is 1 1/2″ above the top of the foundation. In a house with a usable basement, you need at least 7′ 4″ of basement headroom. So, assuming the minimum 8″ above grade to the top of the wall, a standard 4″-thick basement floor and an 8″-thick footing (Fig. 6-7), the excavation for the foundation wall would be no more than 7′ 6 1/2″ below finished grade (8″ + 4″ + 7′ 4″ − 1 1/2″ − 8″). This height is fine if your foundation wall is poured concrete.

It doesn't work, however, if you use concrete blocks. Blocks are either 8″ or 4″ high including the mortar joint. When establishing the height of any foundation wall or pier, then, use a dimension that is divisible by 4″. A common height for a basement wall is 88″, which gives you headroom of 7′ 5 1/2″ in a basement with an unfinished ceiling. The height of a foundation wall around crawl space depends, of course, on the frost line.

For a house built over a crawl space, allow at least 18″ of clearance between ground level in the crawl space and the undersides of floor joists. To be able to move more comfortably, you should allow 30″. You may need more if you heat with a furnace placed in the crawl space; check the manufacturer's instructions for recommended clearance. Ideally, ground level in the crawl space should be no lower than finished grade level, but meeting this ideal often raises the house too high out of the ground to look well.

With a concrete slab the top of the foundation wall should also be at least 8″ above grade. Finished slab floor level is at the same height as the foundation wall itself. With a wood floor structure, however, floor level is anywhere from 9″ to

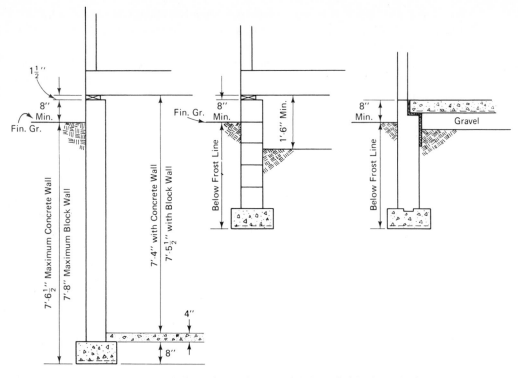

**Fig. 6-7.** Typical dimensions above and below finished grade for foundation walls around a basement (left), crawl space (center), and under a concrete slab (right).

12 1/4″ above the top of the foundation, depending on the depth of wood joists required.

The dimensions shown in Fig. 6-7 are minimums, and they apply at the high point of the grade along the foundation wall. This high point determines the depth of your excavation and the height of floor level above grade. It is also the point from which all surface water will drain. Walk around the cords that outline your foundation and find this high point. At that spot drive in a long stake and mark on it the height of your foundation wall. Be sure to allow for the difference between actual ground level and finished grade. Make the mark bold enough so you can see it from any point around the foundation wall. You refer to it often as you erect batter boards.

## BATTER BOARDS

As soon as excavating begins, the stakes that mark the corners of your foundation will be in the way. So you must use some other method to mark the locations of corners until foundation work is complete. The standard way is with cords strung between batter boards.

A *batter board* is a simple structure made of stakes and cross members (Fig. 6-8). The simplest type (A) consists of a pair of 2 × 4 stakes connected by a 1 × 6 board at least 8 ' long. Set this type of batter board at a 45° angle to the foundation lines. More common and easier to adjust is a pair of batter boards (B), with the 1 × 6s each about 6 ' long, set across foundation lines when extended. On a sloping lot, use a batter board with a center post (C) at low corners.

At this time drive the stakes for the batter boards, which should be at least 3 ' long, part way into the ground. Position the stakes at least 4 ' outside the foundation line and at least 1 ' outside the excavation line. You will add the cross members a little later.

The tops of cross members in type A and B batter boards must be at the same level all the way around the foundation. To establish the level you need some sort of leveling equipment. If you can rent one, use an optical level, commonly called a *dumpy level* (Fig. 6-9). With the level you will also need a tripod and a measuring rod.

**Fig. 6-8.** Of the three common types of batter boards, type A is the easiest to build, and B the most practical. Type C is for use at low corners of a sloping site.

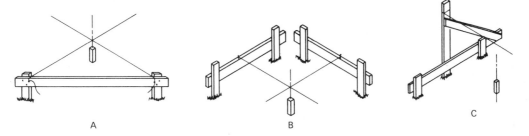

A

B

C

**Fig. 6-9.** A dumpy level is a limited-distance telescope. It rests on a tripod, which must be set exactly level. The level itself can be turned 360° to aim at any point on the site. *Photographer: Leviton Atlanta*

Find some point on the site where you can clearly see all four corners of the house and the stake you drove at the high point of the foundation. Set up your level here, and adjust it until it is exactly level. Then have someone hold the measuring rod against the stake at the high point, with its bottom level with the mark that established the height of your foundation wall.

Look through the dumpy level at the rod and take a reading. Let's say the reading is 4.9′ (the rod is calibrated in feet and tenths of feet), and the mark on the stake is 1.0′ above finished grade. Remember the reading you took; better still, write it down.

Now, without changing its level, swing the dumpy level until it faces a corner stake. Have your helper hold the rod right against the stake and raise or lower it until you read 4.9′ through the lens (Fig. 6-10). Mark the stake at the bottom of the rod and ask your helper to move to the next corner stake. Repeat this process until you have a mark on each stake. The marks indicate the top of the foundation wall at each corner, even though the distance between the mark and the ground varies with the terrain.

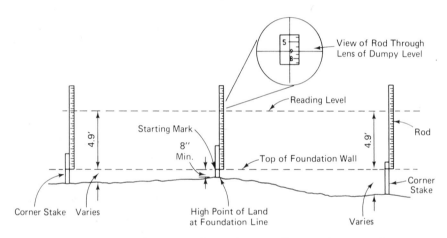

**Fig. 6-10.** With the dumpy level take a reading on the measuring rod at the high point of the foundation. Then transfer the level of the top of the foundation wall to stakes at the corners of the wall.

## Using a Hose As a Level

Just as accurate as a dumpy level, but taking much longer to use, is a homemade level. You need a funnel, a pair of clamps, and at least 50′ of clear plastic garden hose. If you can't see through the hose, you'll also need a pair of glass tubes that fit into the ends of the hose.

Clamp one end of the hose to the stake at the high point of the foundation. Set the end of the hose above the mark if it's transparent. Set the end below the mark if you use the glass tubes. Clamp the other end of the hose to a corner stake.

Through the funnel fill the hose until water level is right at the mark on the stake at the high point. Pour very slowly to reduce as much as possible the wave action that occurs. When the undulation has subsided, the water level at the corner will be exactly at foundation height. Mark this level on the stake, and continue this procedure at all other corners. No matter how irregular the site or how many bends are in the hose, the water levels will always be identical.

## Completing Batter Boards

Now that you have marked the foundation level on a batter board stake at each corner, nail the cross member to the backs of the stakes, with the top of the board on the marks. Use a carpenter's level to make sure you get the boards level. Before stretching cords between batter boards, however, recheck every measurement, recheck your marks, and recheck level. Then you can proceed with confidence. Now is the time to catch and correct any errors.

To stretch cords you need a hand saw and two plumb bobs. Tie plumb bobs to the cord the same distance apart as the distance between the nails in the tops of foundation stakes. This distance is also equal to the overall dimension of one exterior wall of the house. Stretch the cord tightly across the tops of the batter boards until the plumb bobs point directly at the nails in the foundation stakes. Mark the location of the cord on the top of the batter boards and cut saw kerfs in the back side. A *kerf* is the channel made by the saw's teeth. Remove the plumb bobs, tie knots in the ends of the cord, and set the knotted cord in the kerfs. Continue around the house in this manner.

When all cords are in place, hold another length of cord diagonally between the points where the cords cross (Fig. 6-11). Mark this length with chalk on the cord, then measure the diagonal between the other two corners. If the measurements are identical, the house is square. If the lengths are different, go back over all your procedures to find out what went wrong. Cords will stretch slightly,

**Fig. 6-11.** Set the cords outlining the foundation wall in saw kerfs (inset) cut into batter boards. To check your accuracy in making square corners, measure the diagonals. They must be equal in length.

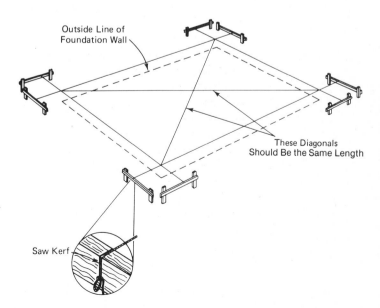

Outside Line of Foundation Wall

These Diagonals Should Be the Same Length

Saw Kerf

but you should have no more than 1/8″ difference in the lengths of the two diagonals. If you measure with a steel tape instead of a cord, there should be no difference at all between the two measurements.

To set batter boards for a wing, refer back to Figs. 6-6 and 6-8. Place half of a type B batter board outside the excavation line at points G and H, and a type A batter board at points K and L. Then stretch cords from G to K, from H to L, and from K to L to outline the foundation of the wing.

The outline of your foundation now floats in midair above the foundation stakes. Before you outline the excavation, use your steel tape to make sure every overall dimension agrees with the matching overall dimensions in working drawings. If everything checks out, you can safely remove the foundation stakes and set them aside for future use.

### Outlining the Excavation

The simplest way to mark the excavation line is with another set of saw kerfs. Excavation lines are easy to locate if you use type B batter boards. Assuming that your excavation line is 3′ outside the foundation line, measure off 36″ on the batter board from the first kerf, moving away from the foundation. In each batter board cut another set of kerfs at this point. Temporarily move your cords into the new kerfs and hang a plumb bob from the points where they cross. Place a stake at each corner just outside the lines, with one edge directly below the plumb bob.

For making the corners of an excavation, use 2 × 2 stakes 3′ to 4′ long. Drive the pointed end half-way into the ground. Then paint the upper 3″ of the stake a bright color that is easy to see for anyone using excavating machinery.

## DIGGING THE EXCAVATION

In most vacation areas it isn't possible to rent excavating machinery. That leaves you with the choice of doing your digging by hand or hiring an excavation contractor. If you want a basement, hire.

If you are building a small vacation house on piers or pilings, or over a crawl space, it's possible to do the work by hand. It is slow, tiring work, however, and can be done by machine much more quickly.

For cutting a trench for a foundation wall, the best equipment is a backhoe. A backhoe operates like an elephant's trunk. It reaches out, scoops up earth toward the operator's cab, then swings to one side to dump the load. Where accuracy of the cut, either in width or depth, is important, a backhoe is the ideal machine. In a few hours a good backhoe operator can dig a foundation trench that would take you a week of work to dig by hand.

For digging holes, a power digger is the best machine. It is a type of drill that bites into the soil and clears out a circular hole big enough and deep enough for setting wood pilings or pouring concrete piers.

Even with machinery to do the heavy work, there is plenty of other work that can be done only by hand with a shovel. Excavating close to trees and roots, leveling the base for footings, shaping vertical cuts, and undercutting banks can best be done by hand. Few power tools exist for such work.

## Solving Excavating Problems

Before the first cubic foot of earth is moved, be ready with answers to five common excavating problems.

First, decide what to do with the soil that is dug up. Store reusable top soil away from the excavation where it can lie undisturbed until you are ready to use it. Cover it with a tarpaulin to prevent washing, and weight the tarp so it won't blow off. Store soil for grading or backfilling around the foundation near the point of use, but not so close that it falls or washes into the foundation trench. Pile excess material and debris to be hauled away close to your access road.

Second, be prepared to take all possible steps promptly to keep water out of your excavation. Water that stands in a trench softens the soil, and you can't pour footings until the soil is dry and firm again, or unless you dig out the heavy, softened soil. The only good answer is to know where you can rent a pump on short notice to pump out rain water or water from an underground spring as soon as it appears. If your foundation is on a slope, leave open the lowest corner of the trench, so that water can flow out of the excavation and harmlessly down hill.

Third, avoid cave-ins by sloping the banks of the excavation as shown in Fig. 6-4. If the soil is too sandy, soft, or moist to hold its shape when cut, shore up the bank (Fig. 6-12). Use 2″ planks driven 3″ into the ground and angled slightly toward the bank. To hold the planks in line against the weight, use

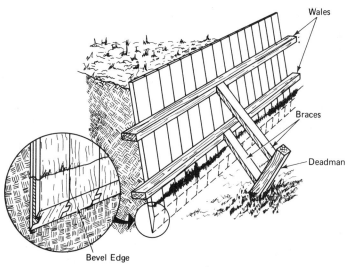

**Fig. 6-12.** Detail of construction for shoring up a bank. Tongue-and-groove boards (inset) make the strongest shoring wall, but ordinary planks will do in most cases. Note the method of bracing.

heavy timbers (4 × 4s or 4 × 6s). Brace as often as needed. The shoring and braces must lie outside the excavation lines when the banks are above finished grade, and outside the footing line if you are shoring up the side of an excavation.

Fourth, you may run into some tree roots, although none should be large if you located your house properly on the site. Cut the roots cleanly with a saw, and seal the cut ends with tree paint. Don't use house paint; it has ingredients that may kill the tree.

Fifth, if you run into rock that isn't soft enough to dig out, there is no good answer. Blasting or chipping with an air hammer is expensive. If you strike a solid rock ledge, you can sometimes build the foundation right on the ledge. It won't heave in the spring the way soil does. The only other solution to a rock problem is to relocate the house on its site.

These problems aren't mentioned here to scare you. They can be headaches if you aren't prepared for them, however. They emphasize the importance of digging test holes around the proposed foundation line, and the need for careful inspection of the site before you buy it.

## OUTLINING FOOTINGS

After all excavation work is completed, and the bottoms of trenches have been leveled, smoothed, and cleaned, the next step is to locate the footings. Begin by adding two marks on each batter board. Let's assume that you plan to build your foundation wall of concrete block on a footing 16″ wide. Then place the first mark 4″ outside the kerf mark for the foundation wall and the second mark 12″ inside the kerf mark. These marks indicate the outside and inside edges, respectively, of the 16″-wide footing. Cut saw kerfs at each mark.

Now temporarily move your cords into matching sets of kerfs for outside footing lines. Where the cords cross you have the outline of the outside edge of the footings in midair. To bring this information to earth, drop a plumb bob on a long string from each crossing. The plumb bob will point to the exact outside corner of the footing. Mark this corner temporarily with a piece of steel reinforcing rod. Repeat the process, using the other new set of kerf marks, to locate the inside corners of the footings.

Finally, drive a pair of 2 × 2 stakes into the ground at each corner just outside the piece of rod. Each stake must line up with a pair of rods (Fig. 6-13). Place a mark on each stake at the height of the footing (usually 8″), and run a continuous cord around all stakes, forming a triangle at each corner. Now you are ready to form for footings.

## FORMING FOR FOOTINGS

Although there are other methods of forming, the on-the-ground method is the most common, and probably the easiest, for the amateur to follow. The procedures that are set forth here are for forming on the ground for footings 16″ wide and 8″ in depth.

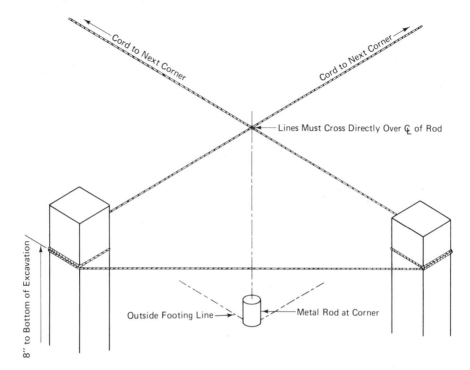

**Fig. 6-13.** At the bottom of an excavation use pieces of metal rod to mark the corners of footings. The cord, which crosses directly above the rod, is wrapped around a pair of stakes at each corner. The cord is at the exact height and location of the tops of footings along their outside edges.

For forming materials you can use 3/4″ plywood, a pair of 2 × 4s placed edge to edge, or a 2 × 8. If you use plywood, buy exterior grade and cut the material in strips 7 1/2″ wide. If you use 2 × 4s, use the straightest lengths you can find. You'll get probably the best results with 2 × 8s, and you will have less cutting and fitting to do. But 2 × 8s for forms are expensive unless you can reuse them later for joists or rafters.

A 2 × 8 is 7 1/2″ wide. Set the forms so that their tops are absolutely level, 8″ above the bottom of the trench, and flush with the tops of supporting stakes. At the bottom leave a 1/2″ gap that serves three purposes. Water can run off quickly without soaking the boards if it rains after you place the forms but before you pour the concrete footings. Second, the gap compensates for any unevenness in level of the bottom of the trench. And third, you can easily sweep out any dirt that falls into the space between forms. A little concrete may seep out through the gap, but not enough to worry about.

Start forming at a corner, building the outside form first. Use the longest and straightest boards available. Butt them at right angles, with one overlapping the other slightly. Line them up plumb, and then drive in a stake behind each board (see Fig. 6-14). With the tops of the 1 × 4 stakes and the form boards flush with the cord, nail the boards to the stakes.

To set the boards in place, hold the form board against the stake with your leg, and raise or lower it with your toe until the top touches the cord. Then nail. It's a good idea to nail the board a little high. You can always pound the stake farther into the ground to lower the form board, but you can't easily raise it.

Recheck the level and plumb of each form board before you move on to the next stake. Complete all corners first, then work toward the middle of each wall. Support form boards every 6′ to 8′ and at each joint. Cut the last piece of board in each form to fit the remaining gap.

To position the inside forms, first cut a measuring stick from a piece of 1 × 4. Make the length of the stick equal to the width of your footing. Use the measuring stick as a spacer between form boards, and follow the same procedures as for outside form boards.

After you have all forms for footings in place, use your carpenter's level for one last check to make sure all tops are level. Then brace the forms so you don't knock them out of place.

Octagonal vacation house has a wood shingle roof, walls of exterior plywood laid vertically, and a deck on three sides. The entire floor structure is supported on posts. Note that the tops of footings are exposed—possible in climates where the ground doesn't freeze, but nowhere else. *Architect: R. Rittenour. Courtesy American Plywood Association.*

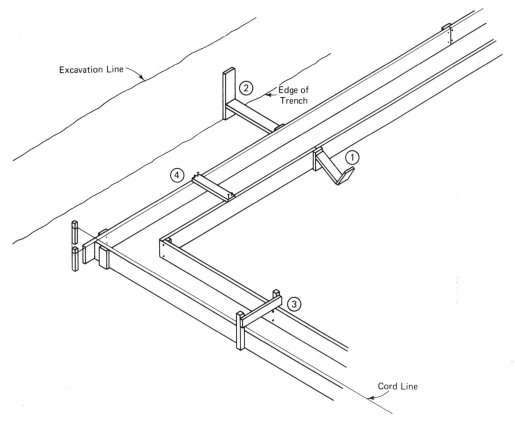

**Fig. 6-14.** The various ways to brace forms for footings. Type 1 is the most common. You can use type 2 against a vertical excavation. Type 3 gets in the way of leveling concrete. A cleat (4) is useful to reduce warp in a form board.

You can brace in any of the three ways shown in Fig. 6-14. Braces prevent the force of wet concrete from pushing forms outward. Methods 1 and 2 are best, because they don't interfere with placing and smoothing concrete. Method 3 does interfere. If any form tends to warp inward, hold it straight with a temporary cleat across the top (4), and add a stake. Nail the cleat just enough to hold, and remove it when you level the concrete.

### Footings for Piers

To make forms for piers, cut a piece of scrap plywood to the exact size of the footing. Then lay 2 × 8s on edge around the plywood, overlapping the boards about 6″ (Fig. 6-15). Nail the four pieces together. Then set stakes against the overlapping ends, and raise the entire form assembly to the correct level.

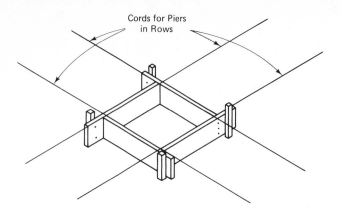

**Fig. 6-15.** Preassemble forms for pier footings around a piece of plywood the same size as the footing. Then stake the forms in place under cords.

Piers lie in rows. Set a batter board at the end of each row at trench level just outside the foundation forms. Then mark and cut kerfs as before, and string cords to mark the locations of footings for piers. You can locate forms for piers more accurately if you place them after you finish work on footings around the perimeter of the house.

### Footings on Sloping Ground

On sloping ground you support a foundation wall on a stepped footing. The process is slow because parts of the forms are horizontal and parts vertical. You can form the entire stepped footing for pouring all at one time, but it is easier to form and pour in sections. To form a good bond between sections, make a key slot in the concrete (inset, Fig. 6-16). Use oiled lengths of 2 × 4, and push them into the wet concrete. Remove them after the concrete has set.

When you lay out a stepped footing, follow two rules. First, the maximum steepness of a stepped footing is 2 to 1. In other words a vertical section can be no more than half as long as the horizontal portion above it. Second, no horizontal section can be less than 24″ long. If the foundation wall is made of concrete blocks, each of which is 16″ long, 32″ is the minimum horizontal run. The minimum thickness of vertical sections is 4″.

The rules for stepped piers are similar but different. First, maximum steepness is 1 1/2 horizontal to 1 vertical. If, for example, the horizontal distance between footings is 12′, the vertical distance between the bottoms of adjacent footings can't exceed 8′. Second, footings for stepped piers can be no closer together than 4′. And third, the bottom of each footing must be at least 3′ below grade at the pier.

### Footings for Chimneys

A chimney is the heaviest part of a house, and it must have its own footing entirely separate from the house's footings. This footing must go below the frost line and rest on firm ground. The working drawings for your house tell you what size footing to form.

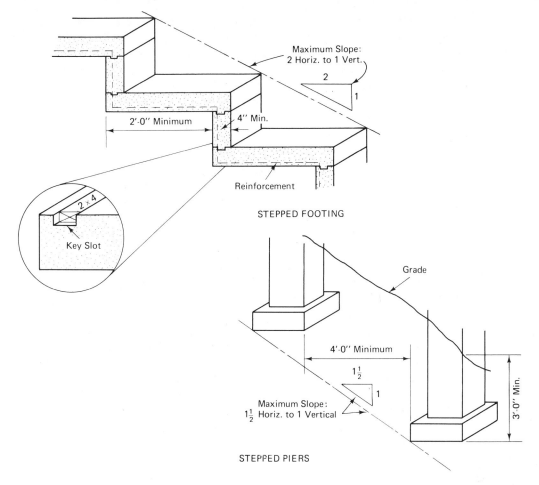

**Fig. 6-16.** Drawings of a stepped footing (top) and stepped piers (bottom) show typical construction and the rules for placement on a sloping site. Use a key slot whenever two sections of concrete meet but are poured separately.

## PLACING FOOTINGS

Concrete is a mixture of cement, sand, aggregate (gravel), and water. For footings the best mix is 1 part cement to 2 3/4 parts sand to 4 parts aggregate no larger than 1 1/2" in diameter. If the sand is wet, add 5 gallons of water per sack of cement. If sand is damp or dry, add 6 gallons per sack. A sack of cement weighs 94 pounds, and contains 1 cubic foot. From one sack you can mix about 8 1/2 cubic feet of concrete, or enough for about 9 1/2 running feet of footing 8" by 16".

Mix the ingredients as close as possible to the point of use. To maintain the proper proportions build a box with inside dimensions of 12″ by 12″ by 12″. Filled, the box holds one cubic foot of ingredients. On the inside of the box draw lines at the 3″, 6″, and 9″ levels. Each 3″ of depth represents 1/4 cubic foot of content.

If your mix for any concrete work is too thin or too stiff, correct the problem by increasing or decreasing the amount of aggregate. *Do not* change the proportions of either cement or water.

### Pouring the Concrete

Pour the concrete mix into forms from as close by as possible. If the concrete has to travel more than 4′ from mixer to form, build a simple wood chute to minimize spills.

As the concrete goes into forms, use a spade, working in an up-and-down motion, to force concrete against the sides of forms to give you solid footings with square corners, and to relieve entrapped air. Fill forms all the way to the top, but not over the top. To level the tops of footings, pull a straightedge in a zigzag motion along the tops of the forms. A *straightedge* is a flat board with a handle on top. To bring excess water to the surface where it can evaporate (this is called *floating*), use a metal or wood float made for the purpose.

You'll get the best results if you pour footings in one continuous operation. But if you have to stop before the job is finished, build a dam the same width as the footing (Fig. 6-17). Stake the dam in place, with its top level with the tops of the side forms. Drill holes in the dam, or otherwise leave room for reinforcing rods to protrude. The continuous rods and the keyway made by the 2 × 4 in the dam provide a good connection between one pouring and the next.

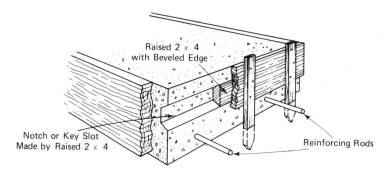

**Fig. 6-17.** If you can't pour an entire footing at one time, build a temporary form or dam across the footing. To the dam attach a 2 × 4 with beveled edges, which will form a key slot. Extend reinforcing rods beyond the dam to tie in the next section poured.

### Reinforcing Footings

Steel reinforcement is advisable in all concrete work, and necessary in most. In footings the standard reinforcement is a pair of 3/8″ steel rods. The rods lie near, but not on, the bottom of the footing. As you fill the forms with concrete, work the rods into the mix until they are about an inch from the bottom, 5″ to 6″ apart, and centered under the wall.

If the concrete work requires any vertical reinforcement, as in a stepped footing, insert it while the concrete is still in a plastic condition.

### Protecting New Concrete

Concrete should be poured and allowed to cure while air temperature is above freezing. In all weather cover the fresh concrete with wet straw, burlap, or any similar material that will hold moisture for a long time. You must let the water in the concrete evaporate slowly. In cool, damp weather, keep the concrete under a moist cover for at least three days. In hot, dry weather, keep it covered for five days.

You can remove forms 48 hours after you pour when the weather is warm, but continue to keep the concrete covered and damp. Leave forms in place for at least four days in cold weather, because concrete sets more slowly at lower air temperatures.

During the curing process check your work at least twice a day. If you have any repair work or patching to do, this is the only time to do it.

## LAYING A BLOCK FOUNDATION WALL

Of the many types and shapes of concrete blocks available, (Fig. 6-18), three will be used more often than the others—stretcher blocks, corner blocks, and cap blocks.

You will use 3-core or 2-core stretcher blocks in straight runs of wall, corner blocks at corners (where else?), and 4″ or 8″ cap blocks atop the wall. Use double corner blocks in exposed piers, jamb blocks beside exterior doors, sash blocks beside steel windows, and partition blocks to divide basement space. All these blocks are either 8″ by 8″ by 16″ or 4″ by 8″ by 16″.

In just a few minutes you can calculate how many blocks of each type you will need. Let's suppose that the overall dimensions of your vacation house are 32′ by 24′. The perimeter of the wall, then, is 112′. Multiply the perimeter by 3/4 (there are 3 blocks in every 4 feet of wall), and the answer is 84. Subtract 2 to correct for the 1/2-block overlap at each corner, and the total number of blocks in each course is 82. Now multiply by the number of courses, which you determined when you worked out the height of the wall.

In a rectangular foundation, 78 of these blocks are stretchers and 4 are corner blocks. All the blocks in the top course are cap blocks.

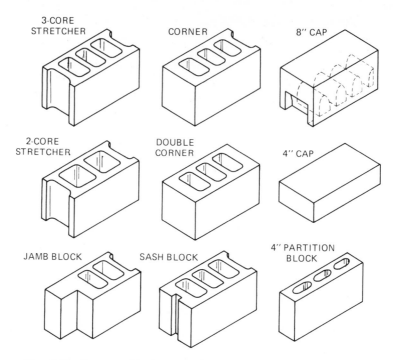

**Fig. 6-18.** Concrete blocks come in many shapes. These are the shapes you are most likely to need in a vacation house.

## Marking the Footings

To guide you in positioning the first course of blocks on the footing, snap a chalk line. First remove the forms and clean them if you intend to use the material in construction. Clean all loose material off the top of the footing. Then, with the help of two other people, two of you stretch a cord rubbed with carpenter's chalk from one end of the footing to the other at a point 4″ in from the outer edge. Have the third person raise the cord at its midpoint about a foot, then let go. The cord will deposit a line of chalk along the entire length of the footing; lay your first course of blocks to this line.

Before you mix any mortar, set a course of blocks on the footing all the way around the foundation to check spacing. Allow for a 3/8″ mortar joint between blocks. You can reduce this spacing to 1/4″ if necessary to avoid cutting a block. But you can't increase the width of the joint without inviting leaks.

## Mixing Mortar

The common formula for mortar in a block foundation is 1 part masonry cement, 3 parts fine sand, and water. The sand must be clean. Using the same box you used for measuring the ingredients for concrete, mix the sand and cement.

Then add water slowly, mixing as you add. Mortar should be firm enough to stand up on the edges of the block, yet wet enough to spread easily and sticky enough to hang on your trowel when you turn it upright. As you mix, give the water a chance to blend thoroughly with the masonry cement and water before you add more. It is easy to add too much water.

You can lay about two dozen stretcher blocks with a cubic foot of mortar. Mix mortar in batches of one cubic foot until you know how many blocks you can lay in an hour. On cool days mortar retains its plasticity for about three hours. On hot days you should use up all you mix in about two hours. Once mortar starts to stiffen, throw it out.

### Laying the First Course

To lay the first course of concrete blocks, spread a bed of mortar a full 8 " wide on the clean footing at one corner. But don't cover your chalk line. With a trowel transfer some mortar from the mixer onto a mortar board, and work from the mortar board. Spread mortar about 6 ' in each direction from the corner. Then make a furrow down the middle of the bed so that the bed is thickest at the inside and outside edges of the blocks.

Lay a square-ended corner block first. Press it firmly into the mortar bed until the dimension from bottom to top of the block is an even 8 ". Use the handle of your trowel to tap the block level, and check its position with your carpenter's level or a mason's level. Also check alignment with the chalk line.

Next lay a stretcher block. Scrape off the excess mortar that has oozed out from under the corner block, using the point of the trowel, and butter one end of the stretcher. Butter only the butting edges. Press the block into the mortar bed, and tap it into position against the corner block. Then check both vertical and horizontal dimensions (8 " and 16 " respectively) exactly. Check alignment and vertical plumb. To check horizontal level, lay your level across the joint between the two blocks.

After you have laid about eight blocks—four in each direction—start the second course and build a pyramid of blocks (Fig. 6-19). Then repeat this process at the other corners. By building pyramids and checking levels constantly, you can then stretch cords between corners as a guide to laying each course.

To the blocks used above the first course you apply mortar differently. Holding the block from underneath, you butter the horizontal face shells and vertical face shells at both ends (Fig. 6-20). Then you turn the block over to lay it. This method, called *face-shell mortar bedding,* gives you full, solid joints between blocks.

As in the base course, you begin all the other courses with a corner block. Set each block at 90° to the one below it, and with the squared end exposed on the corner. When you have finished a wall, the vertical joint between two blocks lies above the midpoint of the block below. This pattern is called *regular bond* or *running bond.*

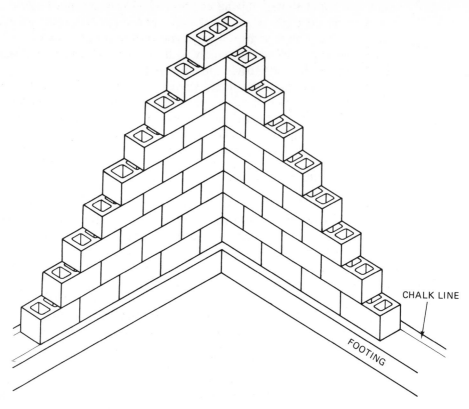

**Fig. 6-19.** Build a pyramid of blocks at each corner; then fill the courses between corners. The pyramids give you a place for attaching cords to guide you to level courses.

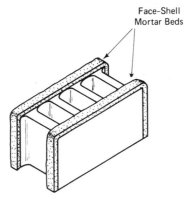

Face-Shell Mortar Beds

**Fig. 6-20.** With face-shell mortar bedding, you apply mortar only to six edges of the block, and then turn the block upside down to lay it in position.

### Finishing Joints

For a strong, weather-tight wall, you must tool all joints. Mortar shrinks as it dries and tends to pull away from a block. Tooling prevents this.

You tool the mortar when it is "thumb-print hard." In other words the mortar is hard enough so that you can see your thumb print when you press it, but no so soft that you can make a dent in it.

You need two tools to finish joints. For horizontal joints, which you tool first, use a *sled-runner*—a steel blade with a handle on it. Sled-runners are made with a rounded blade for dished joints or a triangular blade for V joints. Slide the runner the length of the horizontal joint with enough pressure to compact the mortar. Remove any excess with a trowel.

For vertical joints use a *jointer,* a tool that looks like a narrow-bladed spatula. You press the jointer into the joint and draw it slowly downward. Where vertical and horizontal joints meet, use the jointer to tool the intersection flush.

### Tips of the Trade

To get a professional-looking foundation wall, follow these suggestions:

- Never lay a block with chipped corners or broken edges. Use the good portions for any smaller blocks needed to fill the centers of courses that don't measure out in even blocks.
- Stand unlaid blocks on end so that you can butter the face shells of several blocks at one time.
- Most concrete blocks have a greater core (the amount of concrete between holes) on one horizontal surface than the other. Lay blocks with the greater core surface up, to provide maximum mortar bed for the next course.
- As you lay the base course, drop a little mortar into each hole to help anchor the block to the footing.
- As you set a block, tip it toward you slightly so that you can see the course below. Then swing it into position as if it were hinged. Drop it into place; never drag it through the mortar.
- Never allow mortar that you have spread or buttered to sit for more than half an hour. If the mortar does begin to stiffen before that time, scrape it off and throw it away.
- Take the time to check the plumb, level, and alignment of each block to make sure it is properly positioned before you lay the next block. If you try to reposition a block after the mortar begins to harden, you will create a crack in the joint into which water can penetrate and cause damage.
- Clean off excess mortar as you work. When you stop for a meal or at the end of the day, clean off all work surfaces, including your mortar board and trowel.

## Laying the Cap Course

The top course of the foundation wall should be built of cap blocks. They are solid concrete, keep insects out of the wall, and help spread the load of the floor structure. If you can't buy cap blocks locally, you can use stretcher blocks. But you will have to take some extra steps. In the mortar joint two courses below the cap course (left in Fig. 6-21), embed strips of 1/4″ hardware cloth. Then pour concrete into all holes in the blocks in the course next to the top. The hardware cloth will prevent the concrete from falling through. After you lay the cap course, again fill all holes and trowel the concrete smooth.

If your drawings call for anchor bolts to connect the floor structure to the foundation wall—and they should—set the bolts as you lay the cap course. Anchor bolts fit in the mortar joints of the cap course and into a hole in the course below. Fill the hole with mortar (Fig. 6-21, right) to hold the anchor firm. Anchor bolts are usually placed 8″ or 16″ from the corner in each wall, and about every 8′ between corner bolts.

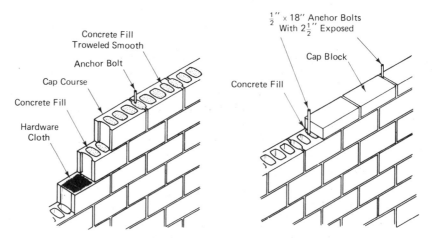

**Fig. 6-21.** To lay a cap course of stretcher blocks, you must lay hardware cloth in the mortar joint two courses below (left), and fill holes in the top two courses with concrete. When the top course is made of cap blocks, set anchor bolts into the mortar joints and a mortar-filled hole in the course below (right).

## Supporting Girders

In most houses a girder runs the long way of the house near the center to support joists in the floor framing system. Where this girder rests on the wood sill at the side foundations, you must fill the holes in concrete blocks with concrete all the way to the footing. The concrete and blocks form a column that carries the weight of the girder itself and the loads on it. The location of the girder is shown in working drawings, usually on the foundation plan or floor-framing plan.

## Filling Openings in the Wall

Every basement and crawl space should have an access door to the outdoors if possible. Locate the door where the wall is highest, so that you have maximum headroom and a minimum of excavating outside the doorway.

Form the sides of the opening with jamb blocks. Set expansion sleeves in the mortar joints so that you have something that will hold screws when you fit the wood door frame. Across the top of the opening lay a steel angle as a bridge to support the weight of blocks above. A 4″ × 4″ × 1/4″ angle is adequate above doors. Use an angle 6″ wider than the door opening. Embed the angle in mortar, and then lay the blocks on the angle in another bed of mortar.

Even if you have no windows or doors in your foundation wall, you will have some openings. Crawl space must be ventilated. Ventilators must be set far enough above grade so that water won't flow into them. If possible, they should be set below wood framing members. With a low foundation you may have to fit ventilators between floor joists.

A ventilator is the same size as a concrete block. Fill the holes in the block below the opening with mortar, and trowel the mortar smooth. Then leave out a block in the course, using the ventilator as a spacer. After the opening is completely surrounded by blocks, fill the holes in the blocks above the opening. Then apply a thick bed of mortar to the bottom and sides of the opening. Fit the ventilator in place, working from inside the wall. Tool the joints to assure a watertight fit, and caulk the top edge of the ventilator to complete the seal.

You may also have to provide a place for water and sewer lines to come through the wall. If you intend to do your own plumbing, plan in advance where these openings should go. If you hire a plumbing contractor, ask him where he wants you to leave openings before you start to build the wall.

Pipes penetrate walls through sleeves. You need a sleeve 6″ in diameter for a waste line and 3″ in diameter for water or fuel lines. To allow space for the sleeve, either cut a stretcher block to size, or use an 8″ × 8″ × 12″ block. For a solid filler use a piece of 4″ cap block. As shown in Fig. 6-22, fill the bottom half

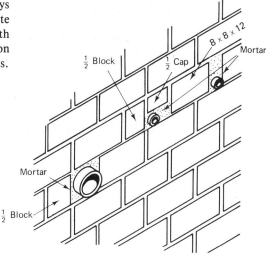

**Fig. 6-22.** Here are three typical ways to set sleeves for pipes into a concrete block wall. The method varies with the location of the sleeve in relation to both horizontal and vertical joints.

of the wall opening with mortar, and set the sleeve in place. It should extend about 2″ from the wall on both sides. Then fill the rest of the opening with mortar. After you run a pipe through a sleeve, fill the remainder of the sleeve with oakum or similar caulking material.

### Building Block Piers

Piers are usually 16″ square. Blocks in even-numbered courses run in one direction and in odd-numbered courses in the other direction. Procedures for building piers are generally the same as for foundation walls. For interior piers you can use either stretcher blocks or corner blocks both below and above grade. If piers are exposed to view, however, use double corner blocks above grade.

It is extremely important to check heights constantly, because all piers must end up at exactly the same height. If the site is close to level, string cords to help you keep courses at the same height. On sloping sites the best way to check the level is to lay a straight joist on edge between piers, and then set a carpenter's level at the midpoint.

## BUILDING A STONE FOUNDATION

If your site abounds with natural stone, you can sometimes use the stone for foundations and piers. To do so may be less expensive, but it is much more difficult than laying blocks.

To be usable for construction, stones should have bearing surfaces that are flat or almost flat. Stones must be cut or trimmed so that they form walls of relatively uniform thickness. At least one horizontal mortar joint must be continuous in every two feet of vertical wall. In this joint you must insert metal bars for reinforcement.

Because of the unevenness of stone surfaces, you will use a lot more mortar. You must also take more time and care than with a manufactured wall material that is consistent in size and quality.

## TOOLS YOU WILL NEED

To stake out the site as described in this chapter, you will need the following tools and equipment as a minimum:

    ax
    steel tape
    nylon cord
    dumpy level or, as an alternate, clear garden hose, a funnel, two clamps, and
        two glass tubes
    hand saw
    hammer
    carpenter's level

Assuming that you hire an excavating contractor to handle all major foundation digging and trenching, you will still need these tools and equipment to complete excavation work and place footings:

spade
tree paint
concrete mixer
water bucket
straightedge
float
trowel
burlap or straw

To build a foundation wall of concrete blocks, you will need the following additional tools and equipment:

mortar board
chalk line and chalk
sled-runner
jointer

# Working Safely

If you are like most people who build a house for themselves, you look forward to the day when the foundation is complete. Then you can start working with wood above ground where your efforts show.

Yet as construction begins to rise, so does the danger of accidents and injuries. People experienced in the building industry know that dangers are always present. Smart workers respect the dangers, know safety rules, and follow them to the letter. Many amateurs don't bother to learn the rules, thinking that they are too wise to get hurt. Unfortunately they are sometimes wrong.

So take a few minutes to study the rules for safety listed below. Then refresh your memory every time you approach the job until you can recite all the rules without error. At best, injuries slow the work. At worst, they stop it completely.

1. Wear safety equipment at all times. Buy a pair of comfortable safety shoes to protect your feet from dropped tools and materials. Wear gloves to protect your hands from splinters, cuts, and blisters. Always wear safety glasses when mixing, hammering, or sawing. And get and wear a hard hat. A hard hat isn't comfortable in hot weather, but it is more comfortable than a fractured skull.

2. Wear tight-fitting clothing. A loose sleeve or billowing jacket can catch on nails or scaffolding or whirling saw blades.

3. Keep sharp tools out of your pockets, and keep everything out of your mouth.

4. Never wear rings or jewelry on the job. They can catch unexpectedly on nails and edges of tools.

5. Never use a power tool without its guard in place.

6. Practice good housekeeping on the site. Keep a garbage container handy for cans, bottles, paper sacks, and wrappings. Place oily rags, scrap lumber, sawdust, and bent nails in a metal container, and empty it when it is about three-quarters full. A clean site is a safe site.

7. Keep walking surfaces clean at all times. Sweep the subfloor every night before you leave. Never set tools or materials or leave scrap in normal walk paths.

8. Work steadily rather than quickly. The old adage that "haste makes waste" could be the truest slogan to post at the site.

9. Use only standard ladders in safe condition. Work only from sturdy, immovable scaffolding.

10. Think safety. And pay attention to what you are doing.

Inattention is probably the most common single cause of accidents. Improper lifting is a major cause of back injury. When you have a heavy object to lift, get help if you can. If you must lift alone, lift with your legs, and keep your back as close to upright as possible.

Improper use of ladders is a prime cause of falls. For using ladders, there is a separate set of safety rules:

- Carry ladders upright, with your hands two rungs apart. On a windy day move the two lengths of an extension ladder separately.
- When raising a ladder, brace one end (usually the lower end), and walk under the ladder toward the braced end, pushing upward as you go.
- The safest angle for a ladder is about 75° to the horizontal. At this angle the ratio of vertical height to the distance between the wall and ladder base is about 4 to 1. In other words, if the point of support of the upper end of the ladder is 16′ above the ground, the base of the ladder should be 4′ away from the supporting wall.
- Both legs of the ladder must be on a solid, level base. If necessary, use a wedge under one leg to achieve this level.
- Allow at least 4′ of overlap where the two lengths of an extension ladder meet.
- If you are working on a roof, let the ladder extend about 3′ above the eave line so you can swing easily onto the roof. Secure the top of the ladder so that it won't slide or blow down, leaving you stranded.
- Clean all mud, oil, or snow off the soles of your shoes before you begin to climb.
- Climb up or down facing the ladder, and always work facing the ladder.

- Never stand on any rung that lies above the upper point of support for the ladder; the ladder could flip.

- Hold onto the ladder with at least one hand most of the time. If you must use both hands momentarily, hook one leg over a rung to steady yourself.

- Never work from either of the top two rungs. You need one to hook your leg over and the other to grab with your free hand.

- If you have to reach so far that your nose is beyond the leg of the ladder, you are reaching too far for safety.

Now that you have read the rules, follow them carefully and get on with construction.

# 8

# Framing the Floor

Just before you finish work on your foundation, place your order for the first load of lumber. When you buy, shop around if you have a choice of suppliers. You don't want to spend any more than you have to, but neither do you want to buy inferior materials just because they are cheaper. You save the optimum combination of time and money by buying the best lumber available within its grade at the lowest price.

You don't select lumber by brand, but by grade. The common grades are select, #1, #2, #3, construction, standard, stud, and utility. For horizontal framing members, such as joists and rafters, order #2 grade. You can use #3, but it can legitimately have some warp, knots, and other defects that can slow your work. For vertical framing members order stud-grade lumber. You can use utility grade for such purposes as blocking, bridging, and bracing, but usually you have enough short cutoffs from other members to fill your needs. Use #1 and select only when the lumber will be exposed on the interior, such as in cabinets, and you want it to be as clear and beautiful as possible.

When you place the order, decide where to store the lumber. Pick a place close to your point of use but also accessible to the supplier's truck. When the truck arrives, and while the driver is still there, check the delivery against what you ordered. Don't hesitate to send back any lumber that isn't exactly what you ordered. Under no circumstances should you accept green (wet) lumber. If you accept inferior material once, you will get inferior material the next time, too.

If the lumber comes banded, leave the bands on until you are ready to use it. Store all material off the ground; on excess concrete blocks is one good method. Cover the stack with a tarpaulin or sheet of polyethylene, which you can buy from your lumber supplier. If the lumber gets rain-soaked on the site, pile it on strips of scrap wood so that air can circulate around it. But because even air-drying fosters warping, take extra care to keep your lumber dry until it is in place.

Lumber warps easily. The warp may take any of several forms—bow, crook, twist, cup, or a combination of any two (Fig. 8-1). You can't straighten a warped board, and you should never use a warped member for structural purposes. By doing so, you build in structural problems that can be expensive to correct in later years.

Don't discard warped lumber, however. You can cut pieces with twist or extreme bow or crook into shorter pieces for use as bridging and firestops. You can rip cupped pieces into narrower boards for bracing.

When you begin to use structural lumber, sort the material according to its straightness, and use the straightest pieces for the main structural members. Sorting takes a little time, but it will save you time in the long run and give you better results.

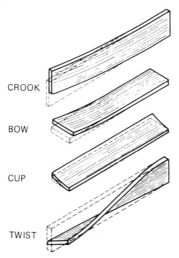

**Fig. 8-1.** A piece of lumber may warp in any of four ways.

CROOK

BOW

CUP

TWIST

## FRAMING ON FOUNDATION WALLS

The first wood you attach to a foundation wall is a series of butted 2 × 6s called a *sill* or *sill plate*. Select your sill members, and lay them atop the foundation to get the spacing right. Plan ahead so that joints between sill members fall between floor joists. Work from the corners toward the centers of walls, and cut midpieces to length where necessary. Then mark the locations of anchor bolts on the sill, and drill holes for them.

Before you do any cutting or drilling, however, look at the main section in your working drawings. Remember in Chapter 5 you read that overall dimensions run from face of stud to face of stud. In some parts of the country it is the custom to include sheathing in the overall dimension, which means that the sill rests, not at the edge of the foundation, but 3/4″ in from the outside edge. The section indicates where the sill members go. You must allow for any 3/4″ offset when you determine the lengths of members and drill holes for anchor bolts.

The sill rests on the top of the foundation wall but does not touch it. Between the wall and the sill you need a sealer that keeps water from seeping into the wood, that seals the joint against wind, and that compensates for any unevenness in the top of the wall. Even if your workmanship is excellent, there will be a few high and low places.

The usual sealer is a bed of mortar, although you can buy gaskets treated with asphalt that work well. Spray the top of the wall to dampen it. Then spread a thin bonding coat of cement and water (no sand) mixed to about the consistency of heavy cream. Before the bonding coat dries, cover the top of the wall with a layer of mortar about 1/2″ thick, using your trowel.

Set sill members into the wet mortar. Over each anchor bolt fit a metal washer 1 1/2″ to 2″ in diameter; then tighten the nut (Fig. 8-2). The tightening process squeezes out excess mortar and assures a tight seal. Use your carpenter's level to keep the top of the sill absolutely horizontal as you tighten the nuts. Then scrape away the excess mortar.

**Fig. 8-2.** Sill members rest on a sealer, usually a bed of mortar, and are held to the foundation by anchor bolts. At corners the two sill members are toenailed together. The termite shield is optional.

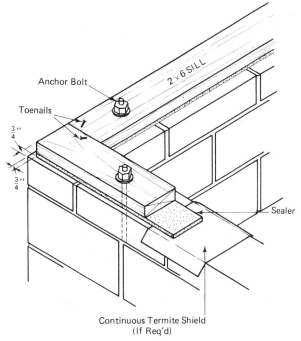

Anchor Bolt

2 x 6 SILL

Toenails

3/4″

3/4″

Sealer

Continuous Termite Shield
(If Req'd)

Start setting the sill at a corner. Toenail the corner pieces together with a pair of eight-penny nails driven at right angles to each other. As with concrete blocks, work from the corners inward. Then any cut pieces, which are the least likely to fit tight, fall in the middle of the wall where they cause the fewest problems.

### Foiling Termites and Rodents

Many types of insects thrive on wood. Termites are the worst of these, because they can't stand light, and therefore you never see them. They live in the ground, build tunnels of earth to reach wood under cover, then eat the cellulose out of it. Eventually the wood can become so weakened that it fails.

You can guard against termites by buying only chemically treated wood, an expensive solution. A better structural answer is to install a termite shield on top of the foundation wall below the seal. A *termite shield* is simply a thin piece of sheet metal that extends about an inch beyond the wall on both sides (Fig. 8-2). Edges are turned down at a 45° angle to prevent any termites from reaching wood.

A chemical answer to termite control is to spray the ground in a crawl space and several feet outside the foundation with a poison formulated for the purpose. The poison prevents termites from living in the soil, but does not harm grass, landscaping, or forest animals. To maintain chemical protection, you must re-spray once a year.

# FRAMING ON PIERS, POSTS, AND PILINGS

In a house supported entirely on piers, use timbers instead of sills. Their size depends on the distance between supports. With a maximum spacing of 12′ between center lines of piers, 6 × 8 timbers are the recommended size.

You set timbers, like sills, either flush with the outside edges of piers or 3/4″ away from the edge. Timbers lie on the centers of center piers. They rest in a sealing bed of mortar, and you hold them in place with anchor bolts set near their ends where two timbers butt together (Fig. 8-3, top). The anchor bolts must be 6″ longer than those used with sills, however, because of the extra thickness of wood they penetrate.

### Framing on Posts

Wood posts are seldom the sole vertical support for houses, even vacation houses. They are often used, however, for center support of girders and edge support of decks. The use of posts under decks is discussed in Chapter 17.

Except in warm, dry climates wood posts should never come in direct contact with either the ground or a footing, even when the timbers have been treated against deterioration. The correct procedure is to anchor the base of the post with a bracket set into a concrete pedestal (Fig. 8-3, right) that is poured separately from the footing. To form the pedestal, which is shaped like a truncated pyramid, you build a frame of exterior grade plywood. Then fit a collar made of

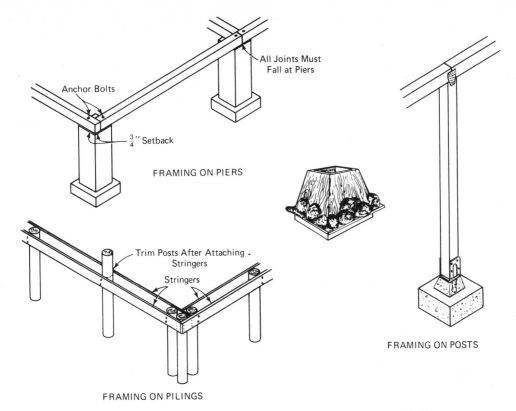

**Fig. 8-3.** Typical methods of framing on piers of concrete block (top left), on wood posts (right), and wood pilings (bottom).

1 × 4s around the base of the form (inset), and weight the collar with stones. The stones prevent the freshly poured concrete from forcing the form upward, spilling its contents.

Set the bracket in the wet cement, making certain that its base is level and its sides vertical. After the concrete has set, push the post into the bracket and nail it securely. But don't place the post until you are sure of its exact length. It's best to wait until you have temporarily positioned the girder and can accurately measure the length of post needed.

### Framing on Wood Pilings

Floor framing for a house built on pilings is quite different. Many vacation houses built on sand, or on tidal ground that floods at high tide, rest on wood pilings treated to resist rot and driven deep into the sand. The depth depends on local custom and requirements. Usually the pilings are 8″ in diameter and spaced 6′ to 12′ apart.

At a level determined in advance of construction, attach 2 × 8 stringers to the sides of the pilings at each post (Fig. 8-3, bottom). Attach stringers with a single nail at one post, and then nail them at the other post after making sure the stringer is level. Position all stringers with a single nail at each post until you are certain that the entire perimeter frame is level. Attach stringers on the other sides of the pilings in the same general way. This time, however, check the level across the pairs of stringers so that all floor joists will bear equally on both stringers. Finally, drill through the whole assembly at each piling, and secure it with corrosion-resistant bolts.

## BUILDING A BOX SILL

Of the various floor framing systems, platform framing is the simplest for the amateur. With platform framing, whether the floor structure rests on sills, timbers, or stringers, the next step is the same; you build a box sill.

A *box sill* consists of header joists and edge joists attached to a sill plate. *Header joists* are the horizontal members set on edge that run across the ends—the heads—of all joists. *Edge joists* are the outside joists set on side sills (Fig. 8-4). Header joists, edge joists, and regular joists are all members of the same size—usually 2 × 8s, 2 × 10s, or 2 × 12s—but their lengths may be different.

Start at a corner (where else?) and set a header joist in position. Place it flush with the sill at the corner. With 16-penny nails, toenail the header to the sill. If the header tends to lean or slide, tack scrap pieces of board to both header and sill to hold it upright. The header joists don't have to be absolutely vertical—yet.

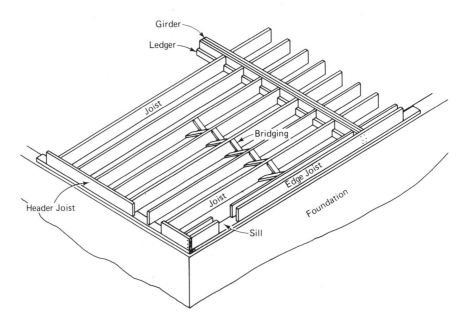

**Fig. 8-4.** Here are the elements of a floor framing system built with platform construction.

One header joist isn't likely to be long enough, and you'll have to *splice*—butt the ends of headers together. Plan your work so that splices fall between regular joists. Since joists are spaced 16″ on centers as measured from the edge of the sill, the length of headers used at corners should be a number divisible by 8″ but not by 16″. A 14′ 0″ (168″) length works nicely, for example. Use another piece of scrap to hold the butting ends together and to the sill. Later, after you have set regular joists, replace the temporary brace with a 14 1/2″ length of scrap joist material as a back block to secure the joint.

After you have both headers in place, set the edge joists. Again start at a corner, and begin with a joist cut square at the end so that you have a tight corner fit. Toenail into the sill, and then use three 16-penny nails to attach the headers to the edge joists. The box sill is now complete.

## WORKING OUT JOIST SPACING

Most sets of purchased working drawings include a floor framing plan that tells you where all joists go. Follow the plan carefully. The designer has determined where heat ducts, piping, and wiring will go, and has allowed space for them.

Without a framing plan to guide you, you must work out these problems yourself. If you intend to subcontract the heating, plumbing, and/or wiring, talk with your contractor before you begin framing to make sure you and he are thinking alike. A failure to plan ahead can bring you both surprises that are no fun and can be expensive.

Heat ducts are the largest item to think about. If you plan a furnace in a basement or crawl space, the main ducts will probably run just beneath the joists, and branch ducts may run between joists. Then they turn and go up through the floor into walls and partitions. Know beforehand where all the ducts go, because you can't cut a joist to make room for a duct.

Sewer piping is the next largest item. The main stack is usually behind the toilet, and it must drop vertically through the floor without hitting a joist. The toilet drain cannot lie directly above a joist, but must fit between joists to allow room for making the necessary connections below. Horizontal drain lines must slope, so horizontal runs should be as short as possible. You can't cut through a joist for a sewer pipe either.

For water, gas, and electrical lines you can notch the top of a joist but not the bottom. Maximum depth of a top notch is 1/6 the depth of the joist. You can also drill a hole through a joist at or above middepth, but the hole's diameter can be no more than 1/6 the joist's depth. In a 2 × 10 joist, for instance, the hole or notch can be 1 5/8″, which is large enough for any such line.

Whatever your source of information on joist spacing, measure with your steel tape or folding rule to mark the locations of joists on the front header. Measure from a corner. If joist spacing is the standard 16″ o.c. (on centers), put the first mark on the top of the header at 47 1/4″. From this mark measure 16″ in both directions until you have marked joist locations for half the floor (Fig. 8-5).

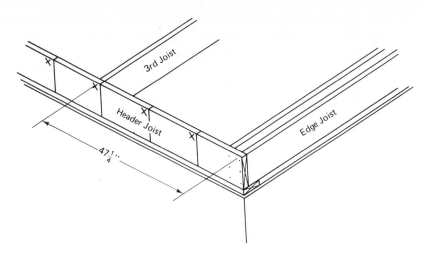

**Fig. 8-5.** The near side of the third joist from a corner is 47 1/4″ from that corner. A series of *X* marks shows on which side of the lines the joists should be placed.

Note that the spacing nearest the corner is less than 16″—15 1/4″ to be exact. The reason is that the material you use for subflooring is 48″ by 96″, and it runs right to the corner of the box sill. The joints between sheets of subflooring must fall over the center of a joist. The third joist from the corner occupies the space against the header between 47 1/4″ and 48 3/4″ from the corner, with the center at 48″. That is why you measure 47 1/4″ to locate the side of the first joist, and not 48″.

Incidentally, make all measurements from the corner, rather than from other marks. If you are 1/16″ off in one 8′ measurement, the error isn't critical. But if you are off 1/16″ in every 16″ measurement, by the time you are 8′ from the corner, your total error is 1/2″. And you are in trouble.

### Odd Joist Spacings

The overall dimensions of most well-designed vacation houses are divisible by 16″, so that your marking comes out even (the last mark will be 16 3/4″ from the second corner). But sometimes a framing plan calls for a joist or two at some spacing other than 16″. Joist spacing varies from standard under three conditions: when the longest overall dimension of the house is not divisible by 16″; at floor openings; and under heavy loads, such as partitions.

Suppose that the overall dimension is 32′ 10″, and you have no framing plan. Look at the floor plan to determine the best place for the odd spacing. It should be toward the middle of the house rather than the end. It should be in a spot either where you have no plumbing or heating lines to avoid, or where you can miss such obstructions with an off-module placement. To mark joists under these conditions, work from one corner to the odd spacing as just described.

Then start at the other corner, placing your first mark at 48 3/4", and successive marks every 16" in both directions.

Figure 8-6 shows typical construction around an opening. For openings up to 48" long a single header at each end of the opening is enough, provided the opening is near the ends of joists. With such small openings there is no need to double joists. With larger openings, as for a stairway, always use double headers at each end. Then add second joists, called *trimmers,* the same length as the joists to which they are nailed.

Under a partition you also add a joist, but you don't nail the two joists together. Instead you separate them with spreaders that allow you to run pipes or ducts between them and up into partitions. The location and size of the utility line determines the length and location of the spreaders.

Note in Fig. 8-4 the extra joist under the side wall, resting on the inside edge of the sill. Although builders sometimes omit this joist, it helps to support the wall and prevents it from leaning inward while you complete roof framing.

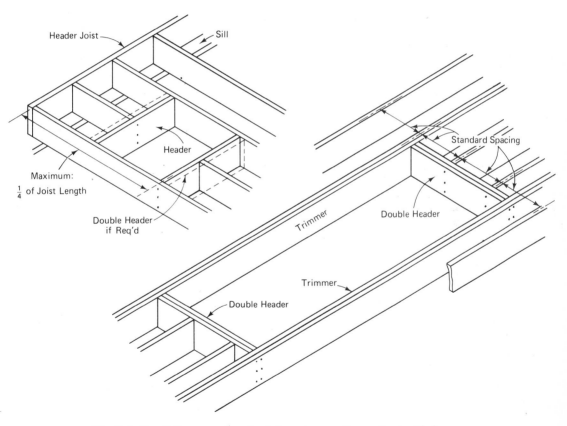

**Fig. 8-6.** Small floor openings (top) do not normally require doubled members around them. Large floor openings, as for a stairway, do.

After you have marked all joist locations, use your square to carry the line vertically down the face of the header. These lines mark the edges of joists nearest the starting corner. Put an *X* beside each mark to remind you on which side of the line to set your joist.

When joists run from header to header, mark the opposite header in the same way. Usually, however, you have a girder that supports the ends of shorter joists in the middle of the house. The next step is to set that girder.

# GIRDERS

The maximum practical length of a single floor joist is 16'. When both outside dimensions of a house are greater than that, some center support is required. That support is a *girder*. Joists usually run the shortest dimension of a house, and girders run parallel to the long walls and midway between them, as in Fig. 8-4.

In those parts of the country that supply much of this nation's building lumber, timbers are often available to use as girders. In other parts of the country you can build your own. A multimember girder, often called a *built-up beam*, has the same vertical dimension as the joists called for in the plans.

The best woods for girders are Douglas fir and Southern yellow pine. A girder is the same length as a header less 3"—the thickness of the two edge joists. If, for example, your foundation is 32' long and you inset the sill 3/4" at the wall, the girder length is 32' 0" less 3/4" less 3/4" less 1 1/2" less 1 1/2", or 31' 7 1/2" long.

You can construct a built-up beam by nailing two or three planks together with 20-penny nails. When the girder is longer than available planks, you must splice. Stagger splices by at least 4' (see Fig. 8-7). You can support joists on girders in two ways. One way is to add 2 × 4 ledgers to each side of the beam, flush at the bottom, and attached with spikes. Joists must be notched to fit over the ledgers. The other method of support is with joist hangers (Fig. 8-8), which will be discussed shortly.

## Setting a Girder

For a floor to be level, the tops of all members that support floor joists must be level. Set the girder—whether a timber or built-up beam—on the sills, and work it into position. Before nailing it to edge joists, make sure the top of the girder and the top of the edge joists are exactly level with each other.

If the girder is low, raise it with shims, one on each side. A wood shingle makes a good shim. After shimming, recheck the level not only with the edge joists but also across the girder to make sure it isn't tilted. That's why you use two shims—so that you can adjust level sideways.

If the girder is high, you can notch its end enough to fit. This is difficult, however, and it is probably better to live with the difference in height unless it is more than 1/8". It is to avoid just such problems that you must check levels both before and after you finish any part of your work.

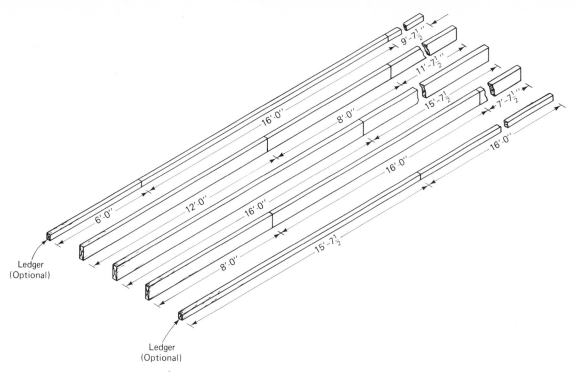

**Fig. 8-7.** A built-up beam is made with three thicknesses of joist material, and joints between lengths must be staggered. The 2 × 4 ledgers support the notched ends of joists, but are not required if joist hangers are used.

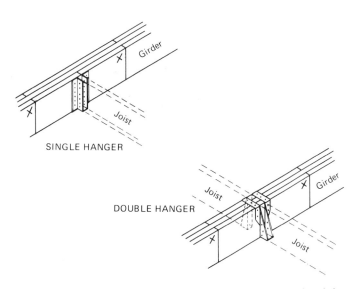

**Fig. 8-8.** Joist hangers are a practical means of supporting joists at a girder. The hanger designs shown are typical.

The tops of piers must be at the same height as the top of the foundation wall. To support a girder at the piers, then, wedge a plank in sealer between the top of the pier and the underside of the girder. The plank should be the same thickness as the sill and at least as wide as the girder. With a built-up beam, use a 2 × 8 as long as the pier for a wedge. Material you used for forms, thoroughly cleaned, works well for girder supports.

After you fix the girder in position at one sill, level it, and temporarily secure it with a nail, you then position the girder over the piers. You don't need to nail the 2 × 8 supports; the weight of the girder will hold them in place. Check and level the entire girder before you nail the opposite end. Then recheck the level before you complete nailing with six 16-penny nails through each edge joist. Either shim or trim the 2 × 8 supports at the piers to adjust the level.

If you are supporting the girder on posts, place a temporary support, such as a building jack, under the girder near its midpoint. Check the girder's level near edge joists, and raise the jack until the girder is level over its entire length. Then measure to the top of the pedestal to determine the length of the post. To set the post, raise the jack a little higher, slip the post into position, and check its plumb. Then drop the girder onto the post and connect it with metal plates.

## PLACING JOISTS

As you pick up each joist, check it for straightness. If it has a little crook, mark the high side with an arrow and set it with the crown up. Look also for knots at the edges; knots are a point of weakness. Always set joists with the knots in the top edge, not the bottom edge.

One other variation in joists can give you problems: dimensional differences. A 2 × 10 joist, for example, may have a depth of anywhere from 9 1/4″ up to 9 5/8″. This dimension is usually consistent from end to end.

To have a level floor, all joists must be the same height at sills. So measure the depth of each joist in the bundle, and with a marking pencil write the fraction near the end of each joist. Then count the number of joists of each size. If you have enough pieces of the same depth, great! If not, use the most common depth as a standard. Notch those joists that are oversized, and shim those that aren't deep enough. In this way the tops of all joists will be at the same level. The undersides may vary, but this is of no concern unless you have a basement with a finished ceiling.

Setting joists is a two-man job. But if you have to work alone, drive a nail at an angle into each end of the joist about half way down from the upper edge. Leave an inch of nail exposed. Rest the nails on the header joist and girder while you line up the joist on its marks. Then remove one of the 16-penny nails and use it to fasten the joist in place. Next, position the other end of the joist and attach it completely before you finish nailing the first end. Recheck position, plumb, and level constantly. If a joist is slightly out of position, you can usually correct this with a couple of well-placed blows with a hammer. If this doesn't work, pull out the nails and start again.

During floor framing a vacation house looks too small to turn around in, much less live in. The system being used here is post-and-beam. Note the deep joists and wide spacing between them. Wood planks are about to be laid in place on the structural framework. *Photography: Richards Studio. Courtesy Lindal Cedar Homes, Inc.*

Set all single joists first. Then come back to set trimmers or short joists that end in headers at floor openings.

### Supporting Joists at Girders

If you support joists on ledgers attached to the sides of girders, you must notch every joist to fit. All notches are identical in size, so it is fairly easy to cut all notches with a power saw at one time before you set the first joist. It's easy, that is, if you are good with a saw.

An alternate method is to use joist hangers (Fig. 8-8). *Joist hangers* are specially shaped metal supports punched for nailing. You line up the inside edge of the slot with the joist mark on the girder, and nail the two flanges of the hanger to the girder. Then drop the joist into the slot, and secure it with cross-nailing. It costs a little more to use joist hangers, but the job becomes much easier, and you save quite a bit of time.

### Cutting Framing Members

Once in awhile there is just no way you can avoid having something interfere with a joist placement, but you should be aware of this before you start framing the floor. In such a case set double headers between the adjacent two joists that remain uncut. Space the headers so that you or your subcontractor have enough room to work on piping and fittings. Then butt two shorter joists against the headers. The process is similar to framing around any other floor opening.

As mentioned before, you can notch the top of a joist to 1/6 its depth, or drill a hole of that size above the center line of the joist. If you must cut a deeper notch or hole, you can do so only within two feet of the supported ends of the joist. Figure 8-9 shows the three acceptable methods of reinforcement. Avoid notching if you can, and you usually can by careful planning. You can't notch a girder under any circumstances.

When a partition lies directly above a joist, you can double the joist, setting the second joist so that the center line of the partition lies as close as possible above the center line of the combined joists. With this doubled support, though, you won't be able to run any duct, plumbing, or wiring into the partition from below. To solve this problem, use spreaders. *Spreaders* are short lengths of joist material. Their length varies from 6″ to 10″, depending on how much space you need between joists to run utilities. Space the spreaders about every 16″, but let the location of the utility line determine the exact positions.

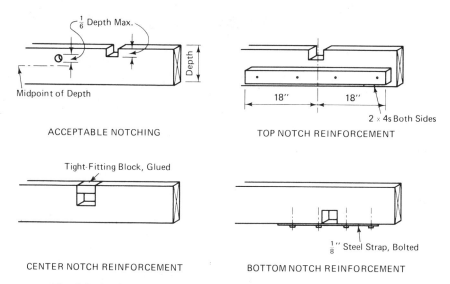

**Fig. 8-9.** Under certain conditions you can notch a joist (top left) without reinforcing the joist. The other three drawings show various approved methods of reinforcing at larger notches. Avoid any notching if you can.

## SUBFLOORING

After you complete your floor structure, remove the temporary braces that held header and edge joists upright. By now, with all other joists in place, these members should be vertical. Cut and fit the back blocks between joists at joints in headers and edge joists.

Now take a few moments to sight across the floor-framing system in all directions. Look for joists that aren't absolutely plumb, especially those that will support joints in subflooring. You can't have a level floor if joists are cocked. Look for joists that weren't set with their crowns up, particularly if they happen to be next to joists that *were* set with crowns up. Finally, check around all floor openings to assure that they are square and that you built them properly. Make any corrections now before you lay the subflooring.

Today most subflooring is 1/2" or 5/8" CDX plywood. Sheets are nominally 48" by 96". Actually they are about 1/32" smaller, and you must leave a slight gap between sheets to allow for expansion. Occasionally you will find some variation in size among the sheets, so measure before you lay any sheets to make sure their edges fall over the center lines of joists.

To lay a subfloor, start at one corner with a full sheet, laid with the long dimension across joists. Along the edge joist lay alternate full sheets and half sheets, as shown in Fig. 8-10. Nail each piece at the four corners with 16-penny nails. Finish attaching with eight-penny nails, spaced about 6" apart at the ends and about 12" apart into other joists.

What you do next depends on what you plan to use as finish flooring. With a prefinished wood floor, such as planks, you have nothing further to do. With carpeting, you will need to add 2 × 4 blocking between joists at all unsupported

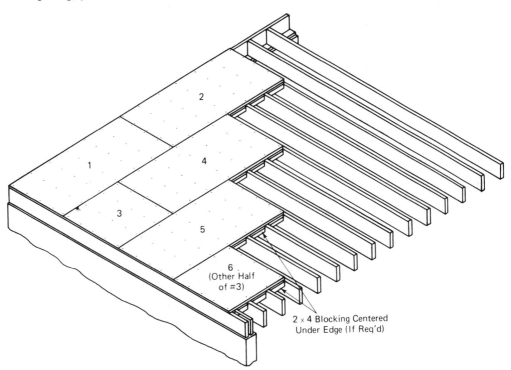

**Fig. 8-10.** To lay subflooring, begin in a corner and lay the sheets in the numbered order shown. Blocking is needed under unsupported edges if no finished flooring material is to be laid.

edges. With linoleum or composition tiles, you will need to apply underlayment over the subflooring, but not until after the house is enclosed and protected from weather.

### Particleboard

An increasingly popular material for subflooring is *particleboard,* a manufactured product made of wood fibers and binders. It is 1 7/8″ thick, but it is no heavier than plywood and is easier to nail because it is softer. It comes in sheets 4′ by 8′ and 2′ by 8′, with edges either square or tongue-and-groove. Check local ordinances to make sure its use is permitted where you are building.

The application procedure is across joists as with plywood, but the nailing procedure is different. Drive the first nail in the middle of the long grooved edge or either long square edge. Then nail along that side toward the ends, alternating on either side of the first nail. Next, work across the center of the board, but stop short of the tongued edge. As in the first row, work outward from the center nail in the middle rows toward the ends. Nail the tongued edge after you fit the next grooved edge of particleboard onto the tongue.

# BRIDGING

*Bridging*—a series of struts set between floor joists—isn't a structural necessity. The floor of your vacation house will be much sturdier if braced, however, and it won't vibrate as you walk on it. There are three types of bridging (Fig. 8-11). Steel bridging is an extra expense, but the job of putting it in place goes quickly; all you do is nail it in place through predrilled holes in the ends.

Solid bridging, made of 14 1/2″ lengths of joist material, takes cutting and nailing. It is economical only if you had to trim standard length joists to fit and have a lot of short pieces left over. You offset the pieces and nail into the ends. The disadvantage of solid bridging is that you have to cut or drill it for any horizontal runs of pipe or wiring.

Cross-bridging is the least expensive, uses the least material, but takes the most time. It requires a lot of bevel cuts that you can easily make in a miter box or, if you have it, on a power saw with an adjustable-angle blade. With joist spacing of 16″, cut the struts at a 62° angle between 2 × 10 joists, and 55° between 2 × 12 joists. Strut length (see inset in Fig. 8-11) is 17 1/8″ and 18 5/8″ respectively.

Before laying the subflooring, attach only the tops of steel bridging and cross-bridging; go back after the subflooring is in place to complete the nailing. In this way you avoid setting up stresses in the subflooring that could cause humps in the finished floor.

Place bridging on either side of the midpoint of joists 12′ long or shorter. With longer joists you need two rows, spaced at about the one-third points of the length of the joists.

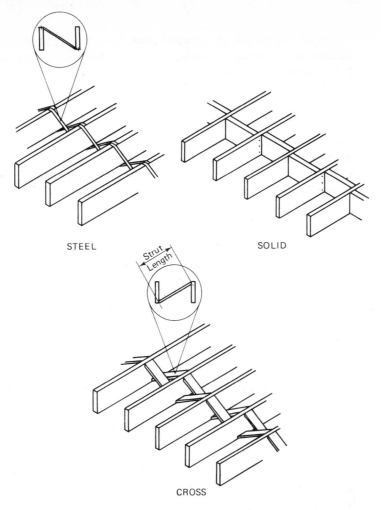

STEEL

SOLID

CROSS

Strut Length

**Fig. 8-11.** The three types of bridging. All bridging is laid on alternate sides of a line either at the midpoint or third points of joists to eliminate floor vibration.

## DOOR SILLS

The chances are that the exterior doors you buy will already be in their frames, ready to install. With most doors you also get a hardwood door sill that has a sloping top to shed water and a flat bottom that rests on the header or edge joist of the box sill.

Get the dimensions of the sill from your door supplier, and mark its location on the joist. The subflooring stops at the inside edge of the door sill, and you must know in advance where this point is. You may even have to notch a header joist, so that the top of the sill is at the same level as finish flooring. Cover the sill with a piece of exterior plywood to protect it from wear during construction.

With a door sill of extruded aluminum, you must extend the subflooring all the way to the edge of the box sill. The door sill fits over the subflooring and butts against finish flooring.

# OTHER FLOORING SYSTEMS

So far we have discussed only conventional construction, with joists 16″ on centers. Alternates worth considering are post-and-beam construction and Mod 24 construction, which is a combination of conventional methods with the post-and-beam system.

## Post-and-Beam System

In post-and-beam construction the module is not 16″ but 48″, 72″, or 96″. You start with a box sill, but use heavy beams instead of joists (Fig. 8-12). Wall members, usually 4 × 4 posts spaced 48″ apart and with no more than one stud between, support roof members. Ceiling joists and rafters are also big beams. Subflooring is made of tongue-and-groove planks instead of sheet materials. So is roof sheathing. In other words, structural members are heavy and widely spaced, and the material covering the structure is an integral part of the structural system.

Post-and-beam construction is often used in vacation housing, but the floor plan must be designed for the system. The locations of structural members are fixed; you can't relocate windows and doors as you can in conventional construction. If you decide to build with this system, be sure that you can get all the structural members locally; they are not always readily available.

The main advantages to post-and-beam construction are that you use fewer pieces and that the house is architecturally interesting. The disadvantages are that individual members are heavier and harder to handle, and greater care must be used in erection. Total material cost may be a little higher or a little lower, depending on the area of the country.

## Mod 24 Construction

In the Mod 24 (short for 24″ module) system the base is again a box sill. All structural members are spaced 24″ apart instead of 16″. Horizontal members—joists and rafters—must be deeper. If plans call for 2 × 10s, you need either 2 × 12s or a stronger grade of 2 × 10s. Because you use fewer members, however you save about 6% of the overall cost of materials.

Aside from the size of members, the greatest changes are in the floor system. At girders, which must be lower and recessed into the foundation wall, joists butt against each other. Subflooring is 3/4″ tongue-and-groove plywood, interior grade with exterior grade glue. You apply the subflooring with glue—a bead along the top of each joist and in the groove at the joints. Gap sheets of plywood about 1/16″ at all joints, and drive eight-penny nails 12″ apart into bearing points to hold the plywood in place until the glue sets.

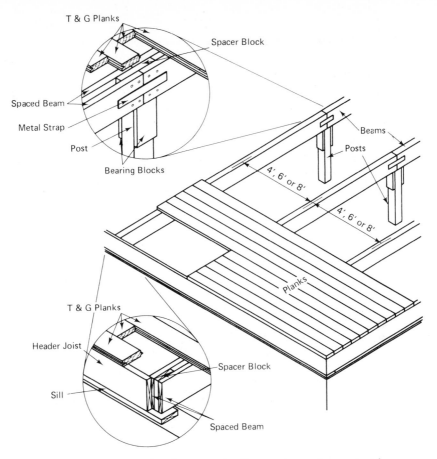

**Fig. 8-12.** Here are the elements of a floor system using post-and-beam construction. Inset details show alternate method using spaced beams instead of solid timbers.

Incidentally, if you use any tongue-and-groove material anywhere in your house, handle it very carefully. Fit the tongue into the groove by hand, and then complete the fit by holding a piece of 2 × 4 against the edge and pounding it with a heavy hammer or sledge. Never hit the edge of the plywood itself; once you damage the edge you can never get a good fit.

### Concrete Floors

There is a time element involved in concrete work that makes it a difficult material for amateurs to use. Like the two-minute drill in football, you are working against the clock under great pressure. Concrete sets whether you want it to or not. It isn't too difficult to pour your own concrete footings, stoops, steps, and walks. But with large slabs you must work fast, accurately, and have a variety of finishing tools. Finishing a slab is one other job that is better subcontracted.

But if you are determined to try it yourself, here are the basics.

The simplest construction is the unsupported slab. The foundation wall must extend at least 8″ above grade, and ground level inside the wall can be no lower than finished grade outside it. Inside the wall place a layer of gravel at least 4″ deep, and tamp it level (Fig. 8-13). Then, where the slab meets the wall, lay rigid insulation at least 1″ thick. Run it down the side of the foundation wall 6″ below the gravel, or horizontally under the slab and gravel 16″. Over the gravel lay a vapor barrier of polyethylene, overlapping about a foot at all joints. The gravel and vapor barrier prevent moisture from entering the finished slab, and the insulation helps to keep the floor warmer in cold weather.

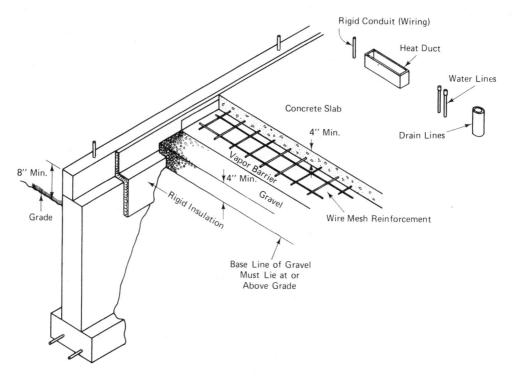

**Fig. 8-13.** This cutaway view of a concrete slab floor shows the basic information you need in order to place a slab.

Before you order any concrete, have reinforcement, sill bolts, and all tools ready to go (Fig. 8-14). Make sure also that all water, sewer, fuel, and power connections that come up through the slab are in place, in the proper place, and stubbed in far enough above floor level so that you won't accidentally fill them with concrete. Cover exposed ends with duct tape.

You will need more concrete for a slab than you can mix yourself unless you have an army of friends to help. It's better to order concrete from a ready-mix plant, so that all you have to worry about is the slab and not its ingredients.

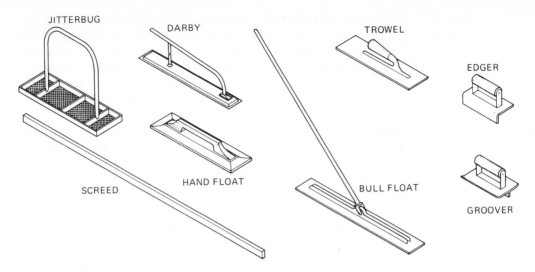

**Fig. 8-14.** Among the concrete you need for finishing a concrete slab are a jitterbug, screed, darbies, floats, trowels, and edger, and a groover.

Once slab work starts, it should be finished without interruption. Before you order, be sure the truck can reach the foundation at several points for pouring.

When you order concrete, tell the ready-mix plant operator that you are doing the work yourself, and how many people will be helping. He can then adjust the mix to give you the maximum working time. The standard mix of concrete for slabs is 1 part portland cement, 2 1/4 parts sand, 3 parts crushed rock or stone, and 6 gallons of water, including any water in the sand. If the ready-mix plant is more than an hour from the site, the amount of water may be slightly higher to allow for evaporation in transit.

### Finishing the Slab

Unlike the reinforcement in footings, you place the reinforcement for a slab before the concrete arrives. Use 6″ × 6″ 10/10 wire mesh; the squares are 6″ on a side and wire strands are 10-gauge steel both directions. The mesh comes in rolls 6′ wide and 50′ long. You simply unroll it over the vapor barrier under the entire slab. Cut to length and overlap 6″ where one strip of reinforcement meets the next. The mesh helps to protect the vapor barrier from damage, since you will be walking on it.

As concrete is poured, water tends to rise to the top because it is lighter than all other ingredients. This process is called *bleeding,* and you prevent it by screeding and darbying.

***Screeding.*** A *screed* (Fig. 8-14) is a long 2 × 4 or 2 × 6 that you pull back and forth over fresh concrete to level it. You rest the end of the screed on the foundation wall. If the distance between walls is longer than your screed—and it usually is—place temporary forms in the middle of the slab to support the other end of the screed. These temporary forms are like forms for footings. They should be the same height as the thickness of your slab (usually 4″). Hold the forms in place with stakes driven below the level of the form so they don't interfere with screeding. After you have screeded one section of the slab, remove the temporary form and reuse it to form the next section. The edge of the first section of the slab then becomes one form for the next section.

Screeding takes three people. One uses a spade or shovel where the fresh concrete is being poured, spreading it as evenly as he can and forcing it against the forms to eliminate any air pockets. The other two work the screed, wiggling it back and forth in a sawing action. The screed levels the wet concrete and trims off high spots. The person with the spade watches this action and fills low spots before the screed gets to them.

As you screed, look for any pieces of coarse aggregate near the surface. Force them farther into the mix by tamping. The tool to use is a *jitterbug* (Fig. 8-14). You can make one out of fine wire mesh attached to a 1 × 2 frame, with a handle of 2 × 2s. As concrete cures, large stones are forced upward and, if they are too near the surface, they may cause humps in the finished flooring material.

*Darbying.* Immediately after you finish screeding a section of slab, continue compacting the concrete surface with a darby (Fig. 8-14). A *darby* is a finishing tool with a slightly curved blade. Lengths vary. The darby you use should have a handle long enough so that you can reach the center of the section of slab from outside the forms.

Concrete must be screeded as soon as it is poured, and darbied as soon as it is screeded. Therefore make the sections of slab no larger than a size you can finish quickly. Sections 12′ square are about the maximum for an amateur crew of three. After you darby one section, begin to work on the next. At this time, set any anchor bolts needed for walks and partitions in the fresh slab.

*Floating.* As concrete begins to set after darbying, water in the mix will continue to work its way to the surface and form puddles. Let this water disappear before you touch the surface again; by then the concrete has started to stiffen. When the surface is firm enough to walk on, but fine sand is still coming to the top, begin the final two steps in finishing. During final finishing it's a good idea to kneel on a piece of plywood that distributes your weight over the surface.

First you use a pair of *floats*—tools similar to a darby with a metal blade. Work with one in each hand, leaning on one while you further smooth the surface with the other. The floats clean up uneven spots, embed large aggregate near the surface, and remove marks left by the darby.

The final step is troweling. You can save energy (yours) if you float and trowel one section, then move on to the next. Trowel with the blade as flat against the surface as possible.

How many times you trowel depends on how you cover the slab. If you carpet, leave the surface slightly rough to keep the carpet pad from slipping. If you tile, trowel the surface as smooth as you can get it. Each troweling after the initial operation further smoothes the surface. Use successively smaller trowels so that you can increase pressure on the blade. Allow time between trowelings to let the concrete set a little more. When the slab hardens to the point where fine sand is no longer rising to the surface, complete the final troweling.

*Curing.* During the curing process, concrete must be kept damp and as close as possible to 70°F (21° Celsius). Concrete generates heat as it cures, so if the outdoor temperature is likely to fall below 40°F (4°C), cover the slab with a thick layer of damp straw; the straw will hold the heat in.

When there is little wind or sun, and outdoor temperatures range from 50° to 80°F (10° to 27°C), spray the surface with water around noon, and check the slab occasionally to make sure it shows no signs of fine cracks. In even warmer weather or on days with a good breeze, spray the surface and cover it with a sheet of polyethylene or heavy kraft paper. Weight the edges so that the cover won't blow away and expose the concrete.

Curing takes about five days. If you have any doubt as to whether a slab has cured, it is far better to allow more time than is needed than not to allow enough.

### Outdoor Concrete Work

The general process for finishing outdoor slabs—walks, driveways, and patios—is basically the same as for floor slabs, with some important differences.

Usually you will need to install expansion joints somewhere. An *expansion joint* is a length of lumber or an asphalt strip made for the purpose. You need an expansion joint wherever

- a driveway meets a garage floor
- a walk meets a driveway, patio, or steps
- any outdoor concrete meets the house
- a slab of concrete is 30 or more feet long.

Trim an expansion joint to fit requirements, and set it in place as a form for one edge of the concrete. The joint prevents the concrete from pushing against other concrete in hot weather, causing it to break or crack.

If the slab has an exposed edge, you use an *edger* (Fig. 8-14) to round the edges and prevent them from chipping. Apply only enough pressure to compact the edge, and leave only a light impression in the slab's surface.

Use the edger just before floating; use a *groover* at about the same time. A groover cuts a control joint, which prevents cracking elsewhere. If the slab is g ing to crack from expansion and contraction, it will do so at the joint where it does the least damage. In strips of concrete, such as sidewalks and ribbon driveways, cut a control joint across the strip about every 4'. The depth of the control joint should be about 1/5 the depth of the slab.

You should also cut a control joint in a floor slab if the house is not rectangular. When the house has a wing, do not carry reinforcement across the junction of house and wing. Stop it about 2" short, and then cut a control joint after the slab is in place.

# TOOLS YOU WILL NEED

To complete a wood floor structure you will need these tools:

    power saw
    crosscut saw
    rip saw
    folding rule
    steel tape
    power drill
    trowel
    carpenter's level
    wrench (for anchor bolts)
    hammer
    metal shears (for termite shield)
    carpenter's square or framing square
    wood chisel
    building jack

To finish a concrete slab, you will need these items as a minimum:

    hand saw (for cutting insulation)
    metal shears
    spade or shovel
    screed
    darby (6 ')
    two floats
    two or three trowels

# Framing Walls

Of the three types of wall framing systems—braced, balloon, and platform—the platform system is by far the most common and the simplest to build. All walls rest directly on a finished subfloor. You build the walls flat on the subfloor, and then tip them into place.

The corners of the box sill establish the length of walls. As to height, standard manufactured wall materials are 8′ long. They go into place after finished ceiling materials but before finished flooring. You must allow for a little expansion. Therefore you calculate the height of your walls and partitions this way:

Thickness of ceiling material + gap between wall and ceiling materials (usually 1/4″) + height of interior wall material + gap between wall material and finished flooring (usually 1/2″) = Height of wall frame

Suppose that you use 1/2″ gypsum wallboard for the ceiling, composition tile for flooring, and plywood paneling on the walls. Then your wall height is

$$1/2'' + 1/4'' + 96'' + 1/2'' = 97\,1/4''$$

In this height you have a bottom plate, studs, and a double top plate (Fig. 9-1). Plates are 2 × 4s laid flat, each with a thickness of 1 1/2″. Total thickness of the three plates is 4 1/2″. Therefore the length of stud needed is 92 3/4″.

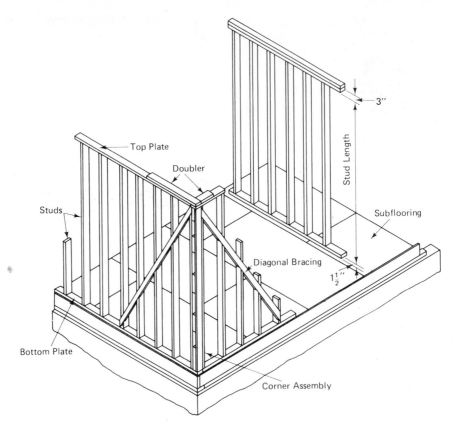

**Fig. 9-1.** Typical wall and partition construction in the platform framing system.

Some dealers will cut studs to length. You state the length of stud you want, and how many, and the dealer delivers them 92 3/4″ long, or whatever dimension you give him. Usually he will charge for this service. If you cut your own studs to length, take a moment to figure out the best length of lumber to order.

If a materials list is included with the drawings, it will specify what to order. But study the framing plans in the drawings yourself, and make your own list to double-check. Then find out what lengths your dealer carries and what his prices are for these lengths, and work out the best lengths to order.

You can order 8′ lengths, of course, but when you trim them to the length you need, you end up with a lot of little 3″ blocks you can't use. You may be able to get 16′ lengths of 2 × 4 at a better price and have only half as many blocks left over. There is some use for 6″ blocks.

The point is: study the plans before you order to find out what lengths of scrap you *can* use. There's no sense in paying for lumber you have to throw away if you can avoid it. Some scrap is unavoidable, of course. If you bought 18′

lengths of 2 × 4 for studs, you could cut two studs and two 14 1/2″ lengths (usable for blocking and firestops) out of each length. Allowing for 1/8″ saw kerfs, you would have only 1/8″ of scrap.

Now that's economy! The only trouble is, 18′ lengths are sometimes hard to find.

# PREPARING WALL COMPONENTS

Except for long plate members and precut studs, every stick of lumber in a wall either must be cut to fit, or it is part of an assembly. Before you start to put wall components together, preassemble corner posts and window and door frames.

### Preassembling Corners

You will need a corner post at every inside and outside corner of the house. A corner post consists of a pair of studs (A and B in Fig. 9-2) separated by four spacers (C), which are pieces of scrap 6″ to 12″ long. Stud B provides a nailing surface for wall materials after the abutting wall, ending in stud D, is in place. The spacers keep stud B straight. Blocks (E) help to form a sturdy corner post.

**Fig. 9-2.** Typical construction at a corner. Studs A and B rest at the end of one bottom plate, and stud D is the end member of the adjoining wall.

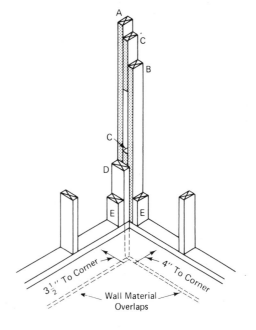

### Preassembling Window Frames

Your dealer can supply you with windows that come from the manufacturer already in their millwork frames, and even with the glass panes inserted. All you have to do is set the frame in its rough opening, and nail it securely. The manufacturer's literature tells you what size of rough opening to build. In the window schedule of most sets of drawings is a column that gives rough opening sizes.

A *rough opening* is the size of the hole you leave in the wall structure, measured from jamb stud to jamb stud and from sill to header (Fig. 9-3). If the rough opening required by the window manufacturer and the rough opening called for in the plans don't agree, use the manufacturer's dimensions. If you

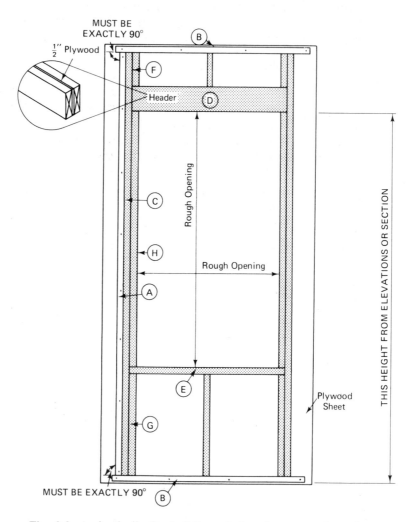

**Fig. 9-3.** A simple jig for building window frames consists of a three-piece frame (parts A and B) attached to a sheet of plywood. The dimensions of the rough opening and the height of the header above the floor appear in your drawings. Inset shows typical construction of a window or door header.

must change the position of a window horizontally, adjust the locations of both jamb studs; always maintain the center line. If vertical height must change, maintain the header position and adjust the height of the sill.

It is very important to build all window and door frame assemblies absolutely square. Otherwise windows and doors won't open and close properly. The best way to build frames is in a jig on a sheet of plywood. You can use the subfloor for this purpose if you're careful not to damage it. To the plywood nail three straight pieces of 1 × 2 or 2 × 2 (Fig. 9-3). Piece A must be the exact length of a stud, and the other two (B) at least as long as the width of your largest rough opening. Make sure all corners are square.

Build the window header first. A *header* above an opening in a wall consists of two vertical members with a piece of 1/2″ plywood between (inset, Fig. 9-3). The plywood is a spacer that brings the thickness of the header to the same dimension as the width of a stud (3 1/2″). The length of a header is the rough opening width plus 3″. Use the table below to determine the proper header height.

| For Rough Opening Widths | Use A Pair Of |
|---|---|
| Up to 2′0″ | 2 × 4s |
| From 2″0″ to 4′0″ | 2 × 6s |
| From 4′0″ to 6′0″ | 2 × 8s |
| From 6′0″ to 8′0″ | 2 × 10s |
| From 8′0″ to 12′0″ | 2 × 12s |
| From 12′0″ to 16′0″ | 2 × 14s |

Next cut all window frame parts to length. To assemble the frame, drop a stud (C in Fig. 9-3) into the jig tight against stud A. Then set the header (D) and sill (E) roughly in place, and fix their positions with top and bottom cripples (F and G) and a jack stud (H). Next drop in the cripples and studs on the other side of the opening.

Make sure that the header and sill are square with the stud at the open end of the jig. Then nail them in place with 10-penny nails—four into the header and two into the sill. Repeat the process at the other stud, using only one set of nails (the jig is in the way of the other set at this point). Then fasten the jack studs, nailing from inside the window opening. Stand on a scrap block used as a brace when you hammer so that you don't loosen nails you've already driven.

You must determine stud spacing, discussed below under "Marking Wall Plates," before you can properly locate other cripples. When you do know their locations, position the bottom cripples and nail through the sill to secure them. If the sill consists of two 2 × 4s, you must toenail. Locate accurately any cripples that carry joints between wall panels. Make sure the cripples are not cocked and are flush with the face of the sill against the jig. As a final step, position top cripples and toenail them into the header. Nail into the edges, not the sides, of the cripples.

Now turn the assembly over, fit it back into the jig, and complete the nailing. You still have a set of nails to add at one side, and one toenail into each top cripple.

### Preassembling Door Frames

The procedure for assembling a door frame is the same as for a window frame with one exception: the window sill acts as a stiffener in a window frame assembly, and you don't have this stiffness in a door-frame assembly. To compensate, make doubly sure that all members are square. Then, before removing the assembly from the jig, add two temporary braces, one horizontally near the bottom of the opening and the other diagonally (Fig. 9-4). Use lengths of 1 × 6 or 1 × 8 for braces. Attach them with eight-penny nails driven part way in or with doubleheaded nails so they can be easily removed. Brace on the outside of the frame.

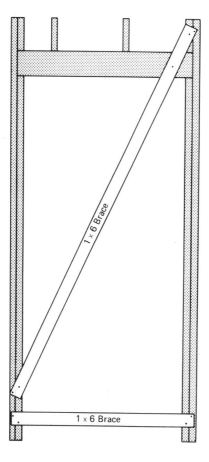

1 × 6 Brace

1 × 6 Brace

**Fig. 9-4.** Door frames must be braced horizontally and diagonally to hold their shape while being moved from jig to wall assembly.

# MARKING WALL PLATES

Customarily the longest walls of the house (usually front and rear) extend from one edge of the box sill to the other. Side walls are set between the longer walls and therefore are 7″ shorter—the thickness of framing at both ends—than the side dimension of the box sill. Build the longest walls first.

If possible, use a single length of lumber for top and bottom plates; otherwise you will have to splice. The best place to splice is between studs and between joists—usually studs and joists line up. This assures you of a strong splice and reduces the chance that you will hit a splicing nail later in construction.

Lay the bottom plate along the edge of the box sill. Then, to determine where the studs fall, study the wall-framing plan in the drawings. It shows the general locations of studs, openings, and butting partitions, but seldom with dimensions. You must work those out yourself.

Mark stud locations on both top and bottom plates at the same time. Lay the 2 × 4s that form the top plate directly atop the bottom plate to make marking easier. Be accurate. Studs must touch top and bottom plates at the same points or your wall won't be square.

First mark the locations of corner studs at both ends (A in Fig. 9-5). Then mark the insides of rough openings for all doors and windows (B). Again, you will work from the center lines shown in the plans. If the width of a rough opening is 2′ 6″, for example, you find the center line, then measure 1′ 3″ in each direction from it and make a mark. As you mark, always add an *X* to show on which side of the line a stud should go.

Next mark the locations of the center lines of partitions that touch the exterior wall (C). Use the symbol ₵ on this line; it's still too early to mark stud locations here.

### Where Seams Fall

The next step takes careful thought and a lot of planning. It is to mark the locations of studs that will support seams between sheets of interior wall material (D in Fig. 9-5). The edge of the corner sheet will lie either 3 1/2″ or 4″ from the corner of the wall (refer back to Fig. 9-2), depending on which wall you cover first. From the line marking the edge of this sheet, stretch a steel tape along the plate and see where every 4-foot measurement falls.

If you are very, very lucky, these 4-foot measurements will hit on the center lines of studs beside openings, and they will end 3 1/2″ or 4″ from the other end of the wall. But don't expect this miracle. Windows, doors, and partitions are located where they will look best and help the house plan function best. This isn't necessarily related to standard 16″ stud spacing, although good designers do try to relate the two. Don't try to relocate windows or doors to make stud spacing work out. You could seriously affect some other aspect of the design, such as fenestration, the plumbing system, or roof framing. It's cheaper and wiser to add a stud where necessary to support a joint in wall materials.

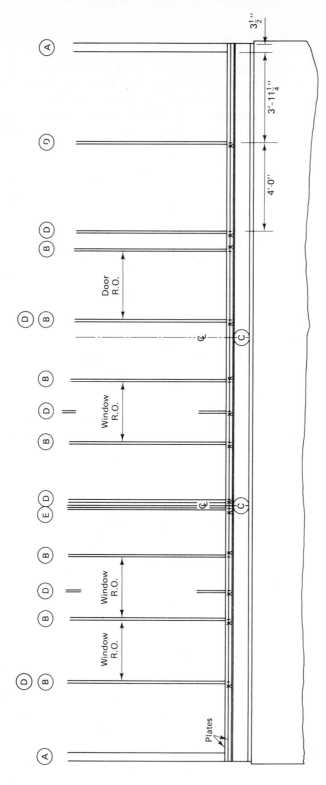

**Fig. 9-5.** On bottom and top plates you simultaneously mark the locations of corner assemblies (A), rough openings (B), center lines of partitions (C), seams in interior wall materials (D), and extra studs for attaching partitions (E).

Nevertheless, if stud spacing doesn't work out well when you measure from one corner, try working from the other corner, and then from other fixed stud locations. When you have decided on the best and most economical arrangement of 4-foot spacing, mark the locations of these studs on the two plates.

### Where Partitions Butt

With a chalk line or marking pencil, mark on the subfloor the thicknesses of stud partitions that meet exterior walls. Work from the center lines you have already snapped, measuring 1 3/4″ on either side to see where the faces of studs will lie.

When a partition happens to fall at a stud in the exterior wall, with at least 3/4″ exposed for the attachment of wall material, you simply add another stud (E in Figs. 9-5 and 9-6, left) 3 1/2″ away from the first stud. When the partition falls between studs, either add two studs or build a ladder of 2 × 4s 14 1/2″ long and spaced about 26 1/2″ apart (Fig. 9-6, right). The ladder parts, set on edge, must be inset 3/4″ to leave room for a 1 × 8. Tack the 1 × 8 to the ladder first, and then slip the assembly into place and nail through the studs. The 1 × 8 serves as a nailing surface for the end stud of the partition and for wall materials.

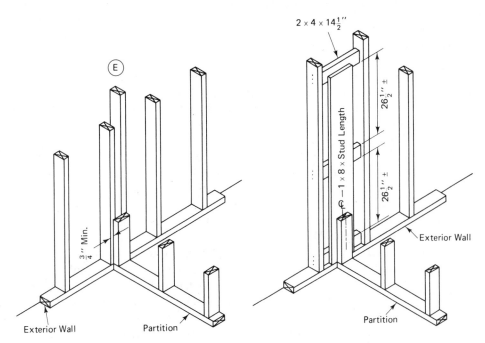

**Fig. 9-6.** When a partition intersects a wall at a stud (left), add another stud (E) for support. When the partition falls between exterior studs, the end support is a ladder (right).

# ASSEMBLING THE COMPONENTS

With all critical stud locations marked on both top and bottom plates, begin to assemble the wall components. Lay the bottom plate on edge on the subfloor about 6" from the long edge of the sill, with the marks face up. Position the corner assemblies next, and then add the top plate. Next lay in all studs with fixed locations—those around openings and those supporting joints in interior materials.

Check each stud for straightness before you lay it into place. Set aside any with twist or crook; to use them is to build in trouble. Lay any studs with a bow in them flat on the subfloor. If the bow measures more than 1/2" at the maximum, set that stud aside, too. Bows of less then 1/2" can be corrected with blocking.

Before you begin to nail the pieces together, recheck all locations for accuracy, especially those that support wall materials. Then, using a pair of 16-penny nails at each stud, nail through the top and bottom plates into the ends of studs. As you nail, make sure that each stud is on its mark, on the correct side of the mark, and flush with both edges of both plates.

Again check your work. Sight down each stud for straightness, then sight across the entire assembly, looking for high spots and low spots. Make any adjustments now. Then set intermediate studs—those that provide only structural strength. They don't have to be exactly on their marks, but they must be straight and not cocked. Use your square and level frequently during the assembly process.

# BRACING

Good construction calls for bracing wall frames at corners, especially in windy communities. *Diagonal* or *let-in bracing* consists of a pair of 1 × 4 boards at each corner of the building, set into notches in studs (Fig. 9-7) at about a 45° angle. Notching is a slow job, because the 1 × 4s must fit tight to do their job. But it is a job worth doing.

To notch studs, lay a 1 × 4 against the framing in proper position, and carefully mark the ends for cutting. Then check the fit. Next hold the diagonal across the studs and mark the location of the notch at each stud. Use a wood chisel to cut each notch as close to 3 1/2" wide and 3/4" deep as you can. Braces must be flush with the surfaces of studs. Nail at top and bottom with three 8-penny nails. Use two 8-penny nails at each stud.

After you complete the entire wall frame, measure its diagonals with your steel tape. They should be identical in length. If you don't use let-in bracing, tack a pair of 1 × 6 braces on the outside of the assembly. The braces help to bring the wall into square if the diagonal measurements weren't exactly the same; they will also prevent racking as you raise the wall.

Before raising the wall, nail three short lengths of 2 × 4 vertically to the side of the box sill. Let them extend about 6" above the subfloor. These stops will prevent the wall from sliding off the subfloor as you raise it. At the same time place three 12' lengths of 1 × 6 where you can reach them in a hurry. These will support the wall after you raise it and hold it in position while you nail it down.

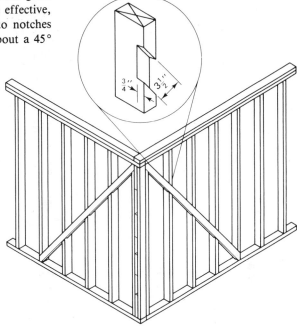

**Fig. 9-7.** Let-in bracing adds great stiffness at corners. To be effective, braces must fit tightly into notches (inset) cut into studs at about a 45° angle.

## RAISING WALLS

If you are going to have help in raising the walls, add window and door assemblies while the wall is flat. They add considerable weight to a wall, however, and you'll need plenty of muscle available.

It takes at least three people to raise a wall properly and slide it into position—one near each end and you in the middle. You must all lift at the same pace. Let the wall slide slowly toward the stops and avoid shaking or wiggling it to position it exactly. A few well-aimed blows of a hammer are usually enough to correct to the last fraction of an inch.

While your two muscular friends hold the wall upright and in place, you check the positioning. Then nail the side braces to the wall (Fig. 9-8). Now nail through the bottom plate into the header, but only at the end of the wall. Then, while your helper holds his end of the wall plumb (absolutely vertical), nail the other end of the corner brace to the side of the header or edge joist. Repeat this process at the other corner. Again nail only at the end of the bottom plate.

If you know that you are going to have to raise the walls all by yourself, you must take two steps to make this possible. One is to leave out all window and door frames until the wall is up. The other is to build the wall in sections small enough to handle alone; then nail the sections together after they are in position and plumb. Plan lengths of sections so that they meet between studs. Add splices to the bottom and top plates after the sections are securely nailed to the floor.

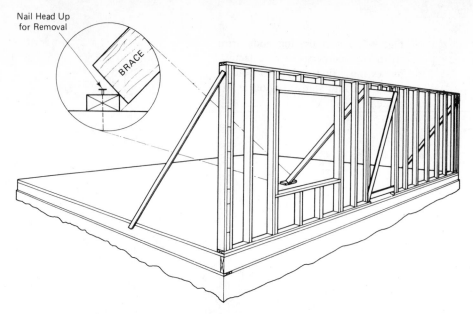

**Fig. 9-8.** To hold a wall upright while it is straightened and nailed down, use temporary braces between end studs and edge joists. Intermediate braces run from a stud to a stop nailed into the subfloor.

To brace at the end of a section, or at midwall of a long section, use a piece of scrap 2 × 4 as a stop (inset in Fig. 9-8). Line it up with the end stud in the section and run a brace between stud and stop to fix the wall's position. Then, with the wall plumb, nail the 2 × 4 stop through the subfloor.

It still isn't time to finish nailing the bottom plate. First check all walls for straightness. To sight down the top plate isn't good enough. The best way is to cut three small blocks of 1 × 2 material. Tack a block on the outside face of the top plate at each corner and stretch a cord between the blocks (Fig. 9-9). At various points along the top plate slide the third block between the plate and the cord. If the wall is straight, the cord should just touch the block. If the cord bends over the block or doesn't touch it at all, you must rebrace the wall. Remove the temporary brace at one end, adjust it until the wall is straight, then renail the brace. If the wall isn't straight near the middle, add an extra brace near the points where partitions will butt.

Only after walls are absolutely plumb and straight should you complete nailing. Nail into the header or edge joist between all studs about 3/4″ in from the outside edge of the plate. Along the inside edge nail into joists. If floor joists lie directly below wall studs, as they often do, toenail through the plate and subfloor into joists as shown in Fig. 9-10. When you have finished all nailing, crawl under the joists and look up above the foundation wall. If you see the ends of no more than half a dozen nails, you have done an excellent job. Too many exposed nail points indicates a weak structure.

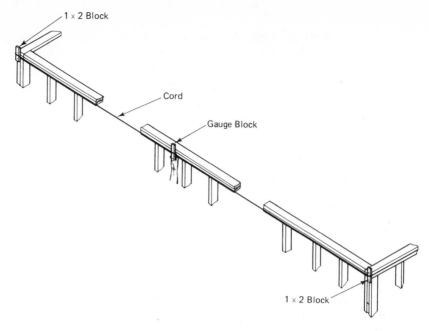

**Fig. 9-9.** To test the straightness of a wall, run a cord between corner blocks. The cord at the gauge block should just touch it at all points along the length of the wall.

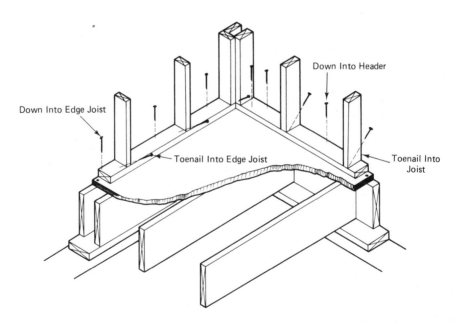

**Fig. 9-10.** Detail of where and how to nail exterior walls to the floor structure. Points of nails should not be visible from underneath the subfloor.

If you are raising a wall on a concrete slab, drill the bottom plate of your wall assembly for anchor bolts before you raise the wall. While drilling you must be accurate in marking centers at the right places and drill holes large enough to fit over the bolts, but small enough so the washers cover the hole. Remember to remove both washers and nuts before you set the wall. Tighten the nuts after you straighten it.

## COMPLETING EXTERIOR FRAMING

With the first long wall in place, assemble the remaining exterior walls, following the same procedures as for the first wall. Build the wall opposite the first wall next, then the two end walls. Leave walls around a wing until last.

When you finally have two walls in place that meet at a corner, check the corner for square and for plumb. Then nail through the end stud of the shorter wall into the corner assembly with 16-penny nails. Next add the doubler over the top plate. Lay the first length of doubler so that it overlaps the top plate of the other wall (Fig. 9-11). The ideal doubler is a single straight 2 × 4 that runs without a splice from the outside of one long wall to the outside of the other. Do not use short pieces for doublers; they have no strength.

If you must splice a doubler, the splice should never be closer than 48″ to any splice in the top plate. Attach the doubler with 16-penny nails. Nail about 3/4″ in from the edge of the doubler at 24″ intervals down either side, but stagger the spacing from side to side, as shown in Fig. 9-11. Wherever a partition meets the outside wall, leave a 3 1/2″ gap in the wall doubler for a partition doubler that overlaps onto the wall.

**Fig. 9-11.** At corners, one wall doubler overlaps the top plate. The doubler of a partition overlaps the top plate of a wall. Stagger nail locations from side to side.

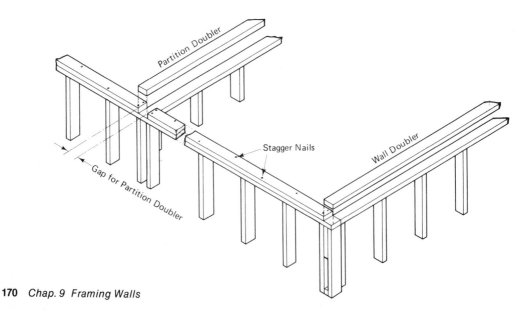

Start nailing the doubler at one end and push or pull it so that it is absolutely flush with the top plate before you nail at any point. If the crook is too great to correct by hand maneuvering, remove the doubler and select a straighter piece. Never ignore the problem and continue to nail. You will build up stresses in the wall that will eventually put a permanent bend in it.

# PARTITIONS

Partitions are walls between spaces in the house. There are two types—bearing and nonbearing. A *bearing partition* supports at least part of the structure above it. A *nonbearing partition* supports nothing, and can be moved or removed without creating any weakness.

How can you tell a bearing from a nonbearing partition? From the drawings. In a one-story house the only likely bearing partition runs parallel to the long exterior walls of the house and lies under the main ridge of the roof. In a house where the roof is supported on trusses, even this partition is nonbearing.

In a split-level house the wall that separates any two levels is always a bearing partition. In a two-story house the center wall is almost always a bearing partition unless the house is so narrow that the joists span from exterior wall to exterior wall. First-floor partitions that run parallel to joists and have another partition directly above are also bearing partitions.

Structurally, bearing partitions are similar to exterior walls. The difference is at door openings. You continue the bottom plate through a door opening to keep the partition straight while you position it. With a power saw set to cut only 1 1/2″ deep, cut out the section of plate between door jambs after the partition is securely nailed.

Treat sills of doors in nonbearing partitions in the same way. Above the door opening, however, you can use a 2 × 4 laid flat as a header.

The actual length of a partition is seldom given on drawings. Dimensions run from the outside face of an exterior wall to a center line, or between the center lines of two parallel partitions. You have to subtract either 1 or 1 1/2 thicknesses of wall to arrive at the actual length.

One way to assure building partitions to the proper length is to lay them out with chalk on the subfloor. Snap the chalk line, not on the center line of the partition, but 1 3/4″ away to mark one edge. This makes it easier to set partitions accurately. Be sure the chalk lines are straight.

### Building Standard Partitions

Build bearing partitions first. They are usually the longest and most important. After that, build on the largest clear floor area you have remaining. Start setting partitions at the most distant part of the house and work toward the largest room. Leave partitions around closets until the very last.

You should build most partitions with 2 × 4 plates and studs, but there are two possible exceptions. The wall behind the toilet, called the *stack wall,* is usually built of 2 × 6s. It hides the main plumbing stack, which won't fit in a partition of standard thickness. Short nonbearing partitions, such as those around and between closets, may be built with 2 × 2 studs. Unless you save enough space to justify the weaker studs, however, stick with 2 × 4s here.

Where partitions intersect exterior walls, you have already made provision for anchoring the end. After you position each partition, nail through the bottom plate at the ends first, and then nail to exterior studs or the ladder. When you set the doubler, lap it over the top plate of the wall for a solid connection.

### Building Partitions Under Roof Trusses

If you plan to finish ceilings with a sheet material, such as plywood or gypsum wallboard, and you are framing your ceiling with roof trusses, hold off on building partitions until the house is under roof and protected from weather. By waiting, you can finish the entire ceiling at one time without anything in your way; this saves a lot of cutting and fitting. After the ceiling is finished, you then erect partitions.

The problem then becomes how to avoid damaging a finished ceiling as you set partitions. To prevent damage, lay out on the subfloor 2 × 4 bottom plates for all partitions and nail them in place. Omit the plate at door openings.

Then build partitions with studs 1 1/4″ shorter than those in exterior walls. At the lower ends of the studs use a 1 × 4 as a bottom plate. At the upper ends add the doubler. Set each partition cautiously on the 2 × 4 plate, hold it upright, and slowly raise it toward the ceiling on shims. When the partition just touches the ceiling, nail through the 1 × 4 plate into the 2 × 4 plate. To hold the tops of the partitions, set blocking between trusses about every 4′, and nail down through the blocking into the doubler.

## MOD 24 WALL FRAMING

Wall construction and assembly with the Mod 24 system are virtually the same as conventional construction, except for a stud spacing of 24″ instead of 16″. If your working drawings call for conventional construction, you may have to adjust the locations of doors, windows, and partitions slightly to achieve savings in materials. You must preplan every step of your work to make sure that you have a stud where you need it for attaching wall materials.

## POST-AND-BEAM FRAMING

In standard construction rafters do not have to rest directly above studs. In post-and-beam construction, roof beams must bear directly on posts. Posts may be a single 4 × 4 or a pair of 2 × 4s. The usual spacing in walls that parallel the roof ridge is 48″ on centers. The weight of the roof is carried on the roof beams (Fig. 9-12) that rest on a ridge beam, which in turn bears on a post in the center of each end wall. This post rests on the plank floor and is supported by an

Erection goes rapidly in this precut house built with post-and-beam construction. Wall sections come ready to install and are set in place at the same time as roof framing. Note the extensive use of braces at both floor levels. This is the same house shown in the previous chapter during floor framing. *Photographer: Richards Studio. Courtesy Lindal Cedar Homes, Inc.*

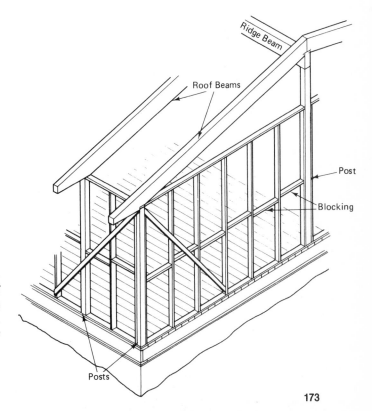

**Fig. 9-12.** In post-and-beam construction the entire weight of roof framing is carried on posts. Doublers are not needed, but corner bracing is. Spacing of standard studs is usually 24″ on centers.

edge joist and a block between the planks and the sill. Use spikes to toenail the post to the floor.

Note in Fig. 9-12 that walls in plank-and-beam construction have only a top plate, and no doubler. Studs are therefore 1 1/2" longer than in conventional construction and are usually spaced 24" o.c. Heavy headers are not required over window and door openings. Blocking is needed between studs, however. Place it near the midpoint of the vertical height of the wall, and stagger locations for easier nailing.

You can build front and rear walls on the floor and raise them as in conventional construction. End walls must be built in sections, however, since they butt against the center post. The order of assembling and erecting walls is the same as in conventional construction, too.

## ASSEMBLING PRECUT WALLS

Manufacturers of precut homes send you not only all the parts for exterior walls, but illustrated instructions on how to put the parts together. Partitions may or may not be included in the package. Some types of precut walls are put together like conventional walls; others follow post-and-beam principles; and still others are built like log cabins.

The method of building log walls is somewhat like laying a concrete block wall. The first log rests on the subfloor. It is flat on the bottom and grooved at the top and ends. In the longitudinal groove you place splines of hardboard that fit into a groove in the bottom of the next log. Splines also hold the grooved ends of logs in line. On both sides of the splines (Fig. 9-13), you hand-staple a gasket to seal out wind and moisture. At corners, the logs fit together in mortise-and-tenon joints.

Fig. 9-13. Today's log cabin is much different from those in Lincoln's day. Logs are debarked and trimmed to shape, then treated with preservative. Splines of hardboard fit into grooves to keep logs in line. Foam gaskets seal the joints between logs. *Courtesy Carolina Log Buildings, Inc.*

All logs are 8″ to 11″ in diameter, precut to length, notched, grooved, and treated with preservative. All you have to do is set them in place according to instructions. The manufacturer provides all splines, gaskets, snow blocks, and spikes. The logs are exposed on both sides as the finished material. No further wall treatment is necessary except for staining.

# SHEATHING

Application of sheathing to, and insulation in, exterior walls of conventionally built houses normally follows completion of the roof structure. Procedures are discussed here only because they relate to wall construction. It is important to get the roof on and watertight as soon as possible to protect the rest of the house.

Sheathing serves four purposes. It protects the structural members of the house from weather. It strengthens the structure, and is vital with the post-and-beam system. It has some insulating value. And it acts as a nailing surface for exterior finish materials.

Sheet materials are most commonly used for sheathing, and you have several choices—plywood, gypsum, and insulating sheathing.

### Plywood

The grade of plywood to use for sheathing is CDX. Order the type made with exterior glue; it holds up better when exposed to weather until you put finish materials in place. Type CDX comes in sheets 4′ wide, in lengths of 8′, 9′, 10′, and 12′, and in thicknesses from 5/16″ to 3/4″. Edges may be square, lapped, or tongue-and-groove.

You can apply plywood sheathing either vertically or horizontally. With vertical application a 3/8″ thickness with square edges is strong enough. Sheets should cover from the bottom of the sill to the top of the doubler. Edges must meet on the center lines of studs.

For a stronger application apply 1/2″ plywood horizontally, again covering from sill to doubler. Butt plywood ends at studs, but stagger the joints so that no two pieces of sheathing end on the same stud except at corners, where you overlap. If edges of sheets are square, add 2 × 4 blocks as nailing strips between studs behind horizontal joints. Blocks are not necessary with lapped or tongue-and-groove edges.

Apply the plywood with six-penny nails. Space nails 6″ apart at edges and 12″ apart into all other structural members. If your vacation house will be subject to high winds, you can increase the strength of the walls 50% by applying a bead of waterproof glue with a glue gun to plates and studs. Press the sheathing firmly into the glue before you nail.

### Gypsum

The main advantages of gypsum sheathing are that it is economical, does not burn, won't absorb water, or warp. It isn't as strong as plywood, however. Sheets are 1/2″ thick and comes in sizes 2′ by 8′, 4′ by 8′, and 4′ by 9′.

The 4-foot-wide panels must be applied vertically. They have square edges, and you butt them together over studs as with plywood sheathing. Space fasteners every 4" around the perimeter of each sheet and every 8" into other framing members. For fasteners use 1 3/4" galvanized roofing nails or 16-gauge divergent point staples with a 1 1/2" leg and a 1/2" crown. Stapling is much faster, but requires a staple gun and a source of compressed air. Drive staples parallel to framing members—vertically into studs and horizontally into plates, sills, and headers.

Apply 2-foot-wide panels horizontally. They have square ends but V-shaped edges on the long sides. Place each panel with the V upside down to keep out rain water, and space fasteners every 4" into studs. Backing is not required behind horizontal joints, as it is with square-edged plywood.

### Insulating Sheathing

Made of a variety of fibers pressed into sheet form, insulating sheathing is strong and the lightest in weight of all sheathing. It does not have good nail-holding strength, however, and you must add nailing strips over insulating sheathing for attachment of wood siding. Sheets come 2' and 4' wide, 6' to 12' long, and 1/2" to 1" thick. Order 3/4" thick material.

As with gypsum sheathing, you apply 4-foot-wide sheets vertically and 2-foot-wide sheets horizontally. Use 1 3/4" roofing nails spaced 3" apart along edges and 5/8" from the edges. Elsewhere space nails every 6". Gap about 1/8" between sheets at studs. The sheets are slightly less than 4' wide to accommodate gapping and to allow for expansion in damp weather.

The 2-foot-wide sheets have interlocking long edges that eliminate the need for backing. Nail every 4 1/2" into studs—6 nails per stud. You can increase this spacing to every 8" if you intend to use wood siding. Siding nails provide the added holding power.

Begin any sheathing job at a corner and work continuously toward the next corner. At openings it is easier to sheathe into the opening and rout out the excess material than it is to precut and fit odd-shaped pieces.

# INSULATION

Like sheathing, insulation serves four important purposes. It keeps heat out of your house in summer and holds heat in in cold weather. It helps prevent condensation problems. It retards the spread of fire in walls. And it reduces the amount of outdoor noise that penetrates into the house.

You can buy insulation in sheets, bags, rolls, or bundles. The most practical type for the walls of a vacation house is blanket batts that come in bundles of seven lengths to the package. Blanket batts are usually 8' long to fit between top and bottom plates without cutting, and in widths to fit between standard stud spacings.

Most insulation is made of mineral fibers that won't burn. Don't use any other kind. Dead air space between the fibers makes insulation function. The fibers come wrapped in a sleeve; one side of the sleeve is thin paper with tiny holes in it that let the insulation breathe. This side faces toward the outdoors. The other side of the sleeve is a heavier paper that acts as a vapor barrier. This side faces indoors and has flanges that you attach to studs. This face paper may be asphalted kraft or reflective aluminum foil.

## Insulating Value

The value of insulation is expressed in the industry by an R factor. An *R factor* is the resistance of any material to transmission of heat. The higher the R factor, the better the material is as an insulator. As concern has increased over our use of energy, building officials have increased the recommended R factors for insulation used at various points in the house. The R factor of blanket batts is clearly marked on the bundle, and the number of lengths inside goes down as R factor and thickness go up.

The R factor you need depends largely on your use of the house. A house in the woods used primarily in summer needs less insulation than a house used year-round, or one that sits exposed to the sun along the shore. But insulation is not expensive, and you are better off insulating thoroughly when you build. Once you have installed insulation and finished the walls, it is expensive to increase the R factor. R factors recommended as minimums are R8 in walls, R16 in the ceiling, R10 in the floor of a house built on piers, and R8 in the floor over a crawl space.

## Condensation

To be effective, insulation must fill all cavities between structural members— even spaces only a few inches square. If you don't fill them, moisture inside the house will head straight for them, and you may have condensation problems in the wall.

*Condensation* is the action that occurs when warm air cools. All air contains some moisture, even in the desert. The higher the air's temperature, the more moisture it can hold. When warm air moves, it always moves toward cold. The moisture that forms on the outside of a glass of iced tea on a summer day is condensation resulting from warm air moving toward a cooler surface.

Condensation can be a problem when the air in a house is warmer than the air outside it. The warm inside air is attracted toward the cooler outside walls. If the wall is uninsulated, the air cools rapidly as it touches the wall and loses some of its moisture. This moisture will condense in or on the wall and in very cold weather turn to ice. Eventually the moisture or ice evaporates, but not before causing structural damage and ruining exterior paint.

If the wall is insulated only, the air cools less quickly as it reaches the wall and loses less moisture. The moisture lost, however, condenses in the insulation.

Here it fills the air cells that make the insulation work, thus reducing its effectiveness. The moisture evaporates more slowly, and can cause even greater damage.

If the wall has insulation with a vapor barrier on the warm side, the barrier effectively prevents moisture from entering the wall. The better the job of insulating you do, the less moisture will find its way into the walls.

### Applying Insulation Between Studs

The easiest way to apply blanket insulation is with a hand-operated staple gun made for the purpose. You can usually rent one from the insulation supplier, along with a supply of 9/16″ staples. Fit each length of insulation into its cavity so that it touches the top plate firmly and stretches to the bottom plate. Tuck the flanges against the studs, but leave a little space between the insulation and sheathing to allow for air circulation.

Staple through the flange into the sides of studs. Staple the top of each side, then work down, spacing staples 6″ to 8″ apart. Keep flanges as flat as possible for an air-tight fit.

If possible, use a single batt of insulation in every cavity. If a cavity is narrower than standard, slit the thin backing paper at one edge (Fig. 9-14). With a utility knife strip away the excess insulation, leaving the paper backing in place. Then trim the heavier face paper to the correct width; remember to leave a flange. Fold the excess backing paper against the back of the flange, and staple through both paper surfaces into studs.

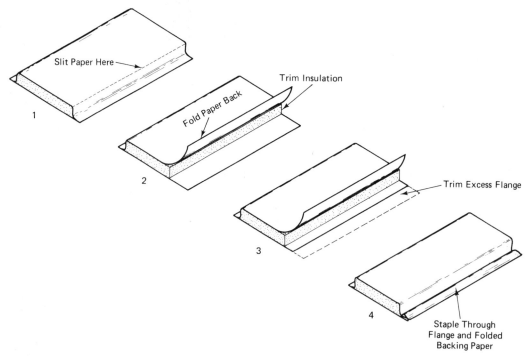

**Fig. 9-14.** Here are the four simple steps needed to trim a piece of blanket insulation to fit an opening of less than standard width.

In very small or odd-shaped cavities, you can strip all the paper off the insulation and stuff the cavity full. Then apply a piece of polyethlyene or heavy face paper from the insulation over the opening as a vapor barrier. This time staple to the faces of studs, but make sure the crowns of the staples don't protrude.

### Applying Insulation Between Joists or Rafters

You should insulate between ceiling joists above all rooms. If the ceiling follows the roof line, insulate between rafters. Use the same procedures and care as for wall application.

For horizontal application, rolls of insulation work better than blanket batts. Rolls are 50' or 60' in length, and you trim to the length you need. Some rolls come perforated every 4' or 8' to make cutting easier.

Insulating a ceiling is an awkward job. You attach the insulation from below, and the weight of the roll makes it difficult to maintain a tight fit. Having someone feed you the insulation as you work is a big help. If you work alone, tack a short board across joists about the midpoint of the span, and thread the roll over the board. This helps to reduce the pull of gravity.

Insulating a floor is an equally awkward job. You can't staple blankets or batts, because the flanges and vapor barrier are on the wrong side. One common solution is to support batts on lightweight screening, such as chicken wire. Begin at one header joist, and staple or nail a 4-foot-wide strip of screening across the undersides of floor joists. Fit batts between all joists with the vapor barrier face up. Then add more strips and more batts, gradually working your way to the other header joist. Slide the insulation in from the open end, and butt ends tightly. Don't leave much of a gap between strips, or the insulation will sag after a time. Hold off insulating the floor until all pipes and ducts are in place.

## PREPARING WALLS FOR HEATING

If you are having a subcontractor install a furnace and the necessary plumbing in your vacation house, give him a call after you have erected all exterior walls and partitions. Now is the time to make sure that you haven't caused him any problems that might require a change in structure. If you have a good working relationship with your subcontractors, and they don't live too far away, they will probably stop to look at your work whenever they are nearby. They want to avoid problems as much as you do.

If you are installing a heating system yourself, mark the locations of holes for ducts and registers. Holes through the subflooring must miss joists. You can tell by the rows of nail heads in the subfloor where the joists are. If ducts rise through plates of walls or partitions, mark their locations on these members. Where ducts end at a wall register, mark the location on the flanking studs. There's no need to make any cuts yet. Just verify that the locations will work, and then mark them. Make the cuts after the house is under roof.

If the furnace is in a basement or crawl space, or is the downflow type located on the first floor, ducts rise from below. Where they rise into an exterior wall, notch the bottom plate and subfloor with a power saw just to the edge of the header or edge joist (Fig. 9-15, right). A shortway elbow connects the lengths of ducts below the floor and in the wall, and will just fit in the hole. The ideal location for registers is about 4″ above finished floor level and centered below windows, provided they aren't covered by full-length draperies.

When the furnace is in an attic space, or is an upflow type on the main floor level, ducts come down through doublers and top plates. When you cut the top plate, you weaken the wall or partition. To replace the lost strength, attach a pair of 16-gauge metal straps (Fig. 9-15, left) to the sides of plates at the opening. Cut the straps twice as long as the width of the opening, drill eight holes, and nail or screw the straps firmly in place.

Remember, you can't cut a joist for a duct under any circumstances.

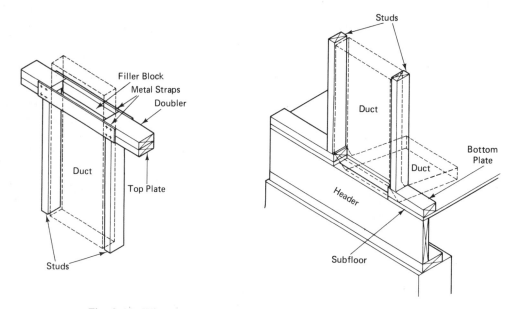

**Fig. 9-15.** When heat ducts come down through the top plate of a wall, you must reinforce at the cut (left). When ducts come up through the bottom plate, no reinforcement is necessary, but you may have to notch the header.

## PREPARING WALLS FOR PLUMBING

With each plumbing fixture he ships, the manufacturer provides a diagram that gives the locations of supports, the size and locations of water supply lines, and the size and location of the drain line. You must provide blocking to support a lavatory or its cabinet. You must block for a showerhead, and a shower curtain rod or shower door frame. You must block around a bathtub and a medicine cabinet. You must notch the subfloor for the bathtub and water closet drains.

You must drill for water and waste lines. At this time also add blocking behind kitchen cabinets. Details are covered in Chapter 15.

Plumbing work is done in three stages. Most of the first stage takes place outside the house. It includes digging a well and installing a septic system. At this time water lines are run from the water source through the foundation wall. Drain lines are carried from inside the basement or crawl space through the foundation wall to the point of disposal.

The second stage is called *roughing-in*. At this stage all piping continues upward from the first stage to the points of connection with plumbing fixtures. Bathtubs are set in place during roughing-in. This work continues off and on over quite a period of time while other construction is under way. In the final or *finish plumbing* stage, all remaining plumbing fixtures are set in place, all fixtures are connected, and the water and drainage systems are tested.

You have reached the roughing-in stage now. First mark the center lines of the hole for the soil stack; this is the largest pipe. It runs vertically from below the first floor, inside the 6″ wall behind the water closet, and straight up through the roof. It must clear all joists and rafters, and fit within the 6″ partition you built for it. The usual location for the stack is directly behind the water closet, on the same center line as the hole for the *closet bend*—the piece of drain pipe connected to the water closet itself.

Working from the point where center lines cross (see Fig. 9-16), scribe a circle large enough to let the soil stack pass through. With a 3″ stack, which has an outside diameter of 3 1/2″, you need a hole 4″ in diameter. With a 4″ stack you need a 5″ hole. Through the center of the circle drill a small hole just large enough to slide a cord through. Secure the top end of the cord to a stud and then get under the floor and tie a plumb bob to the other end.

The main drain below the soil stack should already be in place at this time. Your plumb bob should hang directly over the center of the drain. If not, determine how far off you are and adjust the location of the center lines of the hole on the partition plate above. Only after you are sure of the correct location of the hole can you safely cut into the floor.

The center line of the toilet drain is usually 12″ from the *finished* surface of the partition wall. Therefore you need to cut a rectangular hole about 4″ wide and 19″ long for a 3″ soil stack, and 5″ by 20″ for a 4″ stack. Figure 9-16 shows how to relate the location of the cut to the center line of the stack. Check these dimensions with your plumbing contractor before making the cut.

You need to make a similar cut below the drain of the bathtub, if you have one. A shower stall normally drains straight down, and the cut for its drain pipe is circular.

Most modern bathtubs are supported on the unfinished long side by a metal frame. Some have no support on the back, however, and you must provide that support under the rim with blocking attached vertically to studs. All bathtubs have turned-up rims or flanges with holes in them through which you nail or screw the tub to the wall. Provide blocking along the entire rim. Manufacturer's instructions indicate the height above subfloor level of the holes in the rim. For

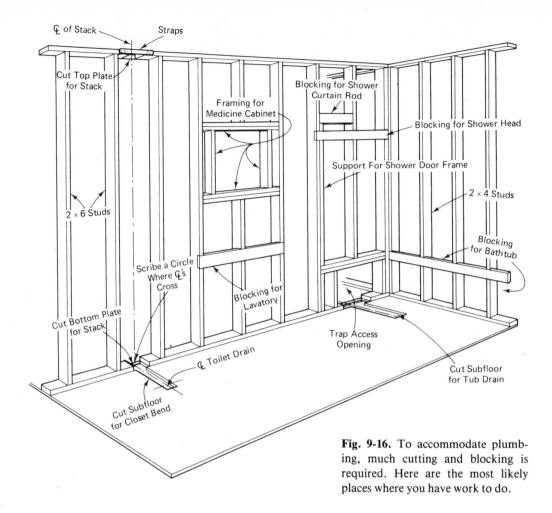

**Fig. 9-16.** To accommodate plumbing, much cutting and blocking is required. Here are the most likely places where you have work to do.

blocking you can use either a 1 × 4 notched into studs or short 2 × 4s set between studs and staggered for easier nailing. Set the blocking so that its horizontal center line is as close as possible to the center line of holes in the tub's flanges.

At the front of the tub, between the floor and the tub rim, provide an access opening so that you can get at the trap to clean out a clogged drain. Typical framing for the access panel is shown in Fig. 9-16.

As you can see, the partition that contains plumbing is much more complex than any other you build. You can save yourself some time and perhaps frustration by accurately drawing an elevation of this wall. On the drawing, mark and dimension the locations of all blocking and cuts. Then you can cut cripples to length and notch for thin blocking before you assemble the partition.

Unlike joists, you can notch studs up to 1/3 of their depth—1 1/8″ into a 2 × 4 and 1 3/4″ into a 2 × 6. Building codes generally permit you to notch two adjacent studs without reinforcing the cuts, provided the cuts are not in the middle third of the length of the stud. Figure 9-17 shows two common ways to reinforce. When you determine the size of a notch, remember to allow not only for the pipe itself, but also for the diameter of the thicker hubs that receive the next fitting in the piping system.

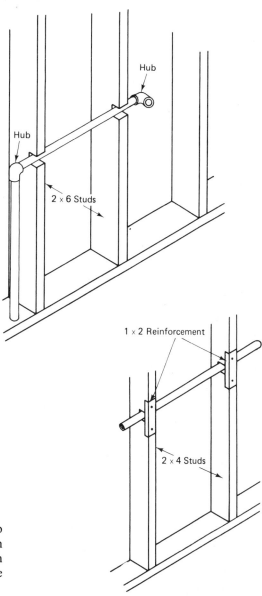

**Fig. 9-17.** You can notch studs up to 1/3 their depth if the notch isn't in the middle third of the stud's length (top). Otherwise you must reinforce at the notch (right).

## TOOLS YOU WILL NEED

To assemble and erect walls as described in this chapter, you will need the following tools and equipment as a minimum:

power saw
crosscut saw
hammer
carpenter's square or framing square
folding rule
steel tape
chalk line
carpenter's level
wood chisel
nylon cord
stepladder (6′ to 8′)
staple gun
utility knife (for cutting insulation)
power drill
hacksaw
screwdriver
compass or scribe
plumb bob
keyhole saw (for circular cuts)

# Framing the Roof

Installing ceiling joists is a fairly simple operation. Working drawings indicate the size of joists to use and the spacing between them. All you have to work out is the correct length. Ceiling joists in a one-story vacation house are smaller than floor joists because they carry a much lighter load. In a two-story house the ceiling joists between first and second floor living space must be the same size as first floor joists.

The actual length of ceiling joists depends on the amount of overlap at bearing partitions, as well as the treatment at the eaves of the roof. Ceiling joists usually run in the same direction as floor joists. They always run in the same direction as rafters of the main roof. Joists must bear fully on bearing partitions. Those above half the floor area overlap those above the other half by at least 6″. So consider the starting point for measuring length as 3″ beyond the center line of the bearing partition (Fig. 10-1).

As long as the pitch of the roof is not greater than 5 in 12 and the roof overhang is not more than 24″, the outside ends of ceiling joists can fall directly over the outside edge of the doubler (top, Fig. 10-1). With steeper roof pitches and greater overhangs, the eave begins to interfere with light into windows below and the view out of them. In such cases it is usually better to continue the joists to the edge of the eave (bottom, Fig. 10-1). Ceiling joist length, then, is 3″ plus the distance from the center line of the

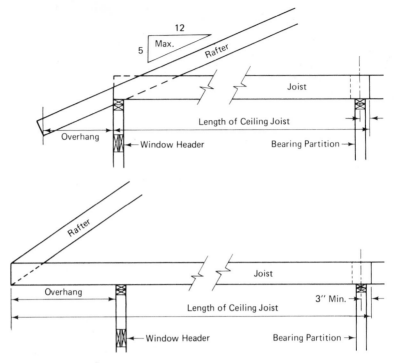

**Fig. 10-1.** Rafters usually rest on rafter plates (top) when roof pitch is low and overhangs permit. Rafters may also be supported on ends of ceiling joists, however (bottom). Note in both drawings the measuring points for determining the lengths of joists.

bearing partition to the outside of wall framing, plus the amount of any overhang. If there is no bearing partition, the ceiling joist length is the overall dimension of the house or wing at that point plus the amount of two overhangs.

## TRIMMING JOISTS

Where the ends of ceiling joists meet rafters, they often protrude above the roof line (Fig. 10-1, top). You must trim off a little triangle of wood so that the cut end of each joist lies flush with the upper edge of its rafter. It's simpler to mark the joist for cutting after it is installed, but it's a lot easier to trim all joists before you set them.

While building a roof, you will make a number of angled cuts in roof framing members, all of which have similar angles. To save yourself time in marking these similar cuts, make yourself a pitch board. A *pitch board* is nothing more than a triangle cut out of a sheet of plywood. The length of the bottom side is 12″. The length of the short side, which is at right angles to the 12″ side, is the same as the first number in the roof pitch. If the pitch shown on the section or elevations in the drawings is 5 in 12, then the height of the short side is 5″. Use a carpenter's square or framing square to make sure the angle between the two sides is exactly 90°.

Before you trim joists, sight down each one for straightness. Look particularly for any bow. Like floor joists, ceiling joists should be installed with the crowns up. As you check each piece, lay it on a stack so that all crowns are facing in the same direction. Then mark and trim all joists at the same time.

To mark the trim cut, measure in 3 1/2″ from the end of the joist along its bottom edge (Fig. 10-2). From this point draw a line along the pitch board, moving upward at the angle of pitch and away from the end of the joist. Next, at right angles to this line measure off the depth of a rafter and mark the point. Remember, a 6″ rafter has an actual depth of 5 1/2″, and an 8″ rafter is actually 7 1/2″ deep. Again using your pitch board draw a line through this point, parallel to the first pitch line. The triangle of wood above this second line is the scrap to be trimmed off.

Usually you won't need to trim the end of a joist above a bearing partition. You trim only under two circumstances. First, if you plan a second story with a finished floor, and the tops of overlapping joists aren't flush, you must trim.

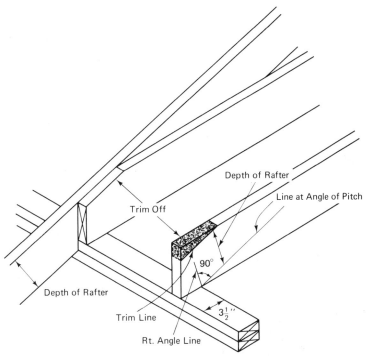

**Fig. 10-2.** Shaded area of the ceiling joist must be trimmed off before you can sheathe the roof.

Otherwise you will have trouble laying a subfloor over the uneven tops. Second, let's say that the shortest joist length you can buy is at least 13 1/4″ longer than the joist length you need. Trim off this much excess, and use the 13″ cutoffs for blocking between joists over bearing partitions (Fig. 10-3).

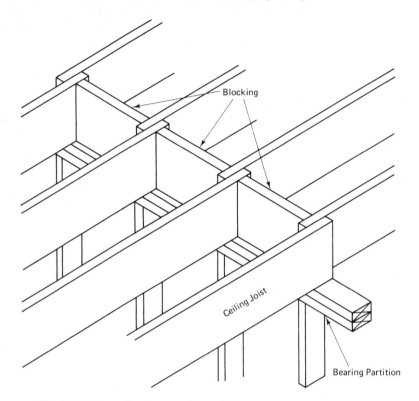

**Fig. 10-3.** Over a bearing partition ceiling joists must lap at least 6″. Blocking keeps joists plumb and deters the spread of fire.

## INSTALLING CEILING JOISTS

Ceiling joists usually lie over studs—if not directly above then close to it. Mark joist locations on the doublers of both exterior walls and any bearing partition. Measure 15 1/4″ from the corner to the first mark, and a full 16″ thereafter. The ceiling joists over half the house will lie on one side of this mark, and on the other side over the other half of the house. Joists overlap on the mark at the bearing partition, as in Fig. 10-3.

For a change, you don't begin installation at a corner, but at the first mark. If the spacing doesn't come out even, adjust in the middle of the long wall or at a ceiling opening, such as for a stairway or access door to attic space. You don't install end joists until you begin roof framing, because the exact location varies with the type of roof and the amount of side overhang.

Set all joists with their crowns up, and position them accurately. Toenail each end to the doubler on one side only—the side away from the mark. In this way nail heads won't be in the way of setting rafters or the remaining joists. Use a pair of ten-penny nails with rafters less then 6″ deep, and twelve-penny nails with heavier rafters. Make sure you stay on the marks when you nail. This is more important than having joists absolutely plumb. You can straighten them later when you install rafters.

As you set joists over the second half of the house, install blocking over bearing partitions. The blocking helps to maintain proper spacing, keeps the ends plumb, and prevents the spread of fire.

### Framing at Openings

You frame openings in a ceiling in the same way that you frame openings in a floor. Use double joists at the sides of large openings, use double headers at the ends, and add trimmers to reduce an oversized opening to smaller dimensions. If you plan an access door to attic space (Fig. 10-4), cut a section 30 1/2″ long out of one joist and use it as a header between uncut joists beside the opening. Use a single header when the opening is not more than 24″ from a joist support; otherwise double the header. Add 1 × 4 ledgers around the opening to support the access door.

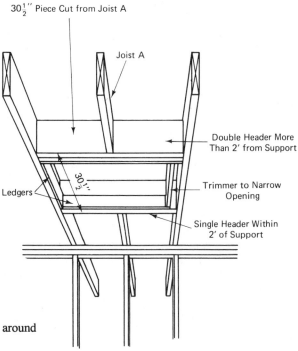

Fig. 10-4. Typical construction around an access door to attic space.

Any opening for a chimney or furnace flue must be at least 4″ larger than the chimney so that no wood structure is within 2″ of it on any side. Sometimes framing drawings indicate the size of opening needed at ceiling level. If not, you must work it out yourself. Details of fireplace and chimney construction are covered in Chapter 11.

### Nailing to Partitions

Where joists run at right angles to a partition, toenail through each joist into the doubler, using an eight-penny nail on each side. Where joists run the same direction as a partition, and the partition lies directly below the joist, toenail in the same way. Where the partition lies between joists, build a ladder, similar to the ladder where a partition and exterior wall meet (Fig. 9-6). First center a 1 × 6 over the length of the doubler and nail it down. This piece serves as a nailing base for ceiling material. Then lay 2 × 4 cross blocks flat on the nailing strip, spaced every 16″ to 24″. Nail the blocks to the strip, and then nail through the joists into the ends of blocks to complete the job.

# ROOF DESIGN

Of the seven basic roof styles, the most common is the gable roof. It has a ridge and slopes in two directions from that ridge. A *gable* is the upper part of an end wall between the ridge and the doubler. The simplest type is the shed roof. Unlike a gable roof, a shed roof has no ridge, and slopes in only one direction. Therefore one supporting wall is taller than the other, and eaves are at different heights. A hip roof has a constant eave height; the roof slopes in four directions from a ridge that is shorter than in a gable roof. A flat roof has no ridge and no slope.

The other three roof styles—mansard, gambrel, and butterfly—are more complex variations of the other types, and are difficult for most amateurs to build properly.

### Roof Parts

Before you can cut the parts for a roof and follow instructions for assembling it, you need to know roof terminology (Fig. 10-5).

A *common rafter* is a roof framing member that runs from ridge to eave of a gable or hip roof, or from eave to eave of a shed or flat roof. All common rafters are identical in any one roof slope.

A *ridgeboard* is the uppermost horizontal framing member in a gable or hip roof. It lies between rafters on opposite roof slopes. It isn't required to make a roof structurally sound, but it does simplify the task of assembly. Flat and shed roofs have no ridgeboard.

A *fascia* is the board that covers exposed ends of rafters at eaves. It simply adds a nice finishing touch to some styles of houses. Rustic vacation houses seldom have fascias.

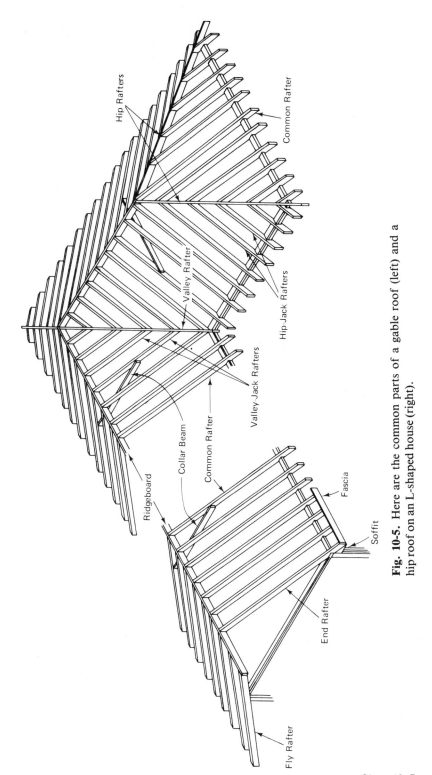

**Fig. 10-5.** Here are the common parts of a gable roof (left) and a hip roof on an L-shaped house (right).

Hip Rafters

Common Rafter

Valley Rafter

Hip-Jack Rafters

Valley-Jack Rafters

Collar Beam

Common Rafter

Ridgeboard

Fascia

Soffit

End Rafter

Fly Rafter

A *soffit* is the underside of a roof overhang. Like a fascia, a soffit dresses up the eaves. If you have a soffit, you must have a fascia.

A *collar beam* is a board that runs between butting common rafters in a gable or hip roof. It is like the cross stroke in the letter A and acts as a stiffener.

Roofs, like floors, also have headers and trimmers. In addition, each roof style has its own special rafters. In a gable roof, for example, the outermost common rafter is called an *end rafter* if it rests on the doubler, and a *fly rafter* when the roof overhangs the gable wall.

A hip roof has several special rafters. A *hip rafter* runs diagonally from the outside corner of an eave to the end of the ridgeboard. A *valley rafter* runs from an inside corner of an eave to the ridgeboard. You have a valley rafter in a hip or gable roof only when the house has a wing; it lies in the intersection of the two roofs. A *jack rafter* runs from a hip rafter down to the eave, or from a valley rafter up to the ridgeboard. All these special rafters have at least one beveled end.

### Roof-Framing Terms

Every roof has a pitch, span, run, and rise (Fig. 10-6, top). *Pitch* is the slope of the roof. It is usually noted on elevations in working drawings as an upside down triangle, with the pitch indicated by two numbers. One number is always 12. The other varies from 0 for a flat roof to as much as 12 for a steep slope. What this means is that for every 12″ of horizontal dimension, the roof rises so many inches in vertical dimension. Thus a roof with a pitch of 3 1/2 in 12 rises 3 1/2″ vertically for every 12″ horizontally.

The *span* of a roof is its total width from outside edge to outside edge of supporting doublers. The *run* is the distance between the outside edge of a doubler and the center line of the ridge. In a roof with the same pitch on both sides of a ridge, the run equals half the span. A flat or shed roof has no run; it is the same as the span.

The *rise* is a vertical distance measured upward from the top of the doubler. If you drew a line parallel to the pitch from the edge of the doubler to the ridgeboard, that line would hit the ridgeboard somewhere below its vertical midpoint. This point is the other end of the measurement of rise. The ratio of rise to run is always the same as the pitch.

### Rafter Parts

A rafter may have two parts that determine its actual length (Fig. 10-6, bottom). The *body* of a rafter is the length between supports—usually the ridgeboard and the doubler (called a *rafter plate* by roofing carpenters). The *tail* of a rafter is the length that extends beyond the rafter plate to form the overhang. Not all rafters have tails.

The *length* of a rafter is the combined length of body and tail. The *actual length* of a rafter is even greater, as you will see shortly.

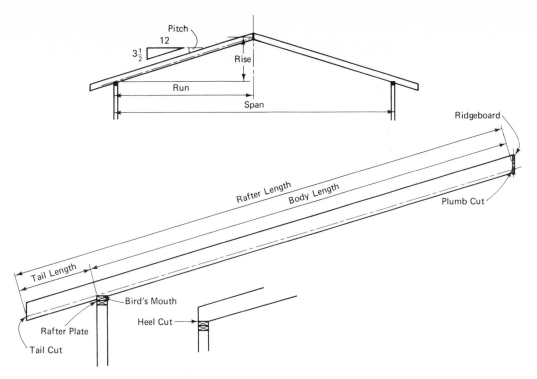

**Fig. 10-6.** Here are the common roof framing terms (top) and parts of a rafter (bottom). Note that the calculated length of a rafter, marked here as *rafter length,* is slightly less than the actual length that you must cut.

### Rafter Cuts

Every rafter has to be cut. Some cuts are simple and some are complex. A *plumb cut* is a vertical cut, such as at the upper end of a common rafter where it meets the ridgeboard. A *bird's mouth* is the notch in the underside of a rafter where it fits over the doubler or rafter plate. A rafter that ends at the rafter plate without any tail gets a heel cut instead of a bird's mouth. A *heel cut* is a horizontal cut. A *tail cut* is any cut made to shape the lower end of a rafter. Rafters in a roof without a fascia usually have square ends with no tail cut. With a fascia but no soffit, use a plumb cut so that the two ends of the rafter are parallel. With both fascia and soffit, use a plumb cut and a heel cut at the end of the tail.

## LAYING OUT A COMMON RAFTER

In roof construction the steel square is a more valuable tool than a saw or hammer. Its long side, called the *blade,* is 24″ long and 2″ wide. Its short side, called the *tongue,* is 16″ long and 1 1/2″ wide. Outside edges are marked every 1/8″; inside edges are marked every 1/4″.

Lay out rafters with the square using unit measurements—the unit run, unit rise, and unit length. The *unit run* is always 12″. The *unit rise* is the rise per foot of run—3 1/2″ for a roof with a 3 1/2 in 12 pitch. The *unit length* is the hypotenuse of the right triangle formed by the unit run and unit rise.

To show how to use unit measurements, suppose that you are building a gable roof with a span of 30′ 0″ and a 4 in 12 pitch. The run of the roof is half the span, or 15′ 0″. The rise of this roof is 4/12 of the run, or 5′ 0″.

Converted to unit measure, the unit run is 12″—it always is. The unit rise is 4/12 of the run, or 4″. The unit length, calculated by the Pythagorean theorem, is the square root of $4^2 + 12^2$, which is 16 + 144, or 160. The square root of 160 is 12.649.

In this example the actual measurements are 15 times the unit measurements. Therefore, the length of the body of a common rafter is 15 × 12.649, or 189.735″. Converted to feet, the length is 15′ 9 3/4″. This is the length used to calculate roof loads.

To find the overall length for purposes of ordering rafter stock, you add the length of the tail. Suppose that the roof overhang shown on drawings is 1′ 9″; this is the run of the overhang. Since this run is 1 3/4 times the unit run, the length of the tail will be 1 3/4 times the unit length, or 22.136″—slightly more than 1′ 10 1/8″. Add the tail length to the body length, and the overall length of a common rafter is 17′ 7 7/8″. Rafter stock comes in multiples of 2′ lengths, so it looks as if you can use 18′ lengths with little waste.

But don't order just yet. Note in Fig. 10-6 that rafter length is measured along the dotted line that passes through the bird's mouth. Because of the angled cuts at ridge and eave, the rafter is actually a little longer than its calculated length. When cut to fit, the rafter in the example will be about 17′ 10″ long. Keep this in mind if your calculated dimension is close to the length of rafter stock available. If the cut length comes out 18′ 1″, you could save money by reducing the overhang an inch, rather than by wasting 23″ of 20′ rafter stock.

### Marking the Cuts

To simplify cutting common rafters, build a sample rafter. Pick out the straightest, smoothest piece of stock you can find, and set it across a pair of sawhorses with any crown in the edge nearest you. Mark the crowned edge with an arrow so that you always know which is the top edge of the rafter. Also make a little mark about 1/2″ in from the right end at the bottom edge.

Lay your square on the rafter as shown in Fig. 10-7—with the blade to the left, the tongue to the right, and the heel away from you. Place the tongue so that the unit rise (4″ in the example above) points to the pencil mark near the end of the rafter. Then swing the blade until the 12″ mark (the unit run) lies exactly at the bottom edge of the rafter. When both marks are lined up properly (inset in Fig. 10-7), draw a diagonal line along the tongue. This line marks the center line of the ridgeboard.

You can use either the inside or the outside of your square to measure the unit rise and unit run, as long as you make both measurements on the same side.

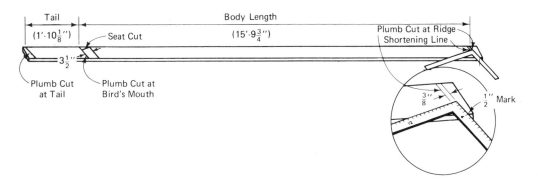

**Fig. 10-7.** Details of how to mark a common rafter for cutting. Lay the square with the 12″ mark on the blade set at the edge of the rafter (inset) and with the unit rise on the tongue. Set the square in the same position when you measure by the step-off method.

It's easier to balance the square on the rafter if you mark on the inside, but it's harder to draw the cut lines. The best way is to mark on the outside of the square and support its ends on another piece of rafter stock laid across the sawhorses.

From the plumb cut line you have just drawn, measure off the length of the body along the bottom edge of the rafter and make another mark. In the example shown this measurement is 15′ 9 3/4″. At this point, using the same procedure as for the plumb cut, draw a second line. This line marks the plumb cut at the bird's mouth (Fig. 10-7).

To mark the seat cut at the bird's mouth, measure off 3 1/2″ at right angles to your latest line toward the top of the rafter. With your square, draw a line through this mark parallel to the plumb cut. Now lay the heel of your square exactly at the point where this line touches the bottom edge of the rafter (the edge away from you), and draw a line between the two parallel lines and at right angles to them. This line marks the seat cut of the bird's mouth.

From the plumb cut line for the bird's mouth, measure off the length of the tail, which is 1′ 10 1/8″ in the example. If you plan a plumb cut at the tail, measure this distance on the edge of the rafter *away* from you, and draw a line parallel to the other plumb cuts. If you plan a square end, measure the tail on the edge *closest* to you, and draw a line at right angles to the edge of the rafter.

The final line to draw is the *shortening line*. Remember that you calculated the overall rafter length to the center line of the ridgeboard. Assuming that you use a 3/4″-thick board as a ridgeboard, measure off 3/8″ at right angles to your plumb cut line at the ridge, working toward the tail of the rafter. Then draw a line parallel to the plumb cut line. This is the line you cut on, not the plumb cut line.

**Checking Measurements by the Step-Off Method.** But before you cut this sample rafter, recheck all your calculations and marks. One way is to lay your square against the plumb cut line at the ridge (not the shortening line) as you did to start the marking process. Mark the edge of the rafter at the 12″ line on the blade. Now move the square until the unit rise dimension on the tongue touches this mark, and make another mark at the 12″ line on the blade. Continue this process down the rafter.

Earlier you determined that the actual body length of the rafter was 15 times the unit length in the example, and the tail was 1 3/4 times the unit length. If you have measured and marked accurately, the 12″ mark on the blade should fall right on the plumb cut for the bird's mouth after 15 moves of the square. To check the tail cut, first make one full move and then another with the square set at 3 and 9 instead of 4 and 12. This procedure is known as the *step-off* method of measuring rafters.

You can save yourself some time in marking the rest of the rafters, and increase your accuracy in layout, by making a *layout tee* (Fig. 10-8). The stem of the tee is a 1″-thick board with the same depth as a rafter. The tee should be about a foot longer than the overhang. The top of the tee is the same length and width as the stem, and it can be cut from the same board.

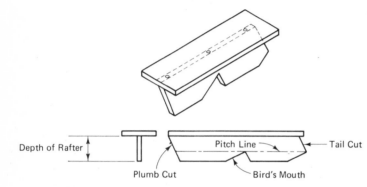

**Fig. 10-8.** A layout tee. The length between bird's mouth and plumb cut isn't important, but the shape of the tail should be exact. The tee's top and stem can be cut from the same board.

Depth of Rafter    Pitch Line —    — Tail Cut
Plumb Cut    Bird's Mouth

Mark the tail cut at one end of the layout tee. Then mark the bird's mouth the same distance from the tail cut as it is in a rafter. You can mark the plumb cut at the ridge anywhere at the other end of the tee. Carefully and very accurately cut along the marks; if you don't cut accurately, every rafter will be off fit. Then center the top over the stem and nail or screw it tight.

To use the tee you need to mark only the length of the body on each piece of rafter stock. Then you slide the tee along the rafter until the proper cut lines up with its mark.

### Testing the Sample

The best way to test sample rafters for accuracy of measurement and tightness of fit is on the clean subfloor before you erect the walls. You need two sample rafters, marked but not yet cut. Since one of the rafters will lie face down on the subfloor, carry your markings to the opposite side. Find the center line of the floor below the ridge and snap a chalk line. Along the chalk line measure the rise of the roof (it was 5′ 0″ in the example) and make a mark. Then snap chalk lines from this mark to the corners of the subfloor (Fig. 10-9).

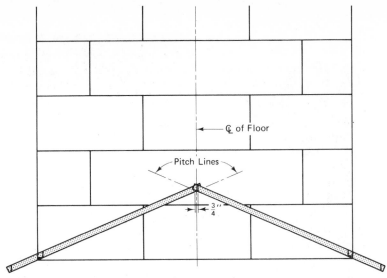

**Fig. 10-9.** To test a sample rafter, lay it, uncut, on the subfloor. The bird's mouths should fit at the corners of the floor, and the plumb cuts should overlap on the center line of the floor.

Lay the sample rafters on these two pitch lines. Let them overlap at the center, but set the lines for the plumb cuts at the ridge 3/4″ apart. Check both bird's mouths first. The plumb cuts should lie exactly on the long edges of the floor, and the seat cuts should be parallel to the short edge. Then check at the ridge; the two shortening cuts should be parallel.

If the fit is good at all points, go ahead and cut the rafters. If the fit is only close, you can usually obtain a good fit by adjusting at the ridge. If this doesn't work, start over. It doesn't pay to force a good fit or to use rafters that don't fit properly.

Make the shortening cut at the ridge first. Then retest the fit, using a scrap piece of ridgeboard as a spacer. If the fit is still fine, complete the two cuts at the bird's mouth and any tail cut. Use the sample rafter to mark all other common rafters, marking with a sharp pencil. And of course plan to use the sample rafters in the roof structure.

With a flat or shed roof, you start assembling the roof after you have cut all rafters. With a gable or hip roof, the next step is to cut the ridgeboard.

## LAYING OUT A RIDGEBOARD

The standard ridgeboard is a board 3/4″ in actual thickness and 2″ deeper than a common rafter. If drawings call for 2 × 6 rafters, use a 1 × 8 for a ridgeboard. The length of a ridgeboard is equal to the length of the rafter plate running parallel to it, plus the widths of side overhangs. When planning length, it's better to build the ridgeboard a little long and cut it to length after the roof is assembled.

You'll probably have to splice the ridgeboard, and any splice must fit between rafters. Therefore the first step is to mark the locations of all rafters on the ridge-

The roof structure supplied with this log cabin is not standard because the roof is shipped in sections and assembled on the site. Boards below roof structure are exposed as ceilings and covered with a vapor barrier. Rectangles may be filled with insulation. Note the diagonal brace, which will remain in place until sheathing begins. *Courtesy Carolina Log Buildings, Inc.*

board. When rafter spacing is the same as ceiling joist spacing, you can lay the ridgeboard across the tops of these joists above the doubler, marking at the edge of each joist. Then carry the marks across the face of the ridgeboard with an adjustable square.

When you mark, remember three things. First, you haven't at this time set all ceiling joists plumb, so correct for any cocked joists as you mark. Second, rafters fit beside joists, not over them. And third, you must provide a nailing surface beginning 48″ from one end of the roof for plywood sheathing. One side of the roof will be different from the other if joists butt over a bearing partition. The rafters meet at the ridgeboard on opposite sides of the mark.

Splice the ridgeboard before you assemble the roof. At a splice you can use either wood or metal. With either type you must splice on both sides of the ridgeboard and offset the splices the thickness of a rafter.

For wood splices use two 12″ to 14″ lengths of ridgeboard stock, nailing one to each side of the carefully squared ends of ridgeboard. Use five six-penny nails in each board, in a pattern like the fives on a pair of dice. For metal splices buy pairs of splice plates at least 12″ wide and slightly less in height than the depth of the ridgeboard. Splice plates have holes punched in them, with the jagged metal protruding at each hole. You use only a hammer to attach them; the metal burrs grip both boards firmly.

# ERECTING SCAFFOLDING

As you assemble the roof, for the first time you will be working above a level you can reach with a stepladder. For this purpose you need a scaffold that runs the entire length of the roof. In some areas you can rent tubular steel scaffolding that can be assembled on the site. Or you can build your own.

To build scaffolding you need long 1 × 8s or 1 × 10s, 2 × 4s, 1 × 4s, and sheets of plywood. Lay the long 1 × 8s across ceiling joists with their center lines 27″ on each side of the center line of the ridge. Nail them to the joists. On these runners at about 7 1/2′ intervals erect a series of frames (Fig. 10-10) with 2 × 4 legs and a Z-shaped brace of 1 × 4s. Space the legs so their inside edges are 49 1/2″ apart. Set the top horizontal brace so that it lies about 4′ below the top of the future ridgeboard. Use four long 1 × 4s as diagonal braces between frames. Inside the legs, supported by the top members of the Z braces, nail 1 × 4s for a catwalk. Then lay 4′ by 8′ sheets of plywood between the sides, overlapping about 6″ at each supporting frame. You can later reuse the plywood for roof sheathing.

**Fig. 10-10.** You need some sort of scaffolding in order to raise a roof. The design shown here is a section of a scaffold that runs across joists the length of the house. All parts are cut from standard stock, and most pieces are reusable in later construction.

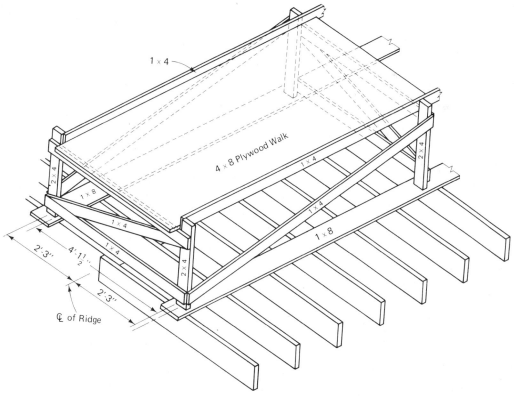

Assembling a roof in midair takes at least four people. You need two to hold the ridgeboard, or three if the ridge is more than 32′ long. And you need someone on each side of the ridge to set rafters.

Pick a day when there is little breeze. Begin by leaning all cut rafters against the rafter plate, with tails down and plumb cuts up, spaced so that you can reach them from the scaffolding. Find the position mark on the ridgeboard for the rafter next to the end, and, with the ridgeboard in hand, hold a common rafter against the mark. With three eight-penny nails, nail through the ridgeboard into the plumb cut. Repeat this process at the mark just before the splice, working on the same side of the ridgeboard.

Now slowly raise the ridgeboard until the two bird's mouths rest on the rafter plate. Jam the rafters firmly onto the plate and tight against the ceiling joist. Nail down into the rafter plate and horizontally into joists with 16-penny nails, using at least six nails. Then nail matching rafters on the other side of the ridgeboard—opposite the first two but on the other side of the marks if ceiling joists overlap. Next attach a pair of temporary 1 × 6 braces between the outer rafters and ceiling joists. At this point the roof looks something like that shown in Fig. 10-11.

Next add a pair of rafters at the unsupported end of the ridgeboard and another pair on the other side of the splice. Again brace at the end. Your roof

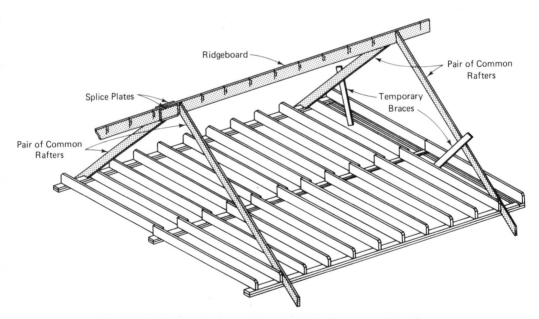

**Fig. 10-11.** Roof structure at the end of the first stage. Note location for temporary braces. Ridgeboard is shown broken, but is continuous to the other end of the house.

structure is now self-supporting enough so you can breathe more easily, even though it is hardly strong.

Before going any farther, check your work. Set a level on the ridgeboard. It should be level if the board itself is straight and you have cut the rafters accurately. Mark any low spots; you can usually take a slight sag out of the ridgeboard as you set additional rafters.

Then, working toward the center of the roof, nail two or three more pairs of rafters in place, including any end rafters that lie directly over end walls. After you have four or five consecutive rafters in place, remove the temporary braces. Check the roof structure for plumb, using either a plumb bob or a vertical board and carpenter's level. When the rafters are plumb, renail the braces at the ends. Then run a 1 × 4 brace diagonally across these rafters at about a 45° angle, and nail it temporarily to all rafters. This brace will hold the roof structure plumb while you add the rest of the rafters.

After you have nailed each pair of rafters, sight down the ridgeboard to make sure it is level and still straight. After all the common rafters are in place, recheck the plumb and sight up each rafter to check its straightness.

### Straightening Rafters

You straighten rafters in the same general way that you straighten joists. Remove one long diagonal brace and mark your rafter spacing on it. Nail this board on a mark to the end rafter at about its midpoint, and work across the roof. Set each rafter on a mark and lightly nail the board with an eight-penny nail into each rafter. This procedure will hold rafters straight until you are ready to sheathe. Leave the braces in place until they get in the way of other work.

At this time you can probably remove the scaffolding. If you are building a chimney, however, leave the scaffolding at that point.

To give your roof greater strength, you can tie pairs of rafters together in two ways. One way is with collar beams placed every 48″—that is, between every third set of rafters spaced 16″ on centers. Place the collar beams about a third of the line length of the rafter down from the ridge. You can shape two collar beams out of one long 1 × 6 by making just three cuts (Fig. 10-12).

The other way is to use 18-gauge metal straps an inch wide and at least 24″ long. You nail the strap to the upper edge of one rafter and carry it across the ridgeboard and down the edge of the butting rafter, nailing every few inches. It is better to tie rafters in this way if you plan to use your attic space. Collar beams get in the way.

**Fig. 10-12.** You can cut two collar beams out of one board by making only three saw cuts. Beam B is upside down.

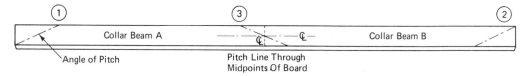

# FINISHING A GABLE ROOF

After the structure for a gable roof is complete, the next step is to build the gables. First find the midpoints of the side rafter plates; they should lie directly below the ridgeboard.

Studs in a gable needn't line up with studs in the wall below. A stud may lie on the midpoint of the gable or 8″ on either side. What goes on in the gable determines which position is preferable. If there is a window centered on the midpoint of the gable, for example, place the studs to suit window framing.

More likely you will need to frame around louvers. To avoid condensation problems you must ventilate the attic. With a gable roof the simplest way is with louvers at the top of each gable. At the bottom of the louver opening you must install a header (see Fig. 10-13). Use your pitch board to mark the beveled cuts that fit against the underside of the gable plate.

Each stud in half a gable is a different length, but the differences in length between adjacent rafters are the same. This is known as the *common difference,* which applies not only to gable studs under gable roofs but to jack rafters in hip roofs. In gable studs the common difference is the unit rise of the roof times the distance between studs measured in feet. In the example used earlier in this chapter the unit rise was 5″. With 16″ spacing the distance between studs is 1 1/3′. Therefore each stud is 6 2/3″ longer or shorter than the adjacent stud— roughly 6 11/16″.

## Building Side Overhangs

Many gable roofs overhang end walls as well as front and rear walls. The ridgeboard ends, not at the gable wall, but at the end of the overhang. Gable studs butt, not against the end rafter, but against a 2 × 4 gable plate. There is no end rafter; instead there is a fly rafter. Each fly rafter is supported at its ends by the ridgeboard and a fascia and in the middle on a ladder.

Figure 10-13 shows the details of construction. Each gable plate runs from the inside edge of the rafter plate to the center line of the ridge. Its top surface is in the same plane as the undersides of rafters. You may have to notch the ridgeboard for gable plates. When you cut gable studs to length, remember to allow for the angled thickness of the gable plate. You can build gables on the ground and raise them into place, but this is difficult since they have no bottom plate. It's better to build them after the roof structure is in place.

To nail gable studs, use a pair of 10-penny nails at each end. Toenail through the sides of studs into the rafter plate and nail through the gable plate into the ends of studs.

The ladder that supports the fly rafter is made of rafter stock, with the parts spaced about 24″ apart. These parts are not set vertically, but are tipped so that the top edges are flush with the top edges of rafters. Toenail at the gable plate and into the ends at rafters. Note in Fig. 10-13 that a fly rafter is exactly like a common rafter except that it has no bird's mouth.

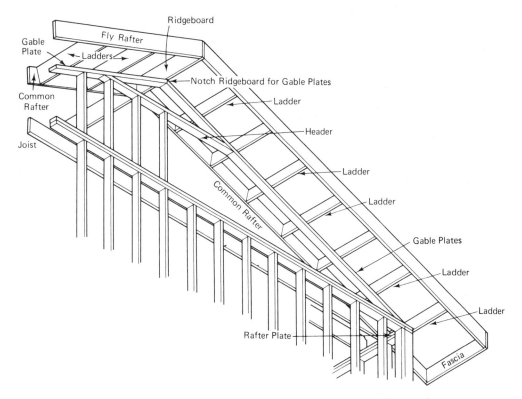

**Fig. 10-13.** Detail of gable wall construction when the roof has a side overhang. The gable plate in effect replaces the end rafter. Note that at its lower end the gable plate does not extend to the outer edge of the rafter plate, but stops at the inside edge.

## FINISHING A HIP ROOF

The center section of a hip roof is built just like a gable roof. At the end of the ridge you brace either with a common rafter running from the end of the ridge to the rafter plate of the side wall, or with a pair of hip rafters.

Hip rafters run at 45° to other rafters. They form the hypotenuse of a right triangle whose other two sides are the length of a common rafter. The hypotenuse of such a triangle is always 1.414 (the square root of 2) times the length of a common rafter. If the length of a common rafter is 17 ′ 8 ″ (simplified from the 17 ′ 7 7/8 ″ in our example), the length of a hip rafter is a hair shorter than 25 ′ 0 ″.

Rafters in hip roofs get different cuts than common rafters, and you mark the cuts differently (A in Fig. 10-14). The common cuts are a single cheek cut (B or D) and a double cheek cut (C).

To mark these cuts you must first find and mark the center line of the long edge of a rafter. To be as accurate as possible, lay your folding rule diagonally

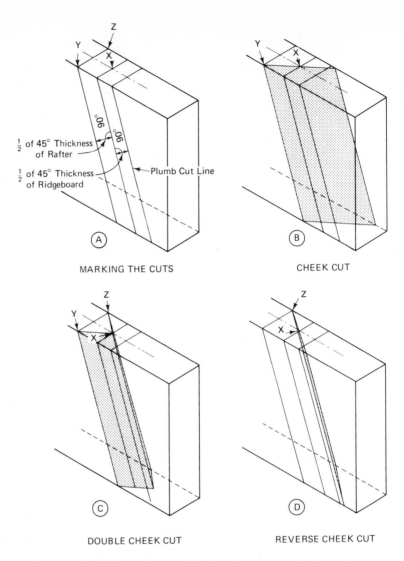

**Fig. 10-14.** All hip, valley, and jack rafters have angled cuts at one end, and sometimes at both ends. All cuts are marked from the same set of lines (A). Typical cuts are a single cheek cut (B), a single cheek cut in the opposite direction (D), and a double cheek cut (C).

across the top edge with the 1″ mark at one side edge and the 3″ mark at the other side edge. With your pencil mark at the 2″ point on the rule at half a dozen spots along the length of the rafter. Then set the adjustable blade of a combination square on any center line mark. Holding your pencil against the blade, pull the square along the edge of the rafter, marking the center line as you go. This line should pass through all your marks.

## Cutting Hip Rafters

When a hip roof doesn't have a common rafter at the end of the ridgeboard, each hip rafter gets a single cheek cut at the upper end. These hip rafters butt against the side of the ridgeboard at its end. When there is a common rafter at the end, as in Fig. 10-15, each hip rafter gets a double cheek cut. The cut at the bird's mouth is shaped like an arrowhead. The tail cut may be a plumb cut if there is no fascia; otherwise it must also be a double cheek cut. You must shorten the hip rafter at the ridge, but the shortening is now half the 45° thickness of the ridgeboard, not the right angle thickness. And you must bevel the tops of hip rafters on each side of the center line. Otherwise the edges of hip rafters will be higher than the tops of common rafters, and jack rafters won't fit properly.

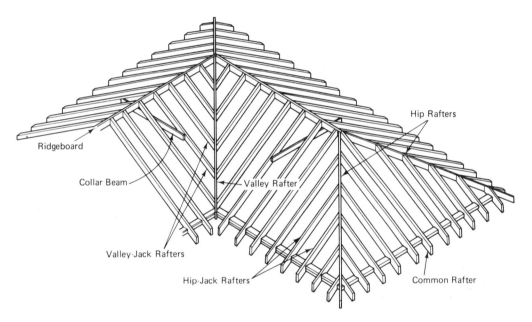

**Fig. 10-15.** The hip roof at the end of the wing shown here has one common rafter that butts against the end of the ridgeboard. Note that wherever a jack rafter meets a hip rafter or valley rafter there is another jack rafter on the other side.


## Cutting Valley Rafters

If your vacation house has a wing, you will need valley rafters where the two roof planes meet. You calculate the length of a valley rafter in the same way as a hip rafter—by multiplying the body length of a common rafter by 1.414. A valley rafter has no tail, however; it ends at the rafter plate (see Fig. 10-15). The upper end gets a double cheek cut.

### Cutting Jack Rafters

*Hip-jack* rafters run from the eave to a hip rafter. They have the same seat and tail cuts as a common rafter. At their upper ends, however, they get a diagonal cheek cut. The difference in length between adjacent rafters is the common difference, as in gable studs. This time, however, the common difference is the rafter spacing stated in feet times 1.414. Measure the common difference on the long side of jack rafters.

*Valley-jack* rafters run from the ridge to a valley rafter. They get a plumb cut at the ridge like a common rafter and a diagonal cheek cut at the tail. They have no seat cut.

Jack rafters always meet each other at right angles, but on the opposite sides of hip and valley rafters. So when you calculate the length of one jack rafter, you always have another of the same length, but with an opposite cheek cut.

## INSTALLING ROOF TRUSSES

Cutting rafters and building a roof is not as difficult as it looks on paper. However, it does require careful calculations, accurate marking, and clean and accurate cutting.

You can avoid some of the work by using trusses. In most areas of the country you can buy trusses made to order. There are dozens of different designs, the most common of which is the single-plane W truss (Fig. 10-16). It consists of two upper chords, each the length of a common rafter, and a heavier lower

**Fig. 10-16.** Typical roof truss. There are many different designs, but the W truss is among the simplest to build and easiest to install.

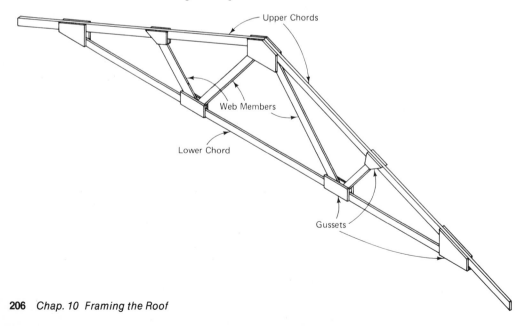

chord like a ceiling joist. Chords are attached to each other with *gussets*—metal or plywood plates that act as stiffeners. Between the chords are web members connected with more gussets at their ends.

The truss manufacturer designs the truss to the dimensions required and for the expected live and dead loads. Trusses are delivered to the site already assembled and ready to swing into place. Hang them on the rafter plates upside down and then pivot them up into position on the marks on your rafter plates. This work usually takes four people, two on the ground and two astride the walls. Once the trusses are in position, toenail at the rafter plate as with any common rafter. Then plumb the end trusses carefully and run a temporary brace across all trusses near the ridge. This brace also acts as a spacer and straightener; a truss roof has no ridgeboard. But trusses don't solve all roof problems. You must still add fly rafters and gable ends to a gable roof, and build by hand the part of a hip roof that lies beyond the end trusses.

## FINISHING A SHED ROOF

In a shed roof all long rafters except end rafters overlap at a bearing partition (end rafters butt). Interior ends needn't be cut. Tail cuts are usually plumb cuts, and each rafter gets a parallel cut at the other end (Fig. 10-17). If the roof's pitch is no greater than 2 in 12, you don't need to cut bird's mouths. With steeper pitches you must cut them in both ends of each rafter.

In the end walls under a shed roof each stud is slightly longer than the one next to it—the common difference again. You can build end walls as ordinary walls with a triangular gable above, or as a single wall with long studs notched to accept the end rafter. In the latter case, however, the bearing partition continues to the edge of the floor (Fig. 10-17) and is as long as the front and rear walls. This partition is bracketed by studs as in post-and-beam construction.

## FINISHING A FLAT ROOF

Flat roofs are similar to low-pitched shed roofs in that the ends of rafters usually overlap a bearing partition at least 6″. Rafters have no bird's mouths, however, and the ends are usually cut square.

Construction at corners is quite different. At a point 32″ from the corner you double the rafter. To the doubled rafter you attach *lookouts*—short lengths of the same rafter material—with framing anchors. Set the first lookout about 16″ from the corner and continue to a similar point at the next corner. Then frame as shown in Fig. 10-18.

There are no angled cuts in a flat roof except for double cheek cuts on the diagonal lookout at the corner. If working drawings call for joists 2 × 10 or heavier, you can improve the exterior appearance of your vacation house by tapering the outer ends of joists and lookouts and using a narrower fascia. A 1 × 6 or 1 × 8 fascia is in better scale than a 1 × 10 or 1 × 12.

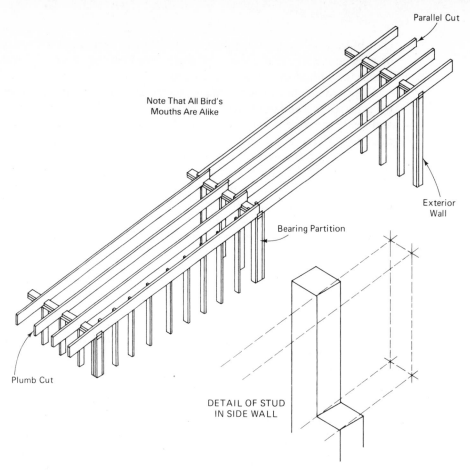

Parallel Cut

Note That All Bird's
Mouths Are Alike

Exterior
Wall

Bearing Partition

Plumb Cut

DETAIL OF STUD
IN SIDE WALL

**Fig. 10-17.** Ends of rafters in a shed roof that meet over a bearing wall are not cut, but outside ends get parallel plumb cuts. If the roof's pitch is steep enough, bird's mouths are needed at the partition. Bearing partitions are flush with the outside edge of the floor and with the end rafter, which is supported on notched studs (inset).

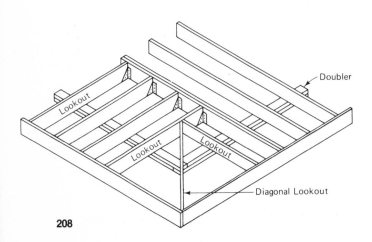

Doubler

Lookout

Lookout

Lookout

Diagonal Lookout

**Fig. 10-18.** Typical construction of a flat roof at the corners and side walls. The length of side lookouts is generally about twice the amount of overhang.

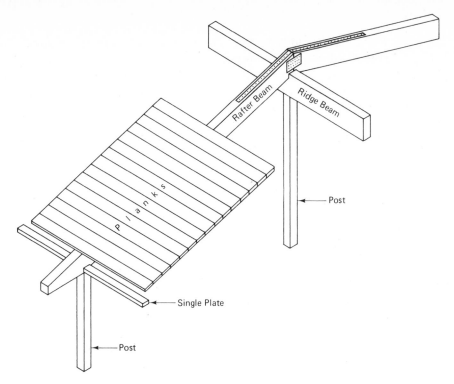

**Fig. 10-19.** A heavy ridge beam is supported by posts in the middle of the house and in the end walls in post-and-beam construction. Rafter beams bear on the ridge beam and posts in end walls. Sheathing is 2″ planks. Note that there is no doubler needed in post-and-beam construction.

## PLANK-AND-BEAM ROOFS

Post-and-beam construction has many variations, but for the amateur the simplest has roof beams supported every 4′ or 8′ on centers. The lower ends of these beams are cut like a common rafter and rest on a single top plate directly above posts (Fig. 10-19). At their upper ends the beams meet over a main horizontal beam and must be notched to fit over and rest on this beam.

Where two beams meet, connect them with gussets on each side and a metal strap across the top. Planks that run at right angles to the rafters form a diaphragm that gives the whole roof structure its required strength. This type of roof needs no sheathing.

## APPLYING ROOF SHEATHING

All other types of roof must be sheathed. Under wood shingles the sheathing must consist of boards with spaces between them. Under all other kinds of roofing materials, including wood shakes, the most commonly used sheathing is

1/2" exterior grade plywood. There's no need to buy the top grade; C–C unsanded grade is adequate for sheathing.

Before you start to sheathe look over the entire roof structure for anything protruding above rafter level. Then pick up a piece of sheathing and check all four corners for square. You must start with an absolutely square piece.

Start sheathing on the unbraced half of the roof. Work from the lower left corner of the roof if you're right-handed. Lefties usually find it easier to start in the lower right corner. Lay each sheet of plywood with the long dimension across the rafters. Set the bottom edge flush with the ends of rafters if you intend to add a fascia; otherwise let the bottom edge overhang about 1/2" to protect the ends of rafters from rain damage.

Set the inner edge of the sheet (the edge away from the roof's edge) on the center line of a rafter, and nail. Let the outer end overhang for the moment. Space eight-penny common nails or seven-penny threaded nails every 12" into each rafter. After each sheet of sheathing is in place, attach H-clips to the open edge between rafters to support the next sheet and to create a tight fit.

Alternate full sheets and half sheets as you work up the *rake* (side edge) of the roof, so that no two adjoining sheets meet on the same rafter. At the ridge let the top sheet overlap; then trim it at the angle of the opposite slope. When you reach the top of the other slope, trim at the opposite angle. After all sheathing is installed, trim the outer edges with a power saw. Snap a chalk line as a cutting guide.

To keep sheathing dry, cover it with building paper immediately. Unroll a roll of two-ply kraft paper along the bottom edge overlapping enough so that water will run off without touching the sheathing. At the rakes of the roof double the paper over about 6" so that you have two layers to nail through. Use regular roofing nails; the only purpose of nailing is to keep the paper from blowing away.

On a roof with a pitch of 5 in 12 or steeper, lap each strip of paper 4" over the layer below it. For lower pitches overlap these amounts: 6" on a 4 in 12 pitch, 9" on a 3 in 12, 12" on a 2 in 12, and 18" on a flat roof.

At the ridge, which you cover last, carry the paper down the other side at least 9" so that you have a double layer on both sides.

When you sheathe a roof with a steep pitch, a series of walking steps can help you keep your footing and give you a handhold when you need it. *Walking steps* are long 2 × 4s laid flat on the sheathing across the roof. Nail the first walking step just above the eave and others about 5' apart as you work up the roof. Nail them through sheathing into rafters for maximum safety. Remove the steps when you finish sheathing, and reuse them when you apply shingles.

### Sheathing Under a Wood Shingle Roof

Wood shingles soaked by rain or snow must be allowed to dry evenly to prevent splitting and rotting. Air must circulate under them as well as over them. Plywood sheathing doesn't permit this air circulation; therefore you must sheathe with boards.

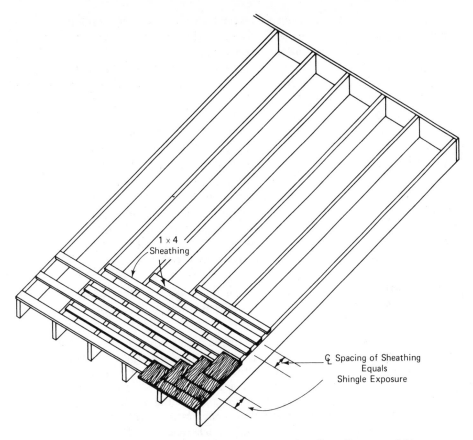

**Fig. 10-20.** Solid sheathing may be used under all roofing materials except wood shingles. Here boards serve as sheathing, and they are spaced in relation to the amount of exposure of the surface shingles.

You can use 1 × 3, 1 × 4, or 1 × 6 boards laid with spaces between them. To determine the spacing, you must first work out the exposure of the shingles (exposure is covered in detail in Chapter 13). Standard exposure is from 5″ to 7 1/2″. Space 1 × 6 boards so that the distance from center line to center line is twice the shingle exposure (Fig. 10-20). Space 1 × 3s and 1 × 4s so the spacing is equal to the exposure.

As with plywood sheathing, the ends of boards must rest on the center lines of rafters, and the joints must be staggered between courses. Two eight-penny nails in each rafter is adequate.

### Special Conditions

When you come to a hip or valley, use your pitch board to determine and mark the correct bevel of cut; this is always the angle between the hypotenuse and the shortest side of the pitch board. Then continue right around the corner with the course of sheathing.

Stop sheathing at the edges of framed openings, as for a chimney. Where a pipe goes through the roof, as it will somewhere, you must do some figuring. As soon as you can determine the exact location of the center of the pipe, hang a plumb bob from the sheathing until it points at that center. Mark the underside of the sheathing with an *X* at this point. Then drive a long nail vertically through the sheathing from below; the nail will guide you in cutting the hole from the roof's surface.

Let's say that you must make a cut for a 3″ vent pipe. To allow a little working room, but still keep the opening small enough to seal easily, plan for a hole 3 1/4″ in diameter. Mark this diameter on the long side (not the hypotenuse) of the pitch board. Also mark the center, which will be 1 5/8″ between the other marks. With your square draw lines from all three marks at right angles to the long side. Then set the hypotenuse of the pitch board *along* the slope so that the center mark lines up with the nail through the roof. The distance between outer marks on the hypotenuse is the length of the oval hole to be cut.

Now set the pitch board *across* the slope with the long side down. The distance between marks is the 3 1/4″ width of the hole. Sketch an oval through the four points on the roof; this is your cutting guide. Remember to make a vertical cut; do not cut perpendicular to the sheathing.

The roof construction shows clearly in this photograph of a partially finished A-frame vacation house. Heavy rafters are spaced 24″ apart and were assembled on the subfloor with two sets of collar beams. The ridgeboard fits into a notch and serves only as a spacer. Rafters are covered with plywood sheathing exposed as a ceiling. Spacers nailed over sheathing into rafters support board sheathing and allow a flow of air beneath the roof's exposed surface. *Photographer: Kelly Severns. Courtesy American Plywood Association.*

# INSULATING A SLOPING CEILING

Where rafters or ceiling beams are exposed in rooms, insulating well is a difficult problem. You can always fit insulation between rafters and cover it with a finished ceiling material. But this is a slow, tedious process, and the effect isn't as exciting as it should be. Only part of the rafters is exposed, and they look weak instead of sturdy.

One solution is to lay finished ceiling material as a sheathing across rafters. You can use plywood, gypsum planks, or rigid insulation, but 2″ planks of redwood, cedar, or cypress look better. Then attach 2 × 4s atop the planks over the rafters, running up the roof (see photograph). These 2 × 4s act as spacers, and you apply sheathing to them. You can fill the areas between 2 × 4s with insulation if you plan much cold-weather use of the house, since it will help somewhat. Otherwise leave the areas empty. In hot weather they act as draft chutes to carry trapped hot air away from the planks. The chutes work best in combination with ridge ventilation.

For a textured ceiling, consider rigid insulation. It may be made of different kinds of foams or mineral wool. It comes in various thicknesses, and in sheets that are usually 2′ wide and 8′ long. You apply it with nails and sheathe directly over it. Rigid insulation may be painted, but it doesn't require it.

# VENTILATING

It isn't necessary to insulate between rafters if you have already done so between ceiling joists. However, it is important to ventilate the space between insulation and sheathing.

In attic space under a gable roof that is not used for living, louvers are the simplest answer. You can buy adjustable metal louvers that fit just under the ridge in gables. Allow at least one square foot of free ventilating area for every 300 square feet of attic floor area. *Free ventilating area* is the area of the louver opening less all obstructions, such as the louvers themselves or screening.

Other types of roof require a different solution. You can ventilate the narrow spaces between rafters effectively with a *ridge ventilator*. This is a metal device with a very low profile that is scarcely visible from the ground. It runs from one end of the ridge to the other. With a ridge ventilator you stop sheathing 1 1/2″ short of the ridge on each side, and cover the gap with the ventilator. Nail through its flanges. Ridge ventilators come in sections that fit together with watertight gaskets. You apply finish roofing material over the flanges.

You can also ventilate at the eaves. This method is the only answer with a shed or flat roof, and it works well in any roof style in conjunction with a ridge ventilator. Figure 10-21 shows three ways of ventilating at the eaves. With exposed rafter ends you must leave a continuous gap in exterior wall materials (A) and cover the opening with screening and a small molding. With enclosed rafter ends, you can set individual vents in the soffits (B) or install a continuous vent (C) manufactured for this purpose.

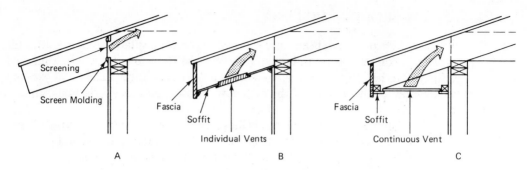

**Fig. 10-21.** You can ventilate a roof at the eaves in three ways: through screened vents in the walls (A), through screened vents in soffits (B), or through a continuous vent in a suspended soffit (C).

## TOOLS YOU WILL NEED

To build the ceiling and roof structure, the following tools and equipment are the necessary minimum:

    power saw
    folding rule
    pitch board (which you make)
    adjustable square
    layout tee (which you make)
    hammer
    crosscut saw
    carpenter's square (or framing square)
    scaffolding (which you can build)
    plumb bob
    chalk line
    stepladder (6′ to 8′)
    extension ladder
    metal shears

# Building

# A Fireplace

Any vacation house that has a fireplace or is heated by any device that burns wood, gas, oil, or coal must have a chimney. The purpose of a chimney is to create a draft that will draw off the gases of combustion and exhaust them well above ground level.

Many factors affect draft. Two relate to the site. A chimney at sea level draws better than the same chimney in the mountains, because the air at sea level is heavier. The flow of air across the top of a chimney helps draft; the greater the flow the better the draft. Therefore a chimney on a meadow will draw better than a chimney in a forest.

One of the conditions you considered when you looked at sites was the prevailing winter breeze. Air needs a path for reaching the chimney and continuing past it. The smoother this flow of air, the better the chimney works. The worst possible condition is an obstruction, such as a stand of trees or a cliff, on the upwind side. Air flows over the obstruction and causes a downdraft in the chimney. Good chimney design reduces problems with downdraft, but it won't eliminate them.

There are two types of fireplaces and three types of chimneys. You can build a fireplace or buy one ready to install. A chimney may serve only a fireplace, only a heating plant, or both.

# PARTS OF A FIREPLACE

A fireplace has four closely interrelated parts—the combustion chamber, throat, smoke chamber, and flue. The chimney is the protective coating around these elements.

The *combustion chamber* is the space where you burn the logs. It is formed by the back and two sides of the fireplace. Dimensions A to F in Figs. 11-1 and 11-2 affect the chamber's shape; the relationship of dimensions is extremely important. The slope at the back of the combustion chamber (height F and depth C reduced to G) is critical. This slope directs the smoke and gases of combustion with increasing speed toward the throat and at the same time throws the flame forward and heat outward into the room.

*The throat* is the narrowed opening between the combustion chamber and the smoke chamber through which smoke and gases flow. Its shape is governed by dimensions A and G. A damper fits across the throat. It controls the upward draft when you have a fire and keeps cold air out of the room when you don't.

*The smoke chamber* is shaped like a truncated pyramid. Its dimensions narrow from a width of H and a depth of I at the base to a width of M and a depth of L at the top. The damper and smoke shelf form the bottom. At the top

**Fig. 11-1.** Parts of a chimney and fireplace, with details of construction. The dimensions denoted by letters are variable; they relate to the chart in Fig. 11-2.

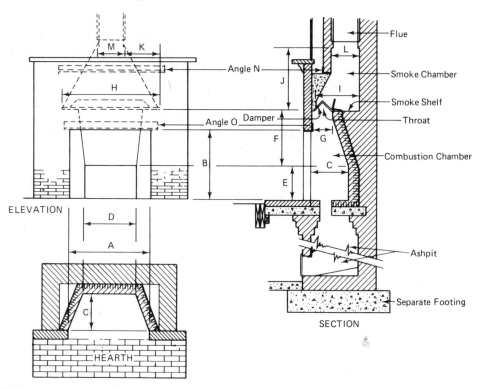

the smoke chamber leads into the flue. The smoke shelf is almost horizontal. Its purpose is to direct any downdraft back up the flue.

The *flue* is the vertical stack through which smoke and gases are carried to the outside air. The flue is lined with clay tiles, which are available in four rectangular, two square, and seven round sizes (Fig. 11-2).

| FINISHED FIREPLACE OPENING | | | | | | | ROUGH BRICK WORK AND FLUE SIZES | | | | | | |
| --- | --- | --- | --- | --- | --- | --- | --- | --- | --- | --- | --- | --- | --- |
| | | | | | | | Other Dimensions | | | | Flue Sizes | | Steel Angles* |
| A | B | C | D | E | F | G | H | I | J | K | L × M | R | N | O |
| 24 | 24 | 16 | 11 | 14 | 18 | 8¾ | 32 | 20 | 19 | 10 | 8 × 12 | 8 | A-36 | A-36 |
| 26 | 24 | 16 | 13 | 14 | 18 | 8¾ | 34 | 20 | 21 | 11 | 8 × 12 | 8 | A-36 | A-36 |
| 28 | 24 | 16 | 15 | 14 | 18 | 8¾ | 36 | 20 | 21 | 12 | 8 × 12 | 10 | A-36 | A-36 |
| 30 | 29 | 16 | 17 | 14 | 23 | 8¾ | 38 | 20 | 24 | 13 | 12 × 12 | 10 | A-42 | A-36 |
| 32 | 29 | 16 | 19 | 14 | 23 | 8¾ | 40 | 20 | 24 | 14 | 12 × 12 | 10 | A-42 | A-42 |
| 36 | 29 | 16 | 23 | 14 | 23 | 8¾ | 44 | 20 | 27 | 16 | 12 × 12 | 12 | A-48 | A-42 |
| 40 | 29 | 16 | 27 | 14 | 23 | 8¾ | 48 | 20 | 29 | 16 | 12 × 16 | 12 | A-48 | A-48 |
| 42 | 32 | 16 | 29 | 14 | 26 | 8¾ | 50 | 20 | 32 | 17 | 16 × 16 | 12 | B-54 | A-48 |
| 48 | 32 | 18 | 33 | 14 | 26 | 8¾ | 56 | 22 | 37 | 20 | 16 × 16 | 15 | B-60 | B-54 |
| 54 | 37 | 20 | 37 | 16 | 29 | 13 | 68 | 24 | 45 | 26 | 16 × 16 | 15 | B-72 | B-60 |
| 60 | 37 | 22 | 42 | 16 | 29 | 13 | 72 | 27 | 45 | 26 | 16 × 20 | 15 | B-72 | B-66 |
| 60 | 40 | 22 | 42 | 16 | 31 | 13 | 72 | 27 | 45 | 26 | 16 × 20 | 18 | B-72 | B-66 |
| 72 | 40 | 22 | 54 | 16 | 31 | 13 | 84 | 27 | 56 | 32 | 20 × 20 | 18 | C-84 | C-84 |
| 84 | 40 | 24 | 64 | 20 | 28 | 13 | 96 | 29 | 61 | 36 | 20 × 24 | 20 | C-96 | C-96 |
| 96 | 40 | 24 | 76 | 20 | 28 | 13 | 108 | 29 | 75 | 42 | 20 × 24 | 22 | C-108 | C-108 |

**Fig. 11-2.** Fireplace dimensions given in inches. Letters relate to dimensions in Fig. 11-1.

*Angle sizes are: $A = 3'' \times 3'' \times 3/16''$; $B = 3\,1/2'' \times 3'' \times 1/4''$; $C = 5'' \times 3\,1/2'' \times 5/16''$.)

# BUILDING THE BASE

Before you reach fireplace level, you must provide a solid chimney base. As pointed out earlier, a chimney must have its own footing totally independent of any other footing in the house. Between the footing and the hearth, inside the base, is an ashpit. The door to the ashpit opens into a basement, or to the outdoors if you build over crawl space or on a slab.

By the time you start to build a chimney, all structural framing is usually completed. It should be; it's easier to adjust the dimensions of a chimney to fit the openings through a structure than to adapt a structure to a chimney.

Build the chimney base centered on its footing. Up to the level of the bottom of the ashpit it should be solid masonry—brick or stone—with all joints solidly mortared. Continue upward another three or four courses on the back and sides, to the level of the top of the ashpit door. Then, using these sides as a form (Fig. 11-3), pour a floor of cement sloping toward the cleanout door.

Across the door opening fit a steel angle. If your drawings don't specify the size, use a $3'' \times 3'' \times 1/4''$ angle and set it as shown in Fig. 11-3. Its length should

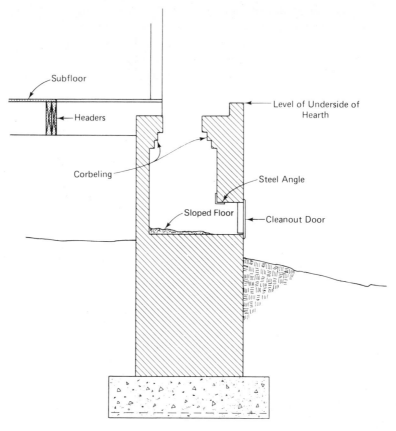

Subfloor

Level of Underside of
Hearth

Headers

Corbeling

Steel Angle

Sloped Floor

Cleanout Door

**Fig. 11-3.** Section through a chimney from footing to hearth.

be the width of the door opening plus 4″. Be sure when you set the frame for the ashpit door in place that it fits tightly against the bricks and the angle, because the slope of the ashpit floor will direct ashes against the door.

With the door in place continue straight upward with masonry until you are about a foot below hearth level. At that point begin to narrow the opening by corbeling the sides. In *corbeling,* you let each course project slightly farther inward than the course below. You want the ashpit large to hold as much ash as possible, but you must provide proper support for the hearth; this is the reason for corbeling.

## LAYING THE HEARTH

A hearth is an extension of the floor of the fireplace. It may be at floor level, but if the floor of the fireplace is raised above floor level, the hearth is usually raised also or omitted entirely. The hearth protects the floor area around the fireplace from damage by sparks and hot coals. With a fireplace screen you don't need a hearth, but the screen absorbs a lot of heat and reduces the effectiveness of a fireplace as a means of heating a room.

The hearth must be supported, and the simplest support is a reinforced concrete slab. One end of the slab rests on a ledger attached to headers at the fireplace opening in the floor. The other end ties into the chimney. Figure 11-4 shows construction of a typical hearth. Its dimensions may vary, but as a rule, a hearth should cover an area that is 24″ from the front of the fireplace and twice as wide as the opening (dimension A in Fig. 11-1).

Let headers around the opening act as forms on three sides of the fireplace; the chimney itself is the fourth form. If you continue the slab beneath the combustion chamber, remember to form for the opening to the ashpit. For a bottom form use 3/4″ plywood, with its surface oiled, supported on 2 × 4s nailed firmly into ledgers with double-headed nails. Remove the form after the slab has cured.

The total thickness of a hearth should be at least 6″. The slab itself should be at least 4″ thick and reinforced with #4 bars 6″ on centers. The total depth depends on the thickness of the hearth material you use. Its surface should be flush with the room's finished floor, not the subflooring, so allow for this difference when you decide on the depth. Set the hearth material in a good bed of mortar and carry it to the edge of the combustion chamber, but not into it.

**Fig. 11-4** Cutaway isometric of construction for supporting the hearth.

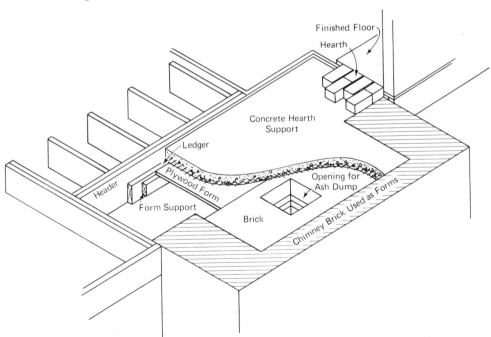

# SHAPING THE COMBUSTION CHAMBER

The floor of the combustion chamber, called the *inner hearth,* must be made of firebricks. A *firebrick* is a brick made of special clay that won't crack or crumble from the heat of a fire. Lay firebricks flat in a bed of *fireclay mortar*—a mortar also specially formulated to withstand intense heat. The total thickness of the inner hearth should be about 3″.

The walls of the combustion chamber are also firebricks, but here they are laid on edge in fireclay mortar. Begin by laying courses of back-up chimney masonry to about the level of the start of the slope at the back of the chamber (refer to Fig. 11-1). Above that point, lay firebricks first across the back of the fireplace, then at the sides. By having the back bricks run behind the side bricks, you let the sides help to support the back on the slope upward.

From hearth level upward lay all chimney bricks or stones (not the firebricks) in a cement mortar; type N is the best for this purpose. The greatest danger in a chimney is a fire resulting from poor masonry work. It is extremely important to lay every stone or brick in a full bed of mortar, with all joints filled flush with the surface of the masonry. This warning applies to all stages of chimney construction, but it is of critical importance where the chimney passes through framed openings in the ceiling and roof.

# FORMING THE THROAT

Continue upward with back-up masonry and firebricks, until you reach the top of the fireplace opening (dimension B in Fig. 11-1). At this point set a steel angle across the back of the opening, with one leg pointed upward and the other toward the room. The correct angle size is shown in the chart (Fig. 11-2) as angle O.

When masonry reaches the level of the throat, set the damper in position so that it is supported level on all four sides. Although the damper must be fully supported, it must not be built solidly into the chimney. Intense fireplace heat will cause the damper to expand, and it must be able to expand freely; otherwise it will crack the masonry around it.

# BUILDING THE SMOKE CHAMBER

The sides of a smoke chamber can be built with masonry formed against sheets of 1/2″ plywood. There is a better method, however: use metal lining plates, which have a smoother surface than masonry and help the smoke chamber operate more efficiently. The plates also act as forms for the back-up masonry around them. The dimensions in Fig. 11-2 that determine the size of the smoke chamber are J, K, and L.

At the top of the inward slope of the front wall of the smoke chamber, set angle N (Figs. 11-1 and 11-2) to support the remainder of the chimney. Shortly above that point you install any mantel. From then upward, except for one bit of corbeling to support the flue, the chimney dimensions are constant.

Some experts in chimney design believe that you can help the operation of a smoke chamber by covering the smoke shelf with a bed of mortar that is rounded at the damper and inside corners (refer to Fig. 11-1). The curves help to aim errant downdrafts back up the chimney as directly as possible.

## INSTALLING THE FLUE

By the time you set the first flue tile, the hardest part of chimney work is behind you. Now accuracy becomes important, and you should check your work constantly for plumb and overall dimensions.

Set flue tiles in type N mortar—the same mortar you use for joints in chimney masonry. Fill all joints full, and smooth them flush on the inside of the flue. Cut away excess mortar with your trowel. After you set each tile, check it for plumb. Build the chimney as you build the flue, stopping a few inches short of each tile joint to give yourself room for setting the next tile.

You'll have some odd-shaped spaces between the flue and chimney masonry, particularly if you use round tiles. Fill these voids with mortar to hold the flue firmly and to prevent any smoke from seeping through poor mortar joints—which you won't have, will you? In large voids you can set pieces of broken brick or stone in the mortar. This not only reduces the chance of cracks but saves on mortar.

Where the chimney passes through the ceiling, be sure to maintain at least 2″ of clearance between it and the wood framing on all sides. Pack the gap with fire-resistant insulation. To support the insulation, form a flexible joint with a strip of metal bent into a U shape (Fig. 11-5). This metal will eventually be hidden behind ceiling material.

As you approach the roof rafters, plan ahead so that the top of a tile lies just below the rafter bottoms. In order to get the heights to work out right, use a half-tile here if necessary. Set the half-tile while you are working in the attic. Set the tile that penetrates the roof while you are working from the roof's surface (its top will be above the roof line, as seen in Fig. 11-5). Make sure you maintain the 2″ clearance as you build the chimney through the roof opening.

## CAPPING THE CHIMNEY

If you have built the chimney of brick, switch from common bricks to face bricks as soon as you break above the roof line. Make the change after two courses of brick are exposed on the ridge side of the roof. You must cover lower courses with flashing anyway, so they will not be visible from the ground. Common bricks and face bricks are structurally equal, but common bricks are less expensive and less attractive in appearance.

Many materials are used for flashing—some good, some not so good—and new ones are being developed all the time. *Flashing* is both a material and a process to waterproof joints where two surfaces meet at an angle. For sealing the opening through the roof at a chimney, metal flashing is the best answer. It may

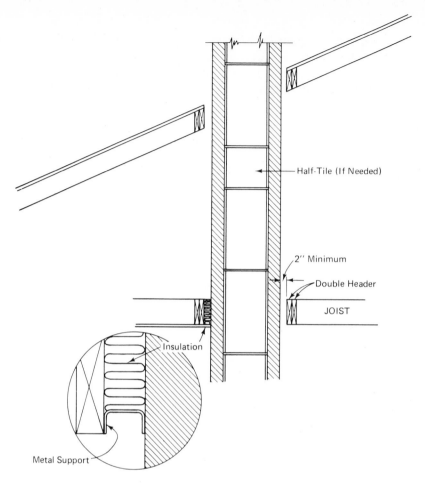

**Fig. 11-5.** Details of chimney construction through openings in the ceiling and roof. Inset shows method of insulating between wood and masonry construction.

cost you more money than other types, but you won't be using enough flashing for its cost to be significant; you may avoid future repairs.

Embed flashing in a mortar joint. Extend the end well into the joint (at least 1″) and put an upward crimp in this end (Fig. 11-6). The crimp keeps water from seeping into the joint between masonry and flue. Bend the flashing over the masonry course below it and fit it tightly against the vertical surface. Extend the flashing 8″ on all four sides; it fits under roof shingles on the sides and up-slope, and over shingles on the down-slope. At the sides bend the last 1/2″ of metal 180° so that water won't run under the shingle.

The top of the uppermost section of flue tile must rise at least 24″ above the highest point of the roof. This is not just where the chimney comes through the roof, but the highest point anywhere—usually the ridge. Complete the flue to its top before finishing the chimney masonry around it.

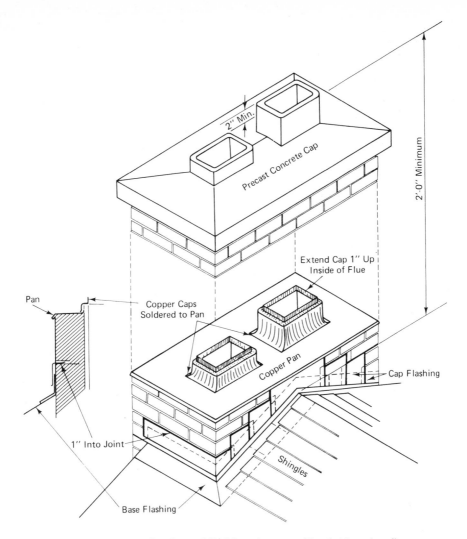

**Fig. 11-6.** Details of metal flashing above roof level. Note that flues are flashed between the top and the next to top lengths of flue tile, and the entire horizontal surface of the chimney is flashed several courses of brick below the top course. As shown in detail at the left, most flashing is done with two sheets of metal, the upper sheet overlapping the lower sheet. Lower ends of flashing are bent double to strengthen and stiffen the edge.

It's possible to cap a chimney with brick or stone laid up with watertight masonry joints. For the amateur, however, a concrete cap is better and surer. In many communities you can buy a precast cap made to fit your chimney. It projects beyond the masonry and has a drip edge on the underside that keeps rain water from streaking the chimney. Where the flue penetrates the cap, fill the joint full of mortar.

# FITTING A SMOKE PIPE

Appliances such as furnaces and wood-burning stoves need a smoke pipe to exhaust smoke and gases of combustion. A smoke pipe may exhaust directly outdoors through a wall, or else it may exhaust into a central chimney through its own flue. It cannot exhaust into a flue from a fireplace, nor can two appliances exhaust into the same flue.

A smoke pipe may be run no closer than 18″ to combustible material. Where it enters the chimney it fits into a metal or clay ring called a *thimble*. Set the thimble in place as you build the chimney, with its inside edge flush with the inside of the flue. The smoke pipe should never extend into the flue itself; this would restrict the flow of exhaust too much.

The top of any second flue in a chimney must be at least 2″ higher or lower than the adjacent flue. This difference in height prevents exhaust from one flue flowing down the other one.

# TESTING CHIMNEY OPERATION

After you complete the chimney and allow all mortar to cure, run a smoke test. Light a smudge fire in the fireplace. When smoke begins to pour out of the chimney, cap the flue with a piece of plywood. Then look over the entire length of the chimney on all sides and at all levels to see whether smoke is coming out at any mortar joint. This is a sign of danger, and you must repair all joints in the area of the leak. Where there is smoke now, there could be fire later.

# OTHER TYPES OF FIREPLACES

Several companies manufacture complete fireplace units that either stand on legs or hang on a wall and are bolted into position. They are attractive, low in cost, and easy to install. They don't provide as much heat as a large fireplace, but they do take the chill from a cool room. Made of metal, they require no footing and no masonry work. They come with a sectional metal chimney, which you install like a smoke pipe. Maintain the clearances specified by the manufacturer at walls, ceiling, and roof.

Some manufacturers also make circulating fireplaces. These are steel units that fit into an ordinary chimney and replace all the chimney parts from hearth to damper. When installed, a circulating fireplace looks much like a masonry fireplace, although its design and operation are different. It can completely heat a small vacation house.

In the wall of the chimney is an air intake. Air entering the intake travels behind the steel rear wall of the circulating fireplace. A fire in the fireplace heats the steel wall, which in turn heats the air drawn into the intake. Heated air then flows into the room through grills in the fireplace's breast. To heat more than one room, you run ducts to grills in other rooms and add a small circulating fan.

Mornings are often chilly in the New Hampshire woods, and this manufactured fireplace removes the chill. It is set in a corner of the living area where it does not block the view of woods and water, and it is angled to heat lounging and play areas. Note that the window above the main entrance door frames a living picture of the forest. *Photographer: Eric M. Sanford. Designer: M. P. Reed.*

## OTHER TYPES OF CHIMNEYS

Chimneys don't have to be built of masonry, although masonry chimneys are usually more appropriate to the appearance of vacation houses. Several manufacturers make prefabricated chimneys for use with furnaces and boilers, and some types can even be used with fireplaces.

Prefabricated chimneys come in sections, usually 18″ or 30″ long. Some types are made of two stainless steel casings with insulation between them. Others have a flue lining wrapped in a wall of lightweight, insulating cement. With both types you stack one length atop the next, sealing and locking the joints as you work upward. The manufacturer provides all necessary parts, and you can complete the assembly with ordinary hand tools.

Manufactured chimneys fit between standard joist and rafter spacings without headers. At a ceiling, set a thimble on ledgers attached to joists and nail through its flanges. Thread the chimney through the thimble from above and lock it onto the section below. At the roof, use a similar thimble that can be adjusted to the pitch of the roof. Flash carefully at this thimble.

Above the roof line you can leave the open pipe exposed or conceal it in a metal housing finished to look like brick. Trim the housing to fit the roof's slope and add the cap that is included as part of the package.

## TOOLS YOU WILL NEED

To build a masonry chimney as outlined in this chapter, you will need the following tools:

trowel
mortar board
mason's level
metal saw
power saw
hammer
wire brush (for cleaning off dried mortar)
plumb bob
metal shears
folding rule
pliers (for crimping metal)

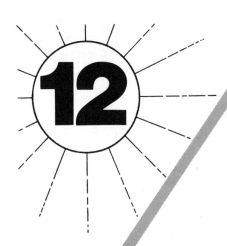

# Finishing Off
# Openings

The windows in a vacation house serve the same purposes as windows in the house back home. They let in light. They provide ventilation. They allow you to see out. This is the order of importance in the city house; however, in a vacation house the order of importance is reversed.

As you study plans for vacation houses, take special note of the window arrangement. Sometimes windows don't do well the jobs for which they are intended, especially the job of letting you see your views. Think of views in the plural, because you usually have more than one. And check the windows for these qualities:

    1.   In living and dining areas window sills should be low enough so that you can see the full view at eye level when seated. This means sills should be at table height in the dining area and as close to the floor as practical in living areas.

    2.   Large uninterrupted glass areas help to make the interior more a part of the outdoors.

    3.   Windows with many small panes may look rustic, but they obstruct the view and make cleaning more difficult. Large glass areas tend to be somewhat self-cleaning.

    4.   One large window does a better job than a group of small ones. The view is better, light is better, and interior light intensity is more even.

5.   The higher the head of a window in a wall, the farther light penetrates into a room. On the other hand, a tall, narrow window lets in less light than a wide, shallow window of the same dimensions. The difference is in the amount of reflected light.

6.   Screens block out both light and view. Therefore, locate operable windows out of the main line of view if possible.

7.   Place operable windows so that they direct a flow of air either at or past the furniture in which you are most likely to be sitting.

8.   In bedroom and bath areas, where privacy is more of a consideration, light is of little importance and ventilation is quite important. The bedroom view to be considered is what you see while lying in bed.

9.   In the kitchen, windows should be close to counter level for best light, and should if possible face a different view than windows in the living area.

10.   Overhangs on the south keep out summer sun—and a lot of light, too. Overhangs on the west and east provide little control over the setting and rising sun.

Large panes of glass march around this living area to give a panoramic view of the world outside. Although windows are fixed, wide doorways provide good cross ventilation. Low window just above bench level provides a porthole view for the short creatures in life—small children, dogs, and cats. *Architect: Charles Moore. Photographer: Morley Baer. Courtesy California Redwood Association.*

Although the plans you have selected call for one type and size of window, there is nothing to prevent you from making changes. But be cautious. Compare the rough opening dimensions shown in the window schedule with the rough opening dimensions of the windows you want to use. There may be only a few inches difference, but those inches may mean changes in the locations of studs and the lengths of cripples.

If you make a change in height, maintain the position of the header and lower or raise the sill. If you make a change in width, try to maintain the center line. Just make sure that, if you widen a window, you won't displace a pipe or heating duct or affect the structural strength of the exterior wall.

Before you make any decision to change windows, take a sheet of tracing paper and lay it over the elevation in the drawings that will change. Trace the base, eave, and roof lines, and the positions of other openings. Then carefully sketch in the new windows. If the change you want to make is slight, the chances are you won't see much difference, and you can proceed. But if the change doesn't look right, don't make it. After all, the designer of the house did have reasons for selecting the windows he drew. Those reasons may be better than your reasons for wanting to change.

## SELECTING WINDOWS

Wood windows are generally more suitable for vacation houses than metal windows. You can buy them in several ways; see your building materials dealer to find out what options you have.

Some windows come already assembled in their frames. All you have to do is set the frames in the rough openings. Sometimes windows even have the glass in place. Or you can buy the windows assembled and the frames unassembled—called *knocked down* and referred to as *K.D.* With this type you assemble the frames on the site, and fit the windows into the frames as you assemble them. K.D. windows are a little less expensive than those already in their frames. Assembly is not difficult, and the manufacturer provides instructions.

Whichever type you buy, you can be fairly certain that the parts are manufactured to close tolerances and will fit well. Nevertheless check the dimensions of all frames carefully upon delivery to make sure they fit your rough openings. If they don't measure to the dimensions the manufacturer specifies, send them back. Your dealer will replace them.

Windows often come with a prime coat of paint or stain on them. If not, apply paint liberally to the sides and ends of all parts. Use a good quality primer, and wipe off any excess paint from those surfaces where windows move in their frames.

### Types of Windows and Their Parts

Windows that don't move are called, quite logically, *fixed windows*. They have no moving parts and no hardware. They provide no ventilation, but are ideal for framing a view. Screens aren't required. In cold climates order fixed windows double-glazed—that is, with two panes of glass separated by a vacuum.

*Sliding Windows.* There are two types of sliding windows. Double-hung windows slide up and down. One movable section, called a *sash,* covers the other section when the window is open. Double-hung windows provide only 50% ventilation—all at the bottom, all at the top, or split between top and bottom. There are counterbalances in the frame that keep sash from moving by gravity. The two sash meet and lock at a horizontal check rail. For hardware you need a locking device and a pair of handles. Screens and storm windows fit on the outside.

Sliding or gliding windows slide from side to side. Sliding windows move in parallel tracks. They provide 50% ventilation—all at one side or the other, or split between sides. Gliding windows on the other hand are side by side when open, but in line when closed. They provide 50% ventilation at one side only. In both types the sash meet at a vertical check rail. Like double-hung windows they require locks and handles. There are no counterbalances. Screens and storm windows fit on the outside.

*Swinging Windows.* Swinging windows operate on hinges or brackets and provide 100% ventilation. There are three types: casements, awning windows, and hopper vents.

*Casements* are hinged at the side. They are designed to swing out, but they can be installed to swing in if you have the clearance in the room for their operation. Casements come singly, in pairs, in groups up to five wide in a single frame, or as pairs flanking a fixed sash. When you order a single casement, you must specify the hand. Order a right-hand casement if you want the hinges on the right as you face the window from the outside. Any casement sash may be fixed or hinged on either side, but adjacent sash cannot swing toward each other. Screens and storm windows fit on the inside.

Casement hardware varies, but it is supplied by the manufacturer. Minimum hardware includes hinges, a pushbar for opening and closing, and a latch. The best hardware includes extension-type hinges, a crank for operation, and a latch to complete a tight seal.

*Awning windows* are hinged at the top. They open out either on a pair of hinges or on pivots and brackets set into the frame. Good quality awning windows have pivots on both sides to prevent racking. You swing the windows out by hand. The handle is a latch that also locks the sash. Screens fit inside, and sometimes have a door that you reach through to operate the latch.

Awning windows are quite versatile. You can install them individually, as in a bathroom. You can use them in a horizontal band, as in a kitchen between counter and upper cabinets. You can use them in a vertical stack, as in a bedroom, for good privacy and ventilation. Or you can group them to fill a whole wall, as in a living room. By building a structural grid (Fig. 12-1) and setting each awning sash individually, you can achieve a strong wall with full ventilation. But you will also have a lot of wood in the way of any view.

A *hopper window* is hinged at the bottom and opens inward. It is actually an awning window installed upside down and inside out. Screens fit on the out-

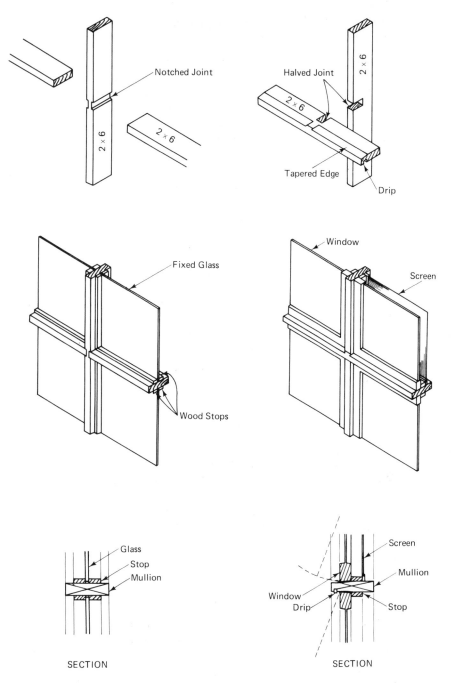

**Fig. 12-1.** A window wall needs some support between panes of fixed glass (left strip) or operating sash (right strip). The drawings show details of jointing (top), the finished window wall (center), and a typical section (bottom).

side. Hopper windows are seldom used by themselves except in basements. More often they are used in combination with other types of windows.

*Combinations.* In living areas a combination of several types of windows is sometimes the ideal answer to the desire for light, air, and view. A band of hopper windows just above the floor lets in ventilation at the proper level when you're sitting down. Just make sure that the hoppers don't interfere with the operation of draperies or other window treatment, and won't be in any traffic pattern where they will cut shins and trip the unwary. Above the hoppers fixed windows let in an unobstructed view. Above the fixed windows a band of awning windows lets out the warm air trapped near the ceiling. Awning sash should be above the head level of anyone walking outside them. If your roof has little overhang, you can leave awning windows open during all but a driving rain. The open sash will shed the rain away from the window opening.

*Jalousies.* A *jalousie window* is made somewhat like a Venetian blind except that the slats are made of glass 4″ wide. The glass slats are fitted into a frame of wood or metal at the factory. When you turn a crank, all the glass plates pivot at or near their centers in the frame. When opened to a horizontal position, jalousies yield about 90% ventilation. When closed, each plate overlaps the plate below for a close fit.

Jalousie windows are usually made to order and are more expensive than other types, but they have one big advantage. When open, they take up no more air space than the wall they are installed in. You can adjust the angle of the glass to suit wind and rain conditions, and lock the jalousies in that position. Screens fit inside.

## ADJUSTING ROUGH OPENINGS

Decide before you begin construction what windows you want to order, but don't schedule delivery until you have the roof completely finished. In the normal sequence of building you will install windows after the roof is shingled but before you apply exterior wall materials. Windows and frames must be protected from the weather and should be stored where they won't accidentally be bumped and knocked out of square.

As you store each window, check its dimensions to make sure it will fit into the rough opening you have built for it. If you find you must adjust any opening, go ahead and prime the window frames. While the paint is drying, make the adjustments.

If you have to adjust the height of an opening, carefully remove the sill member, setting it aside for reuse. Then remove the bottom cripples. Replace them if they are too short, or trim them if they are too long. Then reassemble the framing, this time rechecking your measurements at every step.

If you must narrow an opening 1/2″ or less, add a strip of plywood of the necessary thickness to one side. To correct an error of more than 1/2″, add strips of equal thickness to both jambs. Maintain the center line of the opening.

To broaden an opening, add a stud against the full-length stud forming one side of the structural frame. Then carefully remove the jamb stud (the shorter stud between header and sill) and rip it to the proper thickness, or replace it with a strip of plywood. You must have two full-thickness studs on both sides of any opening; you can't just rip or notch the jamb stud without adding the full-length stud.

## ASSEMBLING K.D. FRAMES

Knocked-down frames come with all parts packaged or taped together. Find the head and two jamb pieces and paint the rabbeted ends where they join. Then fit the three pieces together on the subfloor, using your square inside the frame to guide you to a right-angle fit.

Use 8-penny coated nails with 1″ jamb stock, and 16-penny nails with heavier stock. Drive three nails through the jamb into the head, placing no nail closer than 1/2″ to the edge. Then drive three more nails in the other direction—through the head into the jamb. By nailing from two directions you keep the joints from opening up. Wipe off any excess paint that has oozed out of the joints.

Now nail the sill in place to complete the box. Nail upward through the sill into jambs, making sure that the sill is centered and that you have the correct space between jambs. Then square the frame.

The tongue and blade of a framing square aren't long enough to serve as a tool for squaring window frames. A diagonal rod is better. Cut one end of a 1 × 4 into a right-angle point (Fig. 12-2) and fit the point into one corner of the frame. At the other end of the rod mark the angle with a pencil. Then move the rod to the other diagonal and mark again. If there is a difference between marks, gently rack the frame until the two diagonals are identical in length.

**Fig. 12-2.** The best tool for squaring window and door frames that you assemble yourself is a diagonal rod. One end is cut to fit into a corner of the frame, and you check the square by measuring the diagonals.

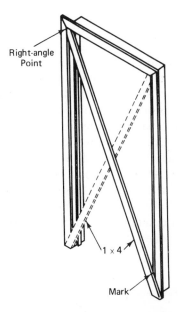

Right-angle
Point

1 × 4

Mark

233

To maintain square, temporarily nail a 1 × 2 diagonal brace across the inside edge of the frame.

Next fit and nail exterior casings and moldings. Cross-nail at corners. Elsewhere space eight-penny casing nails about 9" apart. Countersink nail heads about 1/16" and fill holes with putty as you finish each frame. As you attach casings, be careful to keep all margins constant by measuring accurately. Nail at the ends first. Joints in casings must be tight, but nailed without setting up any stresses in the frame.

The molding that hides the outside edges of double-hung windows and hopper vents, and the inside edges of casements and awning sash, is called a *blind stop* (Fig. 12-3). Often the frame is notched for the blind stop so that you have no trouble locating it accurately. Attach it with six-penny coated nails.

Double-hung windows also have a *parting strip*—a thin molding of wood or metal that hides the inside edges of the upper sash (Fig. 12-3) and forms a groove in which both sash slide. Cut and fit the parting strip at the head first, then fit side strips to hold the head strip in place. Don't nail the parting strip now, however; you would have to remove it to set the sash. Wait until you install the frame in its opening, and then nail the strip with four-penny finishing nails driven into its face.

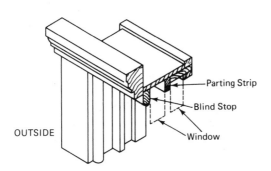

**Fig. 12-3.** Isometric section through the head of a window shows the locations of a blind stop and a parting strip.

Parting Strip

Blind Stop

OUTSIDE

Window

## SELECTING EXTERIOR DOORS

Exterior doors either swing or slide. Swinging doors are usually made of wood and have either flush or paneled surfaces. Sliding doors are made with a metal frame, and run on tracks or in grooves at top and bottom.

Most entrance doors to vacation homes are flush doors. *Solid-core* flush doors have a center of wood blocks laminated with glue under pressure. The surfaces are a veneer of 1/4" plywood. *Hollow-core* flush doors have a center made of cardboard, wood strips, or a honeycomb of paper surrounded by an inner frame of wood. Surfaces are 3/16" plywood. Hollow-core doors weigh only a third as much as solid-core doors, but they do not have as good an insulating value, and they tend to warp when there is a big difference between indoor and outdoor temperatures. Either type of flush door may have small openings for panes of glass.

Swinging doors come in four sizes for exterior use. Heights are either 6 ′ 8 ″ or 7 ′ 0 ″. Widths are either 2 ′ 8 ″ or 3 ′ 0 ″. Thickness is always 1 3/4″. Main entrance doors are usually 3 ′ 0 ″ by 7 ′ 0 ″, and secondary doors are 2 ′ 8 ″ by 6 ′ 8 ″.

Door frames are quite similar in construction to window frames. They come assembled or K.D., but rarely with the doors in them. Because door frames take more stress than window frames, they are built of heavier stock. The best door jambs are rabbeted for the door (A and B in Fig. 12-4). The door fits into the rabbet on one side, and a screen door fits into the rabbet on the outside. Less expensive door jambs have a door stop either mortised into the jamb (C), or attached to its surface (D). Thresholds are a separate item.

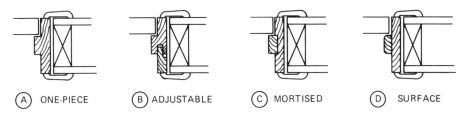

   A  ONE-PIECE       B ADJUSTABLE       C MORTISED       D SURFACE

**Fig. 12-4.** The four common types of exterior door jambs.

# SETTING WOOD-FRAMED WINDOWS AND DOORS

You can set window frames any time after the roof is on and walls are sheathed. Hold off installing door frames until all interior finishing materials are in the house. Otherwise you may easily damage a frame as you bring in materials.

First flash every opening all the way around. Building paper is adequate for this purpose. Use strips about 12″ wide, stapling or nailing them to the sheathing. Flashing should extend a little beyond the edge of sheathing at any opening so that it covers behind the casing of a door or window. Flashing details for various conditions are shown in Fig. 12-5.

## In Stud Walls

In most vacation houses the heads of window frames are at the same height as the heads of door frames. Usually this height is shown on an elevation or section. If not, you can determine it by adding the height of the main entrance door itself, the thickness of finished flooring material, and the thickness of any threshold.

To simplify the job of setting frames at the proper height, make two story poles. A *story pole* is a 2 × 2 cut to the exact height you just calculated. Work-

**Fig. 12-5.** Sections through heads, jambs, and sills of windows and doors in frame construction (left) and brick veneer construction (right) show where to locate flashing. The purpose of flashing is to keep water from entering around joints at wall openings.

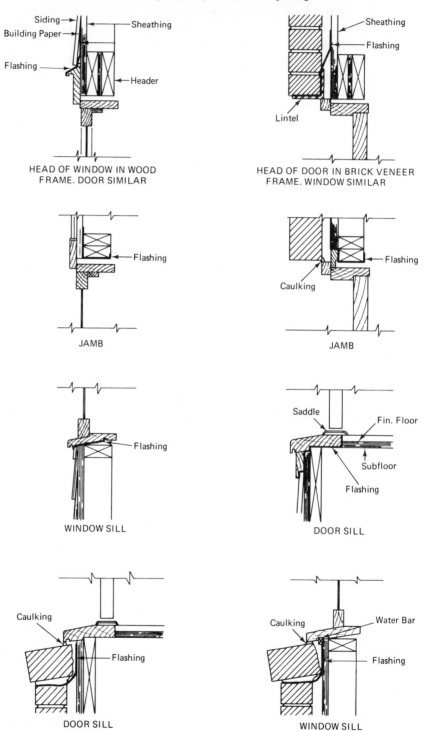

HEAD OF WINDOW IN WOOD
FRAME. DOOR SIMILAR

HEAD OF DOOR IN BRICK VENEER
FRAME. WINDOW SIMILAR

JAMB

JAMB

WINDOW SILL

DOOR SILL

DOOR SILL

WINDOW SILL

ing inside, one person rests the frame on the story poles, while the other sets the frame.

Set the frame in its opening from the outside until it rests on the story poles. Then gradually raise the frame into position and center it in the opening. Place shims under the sill, spaced about 12″ apart. Wood shingles make excellent shims. Set your carpenter's level on the sill and gently tap on the shims until the frame is plumb. Then place a shim behind one upper outside corner of the casing and drive a nail partway through the frame and shim into the header. Drive the nail only far enough to hold the frame in position. At the opposite upper corner place another shim and just start a nail into the casing. Recheck the level of the head of the frame before you drive this nail partway in.

Once again check the frame for square and the sides for plumb. Adjust the shims to establish plumb; as far as possible keep the gaps between frame and jambs equal. When the frame is exactly where you want it, nail part way into the studs and sill at the two lower corners. Again recheck the plumb at the jambs and level at head and sill. Only then is it safe to remove the story pole and complete the nailing.

Nail cautiously, using eight-penny casing nails spaced no more than 12″ apart. Make certain that all nails penetrate into structural members. Stop hammering when nail heads are still about 1/16″ above the surface (1/8″ when you toenail). Use a nailset to drive the nails about 1/16″ below the surface of the casing. If you see a crack develop as you drive any nail, remove it gently. Use a nail puller or claw hammer resting on a block of scrap wood to protect the frame. Then drill the hole and renail. Putty all holes before you move on to the next window. And stuff the cavities around the frame full of insulation.

You should follow these general procedures when you are ready to set frames for wood exterior doors. Support the frame not only on story poles, but on wood or plywood blocks of the same thickness as finished flooring material. If the flooring material is very thin, use a piece of the material itself.

Remove the protective plywood that you placed over the sill earlier. Then recheck the level of the top of the sill. Set the threshold in place and trim the ends to fit the opening if necessary. As soon as you are certain that your door will clear the threshold, remove it; you won't install it permanently until you lay the finished flooring.

As with windows, start work at the top corners with shimming and partial nailing. At one door jamb place shims behind the hinges. The standard locations for hinges on an exterior door are 7″ down from the top, 11″ up from the bottom, and at the midpoint between these two locations. At the other door jamb set wedges opposite the top and bottom hinge locations and also behind the lock and any deadbolt. Standard locations are 36″ above the floor for the lock and 60″ above the floor for any hand-operated security bolt.

Before you complete final nailing, recheck the clearance above the threshold. Then drive and set all nails and putty the holes. Replace the protective cover at the sill; you may need a thinner material now that the door is ready to hang.

## In Brick Veneer Walls

Wood window and door frames made for installation in brick veneer walls are slightly different than frames made for use in stud walls. The casings are only about half as wide at the heads and jambs because they fit into rather than over the opening (see Fig. 12-5). Installation procedures at head and jamb are identical with those for wood walls. After each frame is flashed and set, however, you have to caulk the joints between the frame and masonry to seal out leaks of air and water.

Before you set a window frame in a brick veneer wall, look at the shape of the underside of the sill. Some types have a straight slope with a small rabbet for flashing. Others have a notch cut in them like the bird's mouth of a rafter. This latter type of sill rests on the structural sill; it sometimes requires a small cleat, called a *water bar,* to support the sheathing (Fig. 12-5). Both types of sill extend about an inch over the rowlock course of bricks below. You must caulk fully between the two to seal the joint.

# SETTING METAL-FRAMED DOORS

The standard height of framed glass doors is 6 ′ 8 ″. The standard width for a pair of doors is 5 ′ 0 ″, 6 ′ 0 ″, or 8 ′ 0 ″. The doors themselves are about an inch thick at the edges and 1 1/2 ″ thick where they overlap and interlock. The surrounding frame is about 3 3/4 ″ wide.

Sliding doors are quite heavy, and the supporting sill must be absolutely level in both directions. Following the manufacturer's instructions, set the sill section of the frame first, then the jamb sections, and last the head. Frames are pre-drilled for attachment with Phillips-head screws.

# STAIRWAY DESIGN

Because a stairway slopes, some of the terms in stair construction are the same as in roof construction. The rise of a stairway is the overall height from finished floor to finished floor (Fig. 12-6). The vertical height from step to step—a *riser*— is the equivalent of the unit rise. The run of a stairway is its overall length between the edges of the first and last steps in a flight. The horizontal depth of each step—a *tread*—is the equivalent of the unit run.

Risers and treads are not only distances, but the names of parts of a stairway. Every stairway has treads—the horizontal part of a step that you put your weight on. Most stairways have risers—the vertical part of each step. The diagonal supports under treads and risers are called *strings, stringers,* or *carriages* in various parts of the country.

The design of any stairway between floors in your vacation house has been worked out according to standard rules. As long as you build the stairway opening, run, and rise as called for in the drawings, your stairway will be satisfactory, safe, and comfortable to climb or descend.

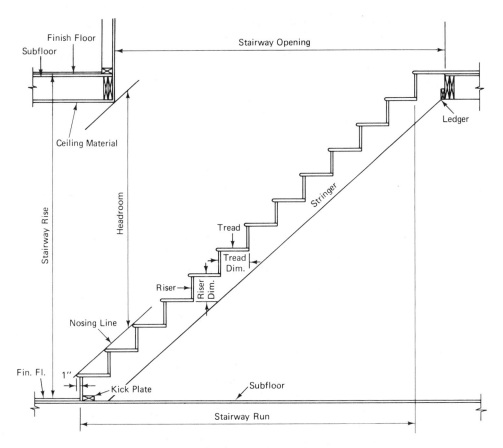

**Fig. 12-6.** In this section through a typical inside stairway are all the parts and terms that you need to know to build one.

But you may be designing your own stairway outdoors—to get from a deck to ground level, for example. Here are the basic rules to follow:

1. Maximum height of a riser is 8 1/4″. A height between steps of 7″ to 7 1/2″ is more comfortable and safer.

2. Minimum depth of a tread is 9″. A depth of 10″ provides better footing for descending.

3. The product of the height of a riser ($R$) times the depth of a tread ($T$) should be about 75 ($R \times T = 75$).

4. The sum of the height of a riser plus the depth of a tread should be between 17 and 18 ($R + T = 17 - 18$).

5. The sum of twice the height of a riser plus the depth of one tread should be between 24 and 25 ($2R + T = 24 - 25$). A stairway with a 7 1/2″ riser and a 10″ tread is just about perfect for meeting rules 3, 4, and 5.

6. Minimum headroom for main stairways is 6′ 8″, although 6′ 4″ is enough for basement stairs. This dimension is measured vertically between the

*nosing line* (an imaginary diagonal line through the leading edge of all treads) and any overhead obstruction, such as a ceiling, beam, or overhang.

7. Hand rails should be attached 30″ to 34″ above the nosing line. All stairways with more than three risers should have at least one hand rail, placed on the right side as you descend.

8. Frequently used stairways should be at least 36″ wide at the tread. If there are hand rails on both sides, 42″ is better. Basement stairways can be as narrow as 30″.

9. Landings between flights should be square if space permits, with each dimension equal to the width of a tread.

## CHECKING STAIRWAY DIMENSIONS

You can buy complete stairways at some woodworking shops, but they may be hard to find in isolated vacation areas. If you don't want to tackle the job yourself, hire a good finish carpenter to do the work. Stairways aren't difficult to build, but there is little room for error.

For that reason, regardless of who builds the stairway, begin work by verifying all major dimensions. First check the stairwell opening for level—across each end and along both sides. If the level is off more than about 1/8″ in width, try to shim the subfloor to establish the correct level.

A handy tool for building a stairway is a *stair pole,* which is somewhat like a story pole. Use a straight 2 × 4 long enough to reach from floor to floor; 12′ is a good length. Set the stair pole in one corner of the stairwell absolutely plumb. On the stair pole mark the exact heights of the finished floors—not the subfloors. Cut two small pieces of finished flooring and tack one down at the head of the stairwell at the edge of the opening (Fig. 12-7). Keep the other piece handy at the lower floor level.

Then on the stair pole mark the ceiling height if you are building an inside stairway, or the height of any obstruction above ground level at the foot of the stairway if you're building outside. Remember to allow for the thickness of any ceiling material. From the ceiling or obstruction mark measure down 6′ 8″ and make another mark. This is the headroom mark. (Measure only 6′ 4″ if you're building a basement stairway).

The distance between the two finished floor marks is the total rise of your stairway. Check this dimension against your working drawings; usually you'll find this dimension on a section through the house.

From a corner of the opening at the top of the stairway drop a plumb bob to mark this point on the lower subfloor. Then on the lower floor at the other end of the stairway mark the location of the first riser. The distance between the two marks is the run of the stairway (Fig. 12-7).

If you don't find the position of the bottom riser dimensioned anywhere in the drawings, you must figure it out yourself. Move your stair pole back into one of the two corners of the stairwell above the lower steps. Hold it so that the

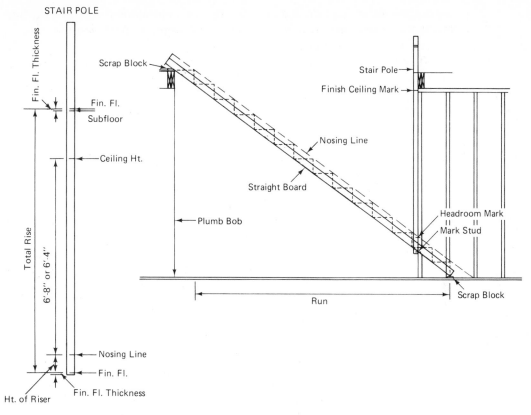

STAIR POLE

Fin. Fl. Thickness

Scrap Block

Fin. Fl.

Subfloor

Ceiling Ht.

Plumb Bob

Nosing Line

Straight Board

Total Rise

6'8" or 6'4"

Nosing Line

Fin. Fl.

Fin. Fl. Thickness

Ht. of Riser

Stair Pole

Finish Ceiling Mark

Nosing Line

Headroom Mark

Mark Stud

Run

Scrap Block

**Fig. 12-7.** A stair pole (left) is very useful in laying out any stairway properly. Section at right shows how to use the stair pole and a straight board to find the run of a stairway and the nosing line.

ceiling height mark is at the future finished ceiling height of the lower story (Fig. 12-7). Then, at the finished floor mark, draw a line across a nearby stud. This line marks the bottom edge of risers at that point.

Next, find a long length of straight board. You'll need at least a 16-footer. Set the upper end on a scrap of flooring and slide the board down the wall until its lower edge crosses the mark you made on the stud. Holding the board against this line, continue to slide it down until its lower end rests on another scrap of flooring. Where the board touches the flooring is the point of maximum stairway run.

When you have located the first riser, measure one tread width beyond this point and set the scrap of finished flooring there. Then measure up the height of one riser above the upper scrap of flooring and mark a stud. Place the long board with the bottom edge touching the new mark at the top and the scrap flooring at the bottom, and draw across all possible studs along this edge. This line marks the nosing line. It must be below the headroom mark you made at the beginning of this procedure.

If this seems like a lot of effort just to check some dimensions, it is. But you can't build a stairway without going through every step. The reason: you must establish and verify the heights of risers and depths of treads before you can cut the supporting stringers. And you can't verify dimensions of risers and treads without knowing the rise and run of the stairway.

Suppose the drawings tell you that your stairway should have 13 risers @ 8" each and 12 treads @ 9 1/4" each. There is always one more riser than tread because the top tread is the upper floor. Therefore the rise of your stairway should be 104" or 8' 8", and the run should be 111" or 9' 3". If the rise and run that you measured aren't the same, you either measured wrong or built something wrong. Go over all your measurements again. If they are still correct, you must develop new dimensions for risers and treads.

To do this, divide the number of risers you want or need into the total rise. Similarly, divide the number of treads into the total run. Be accurate to the nearest 1/16". Remember that the points of measurement for the run do not match the measurements of the stair opening.

## BUILDING A STAIRWAY

The next step is to determine the length of stringer required. To support most stairways you need a pair of stringers cut out of 2 × 12s. Use three stringers when a stairway is more than 42" wide.

The minimum length of each stringer is the dimension of the hypotenuse of a right triangle. The length of one side of the triangle is the rise of the stairway. The length of the other side equals the run plus the depth of one tread. In the example above, then, the length of one side of the triangle is 104" (8.67'), and the length of the other is 111" + 9 1/4", or 120 1/4" (10.015'). Add the squares of these two numbers and you get 75.1 + 100.3, or 175.4 square feet. The length of the stringer is the square root of this number, or 13.25'. Therefore you need 2 × 12s 14' long for the job.

### Laying Out Stringers

The easiest way to mark stringers is with a pitch board like the one you use to mark rafters. Accurately cut a right triangle out of a piece of plywood, with its sides exactly equal to the height of a riser and depth of a tread. The angle between them must be 90°.

Starting at the lower end of the stringer, use your pitch board to mark the angle of the floor line. Carry this line all the way across the stringer (Fig. 12-8). Then, still using your pitch board and working up one edge from the floor line, mark the contours of the stairway on each stringer.

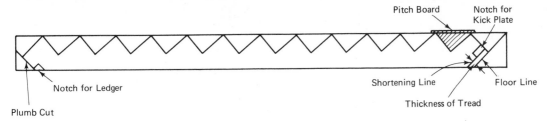

Fig. 12-8. Using a pitch board, mark all the angled cuts required to shape a stringer.

At the back of the top tread make a plumb cut parallel to all riser lines. At the bottom of the stringer you have to shorten the height of the first riser by the thickness of a finished tread.

A strong stairway is supported at both ends by 2 × 4s (Fig. 12-6). Notch the stringers to fit over the ledger at the top and the kickplate at the bottom.

## Attaching Stringers

To give stringers maximum strength, set the upper ends flush with the top of the header at the upper level and nail into joists or trimmers with 16-penny nails. A pair will do for now. Then set the ledger in place against the header, using 16-penny nails at top and bottom, spaced about every 6″, to hold it tight.

At the bottom ends of stringers, position and nail the kickplate through the subflooring and into structural lumber if possible. Then nail twice at each stud and drive two more nails into joists. If the lower floor is concrete, attach the kickplate with concrete nails that require a special power gun.

## Fitting Risers and Treads

Large lumber dealers carry treads and risers as a stock item, and you cut them to the dimensions you need. Risers have a shiplapped edge at the upper end and are rabbeted in one side near the lower end (Fig. 12-9). Treads have a shiplapped end that fits into the rabbet in the riser, and a rabbet that accepts the shiplapped end of the riser. Only the bottom riser and top tread are not rabbeted.

Fit risers first, using six-penny nails. Nail straight into stringers just below the shiplapped end, and toenail into stringers just below the rabbet. As you position each riser, make sure that the back side of the shiplapped end lies as flush as possible with the cut in the stringer for treads.

Glue is the fastener for treads. An aliphatic resin glue provides an excellent bond. Spread the glue liberally into both rabbets. Push the end of the tread well into the rabbet in one riser, and press it firmly onto the end of the next riser below. If you do a good job of gluing, you won't have to nail treads to stringers. The next day, however, after the glue has dried, drive nails carefully at three points into the ends of treads through the backs of risers in order to hold the entire stairway assembly tight. For best appearance add a small cove molding (Fig. 12-9) under the nose of each tread.

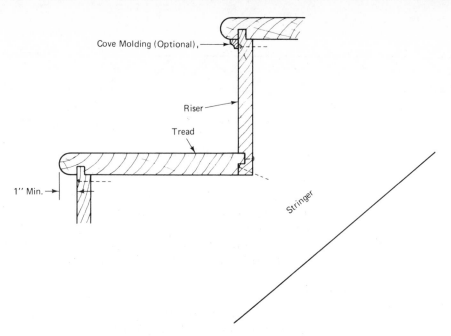

**Fig. 12-9.** Sectional detail through a riser and tread shows how they fit together and where they should be nailed.

A stairway that rises in a room doesn't have to have risers. There are two ways to build a simple stairway of this type. You can cut the stringers as already outlined, and then nail the treads at four points along their edges into each stringer. This method is typical of many basement stairs. For a more finished look, mark the outline of each tread on the stringers, and then mortise out the shape to a depth of about 1/2″. Slide the treads into the mortises from the undersides of the stringers and toenail through stringers into treads. With this second method you may assemble the entire stairway before you fit it into position.

### Adding Hand Rails

When a wall forms one side of the stairwell, attach the hand rail to the wall. Support the rail on brackets fastened with screws driven all the way into studs near each end of the railing and near its midpoint. You attach the hand rail to the brackets with screws also.

When there is no wall to support a hand rail, it rests on a newel post at its lower end. For maximum strength and safety, cut a hole in the subfloor for the newel and nail it to the side of a floor joist (see Fig. 12-11). You can butt a stringer and treads against the newel, but the assembly is stronger if you mortise.

### Building a Landing

Sometimes space does not allow a straight stairway, and it must turn a corner. The safest way to turn a corner is with a landing. A *landing* is a platform between two flights of steps. It has a framework of 2 × 4s either nailed into wall studs or supported on cripples (Fig. 12-10). Upper and lower stringers butt against the framework. Kickplates aren't required.

Build the landing first and attach it with 10-penny nails through the sides into studs and through a bottom plate into floor joists. Then cut the stringers as you would for a straight stairway. Treat the surface of the landing as a large tread.

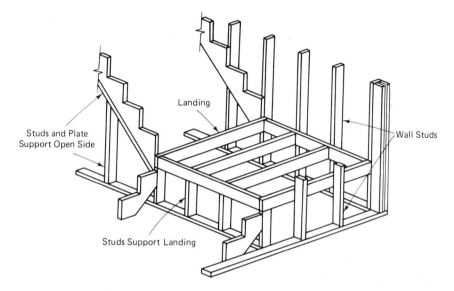

**Fig. 12-10.** Detail of landing construction. You always build and secure the landing before you cut the stringers. Note that the stringer on the open side of a stairway is supported on studs and a plate, similar to construction of a gable under a roof.

## Cutting Winders

When a stairway must turn and there is no room for a landing, you need winders. *Winders* are nonrectangular treads that radiate outward from a newel post (Fig. 12-11). Winders may be a hazard, so avoid them if possible. Two rules govern the shape of winder treads. First, the depth of each winder at its midpoint should be no less than the depth of a standard tread. Second, winders should taper, not to a point, but to a depth of not less than 2".

Build the straight part of the stairway first. Then cut winder risers to length; they get parallel bevel cuts at their ends. Cut and fit treads next and add the newel last. By studying Fig. 12-11 you can see that the stringer won't be straight at its upper edge, and the longer stringer must be built in sections carefully fitted together.

When space is extremely tight, you can buy winding stairways of metal in standard sizes. All treads are winders attached to a center pole which provides basic support. Follow the manufacturer's instructions to determine the proper rise to allow for, and the method of support for the outside edges of treads.

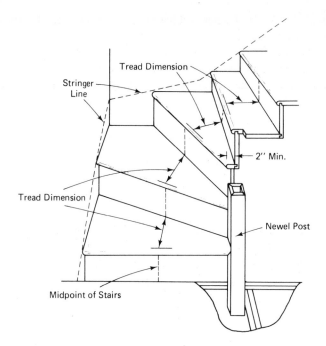

**Fig. 12-11.** Partial cutaway of a stairway with winders illustrates the two rules of design, as well as construction at a newel post both above and below floor level.

## TOOLS YOU WILL NEED

To install windows, doors, and stairways, you wil need at least the following tools:

crosscut saw
nail puller
wood chisels
hammer
paint brush
carpenter's square
folding rule
story pole (which you make)
nailset
power drill
stapler
putty knife
caulking gun
Phillips-head screwdriver
stair pole (which you make)
steel tape
plumb bob
pitch board (which you make)
screwdriver

# Finishing the Exterior

The kraft building paper you laid over roof sheathing for protection won't protect it for long. It needs a finished roofing material. For pitched roofs with a slope of at least 5 in 12 you can use asphalt, wood, or asbestos-cement shingles, or you can use metal. For pitches between 2 in 12 and 5 in 12 you can use only asphalt shingles, metal, or tar and gravel. On flat roofs tar and gravel is the best answer.

In making a selection of exterior materials there are a number of factors to weigh. First and most important, the materials must be adequate for the job of protecting the structure. They must be reasonably easy to apply and reasonable in cost. They must be appropriate to the surroundings. They must be in scale with the size and shape of the house. And all exterior materials must be compatible with each other.

If you respect the limitations of materials and apply them properly, the roof and wall materials you choose will do their job properly. All materials are fragile—even bricks break—but when handled with care and according to standard procedures, they are reasonably easy to apply.

Beyond these two points, where taste and appearance become factors, the choice is a little more difficult. Do you want your vacation house to blend into its site, or stand out from it? You can achieve either result by selecting materials with their scale, color, and texture in mind. Wood siding may look as out of place on a sandy shore line as stucco in the woods. Yet wood is common as an exterior wall material along New England's coast.

One of the secrets of an attractive exterior is contrast. Exterior materials should first contrast in quantity. One must dominate. In an A-frame design, for example, more roof shows than wall. Therefore the roofing material is dominant and will govern your choice of other materials. In a house with a flat or low-pitched roof, the roof may not be a factor at all, and the contrast must appear in the wall materials.

Materials should also contrast in texture—one smooth and one rough—to take full advantage of the beauty of reflected light. In a house with large glass areas, the glass itself counts as a material—smooth in texture, light in tone.

Materials should contrast in tone—one light and one dark. Color is a factor here, too. The general rule for using exterior colors is: one dark, one light, one

Steep roof of cedar shingles reflects the rugged terrain and sheds heavy mountain snows. Shingles are laid with staggered butts as described in this chapter. Note how roof texture contrasts with the smoothness of large glass areas, and how roof angles contrast with the vertical lines of siding and railing. *Photographer: John Fulker. Courtesy Red Cedar Shingle and Handsplit Shake Bureau.*

bright. Again, one must dominate. Usually the bright color is an accent, perhaps on an entrance door or roof trim. If walls are light in tone and color, then the roof should be dark. With dark walls the roof should be light. For good appearance it is very important that colors and textures and tones be noticeably unequal in quantity. Otherwise the eye can't decide which part of the house to look at, and the view brings no pleasure.

Good designers take all these factors into account when they develop exteriors. They vary the quantities and textures, and choose materials in the proper scale. The decision on color, however, is up to you. And the choice usually begins with the roofing material, since it goes on first.

## ASPHALT SHINGLES

For most vacation housing probably the roofing material that is most economical and easiest to work with is asphalt shingles. They are made with a heavy felt base saturated in asphalt, topped with a coating of asphalt sprinkled with mineral chips.

Of the dozen or so shapes in which asphalt shingles are made, the most common is strip shingles. Half of each shingle is exposed, and the other half is covered by the shingle above it. Strip shingles have two, three, or four *tabs*—the exposed fingers of roofing. The mineral chips provide the color on the tabs; the covered half of the strip is solid asphalt. The range of colors is broad—solid colors from white to black, and many variegated color blends. Dark colors absorb heat; light colors reflect it. A dark roof makes a house look smaller and lower than it actually is, while a light roof makes it look larger and taller.

The weight of shingle to order is 240-pound. That is the weight of a *square*—100 square feet of coverage. You order shingles by the square; they come packed in corrugated boxes.

### Applying Strip Shingles

In parts of the country with heavy snowfall, cover the entire edge of the roof sheathing with 4″-wide strips of 26-gauge galvanized metal. Let the strips extend over the edge of the sheathing about 3/4″ at overhangs and 1″ at rakes. Overlap about an inch at joints (Fig. 13-1, bottom). These strips support the edge shingles and prevent them from breaking under loads of snow and ice.

To lay an asphalt shingle roof, start at one lower corner of the roof with a strip of roll roofing called a *selvage edge* (Fig. 13-1, center). The proper width varies according to local weather conditions; your supplier can suggest what width to use. Nail the selvage edge every 6″ along the lower edge, and every 12″ at the upper edge. As an alternative to a selvage edge you can use regular strip shingles laid upside down, with the notches away from the eave.

Each strip shingle has a little notch at the sides. With a roofing knife cut one side square and lay this shingle with the squared edge along the rake of the roof. Set it flush with the metal stripping at the eave if rafters are exposed. If

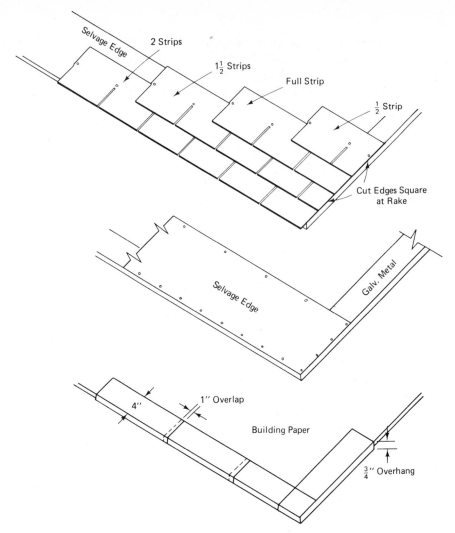

**Fig. 13-1.** An asphalt shingle roof needs metal strips at the eaves and rake (bottom) and a selvage edge over the metal at eaves (center). Top drawing shows the proper method for laying the first few courses and where to nail.

you intend to add fascia and trim, let the shingle overhang the selvage edge about 3/4″ at both rake and eave.

Attach shingles with roofing nails. Their heads should be at least 3/8″ in diameter, and the shanks long enough to penetrate 3/4″ into sheathing. Normal nailing procedure calls for a single nail just above each slit between tabs and at each end in the same line. A three-tab shingle, then, gets four nails (Fig. 13-1, top). In areas of high wind, use a pair of nails above each slit, or a total of six nails in a three-tab shingle. An alternative is to buy shingles with seal-down tabs. The sun's heat softens an adhesive strip on one shingle and seals down the tabs of the shingle above. With seal-down shingles, normal nailing is adequate even on a windy site.

In cold weather, asphalt shingles are brittle and break easily underfoot. In hot weather they soften and tear easily. But you can't shingle a roof without walking on the shingles you've laid. So work on a cool, cloudy day, and stack enough shingles within reach to cover one whole surface before you start work.

Before you continue with the first course, lay a complete row of shingles along the roof's edge to see how the spacing works out. The best-laid roof has full tabs at each end of the first course and every alternate course up the roof. Usually you can adjust any small difference in width as you lay the first course.

You start even-numbered courses with a half-tab, but never with less than half a shingle. Stagger notches between shingles from course to course. Cut the half shingles accurately, or the lines in the roofing will be crooked.

*Laying Courses Straight.* To avoid a crooked shingling job, nail down the first three courses with great care. Then snap a series of horizontal chalk lines across the roofing paper. As the distance between lines use the overall dimension of the three courses you've laid. At the ridge the top of the notches in the upper course should be 4″ to 5″ below the ridge. The ridge is covered in a different way, as you will see in a moment.

Also snap three vertical chalk lines, equally spaced, across each section of roof. Center these lines on notches in the shingles you have laid. The grid of chalk lines gives you an accurate guide for laying the remaining courses. Work in a diagonal pattern, starting at the rake of each section of roof. This way it's easier to check and correct alignment.

If you are shingling a steep slope, lay as many courses as you can from the eave without stepping on the roof. Then nail down walking steps to keep you from sliding on the roof while you nail the next courses within reach. When you remove walking steps, be sure to pull out all nails before you reuse the 2 × 4s on some other part of the roof. Then lift the tabs with the nail holes in them and fill the holes from underneath with asphaltic or plastic roofing cement. Lift the tabs gently to prevent breakage, and seal holes fully.

*Covering the Ridge.* At the ridge there are several treatments possible. If you install ridge ventilation (see Chapter 10), the notches of the upper course of shingles should lie at the edge of the ventilator. Otherwise cover the ridge with roll roofing under the last course of regular shingles. Then add a strip of selvage edge. Over the selvage edge lay shingles specially made for ridges and hips (Fig. 13-2). Bend each shingle gently along its center and lay it with no more than 5″ exposed. Begin work at the end of the ridge away from the prevailing wind that brings rain, and work into the wind. Nail on each side of the ridge, 5 1/2″ from the edge that crosses the ridge and 1″ from each side edge.

If ridge shingles aren't available, cut your own from strip shingles. Make each shingle the width of a tab, and rectangular in shape.

*Covering Hips and Valleys.* Finish a hip as you do a ridge, starting at the eave and working toward the top of the hip. Complete hips and valleys before you work on the ridge.

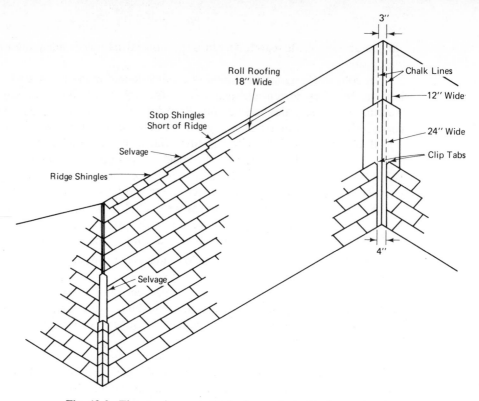

**Fig. 13-2.** The requirements for laying asphalt shingles at the ridge, a hip (left), and a valley (right).

In a valley first lay a 12″ strip of roll roofing, then cover it with a 24″-wide strip (Fig. 13-2). Complete this work before you begin any shingling. Snap chalk lines to mark the stopping points of the shingles. The exposed trough of roofing paper should be about 3″ wide at the ridge and 4″ wide at the eave. Clip the upper tip of each shingle so that water doesn't get trapped under it. Apply a ribbon of roofing cement just outside the chalk lines under the diagonally cut edges of shingles to seal them.

At a chimney, tuck shingles under the flashing on the down-slope side. At all other points lay shingles over the flashing, and seal down the edges completely with roofing cement. Do not nail through flashing; this invites leaks. Where the roof meets a wall, continue the roofing paper up the wall sheathing at least 4″, and then apply a strip of metal flashing at the bend. Run flashing 4″ up the wall and 2″ onto the roofing paper. Apply shingles as you did at the chimney.

## WOOD SHINGLES

Application of wood shingles is quite different from laying asphalt shingles. Standard lengths of wood shingles are 16″, 18″, and 24″. Thicker shingles, called *shakes,* are 18″ and 32″ long. Widths vary from 3″ to 14″. Exposures vary with the pitch and length of the roof.

Wood shingles are treated by the manufacturer with a preservative that prevents decay. The preservative also adds some color that either weathers to a silver gray or turns darker, depending on the wood. You can leave shingles natural or stain them for evener tone. If you stain, dip shingles individually into a container of stain to within 3″ of the thin end, which will be covered by the course above. Stand shingles on the thick butt end to dry thoroughly before you apply them.

### Applying Wood Shingles

The lowest course of wood shingles is a doubled course (Fig. 13-3). Let both thicknesses project at least 1″ beyond edges of sheathing to channel away rain and melting snow. Allow about 1/4″ gap between shingles to speed drying. Nail each shingle with just two nails—no more, no less—regardless of its width. Use three-penny nails with 16″ and 18″-long shingles; four-penny nails with 24″-long shingles, and six-penny nails with shakes. Nail about 1″ above the butt line of the next course to be laid, using a *shingling hatchet*—a tool with a hammerhead at one end and a cutting edge for splitting at the other. Drive nail heads just to the wood's surface, never into the shingles.

Where you lay the second and succeeding courses depends on the exposure. The range is from 3 3/4″ to 5″ for 16″ shingles; 4 1/2″ to 5 1/2″ for 18″ shingles; 5 3/4″ to 7 1/2″ for 24″ shingles; and 8″ for shakes. The steeper the pitch, the greater the allowable exposure. As with asphalt shingles, work out the exposure and spacing you want at this time, and snap chalk lines to assure straight courses.

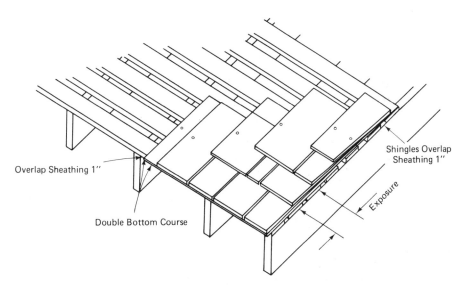

Overlap Sheathing 1″

Shingles Overlap Sheathing 1″

Exposure

Double Bottom Course

**Fig. 13-3.** Wood shingles are laid over sheathing boards, spaced to match the exposure of the shingles. The first course at the eaves is doubled.

To get uniform exposure, rip a long, straight board to a width equal to the exposure. Set one edge of the board flush with the butts of the course you've just laid, and set the next course against it as a stop.

*Covering Hips and Ridges.* The easiest way to cover a ridge is to continue the shingles up the main roof to within 1/4″ of the top. Cover the gap with a pair of shingles of the same width, trimmed and beveled for a tight fit. As with asphalt shingles, begin at the downwind end of the ridge. Lay a double course at this end, with the bevels falling on opposite sides of the ridge (Fig. 13-4, left). Continue to alternate bevels as you work across the ridge.

Complete a hip in the same way as a ridge, starting at the eave with a double course. Where the hip and ridge meet, let the ridge courses overlap the hip courses.

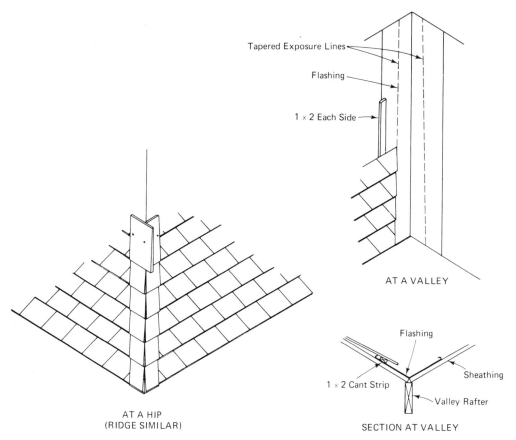

AT A VALLEY

AT A HIP
(RIDGE SIMILAR)

SECTION AT VALLEY

**Fig. 13-4.** The requirements for laying wood shingles at a hip or ridge (left) and a valley (right). Note in the section that the edges of shingles must be raised above valley level.

*Covering Valleys.* Valleys are more difficult than hips, because the butt ends of shingles must be raised above the valley to prevent them from becoming water-soaked. First flash the valley with metal at least 10″ on either side. If you need more than one strip of metal, lap the upper strip over the lower strip at least 3″. Bend the ends upward into a U (Fig. 13-4, section). Upslope from the flashing, on each side, lay a continuous 1 × 2 or a strip of 1/2″ plywood to raise the edges of the shingles. The exposed width of the valley should widen from 4″ at the upper end at a rate of one additional inch of width for every 8′ of valley length.

### Applying Shakes

Unlike wood shingles, which must be applied over gapped wood sheathing, shakes are nailed to solid sheathing. Start work at the eave by applying a metal edge strip, as recommended with asphalt shingling. Cover with a layer of 30-lb roofing felt 18″ wide. Lay the first course of shingles to the edge of the felt. Then, under each succeeding course of shakes, lay another strip of felt. Hold the edge of the felt about an inch back from the butt ends of the covering shingles. The method of nailing and the treatment at ridges, hips, and valleys are the same as for wood shingles.

# ASBESTOS-CEMENT SHINGLES

Asbestos-cement shingles are quite brittle, but they don't rot, decay, or burn. You apply them with 1 1/4″ galvanized roofing nails driven through predrilled nailing holes in the shingles. Asbestos-cement shingles come in several soft colors, but can be painted if you prefer. Because the shingles are so easily broken, the best way to work is from a pair of ladders hung over the ridge and tied together at that point.

### Applying the Shingles

Begin by lifting the first layer of roofing paper that you laid over sheathing; then, at the lower edge of the sheathing, add a 4″-wide metal drip edge. Crimp it as shown in Fig. 13-5. Then lay a course of starter shingles, which are only half the height of regular rectangular shingles. Let their lower edges project 3/4″ beyond the metal drip edge. Now renail the roofing paper.

Begin the first course with a half-width shingle, overhanging the rake of the roof 3/4″. To cut an asbestos-cement shingle, score it with a sharp utility knife and break it along the scoring line. Sometimes you can rent a special shingle cutter from the shingle supplier. Line up the bottom edge of the shingle with the starter course and nail. Nail cautiously until you have the knack. You can shatter a shingle with a misdirected blow.

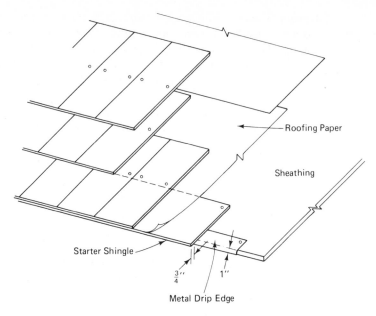

**Fig. 13-5.** Details of an asbestos-cement shingle roof at the eave. Note that both the metal edge and starter course lie underneath the roofing paper.

Complete the remainder of the bottom course with full shingles. Then start the second course with a full shingle and alternate on up the roof so that joints are staggered. When nailing courses, follow the manufacturer's recommendations for exposure. You can't vary the exposure; you must miss the shingles below when you nail.

*Covering the Ridges and Hips.* Continue courses all the way to the ridge. Then, centered over the ridge, embed a 12"-wide strip of 30-lb felt into roofing cement. Figure 13-6 shows the procedure at a hip, which is treated the same way as a ridge. On each side of the ridge or hip lay wood strips 2" wide and the same thickness as shingles. If necessary, set the strips in roofing cement so they maintain the position recommended by the shingle manufacturer.

Cover the strips with another layer of felt, this one only 8" wide. Then apply special ridge shingles, beginning at the downwind end with a half-shingle and continuing with full shingles. Lay one shingle on each side of the ridge or hip, alternating the locations of the seams. Nail into the wood strips; then seal holes and seams with roofing cement and wipe off the excess.

*Covering Valleys.* Lay metal flashing and 1 × 2s in valleys as with wood shingles (Fig. 13-4), with 5" of metal exposed at the ridge, widening an inch for every 8' of valley. Snap chalk lines down both sides of the flashing at the exposure lines, and trim the shingles to fit along the chalk lines.

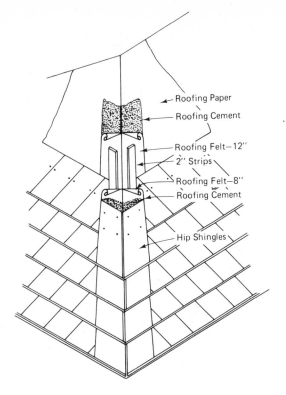

**Fig. 13-6.** Requirements for laying asbestos-cement shingles at a hip. Ridge treatment is similar, and valleys are finished as shown in Fig. 13-4.

Roofing Paper

Roofing Cement

Roofing Felt—12″

2″ Strips

Roofing Felt—8″

Roofing Cement

Hip Shingles

# METAL ROOFING

Most homeowners don't think of using metal for roofs these days, but it has some distinct advantages. The metals most commonly used for roofing are aluminum, galvanized steel, copper, tin (actually tin-plated steel), and terneplate, a combination of lead and tin over copper-bearing steel.

All these roofing materials are highly resistant to weather and corrosion. They are lightweight, easy to handle, and easy to cut and shape. Each metal must be applied with fasteners of the same metal to avoid *galvanic action,* a corrosive chemical reaction between unlike metals in contact with each other. As an alternate fastener you may use screw-type nails with neoprene washers that prevent leaks and keep metals from touching each other.

Roofing metal comes in sheets, and you connect the sheets with seams. The seams may run up and down a slope or across it. When the sheets run vertically, the connection needed is a standing seam. When sheets run horizontally, the connection is a lock seam.

### Making a Standing Seam

To make a 1″ standing seam, begin by putting a 90° bend 1 1/2″ from the edge of one sheet and 1 3/4″ from the edge of the other (step 1 in Fig. 13-7). Butt the two pieces together and fold the longer over the shorter (step 2). The

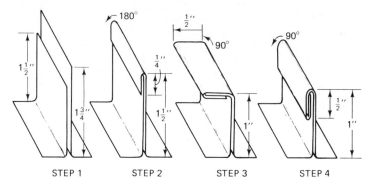

**Fig. 13-7.** The four steps to forming a standing seam in a metal roof. Seams like this run with the slope of the roof.

seam is now 1 1/2″ high. At a point 1/2″ from the top, bend the three thicknesses at 90°, still bending in the same direction (step 3). Finally, bend another 90° (step 4) to complete the seam. Crimp all five thicknesses tightly together.

To attach a standing seam metal roof to sheathing, insert cleats of the same metal into the seams about every 24″, in the manner shown in Fig. 13-8. At the ridge, a hip, a valley, and the eave, bend the end of the seam one more time so that it is nearly flat against the roof's surface.

**Fig. 13-8.** Lock seams run across a metal roof, and cleats hold the roof to the sheathing. To form a simple lock seam, butt the two ends together with cleats between and ends bent 90° to different lengths (step 1). In step 2 bend the longer edge over the shorter. In step 3, fold both edges another 90°, flatten the seam, and solder the joint. Section at lower right is through a strong lock seam.

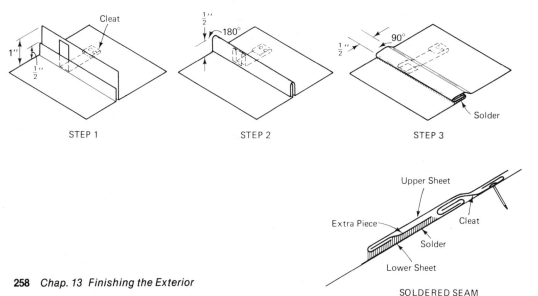

### Making a Lock Seam

The principle of the lock seam is simple. In the ordinary lock seam the edges of metal sheets have reverse 180° bends in them, and the bends hook into each other. A flat-lock seam is stronger, however, and you can make a good one in three steps (Fig. 13-8).

A soldered lock seam is stronger still. The type shown at the bottom right of Fig. 13-8 provides excellent protection against wind damage, but it requires an extra piece of metal. You hold the seams in place by nailing through cleats spaced about every 12″ along each joint.

### Covering the Ridge

At a ridge or hip, trim the sheathing flat (Fig. 13-9, top) and nail a 2 × 2 batten into the ridgeboard. The ideal shape for this 2 × 2 is slightly tapered toward the bottom to allow the roof metal to expand. Run the metal up the batten on each side and add a 180° bend. Then shape a cap strip to fit over the batten and lock into the seams on both sides. The easiest way to install the cap strip is to slide it in from the end. Overlap any joints in the cap about 1″, and solder on all three sides.

### Finishing Edges

When metal runs horizontally, you must stiffen the edges to protect them against the lifting action of wind, and also to hide sharp edges against which you might cut yourself when you clean or paint. Put two 180° bends at the raw

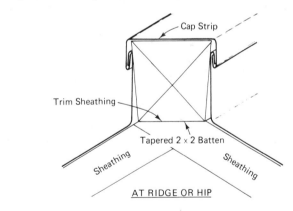

AT RIDGE OR HIP

**Fig. 13-9.** Details of good, watertight treatments of metal roofs at ridges and hips (top), corners (far right), and any exposed edge (right).

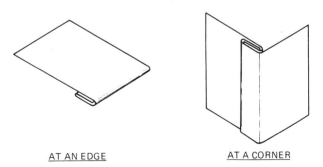

AT AN EDGE                    AT A CORNER

edge (Fig. 13-9, bottom), the first bend 1/2″ in from the edge and the second 1″ in. Apply the roofing with the stiffened edge overhanging the sheathing and bent downward at about a 45° angle.

Occasionally you may have two pieces of metal meet at a corner. Give each edge a 180° bend (Fig. 13-9, center), and then give one piece another 90° bend to complete the lock seam.

### Soldering

*Solder* is a fusible metal alloy. It looks like a heavy, soft wire, comes in coils, and melts under the heat of a soldering iron. As the seal against weather at the seams between pieces of metal, solder must be carefully applied. The process has four basic steps:

1.  Fit the pieces of metal tightly together so that the solder can completely fill all openings. Even a pinhole in a solder joint will let in water. The molten solder is drawn into the seams by capillary action.

2.  Thoroughly clean the surfaces to be soldered. Use steel wool or a wire brush. The metal must be free of dirt, rust, grease, and any other foreign material.

3.  With a small brush apply a thin coat of flux over the entire area to be soldered. *Flux* is a paste that cleans oxides off metal surfaces. It protects the metal until you solder. There is a special type of flux for each metal; read the label to be sure you have the right type. The wrong type can cause a dangerous chemical reaction.

4.  Heat the metal with the soldering iron, and apply solder directly under the iron. Use 40-60 solder; it is formulated from 40% tin and 60% lead. Start at one end of the seam and draw the soldering iron toward you, feeding the solder beneath the iron as you go. The flux on the metal and the heat of the iron will draw the solder into the seam.

When you have a long joint to close, you can make the job easier by tacking the seam about every 4″ with a few drops of solder. Then apply additional solder along the entire length of the seam. Leave finished joints alone until the solder cools—about 15 minutes under most conditions. Then recheck your work thoroughly. If you find any gaps in the solder, no matter how small, add more flux and resolder.

## A BUILT-UP ROOF

Roofs that are flat or nearly flat aren't suitable for shingling. They require a built-up roof—and the term *built-up* describes the process accurately. The roof's surface consists of a number of layers of roofing felt, each mopped into a bed of hot tar. The best roof has as many as five layers of felt at any given point.

A built-up roof requires special equipment, and it is a job that you should subcontract. However, you have some work to do at the edges of the roof before the contractor can begin. Find out what kind of subsurface he wants to work over. He may want you to provide a wood or metal deck over sheathing. Then you must build a dam, called a *gravel stop,* around the entire edge of the roof's surface.

Figure 13-10 shows a typical gravel stop. It consists of a pair of 2 × 4s laid atop each other, with a triangular cant strip on the roof side and a fascia on the other side. Carry the metal base for a built-up roof to the front edge of the fascia. Then bend flashing over the entire assembly and nail into the cant strip, a 2 × 4, and fascia as shown. Apply the flashing after the roof is completed; otherwise it will be spattered with tar.

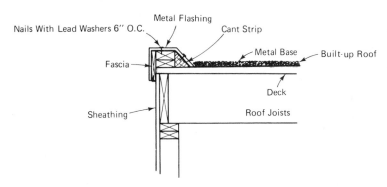

**Fig. 13-10.** When a flat roof receives built-up roofing, a gravel stop is needed around the perimeter of the roof. This section shows typical construction.

# PLYWOOD FOR EXTERIOR WALLS

You have as great a choice of exterior materials for the walls as you have for the roof. You can use sheet materials such as plywood and manufactured composition products. You can use siding of wood, composition, or aluminum. You can use wood shingles. Or you can use brick or stone, provided that you have built the foundation wide enough for masonry.

Of these materials plywood is the easiest and quickest to apply. Plywood for exterior use comes in sheets 4' wide and 8', 9', and 10' long. Its surface may be plain, with edges cut square. Or its surface may be textured in a wide variety of ways, with edges shiplapped. You can buy most types of plywood factory-finished, or unfinished for staining or painting after application.

## Applying the Sheets

Exterior plywood is designed for vertical application. At the foundation wall nail a cant strip through the sheathing into the sill (Fig. 13-11). Overlap the foundation about 1 1/2". A piece of wood shingle about 4" long and 1/2" thick

**Fig. 13-11.** Plywood on exterior walls is applied vertically. It fits over a cant strip at the lower edge that helps water to run off the wall and drip harmlessly away. Point *A* is the lower measuring point for determining the length of sheet required. Point *B* is the upper measuring point when the ends of rafters are exposed.

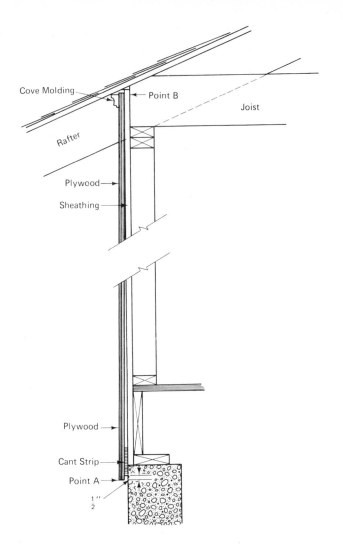

at the lower end makes a good cant strip. Let the plywood lap 1/2″ below the bottom edge of the cant strip so that water can't seep into the sill. Point *A* is the lower measuring line for determining the length of plywood sheet you will need.

If you add a soffit to the undersides of rafters, 9′-long sheets fit without trimming and allow a little gap at the top plate. If rafter ends are exposed, however, plywood must extend to roof sheathing, and you must cut and fit it around rafters. Cover the gap with a cove molding, as shown in Fig. 13-11. With this type of construction, point *B* is the upper measuring point for determining the length of plywood to buy.

Cut each panel to fit around openings and obstructions before you attach it. To assure tight fits you must be accurate in measuring and marking, and careful in cutting. Apply the sheets with eight-penny noncorrosive nails (aluminum or galvanized steel) spaced 6″ apart at edges and 10″ to 12″ apart in the *field*—the middle of the panel. If the plywood is grooved, nail into the grooves to conceal nail heads.

Shiplapped edges require no further treatment. With square-edged plywood, however, you must seal the joints. One common and attractive method is with battens. Battens for this purpose are usually straight 1 × 2s, centered over joints, and nailed into the joint between sheets.

After you have put battens over the joints, stand back and look at the completed wall. For a better appearance, especially on a small vacation house, you may want to add other battens on either a 24″ or 16″ spacing to improve the scale.

At corners, carry the plywood flush with the corner post, and finish the corner with two battens. The application is similar to that shown at the left in Fig. 13-13, except that the battens lie over the edges of the plywood sheets, not between them.

# HORIZONTAL WOOD SIDING

The vertical lines of a board-and-batten exterior make a house look a little taller and a little narrower. Conversely, the strong horizontal lines of siding help a small house look wider and closer to the ground. The effect is about the same whether you use wood, composition, metal, or vinyl siding. Applications are slightly different, however.

Before you order wood siding, see what types your local supplier carries. Beveled siding, also called *clapboard,* is the most popular. Its sides taper, although both edges are cut square. Standard widths are 6″, 8″, and 10″, and the thickness at the butt edge increases with the width.

*Rabbeted beveled siding* is similar to beveled siding, but the exposed edge is shiplapped instead of square, and fits over the top edge of the course below. *Drop siding* is cut from high quality 1″ boards and molded into a variety of shapes that create interesting shadow patterns. Most shapes come in several widths. Drop siding does not taper; it has a constant thickness.

## Treating the Wall at Top and Bottom

The procedures outlined for plywood application as shown in Fig. 13-11 can also be followed with beveled siding. The thinner half of a piece of siding makes an excellent cant strip.

For a more attractive job, however, compare Fig. 13-12. Here the bottom course of siding does not extend below the top of the foundation. At the bottom of the wall instead is a board 1 1/4″ thick and either 5 1/2″ or 7 1/2″ high. This board must be set level, and it should extend about 1 1/2″ over the foundation wall.

On top of the board you set a drip cap and cant strip. The combination of board and drip molding is called a *water table.* The drip cap channels rain away from the joint at the top of the board. The cant strip, which you can make from the thinner third of a length of siding, establishes the slope of the siding. To cal-

**Fig. 13-12.** Section through a wall surfaced with wood siding or shingles. Compare construction at the foundation wall, and the locations of measuring points *A* and *B,* with those in Fig. 13-11.

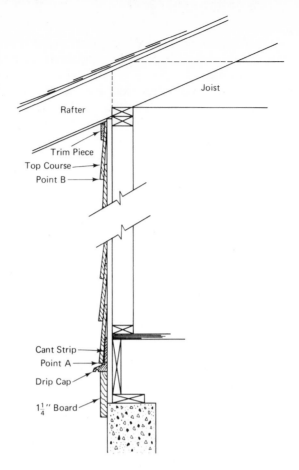

culate the proper exposure for courses of siding, consider the point of bend in the drip cap (point *A* in Fig. 13-12) as the bottom of the wall area to be covered.

At the top of the wall the measuring point for exposure (point *B*) is the butt edge of the top course of siding. Use another piece of siding for the top trim. Rip it to a width that gives you the planned exposure of the course of siding below. Attach this trim piece upside down, with the thin edge down.

### Planning Exposure

The best way to determine exposure is to measure upward from point *A* to the sill line of windows, from that point to the heads of doors and windows (which should be at the same level), and from there to point *B.* The reason for measuring to the tops and bottoms of window openings is to avoid having to notch the siding there. Notching requires great accuracy and careful sealing to avoid leaks.

For the sake of discussion, let's assume that you want to use 5/8″ by 8″ siding, with an exposure of approximately 6″ for each course. The measurements you take are 28 1/2″, 63″, and 8 1/2″. None of these dimensions is divisible by 6, but if you plan five courses in 28 1/2″, you come close. The exposure is about 5 11/16″. Similarly, by planning 11 courses in the 63″ space, each exposure is 5 23/32 ". Nobody will ever notice that 1/32 " difference. At the top simply cut the inverted shingle to a depth of about 2 3/4 " to maintain your spacing.

Before you decide on any exposure, though, try another one. If you plan only four courses in the 28 1/2 ", for example, the exposure becomes 7 1/8 ". Nine courses in 63 " gives an exposure of 7 " even. The 1/8 " difference won't be noticeable in the finished wall either, and you have to apply only 14 courses at about 7 " instead of 17 courses at about 5 3/4 ". With the wider spacing, however, you must use 10 " siding instead of 8 ".

You must judge whether there will be a noticeable difference in appearance between a 5 3/4 " and a 7 " exposure. As a suggestion, stay with the smaller exposure if your longest wall is less than 30 ' long, and go to the wider exposure if the wall is longer.

### Treating Corners

Unless you are an expert at mitering, don't plan to butt courses of siding at corners. There are two simple ways to finish outside corners. One is to buy a 1 1/4 × 8 board (a stock size that is actually 1 " by 7 1/2 ") long enough to run from foundation to eave. Allowing for a 1/8 " saw kerf, rip the board into two pieces, one 4 3/16 " wide and the other 3 3/16 " wide. Overlap the boards at the corner as shown at left in Fig. 13-13 to form a corner post with equal sides. Butt the siding against the edges of this post.

Using the other method, run the siding close to the corner but stop just short of it. Cover the joint with metal corners (Fig. 13-13, center). Slide them on from the bottom and nail at the top of each corner. The nails are concealed, and you have a perfect corner.

At an inside corner rip a square post from 1 1/4 " material. Nail the pieces into the sheathing on both sides (Fig. 13-13, right) and butt siding against them.

**Fig. 13-13.** Typical methods of finishing outside corners (left and center) and inside corners (right) when wood siding is the exterior wall material.

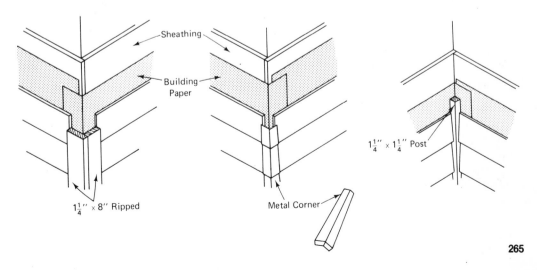

1¼″ × 8″ Ripped

Sheathing

Building Paper

Metal Corner

1¼″ × 1¼″ Post

## Applying Siding

Plywood can be applied directly to sheathing. Wood siding should not. There should be a layer of kraft paper between the two, as shown in Fig. 13-13. Start at the bottom of the sheathing and, at any joint, either vertical or horizontal, overlap the paper at least an inch. Carry the paper over door and window frames for a tight seal. Trim will hide it.

You can apply building paper with 1/2" staples or short nails with broad heads. Apply the bottom layer first, then a few courses of siding, then more paper and more siding. By papering only part way up the sheathing at a time, you can see the lines of nails and use them as a guide to nailing the siding into studs, not just into sheathing.

If you plan to paint the siding, always apply a prime coat to the edges of corner posts, to the water table, and to the cut ends of siding before you attach any of these wood pieces. Otherwise moisture can get behind the siding and ruin your paint job.

Fit corner posts in place first. Use galvanized nails long enough to penetrate at least 1 1/2" into sheathing and studs. Then fit any water table in place, making

This corner detail shows clearly the effect you can get with good materials properly used. Walls are grooved plywood laid horizontally. Joints and intermediate points are covered with broad battens in scale with the size and shape of the wall area. Roofing is clay tile. *Courtesy American Plywood Association.*

sure that the top edge of the drip cap is level along its entire length. Space nails 16" apart into gypsum or composition sheathing, 24" apart into plywood.

The best place to start the first course of siding is at an inside corner. If you don't have one, start at the outside corners and work toward the middle of each wall, or toward a large window or door opening. Cut the last piece in each course to fit very tightly.

Once the first course is in place and level, you can save time in leveling the remaining courses by making a gauge block. To make one, cut a notch in a short length of 2 × 4. The height of the notch should be exactly equal to the exposure you plan. The depth of the notch should be 1/16" less than the thickness of the butt edge of a piece of siding. To use the gauge block, fit the notch over the butt of the lowest attached piece of siding, and rest the next piece against the top of the gauge block. Use your carpenter's level every couple of courses to recheck the level.

***Fitting at Openings.*** Whenever you near the end of your work on any course, stop long enough to plan ahead. Each length of siding should end over a stud, and the piece above it should end over a different stud. No piece of siding should be so short that you can't nail it into a stud at both ends.

As you come to a window, the frame and flashing around the window should already be in place. At the heads of windows and doors butt the lower edge of siding against the flashing. Butt the ends of siding against the flashing at the jambs. At window sills, however, extend the loose flashing over the under course of siding and behind the exposed course just below the sill (refer to Fig. 12-5).

At gables, finding the right line to cut on is difficult because of the bevel in the siding. Use your gauge block to mark the point at which the roof trim on both slopes hits the bottom edge of a length of siding. The distance between these marks determines the length of that bottom edge. Then use your pitch board to mark the slope of the roof on the siding.

If you cut along these two lines, the siding will be too narrow at the top edge. So lengthen the upper edge about 1/8" on either side of the pitch lines you drew and draw new lines. When you cut on these lines, the fit should be almost perfect. Fill any remaining gaps with caulking.

***Fastening.*** Siding is cut from a number of species of wood. Redwood, red cedar, and cypress are the best. Other species aren't as resistant to decay, or they shrink more as they dry. Regardless of the species, predrill for nails near the ends of each piece to prevent splitting. With fir and most pines, predrill all holes. The holes should be slightly smaller than the shank of the nail to allow for shrinkage.

Use eight-penny nails, nailing into every stud. Drive the nail into the thick butt of each piece so that it enters sheathing just above the thin edge of the piece of siding below; don't nail any course near the top. Nails through the trim at the roof line will hold even the top length of siding in place. Countersink nail heads below the surface of the siding, and fill the holes with putty.

# OTHER WOOD SIDING

The procedures for applying rabbeted beveled siding are the same as those for beveled siding, with one exception: exposure is fixed at 5 1/8". The siding itself is 5 1/2" wide. The difference between the two dimensions provides for the overlap and a slight air gap between courses to allow for expansion. The gap is necessary because, unlike beveled siding, rabbeted beveled siding lies flat against sheathing.

With drop siding the amount of exposure is also fixed by the shape of the siding. Each course fits tightly onto or into the course below, depending on whether the joints are shiplapped or tongue-and-groove. With shiplapped joints you nail at the top of every piece, and the course above covers the nails. With tongue-and-groove edges you must nail through the face of the board.

You can also make your own siding out of plywood by ripping sheets lengthwise. Five cuts give you six strips about 7 3/4" wide. Six cuts give you seven strips about 6 3/4" wide. You must use exterior grade plywood, and fully prime all edges. Application is the same as with beveled siding, with three exceptions. First, each course should overlap the course below about an inch. Second, you nail through the bottom of one course and the top of the course below, and then into sheathing and studs. Third, because of this extra thickness of material, you need 10-penny nails. The effect of a wall built this way is quite similar in appearance to beveled siding.

# NONWOOD SIDING

They look very much like wood siding, but they aren't. These are sidings made of insulation board, hardboard, vinyl, and aluminum. Exposures range from 4" to 8", but are rarely adjustable. Most types come from the factory already prefinished. Pieces vary in length from 8' to 16', and are easily cut to length with standard tools.

With all types of manufactured siding you will get manufacturer's instructions. Follow them carefully. Methods of application are similar to those for wood siding, but there are distinct differences. Sidings made of hardboard and insulation board, for example, may bend and break when you nail them unless they are backed by a nailing strip behind the bottom course and by wedges behind all courses. If butt ends don't interlock, you must seal the joints with plastic caulking.

Most types of rigid vinyl siding have a system for interlocking between courses that assures straight alignment. At the bottom of the first course you fit a special starter strip made by the siding manufacturer that guarantees a level start.

Aluminum siding is usually made with a backing already attached, and the courses interlock like vinyl siding. At the ends of siding strips the pieces overlap, with the laps facing downwind. All manufacturers make special shapes for corners and at openings.

The main advantage of nonwood sidings is that they come prefinished. Once you install them, your walls are done and you can get to work finishing the inside of your vacation house. Finishes are available in a number of colors and textures.

# WOOD SHINGLES

If you are interested in texture, you will find it in wood shingles. They combine the effects of the horizontal course lines of siding with a rough-textured finish that looks well in the woods, the mountains, or at the shore.

Of the several approved ways of applying shingles, *single-coursing* is probably the best for a vacation house. Each course is laid as a single thickness, as when shingling a roof. The difference is that on a roof the exposure is small, and each square foot of roof is covered with three thicknesses of shingle to protect against weather. Rain is not as much a factor on a wall, however, so exposures can be about 50% greater, and the wall is covered with only two thicknesses.

### Planning Exposure

You determine the proper exposure in the same way that you determined the exposure of siding. Find the dimensions between the bottom of the bottom course and the undersides of window sills, between the sill and top of the drip cap above windows, and between the drip cap and bottom edge of the top course of shingles. Of these, the least important in shingling is the sill point.

Maximum exposures are 7 1/2" for 16" shingles, 8 1/2" for 18" shingles, and 11 1/2" for 24" shingles. The longer 24" shingles are normally used in *double-coursing,* an application in which each course consists of two thicknesses of shingle, with the outer course overlapping the inner layer by an inch at the bottom edge.

### Applying Shingles

Instead of the cant strip behind the bottom course of siding, use a double undercourse of shingles, similar to the double course used to start shingling a roof. Overlap the foundation wall about an inch with the undercourse (refer back to Fig. 13-11), and overlap the undercourse about 1/2" with the bottom course of shingles. The undercourse places the bottom course at the same slope as later courses above.

Nail each shingle so that the next course above covers the nail heads by about an inch. In shingles up to 8" wide two nails are enough, set about 3/4" in from edges. In wider shingles add a third nail in the center. Use three-penny aluminum or galvanized nails, or staples applied with a stapling hammer. Stagger joints at least 1 1/2" between shingles in successive courses.

Shingles can be laid in several ways. You can fit them tightly together (making a closed joint), or gap them about 1/8" (an open joint). If you intend to fit shingles tight, either prestain them or buy them prestained. You can align all butt edges for smooth horizontal lines, or stagger the butts up to an inch for maximum texture.

Snapping chalk lines as guides doesn't work too well in keeping the courses of shingles straight. A better way is to nail a straight 1 × 4 or 1 × 6 temporarily just below each exposure line. Fit the butts of shingles against the board, attach them, and move the board up for the next course. If you want to stagger the butts, set all shingles on the board as a guide to spacing and nail only every third or fourth shingle at the course line. Come back and fit the staggered shingles before you go on to the next course.

This small two-story vacation house offers an interesting study in tone and texture. Wood shingle roof not only matches the light tone of the sandy soil, but also the texture of native trees. Darker walls are smooth-surfaced plywood with tongue-and-groove edges. This house was built from a stock vacation house plan. *Courtesy Western Wood Products Association.*

# MASONRY

You aren't likely to cover the entire exterior of your vacation house with bricks. But you may want to use some bricks for a chimney, at the top of a foundation, or as a veneer below the sill level of windows. This section gives you only the basic information you need.

For a brick veneer wall the foundation must be 10″ thick. You need 4″ of thickness for the bricks, a nominal 2″ air space, part of which is taken up by sheathing, and 4″ for the stud wall. This means a poured concrete foundation, because concrete blocks do not come in 10″ widths. If you don't like the appearance of concrete at the foundation, you can pour a concrete foundation up to grade, then continue up to floor sill level with face bricks backed by 4″ concrete blocks.

## Preparing Bricks and Mortar

Laying bricks takes a lot of preparation. The bricks themselves must be soaked thoroughly and allowed to drain overnight. Otherwise they will suck moisture out of the mortar too quickly, and you will have weak joints. Soak bricks with a stream of water from a hose until the water runs off on all sides. To be ready for use, bricks should be damp on the inside but dry on the surface. To test, draw a circle about the size of a quarter with a grease pencil on any brick. Put about 20 drops of water inside the circle. The bricks are ready when the water is absorbed in about 90 seconds.

For mortar use ready-mix cement and add sand and water. Instructions on the bag indicate the amount and type of sand to use. The proportion is about one cubic foot of sand per 70-lb bag of cement. Not any old sand will do. It must be clean and coarse, since fine or dirty sand has little strength. Mix the cement, sand, and water thoroughly for about two minutes.

How much water? That's a matter of judgment. The mix should be just short of runny, but firm enough to hang on a trowel tipped at about a 60° angle to the horizontal. If the mix is too stiff, you can always add water. But if the mix is too runny, throw that batch out and start again. Measure carefully the amount of water you use. Then you will know how much to use in the next batch, and all your mortar will have the same consistency.

Mix the mortar in a mortar box, but no more than you intend to use in 2 1/2 hours. Then work from a mortarboard. Water begins to evaporate from the mix immediately, and the mortar will start to set up at the edges of the mound where it is thin. To keep the mix as consistent as possible, trowel the edge mortar back into the center of the mound and replace the water that has evaporated. This process is called *retempering,* and it can be done safely as long as the mortar hasn't begun to harden. Do not retemper large amounts of mortar; throw it out instead.

## Laying Bricks

Work from the edge of the mound of mortar, scooping toward the center of the mortarboard. Pick up enough mortar on the trowel to form a bed for three of four bricks. The movements for picking up mortar and "slinging" it onto the brick are quick, and take some practice. Slinging serves three important purposes: it clears all mortar off the trowel at once. It puts the mortar where you want it. And it provides enough force to flatten the mortar for a good bond.

To spread slung mortar evenly, make a shallow furrow down the center of each bed with your trowel. This puts the thickest mortar at the edges of the bricks below, and makes for tighter joints. Lay each brick with hand pressure—enough to squeeze a little mortar out of the joint on the sides and into the furrow in the center. Use the handle of your trowel to position and level each brick. Check the position and level of every brick with a mason's level before you lay the next one.

Before you lay any bricks, work out their spacing so that you know what thickness of vertical mortar joint to use. Start work at the corners and build brick pyramids as discussed with concrete blocks in Chapter 6. Work in both directions from each corner, laying two bricks at a time in a course. Lay the first brick at each corner into the mortar bed. Then, before laying each succeeding brick, butter the end with mortar from the bottom of the trowel. Work over the mortar board. As you set one brick against the adjoining brick and into the mortar bed, the mortar will ooze out to form a good head joint.

To cut off excess mortar at a horizontal joint, hold your trowel with the point upward and at an angle to the wall. Pull the trowel slowly toward you, while holding the top bricks in place with your other hand. To cut a vertical joint, hold the trowel at the same angle and pull slowly upward. If you move too quickly, you will pull the mortar away from the brick on one side and leave a crack for moisture.

When mortar is thumb-print hard—stiff enough so you can't compact it with thumb pressure but soft enough to show the imprint of your thumb—tool the joints. Tool vertical joints first. Use a jointer just a little wider than the mortar joint, and apply only enough pressure to force the mortar tightly against the bricks on both sides of the joint.

When you lay the *closure*—the last brick in a course—you must break the brick to the right size with a mason's hammer or masonry chisel. Then butter both ends before setting it gently in place. Be careful not to disturb adjoining bricks. Once mortar begins to set, you may crack the joint when you move the brick. If this happens, remove the bumped or out-of-line brick, scrape away all dried mortar in the wall, and start again with a clean brick and fresh mortar.

In every third or fourth course of mortar you must insert wall ties, spaced about 32" apart. *Wall ties* are L-shaped strips of metal that connect the thin veneer wall to the wood structure. Set one end of the ties in the mortar bed and nail the other end into the sheathing if it is plywood, or all the way into studs if it isn't.

*Laying A Rowlock Course.* At a window sill, or at a break between brick on the lower third of a wall and siding above, lay a *rowlock* course—a course with bricks laid on their long edges. Apply flashing over the top course of running or stretcher bond (the standard brick pattern with joints in one course at the midpoints of bricks above and below). The flashing must extend from the window sill down the sheathing (refer back to Fig. 12-5), across the top course of bricks, and over the edge at a 45° angle.

Spread a bed of mortar onto the flashing, filling to the sill at the back. Then set each brick in the mortar at an angle great enough for drainage. Butter the bricks thoroughly on one side, and work from each side of the course toward the center closure. Work out your spacing in advance; you must use only full-thickness bricks in a rowlock course.

## Laying Stones

Stones are more difficult to lay than bricks. If you buy cut stones, you lay them just like bricks. Their thickness is fairly constant, but the widths and heights of individual stones vary. Most stones are heavier than bricks, and you often have to search through a stack to find a piece that will fit. Horizontal joints do not need to be continuous along an entire wall.

If you have stones on your site that you want to use, check locally to make sure they are suitable for construction. You can cut or chip some types of stone into manageable pieces with ordinary masonry tools. To speed the job, try to rent an electric saw with a special cutting blade. Score the surface at the point of breakage, then split it with a chisel and maul.

Laying fieldstone is a slow process because surfaces aren't level. You use the same mortar as for laying bricks, but a lot more of it. Make a bed of mortar for each stone deep enough so that there is at least 1/4″ between stones at the thinnest point. Unless the bottom edges of stones are reasonably straight, and parallel with the top surfaces of the stones below, let the mortar set in one or two courses before you build any higher. Otherwise you could have a stone slide.

After you complete any type of masonry wall, go back with additional mortar to *point* (fill) exposed joints. You can use the same mortar, or you can use commercial sealants that come in soft colors. You can also add coloring to the mortar to achieve the same effect.

## Protecting Incomplete Work

Store all masonry materials on planks or similar supports that keep them off the ground. Cover supplies with a polyethylene sheet, weighted to prevent it from blowing away. Also use polyethylene at the end of each day of bricklaying to cover your work as protection against rain and setting too quickly. Continue to protect your work until you have finished the entire masonry job and the mortar has set.

# TOOLS YOU WILL NEED

These are the tools you are likely to need to finish the roof and exterior walls of your vacation house:

metal shears
hammer
roofing knife
chalk line
putty knife
paint brush
shingling hatchet
utility knife
soldering iron
wire brush
power saw
carpenter's level
adjustable square
gauge block (which you make)
pitch board (which you make)
power drill
mortar box
mortarboard
trowel
mason's level
jointer
masonry chisel
maul

# Finishing Interior Surfaces

By this time the exterior of your house is completely enclosed, although not yet finished. You still have some trim to add and protection to provide. But you have reached the point where you can work regardless of weather. The remaining outside work (discussed in Chapters 15 through 17) can be done during good weather, and on cold, very hot, or rainy days you can work inside.

Work from the top down, completing the ceilings first. Even if you intend to leave the rafters exposed in the main living areas, you probably have some ceilings to install, at least in a bathroom. Wall materials come next, then flooring. Application of trim is the final step before decorating.

Before you decide on a ceiling material, figure out what you want it to do for you. Certainly its key purpose is to hide the rough structure above it. Should it also reflect light or absorb it? Should it reflect sound or absorb it? Is color important? Is the cost of prefinished materials worth the saving in time? Let's look at these questions one by one, because your answers relate also to your choices of wall and flooring materials.

Take light reflectance. A dark-toned ceiling appears lower than it really is, and a light-toned ceiling tends to recede and make a room seem higher. A dark ceiling over a room, say 15' by 20', appears much lower than the same dark ceiling over a room 10' by 10'. If your site is wooded and shaded much of the day, little light will reach the ceiling. But at the shore, sun bouncing off the water and a sand beach casts strong light on the ceiling.

Light walls painted an off-white provide a pleasant contrast with the darker cathedral ceiling surfaced with clear all-heart redwood paneling. Side-by-side fireplaces with raised hearths warm the living area and the secluded room beyond. Redwood is repeated on the divider and around the twin circular flues. *Courtesy California Redwood Association.*

You may want a light ceiling to dispel the gloom in the woods, and a dark or textured ceiling to control glare at the shore.

Contrast, important in the choice of exterior materials, is important inside, too. A room with all light-toned surfaces may be bright, but it is also likely to be dull. It tends to be cool in effect rather than warm, and your focus is in the room rather than outside. A room with all dark-toned surfaces, on the other hand, is warmer and cozier, and focuses your attention toward the lighter world outside. Such a room can also be dull, however, and on rainy days can be rather dreary. A balance of light and dark makes a room more interesting. Of course you can heighten that interest with color and texture.

Most people like to hear the sounds of nature—the boom of breaking waves, the susurrus of wind through trees, the songs of birds, and even the nocturnal footsteps of bears and possums and raccoons. The interior materials you choose have little effect on these sounds, but they should control noise generated in rooms. Normally interior noise isn't a problem except in rooms with hard-surfaced ceilings and walls, and a floor with an easy-to-clean but hard surface. Carpeting, rugs, wall hangings, and soft furniture all absorb sound. Without these absorbents, ceiling tile is worth considering.

Your choice of material to apply to the undersides of joists or rafters is somewhat limited. There are three basic possibilities, with many variations in finish: they are plywood panels, wallboard, and ceiling tile.

# PLYWOOD CEILINGS

For interior surfaces, unfinished plywood comes in sheets 4′ by 8′ and thicknesses of 1/4″ and 1/2″. The sheets have a smooth surface, usually a fir veneer, and edges that are square, shiplapped, or beveled. Prefinished sheets are thinner (4 mm to 5/16″), 4′ wide, and come in lengths from 7′ to 10′. Edges are slightly beveled. The surface may be smooth, striated (combed with vertical grooves), random-grooved, or sand-blasted for maximum texture. Veneers are hardwood in a variety of grains and wood tones. Most interior plywood used today is prefinished, but because of its thinness it has limited structural value.

Order plywood for delivery only a day or two ahead of the date you schedule for beginning application. Store the panels, which come in cartons, flat on the floor out of the way. The day before you begin application, remove the panels from their cartons to let them adjust to temperature and humidity conditions in the house. Keep the panels flat. They bow easily, and a bowed panel is hard to work with. They also scratch easily, so lift, don't slide, a panel off the one below.

## Applying Plywood Overhead

It takes two people to apply any sheet material to a ceiling, and you'll need some means of raising yourself close to ceiling level for fitting and nailing. You can work from sawhorses if you are agile and foolhardy or you can lay planks across sawhorses for a safer and broader working surface. Sometimes you can rent special stilts that lock onto your legs just below the knee and are adjustable in height. They let you move freely around a room. You can't touch the floor, however, so place panels within reach—and hang onto your tools!

For maximum strength run plywood sheets across joists, with ends butting at joists, of course. Take a few minutes before you start work to lay out each ceiling. By knowing in advance where joints will fall, you can often save on material and avoid having to piece around ceiling openings.

Start work in the corner farthest from any ceiling opening. Test the fit first. If the corner isn't exactly square, you must scribe and trim the first panel. Exact positioning of this first panel is critical. Two edges must fit only a knife blade away from studs, and a third edge must lie at the center line of a joist.

Apply a full panel first, attaching it with four-penny finishing nails. Nail 8″ apart at edges, and 12″ apart in the field. If the panel is grooved, nail into the sides of the grooves at a slight angle. Panels are quite thin at the bottom of the grooves and may split if you nail straight in. While your partner holds one end of a panel, fit and nail the other end; then work toward him.

Joints supported at joists should butt smoothly. Gap about the thickness of a knife blade to allow for expansion. To achieve a tight end joint, add 1 × 2 or 2 × 2 nailing strips between joists centered over the joints. If you locate these strips accurately, they are easier to install before you begin to panel. However, you can set them in place as you go.

When you must cut a panel for a light fixture, mark the location on the surface of the panel with a grease pencil. Then use a keyhole saw to cut the hole before you attach the panel. At larger openings you can either cut in advance, or let the panel continue into the opening and rout off the excess later.

Start the second row of panels with something less than a full panel in order to stagger the butt joints. By laying out the ceiling in advance, you can determine what length to use to minimize scrap.

Before you move the sawhorses to the next location, fill all nail holes and repair scratches with putty stick. *Putty stick* is wood putty in stick form, available from your plywood dealer in a wood tone that matches the plywood finish. You apply the putty with a gentle rubbing action, and then smooth it with your finger or a soft rag.

## WALLBOARD CEILINGS

Gypsum wallboard is also known as drywall, plasterboard, and Sheetrock, which is a trade name. It is made of a plaster-like mixture that hardens under heat between two layers of paper. Although it comes in thicknesses from 1/4″ to 1″, the thicknesses most often used in vacation houses are 3/8″ and 1/2″. Sheets are 4′ wide and come in lengths from 8′ to 14′. The long edges of unfinished sheets are tapered or slightly eased for finishing with tape and joint cement. The long edges of finished sheets are beveled or rounded for butting together in a neat joint. Ends of all types are cut square.

The paper backing may be one of three types. One is a heavy paper or thin cardboard that serves no single purpose. Wallboard with this backing is the least expensive and is the type to order for general use. Another backing is reflective aluminum foil, excellent for wallboard used on ceilings and exterior walls. The foil directs the heat of the summer sun away from rooms, but is not as effective as a winter insulation. The third backing is a special water-resistant paper for wallboard used in bathrooms.

The exposed surface paper may also be one of three types. It may be a plain manila paper. It may be a colored paper that denotes specialized use, such as in a bathroom or kitchen. Both types take paint or wallpaper easily. The third type is a vinyl prefinished at the factory. It comes in a range of colors, patterns, and textures, and needs no additional finishing.

Wallboard is heavier than plywood of the same thickness, and it is more fragile until attached to joists or studs. On the other hand wallboard is comparatively low in cost, easy to cut and fit, does not support combustion, and offers a good reflective surface.

### Planning the Job

When planning a layout for unfinished wallboard on a ceiling (or a wall, for that matter), you want as few feet of joint as possible. Finishing joints is not difficult, but it does take time and is completed in several stages. Apply panels across joists if possible for greatest strength. In a 10' by 12' room, for example, you would use three 10' lengths instead of 2 1/2 12' lengths, regardless of joist direction, because you have 4' less of joint.

Here are some other industry recommendations to follow in planning your work:

- In rooms no more than 14' in the shortest dimension, lay wallboard from wall to wall. Avoid butting ends together.
- If ends must butt, stagger the joints as far as possible from the center of the room.
- Join square edges to square edges, and tapered edges to tapered edges. Don't butt a square edge against a tapered edge.
- Edges must meet over joists. Ends must be supported on nailing strips like plywood.

### Cutting and Fitting

Make all cuts before you apply any panel of wallboard. Use a keyhole saw or utility saw to cut holes for light fixtures. Use a wallboard knife for straight cuts.

Measure the cuts with a steel tape, and use a metal T-square with a 48" blade to cut against. Set the tongue tight against the edge of the board to assure a square cut (Fig. 14-1). Support the board on sawhorses while you score the paper, finished side up.

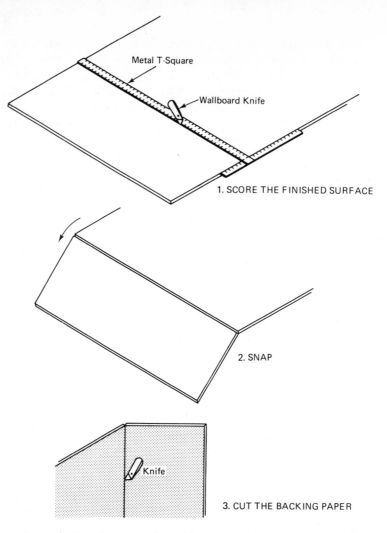

**Fig. 14-1.** The three steps in making a straight cut in gypsum wallboard are (1) score the surface, (2) snap the board along the scoring line, and (3) slit the backing paper along the break point.

To get a clean cut keep the blade of your utility knife razor sharp. Pull the knife toward you along the metal edge of the square, pressing only hard enough to cut the paper and score the gypsum core beneath it (Fig. 14-1, top). Then bend or snap the cut piece away from you (center); it should break cleanly. Next, run the knife up the crease in the back of the panel to cut the backing paper (bottom). Smooth any rough edges with a piece of coarse sandpaper bent over a block of wood. Cut edges should fit either against a wall or at an opening. Avoid exposing a cut edge anywhere in the middle of the ceiling.

## Applying Wallboard Overhead

You can apply unfinished wallboard to a ceiling in two ways. One way is with annular ring nails driven in with a wallboard hammer or a carpenter's claw hammer. A wallboard hammer is the better choice; its nailing surface is scored, slightly crowned, and rounded at the edges. This design allows you to drive nails straight, and puts a slight dimple in the surface without breaking the paper (Fig. 14-2, upper right). The nails have a ribbed shank that resists popping out as framing members expand and contract over the seasons.

You can also apply wallboard with special wallboard screws. The tool to use is an electric screwdriver that has a Phillips head with magnetic tip, adjustable depth control, and a positive clutch. Adjust the head by practicing until you can drive the screw heads enough below the panel's surface to dimple it without breaking the paper. The clutch and depth control let you drive screws just so far and no farther.

It takes at least two people to apply wallboard to a ceiling. You can make the job easier by building a supporting tee to hold the unattached ends of panels. Use a 1 × 6 about 3' long as a horizontal member, and a 2 × 4 as a supporting pole about 2" shorter than ceiling height. Add diagonal braces between the head and stem of the tee for strength.

To finish a ceiling, start in a corner as with plywood, first making sure the panel fits well into the corner. Begin attachment at the center of the panel and work outward. This method will remove any bow in the panel and help to support its weight. Space nails every 7" into joists, and screws every 12". Place fasteners as close to 3/8" from the edges as you can to assure hitting joists (Fig. 14-2, upper left). Now you can see why a bowed or cocked ceiling joist can cause problems.

Where joists meet a wall or partition, attach the panel, but about 8" in from the edge, not at the edge. Let the edge float free to reduce stress; it will be supported by wall paneling anyway.

Prefinished wallboard may also be applied with screws or nails with heads in matching colors. Do not dimple the surface when fastening, however, and drive nails with a plastic-headed hammer that is less likely to damage the surface of the ceiling. Drive fasteners flush with the surface. Butt joints loosely together; do not jam them tight.

## Finishing Joints

Prefinished wallboard requires no joint treatment. Joints between panels of unfinished wallboard and dimples for nails or screws must be finished. Joint treatment consists of wallboard tape and joint compound. The tape comes in rolls 60', 250', and 500' long and about 2" wide. It is made of paper reinforced with fibers, has feathered edges, and is dotted with tiny perforations. Joint compound comes ready mixed in cans of various sizes. It has the smooth consistency of batter, and spreads easily under the blade of a finishing knife.

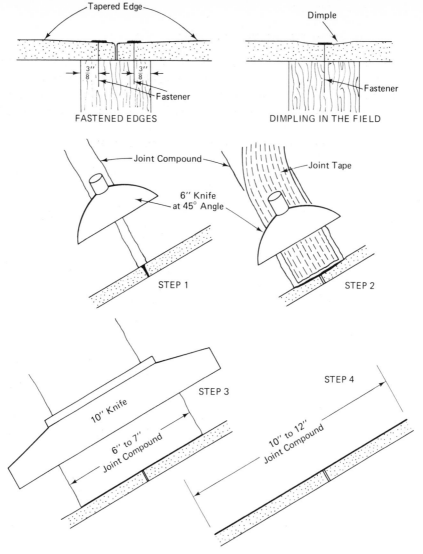

**Fig. 14-2.** Wallboard may be attached with nails or screws. Fasteners are driven at edges (upper left) and elsewhere into joists or studs (upper right) slightly below the surface. Finishing the joints between panels is a four-step process with drying time between steps. Darkened areas show where the joint compound goes in each step.

Before you apply the first layer of joint compound, look over the ceiling closely. Press panels at all fasteners to make sure they are tight. Wipe off all dust and grit—there is likely to be some at any unpapered edge. Run a finishing knife lightly over all fasteners. If you hear it clink against metal, that fastener isn't set deeply enough. Then lay your level across the joints. You won't get a good joint treatment job unless all the edges are at the same level.

Finishing wallboard takes several steps, with drying time between them. To fill dimples and any nicks, use a 4″ or 6″ finishing knife. With the first coat of compound fill to just below the surface, pressing the compound firmly into depressions. A thin second coat should fill the depressions flush. Feather a third coat, also very thin, to a circle about 3″ in diameter. Sand lightly after each coat dries.

At edge joints apply enough compound to fill the groove between panels (step 1 in Fig. 14–2). Wipe off any excess and let the compound dry. The following day fill the channel between tapered edges full of compound. Center the joint tape in the compound (step 2), press it in firmly with your knife; then continue to embed the tape as you unroll it down the joint. Run the tape all the way to the end of the joint, and then cut or tear it. You will get the best results by holding the knife at about a 45° angle to the ceiling surface. Leave enough compound under the tape for a good bond, but only a thin coat at the joint's edges. The compound will ooze through the perforations in the tape. Remove any excess compound; then add just a skim coat over the tape. This skim coat prevents the edges of the tape from wrinkling or curling.

Let this second coat dry thoroughly. Do not sand it. Then apply another coat (step 3 in Fig. 14–2), which should extend about 2″ on either side of the previous coat. Feather the edges. A 10″ knife is better than a 6″ knife for applying the final two coats, because it will give you a thin feathered edge more easily. Let this coat dry, then sand it lightly. Add a final coat (step 4), feathering an additional 2″ on each side of the previous coat. After this coat has dried completely, sand it lightly.

It's hard to say how long it takes joint compound to dry. You can't tell by looking at it. At 55°F—the lowest temperature at which you should work—drying time ranges from one day at 10% humidity to six days at 90% humidity. When the outside temperature is 80°F, drying time ranges from seven hours to two days. Most of the time, if you are working in the summer, allow two days between coats. In winter allow a full week.

Finish butt edges by the same process as tapered edges. To avoid the appearance of a joint, however, extend the feathering a full 9″ on either side of the joint.

# CEILING TILES

Of all ceiling materials, tiles are the easiest to work with because they are manageable in size. One man can do the job alone. Tiles are lightweight and come in 12″ and 24″ squares and rectangles 12″ by 18″, 12″ by 24″, and 24″ by 48″. They may be made of 1/2″-thick fiberboard, a soft wood product, with plain, perforated, or heavily textured surfaces. Or they may be made of molten rock formed into mineral tiles 1″ thick. Fiber tiles will burn; mineral tiles will not. Both types come prefinished, but either kind can be painted.

Square-edged or beveled-edged tiles may be applied with mastic to a flat ceiling of unfinished plywood or wallboard. A less expensive and equally attractive way is to staple the tiles to furring strips. For this application use straight, flat

1 × 2s for furring strips, and mineral tiles with interlocking edges. To protect your ceiling and roof structure from the spread of fire, do not use fiber tiles on a ceiling without a backing of wallboard.

### Planning the Job

A tile ceiling looks best when the tiles at opposite edges of the ceiling are the same width. This takes some planning and measuring. It's easy to cut a tile with a sharp utility knife. But you should never use less than half a tile anywhere. So begin by measuring the dimensions of the room accurately at ceiling level. Put these measurements on a sheet of graph paper and make a drawing of the ceiling as you would look up at it.

Suppose the dimensions of the room are 9′8″ across joists by 13′4″ parallel to joists, and you want to use 12″ by 12″ tiles. If you use nine full tiles across the shorter dimension, you would have rows of 4″ tiles at the walls. This is not good practice. It is much better to use eight full tiles and 10″ tiles at the walls. Similarly, use 12 full tiles and 8″ tiles at the walls across the long dimension of the room.

The center line of each furring strip should fall behind the joints between tiles. In the example, then, the first center lines would be 8″ from each short wall. So measure out 7 1/4″ from one wall (8″ less half the width of a 1 × 2, or 3/4″), and 8 3/4″ out from the other wall (8″ plus half the width of a 1 × 2) as shown in Fig. 14–3. Mark these locations on a joist or plate above one wall, and measure the distance between your marks. The distance should come out in even feet. If not, recheck your measurements and your marks.

### Putting Up Furring Strips

When you are certain your measurements are correct, mark the plate above the opposite wall in the same way. Then snap chalk lines across all joists between pairs of marks. Nail two furring strips (A and B in Fig. 14–3) along the chalk lines—both strips should be on the same sides of the lines. Then nail smaller furring strips across joists against the studs of the shorter walls. These can be 1 × 1s, since you attach only one tile row to them.

Now, on the two full-width furring strips mark center lines going the other direction of the room. At a point 10″ out from each wall along these lines, make a mark. These four marks (C in Fig. 14–3) locate the corners of the first full tile in each corner. The distances between pairs of marks should be in even feet in both directions, and the diagonal measurements between marks in opposite corners should be equal.

If your measurements check out, position and attach the remaining furring strips. Use two eight-penny nails at each joist, driven about 3/8″ in from the edges of furring strips. By placing the nails this way, you won't hit them when you staple the tiles.

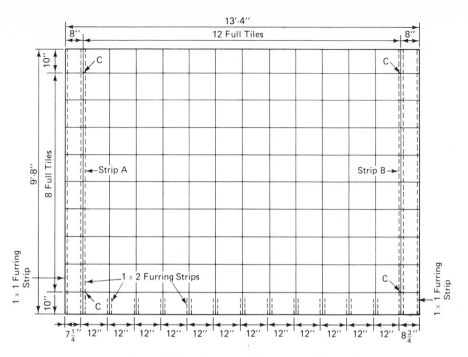

**Fig. 14-3.** Before applying tiles to a ceiling you need to make a layout looking up. Dimensions and details shown relate to the example in the text.

## Applying Ceiling Tiles

Start in one corner with a small tile cut to size. Set it with its flanges toward the center of the room and against the furring strips. Drive three staples into each flange, one at each corner and one centered. At the other edges, where you cut off the flange, carefully drive three finishing nails close to the edges. Ceiling trim will cover the nail heads if you can't hide them in perforations or fissures in the tiles.

The flanges extend about 1/2″ beyond the visible joint between tiles. If you want to line up each tile on its flanges, snap additional chalk lines to allow for the 1/2″ difference. Otherwise, line up the exposed edge of each tile in finished position with existing chalk lines. To keep yourself on the proper spacing, snap additional chalk lines at right angles to the furring strips.

After you attach the first tile, fit the abutting tiles along the walls. Then apply the first full-sized tile. Continue to work across the room in a diagonal pattern. Check frequently to make sure you are staying on the chalk lines, and check the level occasionally to assure that all tiles are in the same horizontal plane.

At the far corner you will again have to cut the last tiles to fit, and face-nail them.

# PLYWOOD WALLS

For wall materials you have a greater choice than for ceilings. In addition to plywood paneling and wallboard, you can use boards, hardboard, or a combination of any of these. If you feel particularly adventurous, you may even want to try your hand at ceramic tiles in the kitchen and bathroom.

Prefinished plywood is primarily for wall application. Order panels to the length you need, so that you have no horizontal joints except in high-ceilinged rooms. Protect the panels while they are stored. You may apply them to studs with four-penny finishing nails, coated nails in matching colors, glue, contact adhesive, or contact cement.

Prefinished plywood is thin, and must be fully supported at all edges. To prevent damage from bumps it's a good idea to add 2 × 2 blocking between studs 3 ' above the floor and 3 ' below the ceiling in heavily traveled areas, such as hallways. Blocking adds considerable stiffness.

### Planning the Corners

Before you begin paneling, lay out each wall so that you know where each joint will fall to assure that you have a stud there. Then decide how you want to handle corners.

At inside corners you can butt panels together. This method works well if your corners are absolutely square and plumb. Otherwise you have to scribe and trim for a tight fit. An alternate solution is to gap panels slightly at the corners, then cover the gap with a length of molding (Fig. 14-4, lower left). Another alternative is to fit a corner molding first; then butt the two panels of plywood against it. With either of the latter two methods the corner panels are likely to be too wide to hit studs at their other edges, and you will have to rip a little off for a fit. Always put the ripped edge in the corner where it is least noticeable.

At outside corners panels will chip easily if the edges aren't protected. The simplest protection is an outside corner molding (Fig. 14-4, upper right). At the ceiling line (upper left) use a small cove molding if the gap between ceiling and wall materials is small, or a larger and fancier cove if the gap is large. If you are careful during application, you will need no molding at vertical joints. Use a thin batten only when necessary to hide a problem (lower right).

### Applying Plywood to Studs

In order to apply plywood to studs with nails, follow the procedures outlined earlier in this chapter for ceiling application. The procedures for glue, contact adhesive, and contact cement are a little different. Most important, you must precut panels to fit. Otherwise you may break the bond.

Apply glue and contact adhesive (they come in cartridges) with a gun to the faces of studs. Lay a bead of glue in a slight zigzag pattern down each stud, but not on any horizontal members. Press each panel against the studs; then pull it away immediately. This spreads a little glue or adhesive on the back of the panel and helps it dry more quickly. Then reset the panel.

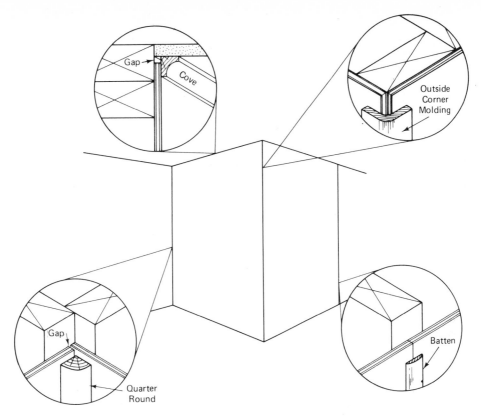

**Fig. 14-4.** Plywood and hardboard on walls must be finished at the ceiling (upper left), outside corners (upper right), and inside corners (lower left). If necessary to hide poor joints in a straight wall, use thin battens (lower right).

The best way to fit a panel is to line it up at the edge of the adjacent panel, use that edge like a hinge, and swing the panel into final position. Tack at all four corners with four-penny nails to hold the panel in place while the glue dries. You can also use nails to eliminate any slight buckling.

Contact cement, unlike glue and contact adhesives, has no open time. In other words, once you position a panel in the cement, you can't move it without destroying it. Mark stud locations on the back of each panel. Then brush two coats of adhesive not only on the studs but also on the backs of panels in strips about 2 1/2″ wide where you marked. Set each panel accurately and swing it into place. To assure a tight bond, pound along the length of each stud with a rubber mallet.

## WALLBOARD ON WALLS

The methods of applying wallboard to walls are similar to those for ceilings. Use the longest lengths you can to minimize the amount of joint. If walls are a nominal 8′ high, lay unfinished wallboard horizontally. Locate any butt joints toward the corners of rooms and stagger them. Make all cuts in advance. Let the fits be somewhat loose; edges will be covered with trim anyway.

There is one important new rule: do not nail wallboard to the flat sides of any wood members, such as window headers. Let panels float at these points. The reason is that wood shrinks more across the grain than it does with the grain, and there is a good chance that cracks will develop if you nail.

When you make a right-angle cut, as at a window, cut the short direction with a keyhole or utility saw, and then score and snap in the other direction.

### Applying Wallboard to Studs

Begin application in a corner. With horizontal placement set the upper panels first—just high enough to support the unnailed edge of a wallboard ceiling. Don't jam panels into place. Set the lower panels firmly against the upper panels, and don't worry about leaving a small gap at the floor line. Support the panel on the toe or sole of your safety shoe to hold it in place while you fasten it. Nail or apply screws from the center outward across the top of each panel, then work toward the floor.

At inside corners butt panels together, but gap about 1/8″ to allow for any unevenness in plumb. At outside corners let one panel overlap the other the thickness of the board so that each corner is as square as possible.

### Finishing Corners

Finish dimples and flat joints in walls the same as in ceilings. At inside corners fold joint tape down the center along the crease provided by the manufacturer. Spread joint compound on both sides of the corner, fit the tape, and embed it by drawing a finishing knife down the joint. Use the corner of the blade to form a sharp corner, holding the knife at about a 30° angle to the wall. Be careful not to slit the tape, however. Like finishing a flat joint, finishing corners is also a four-step process.

Cover outside corners with *corner bead,* a thin strip of metal shaped like a clay tile roof at the ridge. If necessary, cut the bead to length with metal shears. Fit its flanges over the corner and nail it through the wallboard into studs. The corner of the bead is raised and slightly rounded, and you must fill the troughs on both sides with three coats of joint compound. Let each coat dry thoroughly between applications. No tape is required.

# PREFINISHED WALLBOARD

The methods for putting up prefinished wallboard are similar to those for prefinished plywood. The material comes only in 8′ and 10′ lengths. Panels must be applied vertically, but may be attached with adhesive or colored finishing nails. Again, fit cut edges into corners.

There are two differences, however. If possible, use a plastic-headed hammer for nailing to avoid chipping the paint off the nails. And when you cut vinyl-coated panels, score the vinyl surface with a knife before sawing or scoring and snapping.

# HARDBOARD ON WALLS

A manufactured product made of wood fibers and binders pressed into sheets, *hardboard* has many of the characteristics of plywood. It may be unfinished, and as such is either dark brown or tan in color. It may be surfaced in a wide variety of vinyl and printed finishes that look like wood, marble, tile, and even leather. It comes in sheets 4' wide, 8' and 12' long, and 1/4" to 1/2" thick. It cuts like wood, and you apply it with nails or adhesive directly to studs.

But hardboard differs from plywood in several important ways. It expands and contracts more readily, breaks and chips more easily, and doesn't have strong nail-holding power. It is less expensive, however, and you can bend the thinner types around curves. Although hardboard can be applied directly to studs, the best application is over horizontal furring strips, especially if studs aren't exactly 16" on centers.

## Applying Hardboard

Use boards as furring strips. Begin with a 1 × 4 set level about 1/4" above the subfloor. Then add 1 × 2 furring strips on up the wall horizontally every 16" on centers (Fig. 14–5). Use another 1 × 4 at the ceiling. The 1 × 4s give you something into which you can nail the trim. As a temporary support for panels while you fasten them, tack another 1 × 2 over the bottom 1 × 4 close to the floor. Be sure it is absolutely level.

Set the first panel in a corner. Finish at inside and outside corners as with plywood. If you apply panels with adhesive, the methods are identical with those for wallboard and plywood. If you nail, space three-penny nails 4" apart at all edges and 8" apart into furring strips elsewhere. Drive nails carefully and straight. As the name implies, hardboard is hard, and it's easy to bend nails. If you want the best appearance, set the nails just below the surface in predrilled holes and fill the holes with putty that matches the tone of the surface.

## Applying Perforated Hardboard

*Perforated hardboard* is standard hardboard with holes punched in it 1" on centers. It is most often used as a hanging wall. You insert metal hangers through the holes to support tools, pots and pans, and shelves. There are more than 50 different types of hangers, each designed for a specific purpose. Perforated hardboard is applied to furring strips the same way as ordinary hardboard. The open space behind the panels allows you to insert hangers.

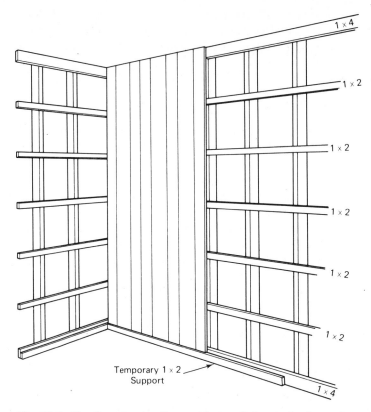

**Fig. 14-5.** Hardboard on walls must be applied over furring strips. Top and bottom strips are wider to provide a nailing surface for trim. Temporary support assures that edges of panels are plumb.

## TWO MATERIALS ON ONE WALL

Suppose you want to use plywood for its durability on the lower part of a wall, and wallboard for its color on the upper part. The question here is how to finish the joints between the two materials; the answer depends on their thicknesses.

When both materials are the same thickness, you can cover the joint with wood molding or fit a thin molding between them (Fig. 14–6). If wallboard is one of the two materials, apply the panels vertically so that you have a square, not a tapered, edge at the joint. Apply wallboard first, then the other material.

When the materials are of different thicknesses, use a molding called a *wainscot cap* large enough to cover the edge of the thicker material. Then add a small cove molding to hide the edge of the thinner material.

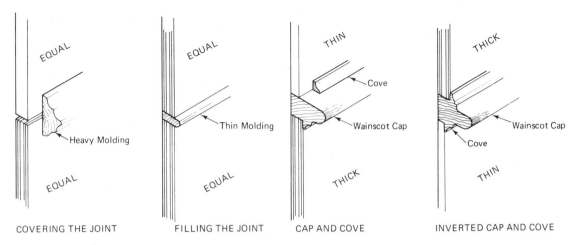

**Fig. 14-6.** Here are four ways to finish a joint between two materials on the same wall. The best method depends on the thicknesses of the two materials.

# THE TUB ENCLOSURE

The best place to start finishing walls is in the bathroom. The work is harder than in living and sleeping rooms, but finish plumbing can't be started until ceilings, walls, and floors are surfaced. After you finish the bathroom, work on the kitchen, which also involves plumbing. Work on the larger but simpler living areas last. Then you and your mechanical subcontractors can work simultaneously, and your house will be ready for occupancy sooner.

You can finish most walls of the bathroom in the same way as any other room. But the tub or shower enclosure requires special treatment. Your choices are varied. You can buy a complete one-piece tub enclosure made of plastic that includes the tub itself and surrounding walls to a height of 6' or 7'. One-piece shower stalls of plastic or metal are also readily available. Neither enclosure requires wall material behind it. Each is equipped with special lugs that you attach to studs. The lugs space the enclosure away from the studs, and the wall material above fits flush at the top.

## Applying Water-Resistant Wallboard

Wallboard with specially treated paper, primarily for use in bathrooms, comes in 8' and 12' lengths and requires special installation techniques. Before you start work the bathtub must be in place, all plumbing must be stubbed through walls, and all blocking installed for soap dishes, toilet paper holders, and other such accessories.

Precut all panels to fit, and also pre-cut all holes for piping. Thoroughly coat all cut edges, including pipe holes, with the sealant that comes with the wallboard. This sealant keeps water out of the gypsum core. Set the first panels horizontally around the tub on a spacer about 1/4″ thick (a shingle works well) in order to keep the edge above the rim of the tub. Fasten with nails every 8″ or with screws every 12″ on centers.

If you plan to paint or wallpaper, finish seams with joint treatment like any other wallboard. If you intend to add tiles, omit joint treatment and simply seal the heads of the fasteners with sealant. As a final step in either case, remove the spacers and caulk the opening between the wallboard and the tub or shower base.

### Applying Tileboard

*Tileboard* is a tempered hardboard with a baked-on enamel surface that sheds water. It is made especially for use in bathrooms and kitchens. Widths range up to 60″ to fit behind a tub without a seam. Manufacturers provide a full line of metal trim for use in all kinds of corners (Fig. 14-7).

Begin by positioning the tub molding (Fig. 14-7, bottom) and attaching it with roofing nails through holes in its flange. Make sure this molding is absolutely level and runs from corner to corner of the long wall behind the tub. Set the tileboard well into the molding, but not so tight that it can't expand. Nail it through the holes in the flange of the tub molding, every 4″ along other edges and 8″ apart into studs.

To finish walls at the ends of a tub, first apply the tub molding. Then butt inside corner moldings over the installed panel (Fig. 14-7, top). Cut end panels to fit. Their width is the distance from the finished surface of the tileboard already in place to the outside edge of studs at the corner, less an allowance for gapping in the moldings. Insert the panels in the inside corner moldings, but before nailing fit the next molding over the open edge. At an outside corner (left) or edge adjoining another material (right), the trim molding slips behind the end panels.

## WALL TILES

Tiling on the walls of a bathroom or kitchen is a nice finishing touch. It adds color and an aura of richness that you might expect only in more expensive, contractor-built vacation houses. Yet tiling is within the scope of most amateurs.

Tiles are made of three materials—metal, plastic, and clay. All three types are applied to an existing wall surface with adhesive. That base surface may be plywood, wallboard, masonry, or concrete. Plywood must be unfinished, exterior grade, applied horizontally. It should be at least 1/2″ thick behind ceramic (clay) tiles, but it can be thinner behind metal or plastic tiles, which are applied with less pressure. Wallboard should be the water-resistant type, again 1/2″ thick behind ceramic tiles.

A wallboard base requires no special preparation, provided that all holes and cut edges are sealed and all joints are fully taped. A plywood base needs a coat of *size,* a thin glazing liquid that helps adhesive to stick better. A concrete

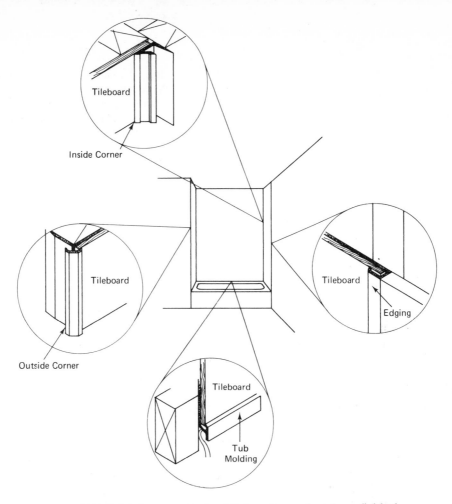

**Fig. 14-7.** Joints between panels of tileboard around a tub are finished with moldings. Insets show how each type of molding fits around or against the panels.

or masonry base requires a sealer to prevent moisture from penetrating from behind and dissolving the adhesive bond.

Whatever the base surface, it must be flat, plumb, and clean. It should not be mirror smooth; a little roughness gives the adhesive something to grab onto. Joints around pipes must be tightly sealed with caulking to avoid moisture penetration.

### Laying Out the Job

Standard tiles are square, 4 1/4″ on a side. You can buy them individually or in sheets 30″ square. Sheet tiles come attached to a webbed backing, and sometimes the tiles have grout between joints. Since the standard tub is 30 1/2″ by 60″, sheet tiles are ideal for finishing a tub enclosure.

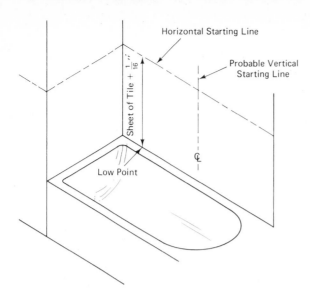

Horizontal Starting Line

Probable Vertical Starting Line

Sheet of Tile + 1/16"

Low Point

**Fig. 14-8.** To lay tiles on a wall around a bathtub you must establish horizontal and vertical starting lines. Measuring points are the low point of the tub's rim and the center line of the longest wall.

To set tiles you need both a horizontal starting line and a vertical starting line. Lay your carpenter's level on the rim of the tub on the long wall. If the rim is level, it can be your starting point. If the rim is not level, find the lowest point and mark it. Then, starting either at the level tub rim or your mark, measure up the height of a sheet of tiles, add 1/16", and mark this height on the wall.

Draw a line at this height on all enclosing walls (Fig. 14–8). Use a straightedge to draw a straight line, and your level to make sure the line is horizontal. Tiles should not rest on the rim of a tub or the edge of any other plumbing fixture. The extra 1/16" is to allow for that space at the bottom of the first sheet. If the tub rim is not level, you must trim the bottom row of tiles to fit the slope.

To establish a vertical starting line, find the center of the long wall above the tub. Mark this center line lightly. Then set a sheet of tiles against the line on each side to see what happens at the corners. With a 60" tub you should have close to an exact fit at both ends. If you have a little too much tile for the space, you must trim the end row to fit.

If you don't get a good fit, check both the plumb and square of the two corners. If both corners are plumb, move the sheet of tiles into the corner nearest the water inlet and draw a new vertical starting line near the center of the wall but at a revised location at the end of the sheet. If only one corner is plumb, move the sheet into that corner and redraw the starting line.

If neither corner is plumb, you must cut tiles at both ends. Ideally, cut tiles should be less than half a tile wide. To achieve this ideal when you have quite a bit of space in the corners, it is usually best to shift the vertical starting line half a tile width in one direction or the other.

On end walls, start measuring at the outside corner of the tub recess. If there is no recess, start flush with the outside edge of the tub. Any cut tiles should be in inside corners where they are least visible.

If you plan to use individual tiles instead of sheets, follow these identical directions. Just substitute the word "tile" for "sheet of tiles."

## Cutting Tiles

To make a straight-line cut in a ceramic tile, first mark the line of cut on the edges of the tile. Then score the glazed surface with a glass cutter, turn the tile over, and break it carefully over a wire; a piece of coat hanger works well. You can cut metal tiles with a hacksaw, and plastic tiles with a fine-toothed coping saw. Cut gingerly, though, because the plastic chips easily.

Cutting a curve in a ceramic tile is a bit more difficult. Mark the curve on the back of the tile with a grease pencil. Where the curve touches an edge, file a notch. Then put on safety glasses and use a coping saw to make the cut. The cut will be clean enough to leave exposed.

When cuts will be hidden behind an *escutcheon* (a circular collar that fits over a pipe at a wall or floor), you can use tile nippers. *Nippers* operate like pliers to nibble away a hole. After filing the edges of the tile and adjusting your safety glasses, carefully chew at the ceramic with the nippers. Nip with the glazed side up. Work slowly and take small bites—no more than 1/8″ in depth. Take too big a bite and you are likely to shatter the tile. Start at a corner and gradually work toward your line, breaking off pieces side by side.

With metal tiles use a coping saw to cut curves. With plastic tiles you can use a coping saw or nippers, or burn in the hole with a soldering iron.

Cutting a hole in the center of a tile is the most difficult operation. You can usually avoid the problem by locating the water inlet pipe so that it comes through the joint between the first and second courses of square tiles above the tub rim, and between the third and fourth vertical courses from the corner. Similarly, locate water controls one course higher and at intersections of vertical courses. Then all you have to do is nip off the corners of a few tiles. Escutcheons will cover any raggedness.

If you must cut a hole in the middle of a tile, follow the procedure shown in Fig. 14–9, a delicate five-step process. If you are lucky enough to be able to borrow or rent a hole cutter, you can do the job more quickly and cleanly. A *hole cutter* is a form of power drill that scribes a hole on the tile's surface. Then you just knock out the plug with a hammer.

**Fig. 14-9.** To make a hole in the middle of a tile, first make a straight cut with a coping saw (1). Then cut the back side of the tile along a perpendicular line (2). Next score the face of the tile along lines 1 and 2 with a glass cutter (3) and snap it into two pieces. Then nibble the hole with nippers (4). Finally, set the two pieces of tile (5) around the hole separately.

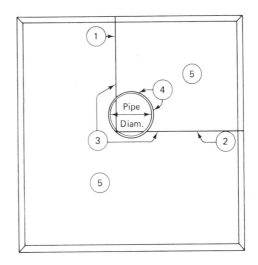

## Spreading Adhesive

When you have cut to size as many tiles as possible, spread mastic on the first section of wall. Cover only as much surface as you expect to tile in 30 minutes. Use a pointed trowel or broadknife to get the mastic out of the can and buttered on the back of a notched spreader. Hold the spreader at about 30° to the wall.

You can spread in any direction you like. Press the spreader against the wall so that the mastic oozes between its teeth, leaving ridges with very little mastic between them. In corners and other spots too tight to coat with the spreader, use a trowel to apply a thin coat. Create ridges with the point of the trowel. The finished coat of mastic should be evenly ridged with no bare or thick spots.

Read the mastic manufacturer's recommendations on how quickly to proceed. While you are reading, take the time to wipe your hands with the cleaner-solvent suggested by the adhesive manufacturer. It's easier to get mastic off your hands than off the tiles. But once you start to set tiles, be careful with the cleaner. It is also a solvent that softens the mastic.

## Applying Tiles

Lay the first tile or sheet of tiles where your two starting lines cross. Press each tile firmly to flatten the ridges and assure a good bond, but avoid pressing so hard that you force adhesive up between the tiles. Use your level frequently to check the accuracy of your progress, resting it on the edge of tiles, not in the mastic.

Always lay full tiles first; then go back to set any cut tiles. Complete one wall before you go on to the next. If the mastic begins to dry before you can set tiles in it, carefully scrape it off. When you are ready to set tiles in corners, use a putty knife to butter mastic on the back of each piece. Then snap it into place.

If you are working with sheets of tiles and have to cut an individual tile, leave the backing on uncut tiles but remove it from all tiles yet to be cut. Only lay up sheets with full tiles in them—set cut tiles individually.

Before the mastic dries, clean the excess out of grooves between tiles with a putty knife and off tile surfaces with cleaner. Apply the cleaner with a damp cloth, using it sparingly. Let the finished wall set overnight before you grout it.

## Grouting Joints

Finish applying tiles to all wall surfaces before you grout joints in any wall. That way you aren't intermixing two separate processes. Use powdered grout— a cementaceous mixture that you mix into cold water. Prepare only as much as you can use in 30 minutes.

Apply grout from the back of the trowel, working the mixture into joints with its edge. Fill as many joints as you can in 10 minutes. Then use a squeegee to draw off excess grout, followed by a damp sponge to wipe off any grout smeared by the squeegee. Be gentle in both wiping operations. The grout in the joints has almost set by now, but it is still vulnerable to vigorous action.

After wiping, compact the grout into the joints. Use something stiff but not sharp, and rather narrow and rounded. A toothbrush handle or the spine of a pocket comb works well. The bottom of the finished groove should be just barely below the surface of the tiles. Clean away excess grout with a damp sponge.

Grout takes about two weeks to cure fully. During this period dampen the wall periodically, but don't use the shower.

With plastic and metal tiles your job is usually done when you have set all square tiles, filled corners, and grouted. For a more finished appearance with any type of tiles—and required with ceramic tiles—fit cap strips along horizontal and vertical edges. *Cap strips* have rounded edges that carry the tile surface attractively back to the surface of untiled walls. They may be square (the same size as standard tiles) with either one or two rounded edges. More often, however, cap strips are 2″ by 6″. Five caps exactly cover seven square tiles. Tile manufacturers make special pieces to fit into inside corners and around outside corners.

# UNDERLAYMENT

Most flooring materials today are set in mastic. Thick coverings such as wood blocks and squares of carpet may be laid directly over subflooring. Thin materials such as resilient tiles and roll goods require an underlayment, regardless of what you use for a subfloor.

*Underlayment* is a thin sheet of smooth material that lies between the subfloor and finished flooring material. Its purpose is to provide a smooth base that will not telegraph through thin flooring the cracks, seams, and other imperfections in the subfloor. Underlayment may be either sheets of hardboard or thin plywood.

## Applying the Material

To prepare for underlayment, sweep the subfloor clean. Nail or screw down any raised edges. If necessary, rent a power sander to knock down ridges and other high spots. Replace any subflooring that has warped badly during construction. You can't get a good flooring job over a poor subfloor, even with underlayment.

The edges of sheets of underlayment must never fall over joints in the subfloor. To avoid this, start in the same corner in which you began subflooring by laying a 2′ by 6′ piece (Fig. 14–10). Then alternate 4′ by 2′ and 4′ by 6′ sheets at one edge, and lay 2′ by 8′ pieces along the other. Lay full-size sheets in the center of the floor.

For fasteners you can use staples or special underlayment nails, spaced 3″ apart at edges and 6″ apart everywhere else. Be sure that the crowns of staples are flush with the surface of the underlayment. They can show through thin flooring, too.

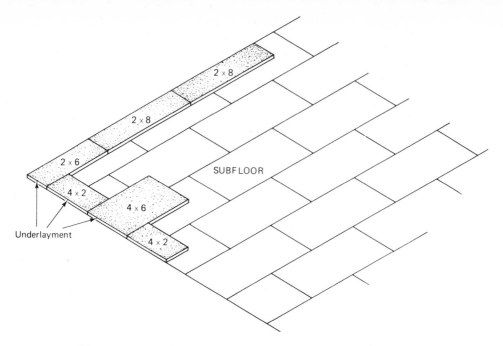

**Fig. 14-10.** A typical starting pattern for applying underlayment. Joints in underlayment must not fall over seams in subflooring.

## RESILIENT FLOOR TILES

Resilient floor tiles may be made of vinyl, vinyl-asbestos, asphalt, linoleum, or rubber, with vinyl the most common. Tile thickness is less than 1/8", and the most popular size is a 12" square. Tiles come in patterns that resemble bricks, wood planks, terrazzo, and—believe it or not—a ceramic tile floor. You can buy tiles with or without adhesive backing. All manufacturers also make *feature strips*—long, narrow strips of material in solid colors—that you can use to devise your own tile patterns.

### Making a Tile Layout

A well-laid floor, like the tile ceiling discussed earlier in this chapter, is symmetrical. Tiles against opposite walls are the same size. To achieve this symmetry, or to make an interesting floor layout with a pattern in it, you must make a floor diagram.

First check all corners of each room for square. Then measure accurately along the base of each wall and write down the dimensions—in feet if you use 12" tile, in inches for anything else. Then find the center of the room by snapping diagonal chalk lines. If the room isn't rectangular, find the midpoints of the two longest walls and measure out from these midpoints to find the center. You must find the midpoint because that is where you will begin tiling. Through the midpoint snap two more chalk lines parallel to the long and short walls.

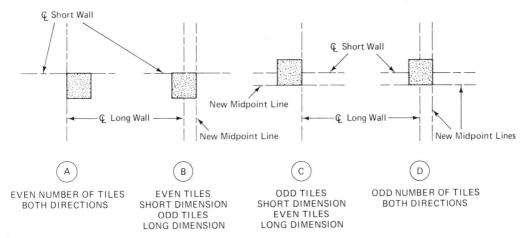

| | | | |
|:---:|:---:|:---:|:---:|
| Ⓐ | Ⓑ | Ⓒ | Ⓓ |
| EVEN NUMBER OF TILES<br>BOTH DIRECTIONS | EVEN TILES<br>SHORT DIMENSION<br>ODD TILES<br>LONG DIMENSION | ODD TILES<br>SHORT DIMENSION<br>EVEN TILES<br>LONG DIMENSION | ODD NUMBER OF TILES<br>BOTH DIRECTIONS |

**Fig. 14-11.** The first tile in a tile floor is laid at one of four points, depending on the number of full tiles required to complete the pattern in each direction.

Suppose the room you start in measures 10′ 9″ by 13′ 6″. To avoid using less than half a tile, you would use nine full tiles and two 10 1/2″ tiles across the short dimension, and 12 full tiles and two 9″ tiles across the long dimension. When the number of full tiles is even in both directions, use as a starting point the point where the center lines meet (A in Fig. 14-11). When either number is odd, move the midpoint and starting point half a tile (B or C). When both numbers are odd, move the starting point half a tile in two directions (D). If necessary, snap new chalk lines parallel to walls through the new midpoint. Now you are ready to lay tiles parallel.

Laying tiles parallel to walls is the easiest way. You can even create a diagonal pattern by using two or more colors (Fig. 14-12), but keep the colors in the same family. White, light green, and dark green will look a lot better together than white, red, and green.

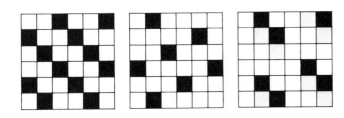

**Fig. 14-12.** Here are just a few of the many diagonal patterns you can create in a tile floor while laying the tiles parallel to walls.

299

## Applying Floor Tiles

Tiles with contact adhesive on the back are the easiest and cleanest to lay, but they are a little more expensive than tiles laid in mastic. Some types of adhesive are applied with a notched trowel, other types with a brush. Follow the manufacturer's directions explicitly.

Lay tiles on a warm day following a warm night. Tiles should be supple, not brittle, at the time of laying. Place the first tile at the crossed center lines, then work outward toward the walls. If you spread your own adhesive, cover about a fourth of the room at a time. Start in a corner and spread toward the center, and then lay tiles in the opposite direction. In this way you avoid trapping yourself in a corner. The adhesive is ready for tiles when it becomes tacky—just slightly sticky to the touch. Resnap chalk lines into the tacky adhesive to get you off to a square start.

Set each tile in position from above; don't twist or slide it. Butt each tile carefully against its neighbors with no adhesive between them. Joints should scarcely be visible. Continue until you have laid all full-sized tiles.

To fit edge tiles, first cut a strip about 1″ wide from a damaged tile, and lay it on the floor against the wall. Then lay a full-sized tile upside down on the strip and the finished floor. Place it tight against the wall or plate, while fitting one edge across the corner where two laid tiles meet (Fig. 14–13).

Along the line of finished tiles score the upside down tile, using a straight-edge for a clean, square line and a utility knife or awl for scoring. Snap the tile along the scoring line, and smooth the rough edge.

Then lay the tile with its cut edge against the wall; it will be covered by trim. Repeat this process for all edge tiles. This method of measuring works even when

**Fig. 14-13.** To fit edge tiles, turn a full tile upside down, score it along the edge of full tiles, and turn the cut tile right side up to lay it.

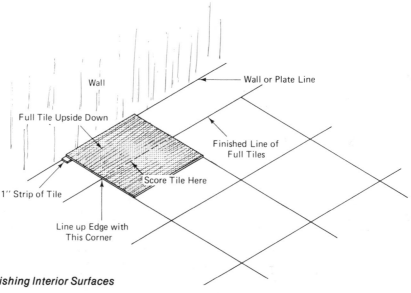

the wall and the edge line of finished tiles aren't parallel. Use the same basic process for fitting tiles at door jambs and at the edge of the bathtub. At kitchen cabinets tile all the way to the wall. The flooring under cabinets protects the absorptive subfloor from damage from leaks in the plumbing or from an overflowing sink.

## ROLL GOODS

Roll goods, of which linoleum is the best-known type, is like resilient tile in sheet form. It is laid over underlayment into mastic. Standard rolls are 6' wide and hundreds of feet long. You buy the length you need. The number of available patterns is vast. Simulated brick and ceramic tile are among the most popular.

Before spreading mastic, unroll the roll goods onto the floor to check for a fit at corners. If you have a door opening in a side wall, allow the roll goods to fit into the doorway as far as the door stop without a break. Trim along one side of the roll and leave a tongue a little wider than the doorway. Make the final cut later.

Determine which way you want to unroll the flooring. Then spread only enough mastic at one end of the room to let you position the roll and hold it in place. Press the end of the roll into the adhesive, and unroll it far enough to make sure you are heading down the room parallel to one wall. To do this, you must precut the roll to width, allowing for tongues at doorways.

When the fit is right, spread mastic only to the first obstacle, such as a waste line in a kitchen or doorway. Cut the linoleum to fit around the obstacle and then apply mastic through the area of the cut. Continue down the room in this fashion.

Cut and trim roll goods with a sharp linoleum knife. At pipes cut a slit from one edge, shape the hole for the pipe, and fit the two cut edges tightly together. Remember that the edges of roll goods will be covered by base trim except at doorways. Here you nail down a metal bar with a hook-shaped section, fit the linoleum into the recess, and press the top of the bar firmly into the roll goods. Fasten the bar to the subfloor with the nails provided by the bar's manufacturer.

## CERAMIC FLOOR TILES

The same type of mounted ceramic tiles for use on bathroom walls is also available for use as finished flooring. Press each full sheet into mastic, being careful not to push a sheet out of position when you walk or kneel on it. To avoid this, work from a 6'-long board wrapped in an old towel. This spreads your weight and saves your knees. Allow a little space between sheets for grouting. Lay full sheets first, then go back and fill in with partial sheets and individual tiles where necessary.

Ceramic wall tiles have slightly rounded edges, and the grout between tiles is recessed just below the surface. Ceramic floor tiles have square edges, and you

The informal interior of this A-frame has several features worth noting and copying. The brick of both the raised hearth and the wall behind a manufactured fireplace adds warmth and color. Walls are unfinished plywood stained to bring out the grain. Simple stairway has stringers and treads but no risers. Flooring is indoor-outdoor carpeting on treads and in living room, and roll goods in the kitchen at right. Note the simple yet effective construction of the railings. *Photographer: Kelly Severns. Courtesy American Plywood Association.*

grout to the top of the tiles for a flush floor surface. Also, you should use a little heavier grout. Follow the same procedures for grouting and cleanup as with wall tiles. Polish with a rough cloth, such as a burlap bag. Do not wash the floor for at least three weeks, and don't use cleaners or waxes for six months.

## PREFINISHED WOOD BLOCKS

Wood blocks are more expensive than resilient tiles or roll goods, but they look it, and provide a rich and warm-looking floor. Blocks vary in thickness from about 5/16" up to 13/16". Set thin blocks in mastic over underlayment, and nail the thicker blocks to subflooring.

Wood block floors come in squares of 9" to 12", in rectangles, and in planks. Some types have butt edges with slightly beveled corners. Others are tongue-and-grooved. They come with or without an adhesive backing.

Application procedures are generally the same as for a resilient tile floor. Check the corners of the room for square, make a layout, and work outward from the center of the room. At the walls, however, allow at least a 1/2" gap at the edge for expansion. Base trim will cover the gap.

# CARPETING

Carpet that comes in rolls and is bought by the square yard is not difficult to lay. But to do the job right you need some special tools to stretch the carpeting tight and avoid wrinkles. A relatively new product, carpet squares, simplifies the laying process. Squares are available in shag, level loop, and other standard weaves.

Carpet squares are 12″ on a side, and are made with a resilient backing that takes the place of a separate carpet pad. They also have an adhesive on the back. You simply pull off the protective paper and set the square in place. The cost per square yard of floor area is a little greater than with standard roll carpeting, but the job of application is much simpler for the amateur. It requires no special tools except a sharp knife for cutting the squares to fit around obstacles.

# TOOLS YOU WILL NEED

To apply interior plywood or hardboard, you will probably use all of these tools:

scribe
putty knife
power saw
steel tape
folding rule
hammer
framing square
grease pencil
power drill
keyhole saw
putty stick
carpenter's level
glue gun (for glue application)
brush (for contact cement application)
rubber mallet

To apply wallboard to walls or ceilings you will need:

framing square
keyhole saw
steel tape
metal T-square
utility knife
coarse sandpaper
wallboard hammer (for nail application)
electric screwdriver (for screw application)
plastic-headed hammer (for prefinished application)
supporting tee (which you make)

small finishing knife (6″)
broad finishing knife (10″)
metal shears
brush (for sealant)

To apply ceiling tiles to furring strips you will need:

steel tape
utility knife
hammer
chalk line
folding rule
stapling gun
carpenter's level

To apply various types of tiles to walls, you will need:

brush (for sizing walls)
carpenter's level
folding rule
straightedge
glass cutter (for ceramic tiles)
hacksaw (for metal tiles)
coping saw (for plastic tiles)
file
safety glasses
tile nippers (for ceramic or plastic tiles)
notched spreader
trowel
putty knife
squeegee
sponge
toothbrush or comb (for finishing joints)

To apply flooring materials with adhesive, you need:

power sander
hammer
staple gun
steel tape
chalk line
notched trowel
brush (for some adhesives)
straightedge
utility knife
linoleum knife
carpenter's square

# Trimming
# and Cabinetry

After the lifting required to finish ceilings and walls, and the kneeling required to finish floors, applying trim is pleasurably light work. The pieces are long and not easy to maneuver, but they are lightweight and simple to cut and fit.

Most houses today have little exterior trim. At the rakes of the roof you may want a fascia, soffit, and small cove molding or quarter-round (Fig. 15-1) to hide exposed roof structure. At overhangs you may want to add a fascia and soffit. You may want to install ventilation at eaves to provide air circulation under the roof. And you may need a rain disposal system to carry water away from the foundation walls.

For fascias, use straight boards of good grade that are free of any large knots. Where boards meet at a ridge, use your pitch board to determine the angle of cut. To protect fascias from rotting and warping, prime the backs and edges before you nail them to rafters. Prime other trim pieces in the same way, and select moldings in scale with the house. They should be large enough to cover the exposed edges of roof sheathing, but should fit about 1/2″ in from the edges of shingles. No molding should cover more than 1/3 of the fascia. Apply trim with finishing nails, countersink them, and fill the holes with putty as you go.

For solid soffits you can use exterior grade plywood in the minimum thickness available, or you can use ordinary gypsum wallboard. For

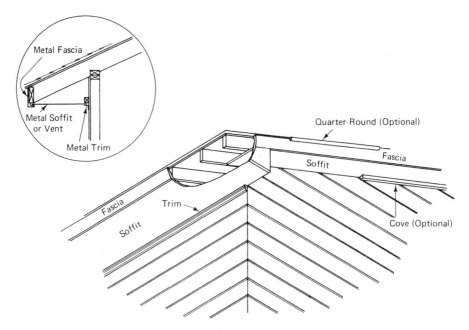

**Fig. 15-1.** Fascias and soffits constitute the bulk of exterior trim at the eaves and rakes of the roof. Note how an eave is boxed at a corner. Inset shows how to trim and ventilate an eave with metal.

ventilating soffits the simplest answer is perforated metal, usually aluminum. It comes in long rolls in various widths, and is crimped for rigidity. You support it either on metal brackets attached to the fascia and wall, or fit it into slots in the fascia and between a cleat and trim at the wall (inset, Fig. 15-1). Feed each roll from the end of the soffit. Where two lengths meet, let one overlap the other a full crimp.

## GUTTERS AND DOWNSPOUTS

All too often gutters are omitted from vacation houses. Yet they are inexpensive insurance against water problems in areas with occasionally heavy rainfall. If you haven't yet made a thorough study of what happens to rain coming off the roof, this is a good project for a rainy day that isn't good for much else.

Gutters are most important on houses with shed roofs and houses on sloping sites with any shape of roof except flat. Half an inch of rain on a shed roof over a house only 32′ by 24′ will spew more than 700 gallons of water on the ground. A gable roof will shed 350 gallons at each eave. Without some means of collection, this water will sink into the ground toward the footings on a level site or wash at foundation walls as it runs downhill on a sloping site. Gutters collect this rain, and downspouts direct it away from the house.

Gutters are made in several shapes and of several materials. The most common shapes are half-round and box. Select a material that requires no upkeep—fiberglass or vinyl in most cases, or wood to match wood shake roofs.

The standard length of a section of gutter is 10', but you can easily cut shorter pieces with a hacksaw. Manufacturers make a complete line of fittings—ends of various types, corners, outlet sections that accept downspouts, connectors between lengths of gutter, and hangers for attachment. Assembly and installation require no special tools.

Gutters more than 30' long should have a downspout at each end. They should slope downward about 1/2" every 10' of length. Provide slope in both directions from the center of a gutter with two downspouts, and in one direction from the high end of a gutter with a single downspout.

Downspouts, also called *leaders* in some parts of the country, come in 8' and 10' lengths. The necessary elbows to change direction of water flow, and the straps for attachment, are available separately. Elbows come in a number of shapes so that you can make a 45° or 90° turn in any direction. Therefore you have to determine before you order any parts at what points rainwater can safely reach the ground for harmless disposal.

## Assembling a Rain Disposal System

Build the gutter to full length on the ground by fitting each section tightly into a slip-joint connector. Caulk the joints fully inside the gutter, but wipe away any excess so that it doesn't impede the flow of water. Add outlet sections and end caps, and caulk them, too. Then fit gutter hangers around the assembly. You need a hanger about 6" on each side of a connector, and about every 36" between.

With the help of a couple of friends or relatives, raise the gutter assembly to the eaves. Set it in position first at the high point, and then work down-slope toward the outlet sections. The inner lip of the gutter must lie just inside the edge of the roof itself in order to catch water dripping off the roof. To catch water running off with some speed, set the outer lip at a point below a continuation of the roof line. The exact point depends on roof pitch (Fig. 15-2). Distances shown are for the lowest point of the gutter.

Attach gutter hangers with roofing nails or screws. Carefully lift the roofing material and fasten into the sheathing through holes in the hangers. Work on a warm day so that you can raise shingles without cracking them. Where you can't nail under shingles, nail into them through a dab of roofing cement that fully seals the hole. Then cover nail heads with the same cement.

Fit elbows and attach sections of the downspout after the gutters are in place. Again, nail hangers through finished wall material, and fill nail holes with sealant that matches the wall.

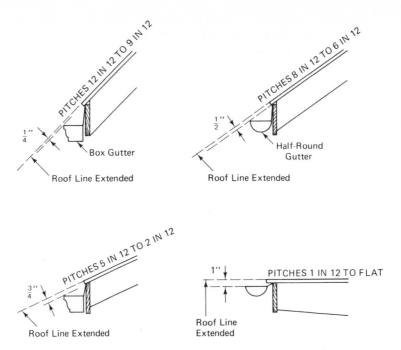

**Fig. 15-2.** Gutters at their low point should be attached a fixed distance below the slope of the roof. The pitch of the roof determines that distance.

## INTERIOR TRIM

Interior trim is both decorative and useful. Its primary purpose is to conceal joints, but the wide variety of trim shapes on the market attests to its secondary purpose of enhancing the beauty of a room. Trim is always needed around doors and windows, where it's called a *casing* (Fig. 15-3). Trim is always needed at the junction of floor and wall materials; here it's called a *base*. Trim may be desirable at the ceiling, where it's called a *cove,* and at the corners of rooms. Hardwood is still the most common trim material, but plastic, vinyl, and hardboard trims are gaining in popularity.

Most lumber suppliers carry trim in random lengths—in even feet ranging from 7' up to as long as 20'. So before you order any trim, figure out the exact lengths of all the pieces you'll need. Then match your needs to the lengths available. If you plan wisely, you can reduce scrap to less than a couple of inches per length.

Order trim only a day or two before you need it. Because the pieces are long and slender, they break easily. Store them out of traffic patterns through rooms, and keep them as dry as possible. Water raises the grain and means extra time spent sanding and smoothing. Moldings applied dry grow slightly in length as they take on moisture, and this helps to close joints between pieces.

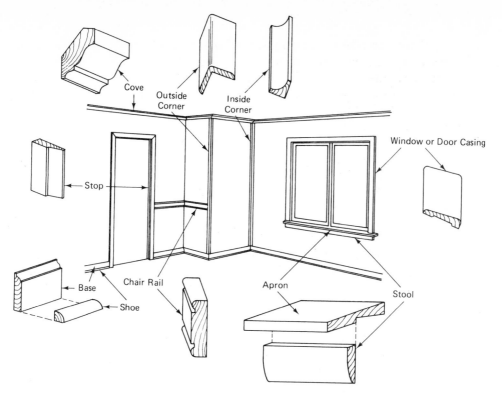

**Fig. 15-3.** In this perspective of a room interior are all the moldings you are likely to need. Details are sections through the various types and shapes.

## Applying Ceiling Coves

Coves are milled in various designs on the exposed face, and are beveled on their backs. They fit across the corner between ceiling and wall, and bridge the gap between materials. The simplest cove is about 3/4" wide on a side, and convex in shape. Fancier coves are sometimes as wide as 6". A simple cove is most appropriate for simple vacation houses.

If you have a miter box, the simplest way to cut the ends of coves to fit at corners is to miter them. Start on one of the shorter walls. To be accurate measure down from the ceiling a distance equal to the height of the molding when it's in position. Then measure the length of the short wall at this level to determine the length of the cove at its longest point—where it touches long walls. Cut the ends at opposite 45° angles, and check the fit. When the fit is good, prime the cut ends.

Attach coves with eight-penny casing nails driven through the lower part of the cove into the wall plate. Be careful not to dent the molding. Select as a point to nail the place where the cove curves outward. Drive nails below the surface with a nailset, and putty the holes. Follow the same process on the short wall opposite.

If you can trim a long wall with a single length of cove, cut it just slightly longer than the measurement between the lengths already in place. Prime the ends. Then fit the cove in place, letting it belly a little in the middle. Nail at the ends first, then at the middle, and then work in both directions alternately from the middle nail. This method takes the belly out of the cove and forces it tightly into the corners for an almost seamless fit.

Where one length of cove won't cover a wall, you can cut the ends of two pieces square and butt them where they meet. But you'll get a better looking and tighter joint if you miter both ends. Let the shorter piece overlap the longer, and nail it first. Then bow and snap the longer piece into place. At the joint nail at a slight angle through both pieces and on into the plate.

Where two lengths of cove meet at an outside corner, miter the corners at 45° first, working with the cove face up (Fig. 15-4, top). Then with a coping saw start just inside the front edge and back-cut at a slightly sharper angle (bottom). The two pieces will touch and fit tightly at the face where they show, but will gap at the back. Use sandpaper or a wood file to adjust the edges for a close fit.

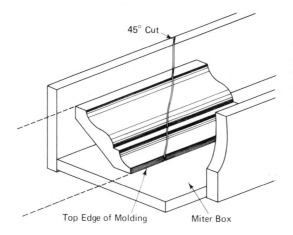

45° Cut

Top Edge of Molding          Miter Box

**Fig. 15-4.** When cove moldings meet at an outside corner, you should cut them in two steps. The first cut (top) is a 45° angle made in a miter box. The second (bottom) is a back cut that helps the pieces fit tightly at their outside edges.

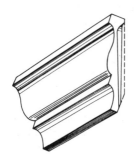

## Applying Corner Trim

The various ways to finish corners were covered in the previous chapter. When you fit corner moldings, cut the pieces so that they stop short of the bottom edge of any ceiling cove. Usually corner molding is thin and butts nicely. But if it is thicker than the bottom edge of the cove, taper the ends to a matching thickness.

Trim looks best if its horizontal lines are continuous, as in Fig. 15-3. As at the ceiling, you can taper ends of corner trim to butt smoothly against the top of the base. But you can also let it run all the way to the floor, like door casings, and butt base pieces against it. If you go this route, be sure to carry the flooring material all the way to the wall to avoid a gap.

## Trimming Interior Doors

The best way to buy interior doors is prehung in their frames. Order by size of door and thickness of wall. Hinged doors are a standard 6' 8" high, and come in widths of 2' 0" and 2' 4" for closets and 2' 6" and 2' 8" for rooms. Order a frame depth of 4" if wall material is 1/4" thick on both sides, or 4 1/2" if wall material is 1/2" thick.

If you make your own frames, keep the above dimensions in mind. The width of the frame opening is equal to the width of the door plus 1/8", and the frame opening height is equal to door height plus 1/2". These are not the same as rough opening dimensions.

Fit the door frame with wedges in the same way you fitted an exterior door. Be sure that the edges of the frame are flush with the wall on both sides. When the frame is nailed, draw 45° lines upward on the wall surface and outward from the top corners. These lines will mark the corners of the casings.

Casings may come as part of the package with exterior doors, but you must select interior casings separately. They are 1/2" to 3/4" thick and from 2" to 4" wide. Their surfaces may be flat, gently rounded, or molded. Choose the simpler shapes and the narrower widths.

Fit casings at the jambs first. Square one end of the long pieces of casing and set the square-cut ends on the floor 1/4" from the edge of the frame. This 1/4" dimension is called a *setback*. Mark each length of casing at the point where it crosses the 45° lines you drew. Cut along these lines, and hold the two pieces back to back. If your cuts are accurate and you have set the door frame square, the match will be perfect.

Set the two lengths in position, remembering to allow for the setback. With eight-penny casing nails driven part way in near the outer edge of the casing, tack the two pieces in place. Then measure, mark, and miter the head casing. Test the fit, and correct any problems with a block plane. As long as the miters fit tightly, you can vary the setback slightly to compensate for any minor variation from the proper length. When all three pieces fit, attach the casing to the frame near the inner edge, and complete nailing at the outer edge.

To prevent the jambs from opening up, cross-nail at the corners—that is, nail down through the head casing into the jamb casings, and nail sideways through the jamb casings into the head casing. Predrill the holes to prevent splitting, and attach with six-penny nails. Fill all nail holes before you move on to the next door opening.

### Applying a Base and Base Shoe

Base moldings for concealing the junction of walls and floor are similar in shape and size to casings (Fig. 15–3). They may be used by themselves if the finished floor surface is extremely level or carpeted. Otherwise add a shoe molding—usually a quarter-round—over the base at floor level.

Applying base trim is the same as fitting ceiling coves, but is a lot easier because the molding fits flat against the walls. Drive eight-penny casing nails through the base into studs at a point about 1/2" down from the top edge. If you don't intend to use a shoe molding, fit the base tightly against the floor or carpet, and toenail a second set of nails into the bottom plate. If you add a shoe molding, gap the base slightly at the floor.

You can nail a base shoe in two ways—into the base molding at about 15° to the horizontal, or into the subfloor at about 60° to the horizontal. The first method is probably preferable if the finished flooring is carpet, roll goods, or resilient tile. The shoe will remain tight against the base in case of structural movement, and any gap will occur at the floor line. The second method is a better choice with wood flooring. The shoe then remains tight to the flooring and slides up or down along the base.

In either case predrill the base to prevent splitting. If you nail down into flooring, drill all the way into the flooring to avoid bent nails.

### Trimming Windows

Window trim has five parts—a head casing, two jamb casings, a stool, and an apron. Because the jamb casings end at the stool and the apron supports it (Fig. 15–3), the stool is the first of the five pieces to be cut and fitted.

Stools are usually notched on the underside to fit over the sills of double-hung windows, and they are shiplapped at the inner edge to fit into the sills of casement, awning, and hopper windows. When window frames are set level, the top of the sill will be level, too. Adjustment is virtually impossible.

The depth of a stool (front-to-back measurement) is determined by the thickness of the exterior wall; you must figure out its length (side-to-side measurement). The length of a stool is equal to the width of the window opening plus two setbacks plus the width of two jamb casings, plus two returns. A *return* is an extension of the stool beyond the casing; this is usually about an inch. Say, for example, that your window opening is 3 ' 4 1/4" and casings are 2" wide. From one side to the other, then, the dimensions would be 1", 2", 1/4", 3 ' 4 1/4", 1/4", 2", and 1". Therefore sill length is 3 ' 10 3/4".

The stool fits into the window opening, and must be notched at the flanking walls. Because an exact stool fit is important to prevent air and water leaks, you must measure accurately and cut notches with no tolerance. This isn't easy because you will be working in midair.

To make marking easier, tack a pair of thin but stiff supports to the sill so that they project into the room beyond the edge of the stool (Fig. 15-5, section). Set the outer edge of the stool on the supports, press the inner edge flush against the wall, and adjust the stool to level. Then, on the inner edges of the stool, mark the width of the window opening between jambs (Fig. 15-5, left). On the top of the stool draw lines from these marks at right angles to the edge.

Next, measure the distance from the surface of the wall to the face of the sash of double-hung windows, or to the face of the grooved sill member of hinged windows. Mark this dimension along the two cut lines, and draw lines from these marks to the ends of the stool. You have now marked the stool for notching.

**Fig. 15-5.** To mark cuts for a window stool, support it on thin plywood (section). Shaded areas in isometric are the pieces to be trimmed off so that the stool fits into the window opening.

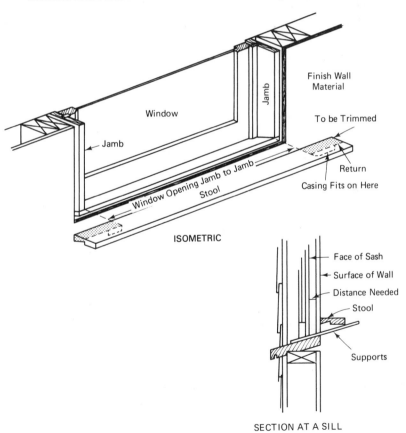

Before you go any farther, however, hold a straight board against the wall across the window opening. If the board is flush with the wall on both sides, you can go ahead and make your cuts. If the board is not flush, you must scribe the sill for a good fit.

Set the *scriber,* a simple compass with a metal point at the end of one leg and a pencil or point at the other, to the exact depth of the notch in the stool. Then, holding the stool level and in position on its supports, set the scriber on the stool with the metal leg against the wall and the other at right angles to the wall. Carefully pull the scriber along the wall. The outer leg will mark the exact shape of the irregular wall on the stool; cut along that line.

After cutting the two notches, test the fit. The stool should not quite touch movable sash; you must allow for thicknesses of paint. If the fit looks good, remove the supports and recheck the fit of the stool in final position; you may have a little planing or sanding to do. Then paint all hidden edges and surfaces. When the paint is dry, nail through predrilled holes into the sill. Use eight-penny casing nails at each end and about every 12" between.

To protect the projecting sill from damage, install the supporting apron next. For an apron you can use a piece of window casing fastened with the thicker edge up. The length of an apron is the length of the stool minus returns. Where they meet the stool, the ends of the apron should be on the same vertical line as the edges of jamb casings above. You can cut the ends square, or give them the same shape as the apron itself with a coping saw.

Attach the apron with eight-penny casing nails. As with cove molding, nail into an outward curve to minimize hammer marks. You may have to toenail slightly upward to assure hitting the sill. Predrill holes, insert nails, center the apron, and complete the nailing.

With the stool and apron in place, you then measure, miter, and attach casings in the same way as around a door opening.

## STORAGE IN BEDROOMS AND BATH

Way back in Chapter 1 you and your family made lists of what you needed to store in your vacation house. A few items are most easily stored on hooks in perforated hardboard. Nearly everything else hangs on rods, rests on shelves, or hides in cabinets. Your working drawings may show details of any special cabinets, but in closets they either say simply "R & S" for rod and shelf, or they say nothing at all.

### Finishing Closets

Begin your planning of closet storage by determining the height of the rod for hanging clothes. Standard height for men's clothes is 66" above the floor to the underside of the rod. For women 62" is standard. Raise a man's clothes rod 1/2" for every inch of his height over 6' 0", and raise a woman's rod 1/2" for every inch of her height over 5' 6". Rods for children's clothes should be at their eye level, and set on adjustable supports. The centers of all rods should be 11″ to 12″ from the door and rear wall of the closet. Allow 3″ of clearance between the top of the rod and any shelf above it.

A 3/4″ metal pipe makes a rigid rod and needs no center support if it is less than 6′ 0″ long. Cut a pair of cleats out of a 1 × 6, and rout out a slot (Fig. 15-6) to accept the rod. Run the cleat the entire length of the side wall, and nail it sturdily to studs. Angle the slot so that you can remove the rod without hitting the shelf above it.

Half-inch plywood makes an excellent shelf. You can leave the edge raw, or finish it with a piece of trim. Support the ends of the shelf on the cleats, and the back on a length of 1 × 2. Make the shelf 14″ deep if you plan only one shelf. If you install two, make the lower one 12″ deep and the upper one 14″ deep. Allow a minimum of 9″ clearance between shelves.

If rod and shelf are more than 6′ long, add a metal support at the center. The best type is triangular in shape, with a hook extension (Fig. 15-6). The long side of the triangle supports the shelf, and the hook carries the rod. The hypotenuse provides bracing strength.

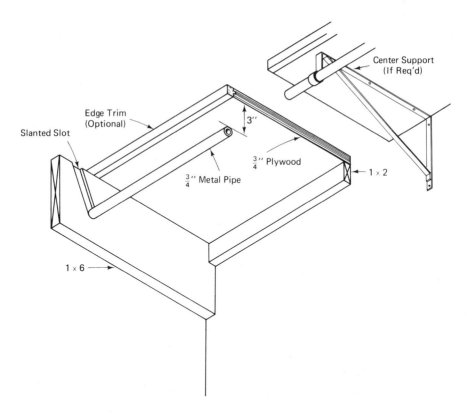

**Fig. 15-6.** Detail of a closet shelf, hanging rod, and their supports at their ends and midpoint.

## Storing Linens

Often overlooked in vacation houses is adequate storage for extra blankets, sheets, pillowcases, pillows themselves, and towels. As you know, you will have weekend guests, presumably but not always invited. A clothes closet is no place to store linen and bedding. The shelves can't be wide enough, and you can't protect them from dust and mildew.

The best shelves for linens are about 18" deep and 24" wide, supported on *standards* (adjustable brackets), and protected behind a door. Shelves of this size nicely accommodate pillows (about 16" by 22") and folded blankets (about 18" by 20"). They also take two stacks of folded bath or beach towels.

Rather than buy dressers and chests of drawers, or haul them from home, consider storing flat clothing on shelves in cabinets built into or onto bedroom walls. Fit the cabinet into a double stud spacing. This gives you a clear inside width of about 28". Remember to install headers both above and below cabinets (Fig. 15–7). A shelf depth of 10" is adequate, although 12" is better. Again, make shelves adjustable for maximum utility.

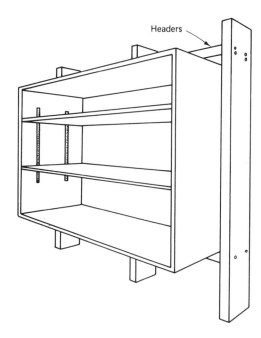

Headers

**Fig. 15-7.** For flat storage, a hanging cabinet in a double stud opening does a good job and takes up no floor space. Shelves are adjustable. Doors may be overlaid or lipped (see Fig. 15-8).

## Storing Bathroom Supplies

Cabinets in the bathrooms should provide three kinds of service. You need a place to store medicines, first aid supplies, and the tools of daily hygiene. You need a larger space for bulkier items such as towels, toilet paper, and tissues. And you need a work surface for washing out clothes (especially if you don't plan laundry equipment) and general utility.

There are two types of medicine cabinets—those that fit into the wall and those that hang on the wall. In-the-wall types have a series of shallow shelves (about 3 1/2" deep) behind a mirrored hinged door. On-the-wall types, sometimes called *cosmetic boxes,* usually have a single shelf 5" to 6" deep behind a pair of sliding doors. You fit a mirror above. Cosmetic boxes are the less expensive of the two, and require no special wall framing. You simply attach them through their backs into studs.

You can buy bathroom lavatories as individual units, as part of a countertop shaped out of plastic, or as part of a complete cabinet with countertop and storage space below. If you build your own lavatory cabinet and counter, it should be between 22" and 24" from front to back, as wide as space in the bathroom allows, and from 30" to 34" above the floor. The best height for your family depends on their heights.

The bowl of the lavatory and its water and drain connections take up some cabinet storage space. A toe space 4" high and 2" deep eats up some more. Still, the remaining storage space is worth the cost and is the best answer for bulky items. The cabinets shown in Fig. 15–8 are not difficult to build, and you can easily adapt them to your own bathroom requirements by changing heights, widths, and depths.

# KITCHEN CABINETS

The floor plan in the working drawings for your vacation house shows the arrangement of cabinets and appliances in the kitchen. Most sets of drawings also include fully dimensioned elevations giving the height, width, and depth of both base and wall cabinets, and their heights above the floor.

You can buy cabinets that will fit almost any kitchen with minor adjustments of no more than 1 1/2". There is a wide range in quality. Well-built cabinets are expensive, but they are built of sturdy materials, are well designed, have tight-fitting joints, good hardware, and an attractive finish. Many of the less expensive cabinets are little more than storage boxes. If you enjoy cabinetry, you can do as well to build your own to the specific needs of your family.

## Assembling Base Cabinets

The narrowest manufactured cabinet is 12" wide. Widths increase in 3" increments all the way up to 33". Sometimes you can find cabinets in 42", 48", and 60" widths. If not, you can combine a couple of narrower cabinets to fill openings greater than 33".

Standard depth of base cabinets is 24", and height is about 35" without countertop. The countertop brings the total height to 36". Yet this height is not the most comfortable for all women, and a woman on vacation should be comfortable. Ideally, the level of the counter should be 3" below a woman's elbow when her arm is extended as if to shake hands. To adjust the height of manu-

factured cabinets, modify the toe space—adding taller supports to raise the
counter level, and trimming toe space to lower it.

The isometric in Fig. 15-8 (top left) shows a typical frame for a base cabinet.
The three sections show the common types—one with drawers only, one with
shelves only, and one combining the two. Note that doors and drawer fronts may

**Fig. 15-8.** Isometric (top) shows typical construction of a base
cabinet for kitchen or bathroom. Sections below show typical
dimensions for the three common types of cabinets, and the ways of
handling door and drawer fronts. The fronts may be adapted to
any cabinet design.

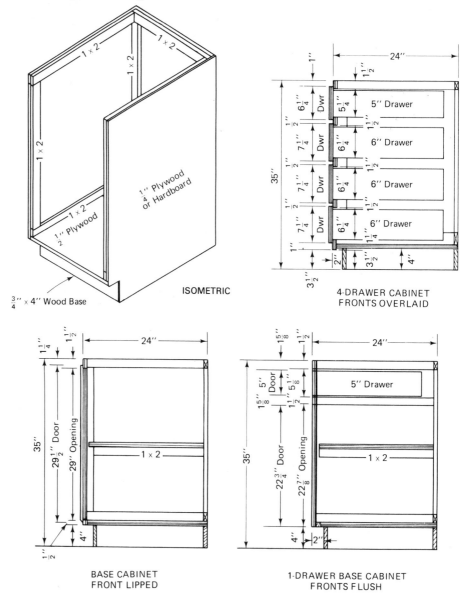

be built in three different ways—overlaid, lipped, or flush. Lipped and flush drawers and doors require knobs or pulls. Overlaid drawers do not; the bottom and side edges must be beveled to provide a finger grip.

Finish shelf edges with a thin batten, or else nail and glue a small piece of board, cut to fit and carefully smoothed.

### Assembling Wall Cabinets

Widths of standard wall cabinets are the same as for base cabinets. Depth is generally about 12″, however. Wall cabinets come in three basic heights: 15″ to 18″ for use above a refrigerator and range; 21″ to 24″ for use above a sink or laundry equipment; and 30″ to 33″ for use elsewhere.

In most kitchens the tops of wall cabinets are 84″ above the floor. This height permits the standard clearances developed to assure maximum safety and utility of space. Small wall cabinets should clear the top of a refrigerator by about 9″, allowing air circulation to carry off heat from the compressor. A small cabinet should clear a range by at least 30″, allowing the installation of a range hood below it. A medium cabinet should clear a sink by 24″. A tall cabinet should clear a counter by 15″, and 18″ is even better.

Above wall cabinets you must furr the ceiling. *Furring* is a light framework that fills the space between the ceiling and the cabinet tops and provides a horizontal surface for attachment. You build the framework of 2 × 4s and surface it like other kitchen walls (Fig. 15–9).

**Fig. 15-9.** Storage space more than 7′ above the floor isn't easily accessible. Furring (isometric) fills the gap between the tops of wall cabinets and the ceiling; it is surfaced like walls. At right is a sectional view through a typical wall cabinet and furring.

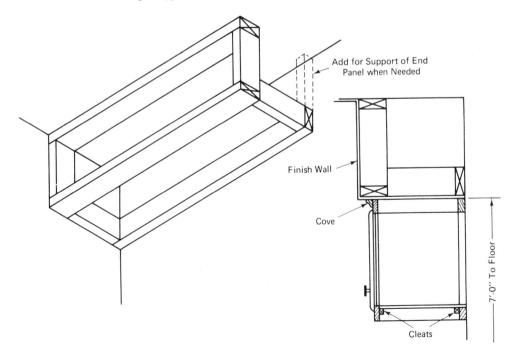

Add for Support of End Panel when Needed

Finish Wall

Cove

Cleats

7'-0" To Floor

## Setting Base Cabinets

Using chalk lines, lay out the arrangement of base cabinets on the finished floor. Check the room corners for square. In determining widths for cabinets allow small gaps at free-standing appliances. You want a tight fit to keep out dust and dirt, but you must also leave enough room to move the appliances when you connect them and make repairs.

Fit the cabinets on the chalk lines, starting at one corner. When all cabinets fit and line up both at their fronts and tops, attach them at three points with wood screws. Predrill all holes. Screw downward at about a 30° angle to the horizontal through rear cleats just above the bottom shelf into studs (Fig. 15–10). Screw upward at about 30° to the horizontal through upper rear cleats. It's best to screw into blocking, because there may not be a stud where you need it. Set 2 × 4 blocking on edge and stagger its height for easier nailing. The point at which the screws enter is about 33 1/2" above the subfloor when the counter height is 36".

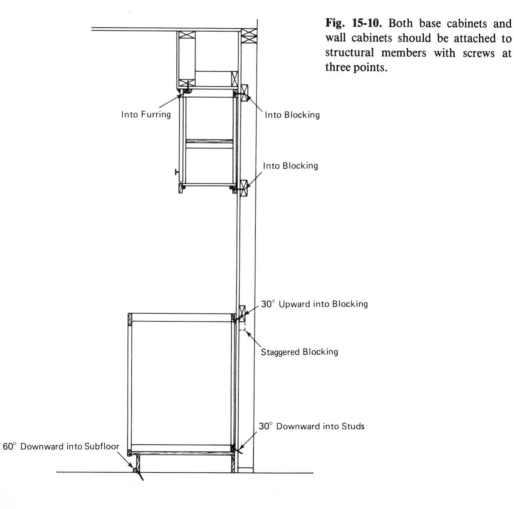

**Fig. 15-10.** Both base cabinets and wall cabinets should be attached to structural members with screws at three points.

Into Furring

Into Blocking

Into Blocking

30° Upward into Blocking

Staggered Blocking

30° Downward into Studs

60° Downward into Subfloor

Finally, drive screws at a 60° angle through the toekick into subflooring. Countersink these screws and cover the holes with shoe molding.

### Hanging Wall Cabinets

When setting base cabinets, keep the tops level and shim at the bottom. When hanging wall cabinets, keep the bottoms level and shim at the top. You can cover any gap at the furring line with trim. Mark the locations of the undersides of cabinets on the wall, and set the cabinets against these horizontal guide lines.

Attach wall cabinets with screws at two points (Fig. 15-10). Inside the cabinet screw horizontally through the upper cleat into blocking. Outside, screw as horizontally as possible through the cleat that supports the bottom shelf, again into blocking. If your cabinets have a cleat just inside the rail above the door, add a third screw upward into the furring.

Setting cabinets takes two people—one to hold the cabinet in position and the other to operate the screwdriver. You should always start at the corners, because most problems occur there. Once the first cabinet is properly set, all others should fit square and plumb.

Nevertheless, check the plumb and level constantly. Joints between base and overhead cabinets should line up vertically if possible; the job looks more professional when they do. That's why it is better to set base cabinets first. You have less leeway to make adjustments. On the other hand it is easier to hang wall cabinets when you don't have to lean over base cabinets. You can have the best of both worlds if you make and attach the countertops before you install the wall cabinets.

### Making Countertops

You can buy countertops made to order, but they aren't hard to make if you have the right tools. They have a base of 3/4" plywood or particleboard topped by a thin layer of plastic laminate attached with contact cement. Most countertops have a finished edge at the front and any exposed sides, and a backsplash against the wall to protect it from water, grease, and damage.

Cut the countertop base for a tight fit at walls. Allow a 1" overhang at the front edge, a 3/4" overhang at an exposed side edge, no more than 1/2" overhang next to the refrigerator, and about 1/8" on each side of a free-standing range. Use a single piece of base for each section of counter; kitchens are almost always designed so that this is possible.

Cut each piece of plastic laminate 1/8" to 1/4" oversize at all edges. Laminates come in 8', 10', and 12' lengths, and usually wider than 48", so that you can cut two widths of countertop out of a single sheet. You can cut laminate with a power saw, a fine-toothed hand saw, or metal shears. If you use a power saw, cut with the finished side of the laminate down. With other tools cut with the finished side up to avoid chipping. Support the laminate as you cut, and saw at a low angle—that is. with strokes close to horizontal.

Check the laminate for fit to the plywood or particleboard base, and adjust the cuts where necessary. Then apply contact cement not only to the smooth base but also to the back of the laminate. Let the cement dry for as long as the manufacturer recommends. Cover the cemented surface of the base with pieces of strong, thin paper about 2' square. Leave just a little cement exposed at the end where you plan to start laminating. The paper won't stick, but it will prevent the laminate from sticking until you are ready to have that happen. When the contact cement on the base and the contact cement on the laminate touch, they are stuck for good—and so are you if you haven't positioned the laminate exactly.

Lay the laminate cautiously on the paper, holding it up off the unpapered end of the base. When you are sure that the laminate is properly placed and overlaps the base at all edges, press down gently. Then warily remove each sheet of paper as you work down the base, rechecking position first and pressing afterward.

When you have full contact, press down hard over the entire surface, starting at the center and working toward the edges. For this step you can use a wood block and a rubber mallet, or a heavy hand roller. You must assure complete contact between the two surfaces over every square inch. If you leave any air bubbles, the result can be delamination.

Usually you can plan your countertop so that each section can be laminated without a seam. If you must join two pieces, the best places are in a corner (with butting edges cut at 45°) or at a countertop range. Avoid seams at sinks. They aren't too visible there, but they can lead to moisture problems and delamination.

*Finishing Edges.* The simplest way to finish an exposed edge is with a metal molding strip attached with screws (Fig. 15–11, left). Sometimes you can buy plastic molding with a T section (right). Cut a narrow slot in the edge of the countertop base and coat the edge with adhesive. Then with a rubber mallet, drive the stem of the T into the slot and pound the trim into the adhesive. Trim the edge of the laminate first, making a vertical cut with a router.

For a more attractive edge (Fig. 15—11, bottom), calculate the front overhang for the base at only 1/4″ instead of 1″, and add a smooth, straight 1 × 2 at the edge to make up the difference in dimension. Glue the 1 × 2 to the edge of the base, and then attach it with finishing nails. After countersinking the nails, apply a strip of laminate to the face of the 1 × 2 and flush with the top edge. Then apply laminate to the top surface as before, with the edge of the laminate extending over the 1 × 2 and its face laminate.

Where two pieces of laminate butt at the edge, you can trim vertically so that the upper piece overlaps the edge piece. Or you can set the router to bevel at 22 1/2°. Smooth the edges with a block plane and hand file.

Set the completed countertop carefully on the base cabinets and shove it slowly but firmly against the walls. Attach it from underneath with flat-head wood screws long enough to go about halfway into the countertop base. Screw through cleats at all four corners of every cabinet. For best appearance, predrill the holes and countersink all screws.

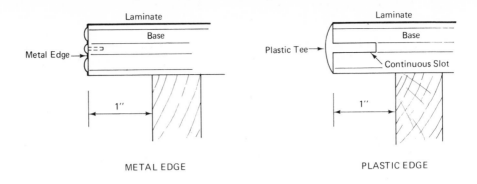

METAL EDGE

PLASTIC EDGE

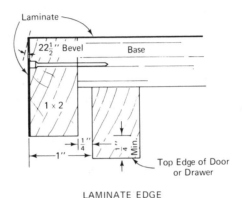

LAMINATE EDGE

**Fig. 15-11.** You can finish the edges of countertops with metal trim (top), a plastic tee molding (top right) or a laminated 1 × 2. If you laminate the edges, be sure that doors and drawers clear the bottom edge of the 1 × 2.

*Adding a Backsplash.* You can make and finish a backsplash in much the same way as a countertop. The base is 3/4″ particleboard or plywood about 4″ wide, and you apply plastic laminate to the top and one side with contact cement. But there is one very important difference. You attach the backsplash to the wall after the countertop is in place, but before you apply any laminate. Fill the crack between countertop and backsplash with sealant, or trim it with a thin plastic cove molding.

## Attaching Cabinet Hardware

Cabinet hardware comes in an almost infinite variety of shapes, sizes, and finishes. There is at least one item of hardware for every purpose you can think of.

Swinging cabinet doors, unless they are the overlaid type with beveled edges, need knobs or pulls for opening them and some method for keeping them shut. Simple, two-piece magnetic catches serve this latter purpose nicely. Place the catch at the center of the stile opposite the hinges, or on the underside of a center shelf. A midpoint location reduces the possibility of warping.

Flush doors require flush hinges, with one leaf attached to the stile and the other to the face of the door (Fig. 15-12, left). Lipped doors require an offset hinge. A decorative leaf fits on the stile, while a broader, plainer leaf goes on the back of the door. Overlaid doors swing well on semi-concealed hinges (Fig. 15-12, right). One L-shaped leaf is mounted on the rear edge of the stile. The other leaf, also L-shaped but at right angles to the stile leaf, fits on the back of the door. You must notch the edge of the door itself to allow the hinge to pivot. Only the pivot is exposed when the door is closed. Use three hinges per door.

**Fig. 15-12.** When the edges of cabinet doors are flush with flanking stiles, they operate on flush hinges. The hinges come in a variety of decorative shapes (on door and on shelf, above). These are black. Semiconcealed hinges for use on overlaid doors (p. 325) are scarcely visible when doors are shut. Note that top and bottom edges of the door are notched to accept the hinge, and the door is slotted for the center hinge. These are brass. *Courtesy American Plywood Association.*

Drawers also require knobs or pulls that match door hardware, and some sort of track to run on. There are three types of drawer guides. One type requires a shelf or ledge on which supporting rollers turn. Another type fits on top of the drawer, while a third supports the drawer at its sides. Find out what is available locally, and decide on drawer hardware before you build your cabinets and drawers. Then you will be sure to have the necessary points of attachment for guides and also the necessary clearances for smooth operation.

## INSTALLING SWINGING DOORS

Of the seven types of door operations, you are likely to run into no more than two or three in a vacation house. Most doors will be hinged and will open in only one direction. Interior doors require a pair of hinges (you always order by the number of pairs), a lockset, and a strike plate. Exterior doors are heavier, and require 1 1/2 pairs of hinges, a lockset, a strike plate, and perhaps a surface latch or deadbolt for extra protection.

Common door hinges have two leaves of equal size, one with two knuckles and one with three. A pin fits through the five knuckles to hold the hinge together. Pins are fixed in less expensive hinges and are removable in better ones. Hinges may be mounted in several ways, but on most doors they are *full-mortised*—that is, one leaf is recessed into the edge of the door and the other leaf is recessed into the jamb casing. Prehung doors come this way.

Every hinged door has a *hand,* determined by the location of the hinges and the swing of the door as you face it from the outside. "Outside" means from outdoors (for an exterior door), from outside a room, or from outside a closet. You are outside a door between two rooms if the door swings away from you.

You order prehung doors by the hand, and you order hinges by the hand. They are installed with their pins up and the three-knuckled leaf attached to the door jamb. A *right-hand door* has hinges on the right, and the door opens away from you. A *right-hand reverse door* has hinges on the right, but the door opens toward you.

### Attaching Hinges

If you intend to hang your own doors, mark the jamb of each door opening that will receive hinges. Then measure the width of the opening at top and bottom. The width of the door itself must be 1/8″ less than this measurement. Plane the door's edge to narrow its width. Leave the edges of interior doors square. Bevel the hinge side of exterior doors about 1/16″ toward the inner face so hinges won't bind. As you plane, replace the door in its opening frequently to make sure you get a good fit.

When the door fits, set it in the opening and wedge it into position. Then, on both the edges of the door and the jamb, accurately mark the location of the top of the upper hinge and the bottom of the lower hinge. These dimensions are usually 7″ down from the head (including 1/16″ clearance between head and door) and 11″ up from the finished floor. Then remove the door and mark the complete shape of the mortise for the leaf on both door and jamb (Fig. 15–13).

Note in step 1 that the leaf doesn't go all the way across the edge of the door. Dimension A should be 1/32″ to 1/16″ greater at the jamb than on the door so that the door won't bind. Dimension B is usually 1/8″ for interior doors that are 1 3/8″ thick, and 1/4″ for exterior doors that are 1 3/4″ thick.

To cut the mortise, use a sharp chisel to outline the two ends (step 2 in Fig. 15–13). Next cut a series of notches just to the depth of the mortise (step 3). This removes about half the wood. Then work along the side cut line to remove the remaining wood, chiseling at right angles to the face of the door (step 4). With careful craftsmanship you can make a very smooth mortise. Follow the same procedures at the door jamb.

Fit the hinges into the mortises, with the head of the pin toward the top of the door. Drive in two screws, set off center in the holes toward the edge of the leaf. This draws the leaf tightly against the back of the mortise. Do the same thing at jambs.

**Fig. 15-13.** The four steps in mortising a door or door jamb for a hinge: marking the cuts (1), defining the ends (2), cutting a series of notches (3), and cleaning out the mortise (4).

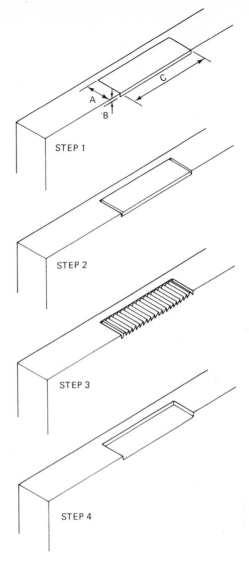

## Hanging a Door

Raise the door into position, inserting pins only far enough to hold it. Open and close the door several times, looking for signs of binding. The door should clear the jamb by 1/16″. If you have more clearance, remove the door and deepen the mortise in the jamb. If you have less clearance, add cardboard shims behind the jamb leaves. When clearances are right, insert the remaining screws and drive them tight, and drive the pin all the way down.

Next set the door *stop*—the square-edged piece of wood trim against which the door closes. The door should clear the stop 1/16″ at the hinge side and fit without clearance at the knob side. The stop across the head of the door will therefore run at a very slight diagonal so that it lines up with both jamb stops. Make sure that the edges of the stop are straight, and that the door butts against the thicker edge. Then attach the stop with four-penny finishing nails 12″ on centers. Countersink the heads and fill the nail holes.

## Attaching Closing Hardware

Of the many types of hardware for opening a door and holding it shut, the easiest to install are the unit lock and the bored-in lock. A *unit lock* is a metal box with knobs on both sides that comes in one piece. It fits into a deep notch in the edge of the door. A *bored-in lock* comes in three pieces, and the pieces meet in the door through two circular holes, one drilled into the edge of the door and the other through the door from face to face. Most prehung doors come already drilled, and you simply insert the lock.

The normal height above floor level to the center line of a door knob is 36″. If you must cut holes for locksets, follow the directions provided by the hardware manufacturer in the shipping box. He includes templates that show full size exactly where to locate holes and cuts. Be careful to drill the holes at right angles to each other and parallel to the floor.

Half a dozen basic types of closing hardware are manufactured, and all fit the same holes. Typical uses of the most common types are:

For closets—a *dummy knob*. It doesn't turn, there is no lock and the latch is spring operated. You simply pull on the knob to open the door. The dummy knob is surface-mounted.

For bedrooms and bathrooms—the *emergency key lock*. A button or thumb latch locks the door on the inside, and a turn of the knob unlocks it. On the hall side the knob has a tiny hole for a special key that unlocks the door from the outside in an emergency.

If privacy is not important, use a *knob latch*. It has knobs on both sides that turn, but has no locking device and no key slot.

For exterior doors—an *exterior door lock* or *all-purpose lock*. Both types lock from inside with a button, and can be unlocked from outside only with a key. To unlock from the inside you turn the button of an exterior door lock, or push the button of an all-purpose lock.

Most locking devices for extra night protection are surface-mounted and require no door preparation.

## Locating the Strike Plate

After you have fitted the lockset in each door, mark the point where the top of the latch hits the door jamb. Carry this line horizontally across the jamb (Fig. 15-14). Then measure the distance between the edge of the door and the flat side of the latch. Mark this distance on the jamb, carrying the line vertically downward from the other line at least an inch. Next, set the strike plate so that the top and edge of the hole in it lie on the two lines. Accurately trace the shape of the plate and its latch hole on the jamb.

Mortise the hole for the latch first, using a small chisel. Start about 1/16″ above the horizontal line and about 1/16″ from the vertical line on the side away from the stop (Fig. 15-14). Make the mortise as clean and square as you possibly can. Then test your work by closing the door. The latch should drop neatly into the mortise.

Next mortise the jamb for the strike plate, working a hair inside the outline you drew. Aim for a fit so snug that the strike plate will stay in its mortise without screws while you again test by shutting the door. The latch should fit close to the top of the hole in the strike plate. Then, if the door sags a little over the years, it will still close and remain latched without rattling when the wind blows.

After you are certain that you have a good fit, attach the strike plate. You can make minor adjustments in its position by placing the screws off center in their holes to pull the plate in that direction.

**Fig. 15-14.** Mortising a jamb for a strike plate is similar to mortising for hinges. Note that the mortise for the latch is slightly larger than the hole for the latch in the strike plate.

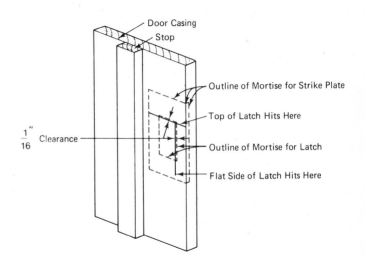

## INSTALLING SLIDING DOORS

Bypass and bifold doors for closets operate on an overhead track. *Bypass doors*— two doors that slide past each other to expose half of the door opening—require a double track. *Bifold doors*—pairs of doors that pivot at the outside and are hinged at the center—require only a single track.

You attach both types of tracks to door headers with Phillips-head screws. Usually the track comes as part of the door package from the manufacturer, along with knobs or pulls to operate the doors and some device to keep them in line while closed or being opened. The track must be straight and as level as possible. If the header is almost but not exactly level, you can adjust the door hangers to compensate.

The hangers for doors that move in a single track fit on the top edge of the door. When you have more than one track—even if the track comes in a single piece—the hangers fit against the back surface of the doors on their top rails. Each hanger has some device with which you can raise or lower the door to adjust for nonlevel track.

Bottom tracks are not required except with exterior sliding doors. But you do need some type of guide at the floor to keep bypass doors from getting out of line and bumping each other. You also need door *pulls*—round or oval cupped plates that fit into recesses in the face of a door at normal knob level (knobs would hit). Use the manufacturer's template for mortising the face of the door for the pulls. They snap into place, so make the cuts for a tight fit.

Bifold doors need knobs. They also require a device for holding doors in line when closed. This device may already be on the door. If not, you can buy types that fit on the doors or are screwed into the floor between them.

## INSTALLING WINDOW HARDWARE

Windows that you buy already in their frames come with some hardware. Most casements, awning, and hopper windows come equipped with hardware. Double-hung windows come with balances, but you must provide a sash lock and lifts for the lower sash.

## TOOLS YOU WILL NEED

To apply exterior and interior trim and hanging interior doors, you will need the following tools:

pitch board
paint brush (for priming)
putty knife
pliers
metal shears
caulking gun
hammer
miter box (which you make)
crosscut saw
nailset
coping saw
wood file
sandpaper
folding rule
block plane
hand drill or power drill and bits
wood chisel
scriber

To build and install cabinets and other storage, you will need:

    hacksaw (for metal rods)
    power saw
    wood chisel
    hammer
    drill and bits
    carpenter's level
    chalk lines
    screwdriver, slot-head
    screwdriver, Phillips-head
    hand saw, fine-toothed
    metal shears (for laminate)
    brush (for contact cement)
    rubber mallet
    router
    block plane
    hand file

# Protecting

# and

# Decorating Surfaces

With the advent of prefinished building materials, and steady improvement in the durability of paints and stains, the task of coating exterior and interior surfaces isn't the long, drawn-out job it once was. But coating is still necessary. You must protect unfinished surfaces against the weather and abnormally early deterioration.

In the course of finishing your vacation house, you may use as many as six different types of coatings. The most common, of course, is paint. You are also likely to stain some wood surfaces. You may use some varnish and lacquer. And you may want to apply a sheet finish, such as wallpaper or fabric. Each coating serves a different purpose.

You probably decided long before you began to build just how you wanted the finished exterior and interior of your house to look. Now that you can see everything in three dimensions, and before you buy any coatings, take some time to plan your color schemes.

## DEVELOPING COLOR SCHEMES

The subject of color came up briefly in Chapter 13 in connection with selecting the color of roof shingles. In any color scheme one color should be dominant. A good scheme has one dark color, one light color, and one bright color.

All colors have important properties that must be taken into account while you develop a color scheme. Every color has a name—its *hue.* Every hue has value and chroma. *Value* is a measurement of brightness or tone. Orange has a light value, brown has a dark value. *Chroma* is a measure of intensity or purity. Electric blue has great chroma; it is pure color. Baby blue, which has a lot of white in it, and slate, which has a lot of gray, have low intensity.

Hues fall into two general categories called *temperatures.* Warm colors—reds, yellow, and oranges—tend to move into the foreground of a view and seem closer than they really are. Cool colors—mostly blues and the bluer shades of green and purple—tend to recede into the background and seem farther away than they are.

## Color Scheming the Exterior

In developing an exterior color scheme, start with any natural materials first. Wood siding in an unfinished state has medium value, low intensity, and warm temperature. A brown stain changes the value to dark, but does not alter intensity or temperature. A gray stain changes the temperature to cool, but does not alter value or intensity. With paint you can change one, two, or all three characteristics. Base your exterior color scheme on the dominant color in the natural material.

If you used no natural materials, begin with the largest surface area. In most houses this is the walls, but on others, such as A-frames, the roof area dominates. When you select a color for the largest area, remember that colors with dark values absorb heat, while colors with light values reflect it. Light, cool colors are appropriate for a shore vacation house; warm, medium-to-dark colors are more appropriate in the north woods.

Bright colors in large quantities are tiring. Usually the dark and light colors in a scheme appear on the walls and roof in either order, and the bright color appears on trim. If roof and walls have warm colors, choose a warm bright color for trim. Conversely, a cool bright color looks best with cool wall and roof colors. You can use white as part of any exterior color combination.

## Color Scheming the Interior

The orientation of a room has a decided bearing on its color scheme. Northern exposure provides a cool light that adds blue to interior colors. South light in the summer is almost white, and merely intensifies room colors. East light in the morning and west light in the afternoon are warm lights that add yellow and orange to interior colors. The light in west rooms in the morning and east rooms in the afternoon is the reverse—a cool light.

Comfort is partly psychological. You feel cooler in a room with cool colors even when the temperature hovers in the 90's. In winter a room with warm colors is cozier than the same room with cool colors at the same air temperature. Because of the effect of color on comfort, use neutral colors in east and west rooms, warm colors in north rooms, and cool colors in south-facing rooms. If a room has two exposures, use warm neutrals or cool neutrals, depending on orientation.

The amount of light entering a room must also be considered. A wall of glass, unshaded by trees, can let in so much light that you may want other walls medium to dark to reduce glare. On the other hand, you may want other walls to be light if the wall of glass is shaded most of the day. Rooms with small glass areas are more comfortable with light wall and ceiling surfaces. Rooms with two exposures can have medium values.

Color schemes are largely a matter of personal preference, but there are some guide lines developed by color experts. Orientation and incoming light have a distinct bearing on the value and temperature of color to use in various rooms. Now those personal preferences take over. If everyone in the family has the same favorite color, the job of developing a color scheme is easy. But even if all the favorites are different there is still hope that you can satisfy everyone.

*Types of Color Schemes.* Color schemes range from the simple to the complex. Most vacation houses, since they are small compared to year-round houses, demand simple color treatment. You can follow the process by which color schemes are put together by referring frequently to Fig. 16-1. In any of the color schemes to be discussed, one color must be dominant. No color needs to be pure; you can use various *shades,* which are gradations of chroma. Any color with high chroma should be used in the smallest quantity of all the colors selected. As on an exterior, you can use white as part of any color scheme.

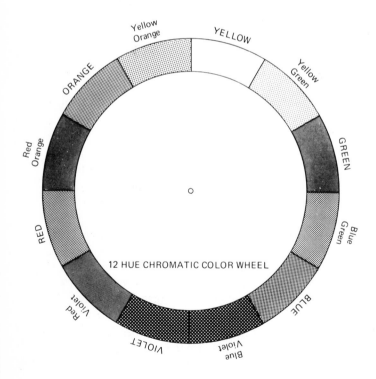

Fig. 16-1 A color wheel is the starting point for developing any color scheme. Start with your favorite color and pick one of the color schemes described in the text.

The simplest of all color schemes is the *monochromatic* scheme. You use only one color, your favorite, in various shades. This scheme works well in a very small room, such as a bathroom or kitchen where the colors of appliances and plumbing fixtures must be taken into account.

An *analagous* color scheme has three colors in it. They can be any three colors that are adjacent to each other in the color wheel. If green is your favorite color, for example, you may choose from three analagous schemes—green with yellow and yellow-green, green with yellow-green and blue-green, or green with blue-green and blue.

A *complimentary* color scheme has just two colors, and they are directly opposite on the color wheel, such as red and green. More common in homes is the *split-complimentary* scheme. Green remains the main color, but instead of using red with it, you use the colors flanking red—red-orange and red-violet.

A combination of two color schemes is the *analagous with a complimentary accent*. The accent color is the one opposite the middle of the three analagous colors, such as blue-violet as an accent with orange, yellow-orange, and yellow.

An excellent color scheme to use with natural wood interiors is the *triad*. It has three colors—every fourth color in the circle. Wood contains shades of several colors, and the triad scheme accents them. With brown-toned woods, for example, you could use a triad of orange, green, and violet. With gray-toned woods you could use blue-green with yellow-orange and red-violet.

Actually there are only two colors that you should not use with your favorite. They are the two at right angles to your favorite in the color wheel. With green, for example, you should not use yellow-orange or blue-violet. All others can be used in one or another of the basic color schemes.

Now that you know the basic premises behind color usage, take a look at the coatings available to help you create your color scheme.

## STAINING

Stains consist of pigment and a vehicle. *Pigments* are the solids that give color, and the *vehicle* is the liquid. Unlike most other finishing coatings, stains do not remain on the surface, but penetrate deeply into the grain of the wood. They allow the wood to breathe—an advantage on wood shingles and shakes.

Stains are manufactured in a wide variety of tones and hues from deep browns to light grays. Some types contain pentachlorophenol to protect the wood against damage from insects and decay. And they have good, uniform hiding properties. Others made with water or spirits as a vehicle penetrate more quickly but not as evenly.

Before you stain any wood surface, test the effect on a smaller piece of the same material to make sure you get the results you expect. Once stain penetrates wood, it is almost impossible to remove it completely, even with much sanding.

Stains should be applied only to raw wood. Its surface must be clean and free of any grease or oil that will cause discoloration or prevent the stain from penetrating. Read the directions on the can of stain you select. Some types must be applied to dry wood, while others work better when the surface is damp. The wood's surface may be smooth or rough. It is much easier to stain a rough surface than to paint it.

You may apply stain with a brush or with rags dipped into the can. With either method you will get some variation in tone, because the cellulose in wood is more dense than the lignin, and they absorb stain at different rates. Most stain manufacturers recommend a three-coat application: a light-toned first coat, a slightly darker second coat, and a similar third coat. The first coat may appear a little blotchy, but the second coat helps to darken places that appear too light. Even after the third coat there will be some variation in tone. This adds life to the wood's appearance, however, and will tend to disappear with weathering.

Allow thorough drying between coats, because stain appears darker when damp. Restain with a single coat every third or fourth summer to renew the finish.

The methods just discussed are for the application of stain to exterior wood. You can get the same variety of tones on interior wood, however, and the procedures are the same. If you want a clear finish that allows the beauty of the wood to come through naturally, you can achieve a beautiful result in several ways. Where you might otherwise use a semigloss paint, use two coats of clear lacquer. On less heavily fingered surfaces you can brush on a mixture of linseed oil and turpentine. You can rub in and polish a paste wax. Or you can buy clear finishes that prime, seal, and decorate the surface in a single brushed application.

# PAINTING

Unlike stain, which is primarily for use on wood, you can find a paint to coat almost any type of surface. Paints are specially formulated for the surface to which they are applied. Each type contains pigment, vehicle, thinner, and drier.

Pigments give paint their color, and you simply order the color you want by the manufacturer's number. You also order by the type of vehicle, also called a *base*. Oil-base paints have been used for many years, and many professional painters prefer them to any other kind. Latex-base paints have an advantage for nonprofessionals: you can clean the paint out of brushes and off your skin with ordinary soap and water. Most of the newer paint formulas use some sort of resin as a vehicle—alkyds, acrylics, and polyvinyl acetates.

### Selecting an Exterior Paint

A good exterior paint must have three important qualities. It must have good *hiding power*—the ability to cover a surface fully and to reflect the ultraviolet rays of the sun. The higher the percentage of pigment shown in the list of ingredients, the better the paint's hiding power.

Exterior paint must be formulated for *chalking*—a slow process during which the weather wears the initial gloss off the paint and turns it to powder. Some chalking is desirable. It allows rain to wash off dirt that clings to the surface, and keeps paint looking fresh and its original color.

Exterior paint should be easy to apply. You can apply most paints with a brush, roller, or spray gun, and the paint you choose should be designed primarily for the method you prefer to use. Although it is the slowest method, brushing is usually best for exterior surfaces. Paints for brushing range in consistency from thin liquids to thick gels that won't spill even when you upset the can. Each has its advantages. Thin paints go on easily, generally adhere well to a surface because they penetrate it somewhat, but tend to run. Thicker paints cover better, but go on less evenly and require more brushing effort.

No matter how good the paint, a paint job is no better than the condition of the surface to which it is applied. A good paint job—proper surface preparation, thorough priming, and well-brushed finish coats of good quality paints—should last ten years.

## Painting Exterior Wood

To prepare wood, rough the surface with steel wool or a wire brush. Wash off all dust and dirt that have accumulated during construction. As you clean, look for knots and sap streaks, and brush on a sealing coat of shellac or aluminum primer. Some undercoats also suffice, but not all of them. Check the label.

Apply a primer-sealer to new wood as a first coat. Brush it well into cracks, splits, and corners. Evenness of the prime coat isn't nearly as important as thorough coverage.

After the prime coat is dry, check the entire surface for unfilled nail holes and other defects. Fill them with putty before you brush on the next coat. Overfill holes a little, because putty does shrink as it dries. Apply one or two finish coats as necessary for good coverage. These coats should be as smooth and even in thickness as you can get them.

For the most efficient painting you will need at least three brushes. On large surfaces use a 4" or 5" brush to make the work go quickly. On trim, at corners, and in other tight spots use a 1 1/2" to 2" brush. Around glass you get the best control and the least cleanup with a 3/4" brush.

## Painting Masonry

To prepare masonry for paint, wire-brush the surface and joints to remove any loose particles. Brush the surface with a solution of muriatic acid to remove any *efflorescence*—discoloration that occurs as a chemical reaction between masonry, mortar, and rain water. Wash the surface thoroughly with a hose, and let it dry completely before you paint. Use only alkali-resistant masonry paints.

## Painting Exterior Metal

You should have little metal to paint, if any. Roofs don't generally require it, flashing should not be painted, and most gutters and downspouts come already finished. Metal windows and doors, however, may come with only a prime coat.

To prepare raw metal for paint, remove any rust with steel wool. Then go over the surface carefully with a wire brush to loosen scale, and with a clean rag wipe off all residue. Then apply a coat of alkyd-resin primer.

Finish primed metal with two rather thin coats of exterior house paint. Metal that is exposed to direct sun will heat up and expand during the day and contract at night. Two thin coats withstand this movement much longer than one coat of the same total thickness.

### Selecting Interior Paints

Chalking ability is not a factor in interior paints, but gloss and reflectance are important. The two terms are interrelated. *Gloss* is the capability of a paint to reflect light. *Reflectance* is a measure of the amount of light reflected.

There are five designations for gloss: flat or matte (the least gloss), eggshell flat, eggshell gloss, semigloss, and full gloss. Generally as gloss increases the amount of pigment decreases. Reflectance ranges from about 80% for white paint down to 9% for dark green.

You will get the best results with the middle three gloss designations. Use an eggshell flat for a softly reflective finish on all ceilings and walls of major living and sleeping areas. Use an eggshell gloss in the kitchen and bathroom. It is more resistant to moisture and is easier to wipe clean. For trim and cabinets that are touched frequently, go to a semigloss, preferably an enamel. Enamel has varnish as a vehicle, which makes the finish durable and washable with soap and water.

### Painting Wallboard

Unfinished wood, masonry, and metal surfaces inside the house are prepared in the same way as exterior surfaces of the same materials. Wallboard requires no special preparation after you complete joint treatment. Look for any small nicks or scratches, however, and fill them with joint compound. Then wipe the entire surface with a damp sponge to remove dust and dried compound.

Apply a primer-sealer to the wallboard first, then add one or two coats of interior paint. If you are using a brush, start in one corner of the ceiling and complete about six square feet before moving on to the next area. On walls work from the top down to minimize the danger of runs.

If you use a roller instead of a brush, use a small brush to paint in corners and around trim. It's hard to roll close to edges, and the difference between roller texture and brush texture is less obvious if you brush first. Then you can roll close to corners and edges without having to roll into them.

## PROTECTING FLOORS

Floors covered with linoleum or resilient tiles require no further finishing. An occasional polishing with an emulsion-type wax is the recommended maintenance. Ceramic tile floors require only an occasional washing.

Stairways and interior wood floors that aren't prefinished, however, require several steps to protect them. If you like the tone of the wood, no stain is necessary.

The floor of this spacious deck is clear-grade redwood without knots, treated with preservatives for maximum wear. The railing and shade roof are built from more economical but equally rugged garden grades of redwood. Roof members are set on edge to let through midday sun, yet also provide protection against low-angle glare in the evening. *Courtesy California Redwood Association.*

To change the tone of hardwoods, such as oak, apply stain with a rag, wiping it on to get as even a tone as possible. To change the tone of softwoods, such as pine, cedar, or gum, apply a light coat of shellac to seal the wood's pores. Then apply stain and let it dry overnight.

Next brush the floor with a wood filler in a matching tone. This coat fills open pores and small dents. Wipe off the excess with a piece of burlap. Then apply a liberal coat of sealer to protect the floor surface from excessive wear. After the sealer is dry, sand the surface lightly with steel wool. Only now are you ready for the final finish.

The basic finishes for wood floors are varnish and shellac. Varnish comes in various glosses, and the higher the gloss the more wear-resistant the finish. Apply two coats according to manufacturer's instructions. Let each coat dry for 24 hours.

Shellac should be applied in three coats. Apply the first coat, let it dry for about four hours, then sand it lightly. Let the second coat dry for another four hours before you apply the final coat.

No matter how you finish an interior wood floor, or if you laid prefinished flooring, apply a good coat of paste wax. Wax itself isn't durable, and must be renewed periodically. But as long as the wax coat is intact, it will fully protect the finish beneath it.

# PRESERVING DECKS AND DOCKS

Wood that is constantly exposed to weather and wear must be preserved and protected. The treatment that you should use depends on the species of wood, the amount of exposure, and the appearance you desire.

You can let wood weather naturally. To do so, however, you must select lumber carefully. You need a high grade, preferably heartwood. Edge-grained decking weathers better than flat-grained. If you use flat-grained lumber for a deck, lay it with the arc of the grain face up. The best species for natural weathering are cypress, redwood, and cedar.

Yet even these species are not consistent in weathering. Untreated woods tend to darken in damp climates during their early months of exposure. Eventually—and it may take years—they turn a warm gray. Timbers not exposed to weather, such as the part of a deck under an overhang, may never lighten. In dry climates redwood, cypress, and cedar are likely to turn a rather dull gray instead of darkening, then gradually lighten to a cool gray.

## Applying Water Repellents

You can preserve both the wood and its natural color with chemical preservatives. There are two basic types. Both types reduce dimensional instability and prevent checking (small splits), rotting, and other similar problems. You can buy lumber already treated under pressure at the mill, or you can soak it yourself at the site. Pressure treatment is far more effective.

One type of water repellent forms a protective film on the wood. The repellent may be clear, it may contain stain or pigment, or it may have a color of its own. Typical of film-forming repellents are creosote, copper naphthenate, and pentachlorophenol solutions. They should be used for protecting wood in constant contact with water or damp soil, such as pilings, posts, and poles.

The other type of water repellent penetrates the wood without forming a film. It should be used for protecting woods alternately exposed to wetting and drying, such as decks, steps, and walkways raised above ground or water level. Repellents must be applied to cut members, notches, and drilled holes after the raw wood is exposed.

*Creosote.* An oily liquid with a base of coal tar or wood tar, creosote has long been used as an effective long-term water repellent. It is a far more effective preservative when applied under pressure. Brushing it on is not recommended. You can let it soak into wood by building a trough of polyethylene formed on four sides with timbers. Creosote darkens wood, has a medicinal odor, and is extremely difficult to paint satisfactorily.

*Copper Naphthenate.* A thinner and more manageable liquid than creosote, copper naphthenate is not as good a preservative, but it doesn't have the drawbacks of odor or method of application. You can soak lumber in a bath of copper naphthenate, you can brush on a liberal coating, or you can dip short members in a partially filled 55-gallon drum. Dip one end, then turn each member over and dip the other end. The preservative has a faint greenish color, but you can paint over it. The chemical does not injure plants.

*Film-Forming Pentachlorophenol.* The effectiveness of this repellent for protecting wood in contact with water or the ground lies somewhere between creosote and copper naphthenate. Soaking or dipping is preferable to brushing, although you should take special care to brush the repellent into defects in the wood and at any point where you have cut the surface.

Be extremely careful in working with pentachlorophenol. It will irritate the skin, so wear rubber gloves. It can burn the eyes and lungs, so work outdoors and wear safety glasses. It is also injurious to plants, so it can't be applied to lumber used in landscaping.

*Film-Free Pentachlorophenol.* Mixed with stains or pigments of various colors, film-free pentachlorophenol is an excellent repellent for decks and deck parts. As a finish coating it helps the wood retain its natural color, although the coating must be renewed every year. Clear pentachlorophenol is formulated for use as a primer-sealer under finish coats of stain or paint. Both types of pentachlorophenol dry in about 24 hours under normal conditions, and have no odor.

## Bleaching

If the lumber you use outdoors is not reasonably uniform in color, you can bleach it to assure faster and more even weathering. Use a bleach that has mildew-resistant additives. Apply it with a brush or roller after construction is complete and after the lumber has been treated with a clear repellent. You can speed the weathering action by dampening the surface periodically with a hose.

### Selecting Deck Paint

If you intend to paint them, treat all parts of decks and other exposed, heavily-used wood areas with preservative and paint primer before you assemble them. Apply finish coats after construction is complete. You can use lower grades of lumber when you paint than when you stain.

Selection of the proper primer is critical. It should be an oil-base paint that is chemically compatible with both the repellent and the finished paint. Study the manufacturer's recommendations for all three coatings before you select any of them.

Deck finishes come in a wide variety of formulations and an equally wide range of prices. Your choice of colors is somewhat limited. Among the better deck finishes is epoxy resin, which comes both clear and pigmented. You apply three coats with a brush or roller. A coat is dry enough to work or walk on in a couple of hours on a good drying day. For a nonskid surface you can add a thin layer of sand or fine aggregate to the last coat as you apply it. After this coat has dried, lightly brush away the excess sand.

## TOOLS YOU WILL NEED

To preserve and decorate exterior and interior surfaces you will need the following tools and protective equipment:

> paint brush (4″ to 5″)
> paint brush (1 1/2″ to 2″)
> paint brush (3/4″)
> rags (for applying stain)
> paint roller
> paint tray
> spray gun
> steel wool
> wire brush
> scraper
> sponge
> burlap (for wood floors)
> sandpaper
> ladders
> dropcloths
> thinners
> solvents
> rubber gloves
> safety glasses

# Building Decks

# and

# Finishing the Site

The finishing touches inside and outside a vacation house usually are applied concurrently. Take advantage of bad weather to finish the inside and to plan exterior work. Work outside as weather permits.

After you have your house enclosed and can see exactly how it looks in three dimensions on its site, take another look at the site plan you drew some months before. Things are likely to look a little different, and you may find that a few changes are in order.

Look first at outdoor living areas, especially decks that are structurally tied to the house. Do they have the view you expected them to have? Do they interfere with views from inside? Do they have sunlight during the hours the family is most likely to want to acquire a tan? Do they have shade during the heat of the day? Are the points of access and egress where they should be?

Next, check out the entrance road or driveway. By now you have had a chance to use it for a few months, and probably know if you should widen it, straighten it, level it, or smooth its surface. Do you have a place for parking that is convenient but that doesn't put cars in the way of a good view? Is the walk between parking and entrance door direct and well drained?

Study drainage thoughtfully during rainstorms. Does water run off away from the foundation? Does it run across the road or walks and make them difficult to use? After you have attached gutters and downspouts, are they doing the job for which you installed them? Is water running off onto a neighbor's property where it will cause him problems and strain relations? Do level outdoor areas drain well so that you can use them again as soon as the sun comes out?

Finally, study privacy conditions from all viewpoints. You may get some enjoyment out of watching the activities of any fairly close neighbors, but do you want them watching you? If the sills of bath and bedroom windows lie below chest height for better light and an intimate study of wildlife, are they or can they be screened against a similar view from outside? Are outdoor living areas as private as you want them to be? Do you have an area screened from everyone's view for setting out trash and garbage until you can dispose of it?

Make a careful review of all site conditions to determine what corrections must be made and the most logical time to make them. Any relocation of structural outdoor living areas should proceed immediately. You can correct problems

Metal stanchions serve as posts and ropes serve as railings around this deck without blocking any view. Decking is laid parallel to the wall of the house at all points. Note how treads of wood steps are shaped to turn the small angle between sections of deck. Exterior walls are faced with horizontal boards and vertical battens. *Courtesy Carolina Log Buildings, Inc.*

with the entrance road after the last delivery truck has gone. You can correct most drainage problems with finish grading. But call your grading contractor now to let him know when you will need him, so that he can work you into his schedule. You can solve privacy problems with planting, screens, and fences at the very end of the job.

# PLANNING A DECK

The plan view in the working drawings for a vacation house usually shows the general locations of decks, and sometimes gives their sizes. Unless the deck is integrated into the structure of the house itself, however, drawings don't often give much in the way of details. The reason is that the size and shape of a deck depend so much on specific site conditions.

Per square foot of area, a deck costs a lot less than the house itself. Yet it quickly becomes the most used part of your living area. So think big, particularly if the house is small. A small deck is a waste of money.

Draw the outline of your deck on the floor plan or site plan to establish its perimeter. Then decide what pattern you would like for the decking. Running the boards parallel to the wall of the house makes for the simplest construction. But for more interesting patterns you can run the boards diagonally, in a herringbone pattern, square parquet, diagonal parquet, or a design of your own creation. Keep in mind, however, that the more complex the pattern the more complex the framing. Each cut end of each piece of decking must be supported.

Decks must be designed and built to the same code requirements as standard interior floor construction. There are three essential parts to any deck: its supports, its platform, and guard rails.

## Supporting the Deck

A deck may be supported in several ways. It may rest on posts, piers, or pilings, and not be connected directly to the main house. It may be supported partly on posts and partly at or on the foundation wall. It may be a cantilevered extension of the interior floor system. Or it may be supported by some combination of methods.

The same rules and procedures that apply to foundations also apply to pier supports. The simplest pier to use is the bell-bottom pier shown in Fig. 6-2. The bottom of each pier must extend below the frost line, and its top should rise at least 6″ above grade. Space piers 5′ to 6′ apart as you go away from the house, and no more than 12′ apart across the front of the house.

The exact spacing of piers depends on the size and shape of the deck and the size and grade of the beams that span between piers. If you use the better grades of 4 × 8 redwood beams, for example, the recommended spans are

9′ 0″ for a deck 6′ wide
8′ 0″ for a deck 8′ wide
7′ 0″ for a deck 10′ wide
6′ 0″ for a deck 12′ wide.

These spans run parallel to the wall of the house, and deck widths are measured from the exterior wall of the house to center lines of piers.

With 4 × 10 beams you can increase the above spans 25%. With 4 × 6 spans you must reduce spans by 25%. As a rule it is better to use larger beams and fewer posts. If you can't find 4″-thick beams locally, make built-up beams out of a pair of 2″ members fastened together with lag screws or bolts.

In the other direction you can use construction heart and construction common grades of redwood or cypress. At a spacing of 16″ on centers, you can span up to

> 6′0″ with 2 × 6 joists
> 9′0″ with 2 × 8 joists
> 13′0″ with 2 × 10 joists.

At a 24″ spacing you must reduce the length of span 1/6 from the spans given above for 16″ spacing.

Only after you have decided on the size of structural members can you determine the lengths of posts. If the level of the house floor and the deck are the same, and you use 4 × 6 beams and 2 × 6 joists, for example, the distance from the interior floor level to the tops of posts will be 14″. That's 1 1/2″ for the decking, 5 1/2″ for joists, another 5 1/2″ for beams, and 1 1/2″ for a cap. A *cap* (see Fig. 17-2) is a piece of 2″-thick material that is the equivalent of a sill plate on a foundation wall. If the deck lies close to the ground, you can omit the caps and rest the posts directly on the tops of piers.

*At the House.* When floor and deck are at or close to the same level, you can attach deck framing to house framing in two ways. One way is to bolt the edge joist of the deck through the header joist of the house (Fig. 17-1, top). As the first step, position the edge joist and attach it. This establishes the level of the tops of beams that support the other ends of deck joists. Hang the deck joists from the edge joist with strap hangers. Unless decking will cover and protect the edge joist over its entire length, flash it.

The other method of tethering deck framing is to anchor a ledger to the foundation wall (Fig. 17-1, bottom). The ledger supports the decking itself if deck joists run parallel to the wall. If they run perpendicular to the wall or at an angle, the ledger supports the edge joists. Toenail the joists into the ledger.

When there is a difference of at least one riser between the main floor and deck levels, it is best to support the entire deck on posts.

*On Posts.* To the top of each pier bolt a cap of 2″-thick lumber large enough to cover—usually about 8″ square. Use weather-resistant lumber such as redwood or cypress; construction heart is the grade to use for caps, posts, and beams. Cut posts to the proper length at the house first, and use their tops as a fixed point for determining the lengths of other posts. Use identical piers and caps at all support points, and let the lengths of the posts vary with the terrain.

Beams may be supported at posts in three ways. Where the two members form a tee, you can use metal hangers (Fig. 17-2, left) or gussets of exterior plywood with their tops flashed (center). Where you want posts to continue up-

**Fig. 17-1.** At the wall, decking is supported by a ledger bolted to the header joist. Supporting joists may butt against the ledger (top) or run parallel to it (bottom). Note that flashing is required when decking does not protect the ledger over its entire length.

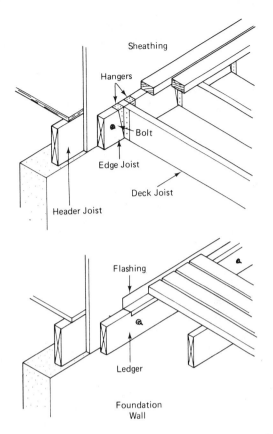

**Fig. 17-2.** Beams may be supported on posts in three ways: with strap hangers (left), with gussets flashed at the top edges (center), and with bolts when the post rises above deck level (right). Caps are not required on piers when posts are less than a foot long.

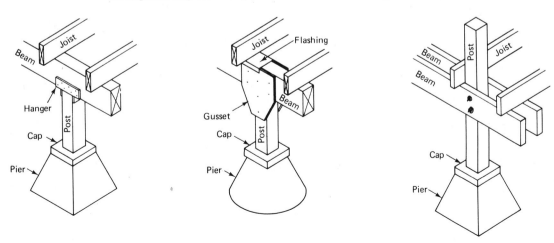

ward to support a railing or bench, the beams must be two thinner members, one bolted to each side of the post (right). If you must splice beams, carefully square the ends for a tight fit, butt them directly over a post, and add a 2"-thick cleat on the hidden side.

Ideally, each joist should be an uncut member. If you must splice, do so over the beams by nailing a 1" board of the same species of wood on each side of the joint. At openings in the deck for stairs or a planter, use the standard header construction shown in Fig. 8-6.

When you cut deck members and position them, it is extremely important that cuts are square, posts are plumb, and beams and joists are level. Have your carpenter's level handy at all times, and use it every step of the way. Use your framing square to assure that the joists are set at right angles to ledgers and beams.

## Laying the Platform

For decking the best lumber is construction common redwood or cypress 2 × 4s or 2 × 6s laid flat. The surface of the deck may be laid flush with the inside floor level, or down one step. It isn't wise to have more than one step down, nor to have a step less than 4" in height.

With *vertical-grain* decking—that is, the grain runs up and down the end when the piece is flat—you can place either side of the decking face up. With *flat-grain* decking, where the grain curves across the end from side to side, place each piece with the annular rings pointing down at the edges. This leaves the bark side of the tree exposed, the side closest to the weather in a growing tree.

If you run decking parallel to the wall of the house, align the first piece at the wall, gapping about 1/8", and at right angles to joists. Precut and preserve all pieces before installation. Precutting requires a little planning so that the ends of decking that butt together meet over joists. Decking should never be spliced.

Attach decking with 16-penny nails. Drive in one nail at each joist. Position the nails alternately near one edge and then the other to overcome any tendency of the wood to cup (Fig. 17-3). Where two pieces butt, nail at opposite corners into predrilled holes to prevent splitting. Use two nails side by side in a piece of decking only at the edges of the deck where the long boards end, or in any short boards that run only between two supports, as in a parquet pattern. Always gap 1/8" between deck planks to allow for drainage.

Poorly galvanized iron and copper nails often stain wood decks badly. Use only aluminum, stainless steel, or hot-dipped galvanized nails throughout deck construction. To make sure no staining occurs, countersink nails below the surface, brush the holes with water repellent, and fill them with an oilless wood filler.

The procedures outlined here apply primarily to decks close to but not on the ground. Higher decks require longer and heavier posts, and diagonal cross-bracing is frequently needed to provide lateral stability. Before you begin to build a deck more than 6' off the ground, have your design checked by an architect or structural engineer for adequacy.

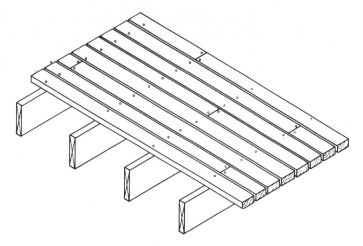

**Fig. 17-3.** Recommended nailing of decking is one nail per joist, alternating from side to side of each plank. Only at the end of the deck do you use two nails per plank.

To lay a deck on the ground, you need a bed of sand about 3″ deep to suffocate weeds and grass and to serve as a base for the deck. If the area does not drain well, put in 3″ of gravel beneath the sand.

Instead of joists use 2 × 4 all-heart cypress or redwood cleats laid flat in the sand and carefully leveled. Space the cleats 24″ on centers under parallel decking, or about 30″ o.c. if you use a parquet pattern. Nail as described for above-ground decks.

### Erecting Guard Rails

Any deck more than 2′ above grade should have a railing. Railing supports toenailed to the decking are not strong enough, so you must do one of two things. Either extend the posts upward through the deck (see Fig. 17–2 for the method of supporting joists) and nail the railing into the tops of posts; or bolt supports to the joists below the deck and notch the decking to fit around them. Railings should be cut from clear, all-heart vertical-grain redwood or cypress, and should be supported every 4′.

The top of a railing should be no less than 30″ above the deck for greatest safety; 42″ is a practical maximum height. The best height for your particular railing is at a point where it doesn't interfere with the view at seated eye level—not only when you are on the deck but also when you are inside the house looking out.

You can treat the apertures formed by railing, deck, and posts in a number of ways. For privacy, insert solid panels of plywood, although they may interfere with the view. For the safety of small children, add a wood or metal grille. The grille prevents them from falling off the deck, lets them see what is going on, and minimizes their desire to climb on the railing to see better. For maximum view when safety and privacy aren't major considerations, leave the space open.

**Building Benches.** On a large deck you can provide seating at very little extra expense by extending the posts upward as one of the seating supports. Figure 17–4 shows one good design. Back supports must be firmly bolted to withstand the outward pressure of seated people.

The forward edge of seating should be about 16″ above deck level, and the seat itself should be about 16″ deep. The height of the back should be 16″ at a minimum and about 22″ at a maximum. Canting the seat and back at an angle of 12° to 15° makes sitting more comfortable. If you expect that the seat will be used more for stretching out full length than for lounging upright, widen the seat to 18″ and reduce its angle to no more than 6°.

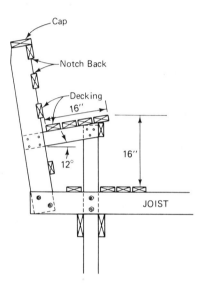

**Fig. 17-4.** Sectional detail of a bench at the edge of a deck. Seat and back dimensions and the angle they form may vary. Note that the back is notched for slats and topped with a cap.

## Cantilevering a Deck

The size of a supported deck is limited primarily by the terrain and your pocketbook. The size of a cantilevered deck is limited by the structure of the house.

A cantilevered deck is carried on joists that are a continuation of the joists supporting the floor of the house. Interior joists that extend outdoors must be of weather-resistant wood over their entire length. As a rule the amount of cantilever should not exceed 1/3 the total length of the supporting joist. Even decks with this short a cantilever are more stable if they are braced against the foundation wall.

When you build a house with a cantilevered deck, omit the header joist. Fill the spaces between joists with shorter lengths of joist material. Cut these lengths with square ends for a tight fit. They will help to keep joists plumb and prevent twisting.

To accommodate the difference in thickness between the decking and the combined thickness of subfloor and finished floor inside, you have three choices.

One is to trim the depth of the long joists outside the foundation wall so that the two levels are the same (Fig. 17-5, top). The amount to be trimmed is about 5/8″ with thin floor coverings and about 3/8″ with thin wood blocks. With thicker wood blocks the two floor levels should be almost identical.

A second way is to add a threshold at doorways (Fig. 17-5, center) to allow for the difference in height and to prevent rain from flowing into the house. If you use sliding doors, simply set the bottom track on a wood strip to raise it above deck level. You must then step slightly downward as you enter the house, but the difference in level is not enough to be dangerous.

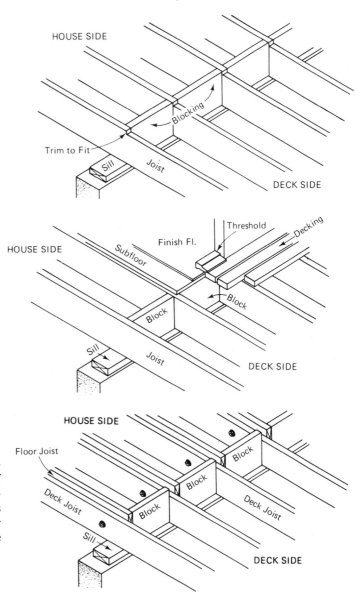

**Fig. 17-5.** You can adjust for difference in level between the floor of the house and the floor of a cantilevered deck by notching long joists (top), adding a threshold at door openings (center), or doubling the joists (bottom).

With the third method you can resolve the height problem by keeping floor joists at their normal length and bolting smaller deck joists to them (Fig. 17-5, bottom). These deck joists, 2″ less in depth, must be at least twice as long as the amount of cantilever. Set the two joists flush at their bottom edges, and bolt them together tightly.

There is usually some vibration is a cantilevered deck, although the amount is minor with good construction. You can further reduce the effect in two ways. One is to add flat braces across the undersides of exposed joists. This spreads the vibration over the entire deck area.

The other way is to add diagonal struts. Fit one end of each strut over another ledger at the foundation wall attached just above grade (refer back to Fig. 17-1). Bolt the other ends to the joists just inside the header joist at the edge of the deck. Braces like this every 48″ will dampen any vibration.

## BUILDING STEPS OUTDOORS

The rules set down in Chapter 12 for interior stairways apply also to exterior wood stairways, but only as minimums. Treads without risers should be no less than 11″ deep—a 2 × 12, a pair of 2 × 6s, or three 2 × 4s. If you notch stringers for treads, let the treads overhang each other about 1″.

For a simple stairway, trim the ends of stringers to fit the slope, and support the treads on cleats nailed to the insides of stringers. Mark the stringers as if you were going to cut them, then set cleats at the horizontal marks. This method can be used on a stairway less than 42″ wide. Broader stairways require a center stringer, and all three must be notched.

### Forming Concrete Steps

The general rules for building concrete steps outdoors are different from the rules for inside stairways. The steps are not as steep. Instead of the 7 1/2″ to 8″ riser and the 9 1/4″ to 10″ tread, the more common dimensions for concrete steps are 6″ and 12″ respectively. If possible, keep flights of steps short (no more than six risers), and break up longer flights with landings.

Details of typical construction appear in Fig. 17-6. Each tread should pitch forward about 1/8″ so that water drains away. To make the stairway safer and easier to climb, slant each riser inward to provide more toe space. If the bottom step is below grade, such as the end of an outdoor access to a basement, provide some means of drainage.

## SHORING A BANK

By studying the effects of heavy rains on your site, you will learn whether you have any problems with soil erosion. You can prevent such erosion with retaining walls that are not only attractive but can help to create privacy.

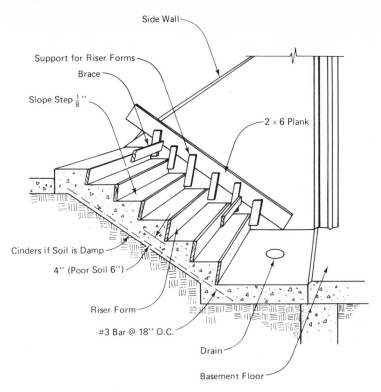

Side Wall

Support for Riser Forms

Brace

Slope Step $\frac{1}{8}''$

2 x 6 Plank

Cinders if Soil is Damp

4'' (Poor Soil 6'')

Riser Form

#3 Bar @ 18'' O.C.

Drain

Basement Floor

**Fig. 17-6.** Section and perspective of a concrete stairway poured on grade shows details for reinforcing, forming, and angling treads and risers for maximum safety. A drain is important if water has nowhere else to flow.

At this point in construction you are probably thinking: "I've done enough for now. I'll build walls later." But there are two advantages to building walls at the time of finish grading. Some grading must be done anyway, and it costs a lot less to grade for retaining walls now while the equipment is on the site than to have a crew return at a later date. Equally important, the washing problem isn't going to improve by waiting. It can only get worse.

A stone or concrete retaining wall isn't that hard to build, but there are some design limitations. The base of the wall should lie 12" below the frost line. Its top should lie no more than 3' above the grade of the lower level (Fig. 17-7, left). The thickness of the wall at the lower grade should be no less than 1/3 the wall's exposed height. The wall at its top should be no less than 12" thick. And you must provide weep holes.

*Weep holes* are small holes through a masonry wall that allow moisture trapped behind the wall to escape. They are placed in the head joints between stones in the first course above the lower grade, about 24" on centers. When you build the wall, set an oiled dowel 1/4" in diameter at a slight angle in the mortar

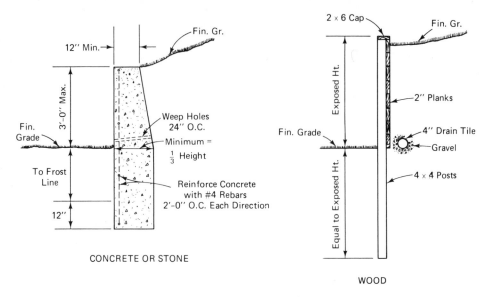

**Fig. 17-7.** Sections through retaining walls of masonry (left) and wood (right) show typical construction and general rules for heights above and below grade.

(or concrete). Remove the dowel just before you tool the joints (or concrete sets), and fill the hole with inorganic insulation. The insulation acts as a wick to draw out moisture; it also keeps out insects.

You can also build retaining walls of rot-resistant wood. All-heartwood lumber must be used. Garden grade is adequate, but when visual appearance is a factor use clear all-heart. Sometimes you can buy the lumber either rough- or smooth-surfaced.

For walls up to 24″ high on the exposed side, use 4 × 4 posts spaced 4′ on centers. For higher walls (up to 48″), space 4 × 4 posts 3′ on centers. The posts must extend as far below ground as they are exposed above (Fig. 17–7, right). To dig the holes, borrow or rent a post-hole digger. An auger digger works best in light soil. Stony or rocky soil calls for a clamshell digger.

The strongest wall consists of 2″ planks nailed on the back sides of posts. Treat all members with water repellent after cutting them to length, and then attach them with corrosion-resistant nails. For a little more attractive wall, attach planks to the fronts of posts with anchor bolts. Apply a 2 × 6 for a cap. You can then decorate the exposed surface with 2 × 2 battens applied vertically, or by inserting 2 × 4s on edge horizontally between planks.

In order to nail planks on the backs of posts, you must dig away the slope, then backfill. To carry off moisture that will accumulate behind the wall, lay a 4″ drain tile in gravel along the base of the wall before you backfill. The only alternative, which is acceptable if you don't object to seepage at the front of the wall, is weep holes drilled into the planks every 24″ at the base.

# IMPROVING YOUR ACCESS ROAD

On most vacation sites finish grading is largely a matter of adjusting slopes to resolve drainage problems and spreading the topsoil you set aside at the beginning of the project. This work may be included as part of your contract with your excavating contractor. If you plan to have some landscaping done, however, finish grading might be better included in a contract with the landscaper or nurseryman.

If your access road has not held up during the months of construction, now is the time to regrade or put in a better road. A good unpaved driveway has four layers (Fig. 17–8, left). The base layer is crushed stone 3 1/2″ to 4″ thick, compacted with a roller. The next layer is identical. You get a much better base by compacting two 4″ layers than one 8″ layer. The third layer, also rolled, is only 3″ thick, and you top it with a 1″-thick layer of finer stone that you don't roll. Shape the top two layers with a slight crown to assure good drainage.

You can leave the top layer of rock natural for appearance, or oil it to reduce dust. For a more durable finished surface add a 1/2″-thick layer of asphalt or some other bituminous product.

A concrete driveway should be a minimum of 5″ thick and reinforced its entire width with wire mesh set 2″ below the surface (Fig. 17–8, right). No special base is needed in warm climates, but the ground below the slab should be compacted with a roller. In cold climates provide a base of gravel at least 4″ thick beneath the slab. If your site is flat, slope the driveway to one side at least 1/8″ per foot of width to provide drainage and to speed drying.

**Fig. 17-8.** Sections through a good unpaved (top) and concrete driveway (bottom). Dotted lines show shape of concrete if driveway is a thickened-edge slab.

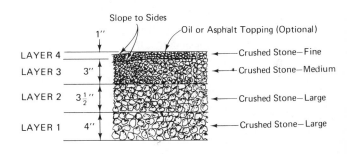

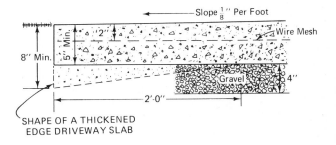

# LAYING WALKS AND PATIOS

Bases for walking surfaces are thinner than bases for driving surfaces. Six inches of gravel topped by 2″ of sand is a good base. Six inches of sand with no gravel beneath it is even better. The sand must be well compacted and bounded by soil, masonry, or treated wood to prevent erosion. The top of this base should be high enough so that the finished walk or patio is at least 1″ above grade for good drainage.

Use a rubber mallet to press each stone or brick into the sand, and level each piece as you set it. Space the stones about 1 1/2″ apart if you want to add topsoil and grow grass between them. Otherwise set them with only a little space between them, and fill the gaps with sand.

# CREATING PRIVACY

On most vacation sites privacy isn't a problem. Where it is, and you need some sort of visual screen, you can build it or plant it. If a screen under 6′ in height will give you the necessary privacy, consider building a fence. It never grows or needs trimming. For anything taller than 6′, you'll need to plant trees.

For fence posts you can use 4 × 4s of cedar, Douglas fir, cypress, lodgepole pine, redwood, or Southern yellow pine. The wood must be pressure treated. Dig holes 12″ in diameter to a point about a foot below frost line. Set the posts in the holes and backfill with concrete or crushed rock to a depth of about a foot. Use a plumb bob and level to make sure the posts are plumb, in line with each other, and evenly spaced.

The best privacy fence is not solid. It shuts out the view but lets through any breeze. Once you have the posts in place, you can develop your own design. Figure 17–9 shows only a few of the many possibilities. Treat all fence parts with water repellent after cutting and fitting them, but before assembly. If you also intend to stain them, apply the stain and let it dry before assembling the parts.

Prior to planting a live screen, seek advice from a local nurseryman. Tell him what you want to accomplish, and ask his recommendation. He knows what grows well in the area, what soil conditions are like, how fast various plants will grow, and whether they need shade or sun. No book can guide you as well as the man on the spot.

# LANDSCAPING

Unless you are a hobbyist, you probably listed cutting a lawn, weeding flower beds, and trimming shrubbery among the things you do *not* want to do on a vacation. If so, keep lawn and planting to a minimum. On a wooded site you have plenty of natural landscaping to soften the lines of the house. On a barren shore site, however, you may feel the need for a little visual relief and color.

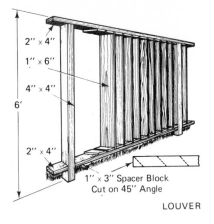

2″ × 4″

1″ × 6″

4″ × 4″

6′

2″ × 4″

1″ × 3″ Spacer Block
Cut on 45″ Angle

LOUVER

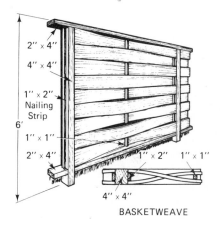

2″ × 4″

4″ × 4″

1″ × 2″
Nailing
Strip

6′

1″ × 1″

2″ × 4″

1″ × 2″    1″ × 1″

4″ × 4″

BASKETWEAVE

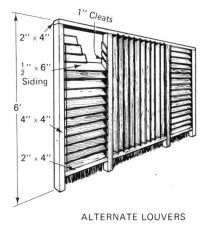

1″ Cleats

2″ × 4″

½″ × 6″
Siding

6′

4″ × 4″

2″ × 4″

ALTERNATE LOUVERS

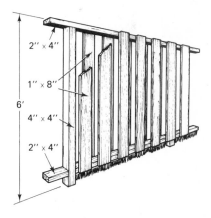

2″ × 4″

1″ × 8″

6′

4″ × 4″

2″ × 4″

BOARD AND BOARD

**Fig. 17-9.** Here are just a few of the many fence designs that block
a view for privacy but do not interrupt a breeze.

Redwood used here for deck, stairway (except for posts), and stair rail is gradually weathering to a soft driftwood gray. Because the deck lies almost at grade, no railing is needed. Note that headers are deeper than joists, and are flush with planks in the deck. *Architect: Richard Stowers. Courtesy California Redwood Association.*

To reduce upkeep, ground ivies of various textures and growth patterns are a delightful substitute for a lawn. For base planting put in shrubs that will be in flower during the times you are most likely to occupy the house. Colorful plants in portable flower beds are excellent for brightening a deck. If you need to plant a tree or two for shade or privacy, again talk to the local nurseryman. He can not only recommend the right tree for the purpose, but for a small fee he will plant it for you.

# TOOLS YOU WILL NEED

In order to build a deck you will need the following tools as a minimum:

power drill
power saw
brushes (for applying preservative)
wrench (for bolts)
hammer
carpenter's level
metal shears (for flashing)
framing square
steel tape
folding rule
spade

In addition, for finish grading and landscaping, you are likely to need

post-hole digger
shovel
roller (for compacting stone)
rubber mallet
plumb bob

# Building

# Over Water

Before you even consider building a pier, boat dock, or float, find out what the local restrictions are, and who has the authority to approve your plans. In almost any situation you could name, somebody somewhere must give you permission to build anything that will affect the water on which your site fronts.

Usually waterfront sites fall into one of three categories. Local real estate agents and neighbors with similar dock or pier facilities can tell you which category your site fits, and where to go for the necessary approvals.

1. *Private lakes.* Where the entire shoreline is privately owned, and there are no public beaches, boat docks, ramps, or other similar facilities, the rules governing what you can build are usually developed by property owners. A board made up of owners establishes restrictions, and it has the right to approve your plans. As long as your pier is no longer or much different than existing piers, approval should be routine.

2. *Public but nonnavigable waterways.* Where the general public has access to the water, your proposed pier or float and the locations of rafts must be approved by an authorized official. This official may be a local authority, but more likely has an office in the Water Protection Division of the Natural Resources Department of the state government in the capital. A permit is usually required before you can begin construction.

This combination deck and boat dock exemplifies good design. The walkway is narrow and has railings on both sides because of its position high above water level. A large lounging deck is isolated from other water activities, but commands a superb view. The redwood ladder, which pivots with tidal movements, carries passengers from boats to dock. Note how the massive railing of redwood timbers cantilevers beyond the posts and houses pulleys for raising boats above water level. Swimming and diving are not common activities here, and little provision was therefore made for them. *Courtesy California Redwood Association.*

3. *Navigable waterways.* A permit is always required from the District Engineer, Corps of Army Engineers. The United States is divided into 11 divisions, each with a headquarters. Each division is further divided into as many as five districts, each with its own headquarters. From any division or district office you can request a pamphlet, *Applications for Department of the Army Permits for Activities in Waterways.* The booklet sets forth procedures for securing a permit.

The jurisdiction of the Corps extends over the entire salt water coast of the U.S., the shores of the Great Lakes, and "all rivers, streams, and lakes which have evidence of past, present, or potential use for interstate or foreign commerce." Sometimes state and local authorizations must be secured before you can receive federal approval, although processing can go forward simultaneously.

Any authority who must approve your proposed facilities is interested primarily in the length of the pier and the durability of construction. Naturally your pier must not interfere with the activities of others, including marine life. For this reason you may need approval even if a lake or pond is entirely on your own property but drains into a stream that runs through the property of others.

You must build piers strong enough to withstand the effects of tides, high water from storms, and damage by wave wash. You have the responsibility for maintaining your in-water facilities in good condition. If you don't, you are liable for the cost of returning the waterway to its original condition.

After you apply for a permit, a public notice is usually issued to potentially interested parties. They have a limited period, often 30 days, in which to raise objections. You must answer and overcome all objections to obtain approval. If your application is controversial, the approving authority may call for a public hearing. If there are no objections at any level, however, you can normally obtain a permit within 90 days after submitting your application. So allow for this lead time. On most applications you must state the approximate date you plan to start work, and the expected date of completion.


## DESIGNING A PIER

The best pier is one designed to serve specific purposes well. A pier may be used for tying up boats, for swimming, diving, waterskiing, sitting, sunning, or any combination thereof. The design of your pier therefore needs input from the whole family.

Technically a *pier* is a fixed platform above the water that does not move with a change in water level. A *float* is a movable platform that floats on the water and remains a constant distance above water level. A good pier will last for years. A good float will not. When differences in water level vary greatly during the vacation season, you may need both a pier and a float with a walkway between.

Design a boat dock so that it protects water craft from the prevailing breeze (Fig. 18-1). To minimize damage to both boats and dock, the breeze should

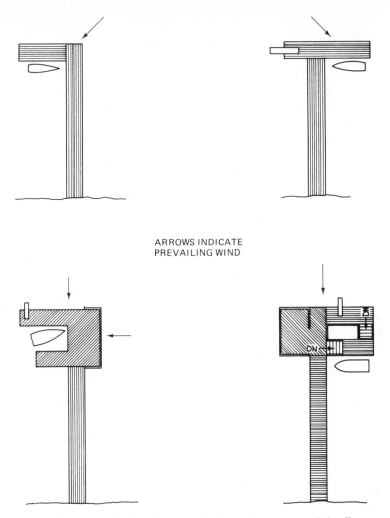

ARROWS INDICATE
PREVAILING WIND

**Fig. 18-1.** To design a pier properly, its various uses and the direction of the prevailing wind must be your major considerations.

blow across the dock toward the boats. If possible, other water-related activities should be isolated from boat operations to reduce the chances of injury. Inactivities, such as enjoying the breeze or the sun or watching water activities, should be planned farther toward shore, away from the splashing of swimmers, divers, and skiers.

Three feet is about minimum width for the part of a pier used only as a walkway. Four feet is better. Areas used for sunning or watching aquatic goings-on should be no less than 6' wide. A boat mooring must be as long as the longest boat you own.

For diving, minimum depth of water at the pier's end is 6' at low tide. This is adequate for all boats except sailboats with a deep keel, which may require a depth up to 12'.

The height above water level of the platform of a pier or float varies with water conditions. On small lakes 22" is about right. On large lakes that get rough in bad weather, set the level so that waves won't wash over the dock. A 30" height is usually enough. On tidal waters plan the deck at 22" above water level at low tide.

On most sites you can locate a pier anywhere between an extension of your property lines into the water. All too often people build a pier in the middle of the shore line, only to discover that it interferes with the view. On the other hand, if you want to observe closely what is happening on or around the pier, locate it so that it is in full view from outdoor living areas and certain control points in the house, such as the kitchen.

## BUILDING A PIER

Pier construction is similar to deck construction. The basic support for large piers is heavy pilings, driven 12' on centers by professionals. Under certain conditions you can drive pilings yourself for lighter docks, spaced 6' on centers.

First, the lake bottom or river bed must be soft—mud or light sand that will give way when you drive the pilings, and reform around them to hold them in place. Second, you must have a firm working surface from which to swing a heavy sledge. This surface may be a portable plywood platform (Fig. 18-2) that rests on the exposed bottom of tidal waters, or of reservoirs that are drained in the fall, or sometimes on beds of rivers and streams when water level is low. In northern climates the platform can be thick ice. You simply cut holes to size in the ice at the proper locations, then drive pilings through the holes.

**Fig. 18-2.** Suggested design of a portable platform from which you can drive pilings to support a pier or float

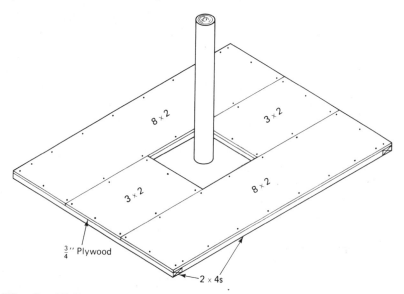

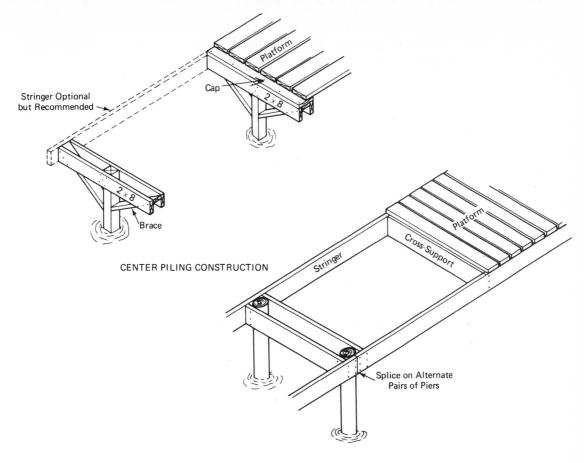

**Fig. 18-3.** Piers supported on a single row of pilings (top) are more economical to build but less sturdy than piers anchored to a double row (bottom).

Pilings should lie inside the edges of the pier so they can't damage a moored boat. And because railings aren't practical on most piers, pilings don't need to project above the dock's deck.

It's almost impossible to get the tops of all pilings at the same level. Just come as close as you can for the sake of appearance. Then attach 2 × 8s on both sides of the pilings, and cap them with a plank wide enough to cover the support assembly (Fig. 18-3, top). Use only bolts or spikes that are unaffected by water.

If you use only a single row of pilings under the center of the pier, add 2 × 4 braces to assure stability. This design is recommended only for walkways. When much action takes place at the edges of the pier, use a double row of piles (Fig. 18-3, bottom). Run stringers the long dimension of the pier between the piles to add longitudinal stability, to trim the edge of the pier, and to support the ends of decking.

Use either 2 × 6s or 2 × 8s for decking. You may lay the decking across the pier from stringer to stringer without additional support as long as it is not more than 48″ wide. With greater spans or with longitudinal decking you must add cross supports between stringers.

## BUILDING A FLOAT

You have as much freedom in designing the shape of a float as you have in designing a pier. You still need pilings, however, to hold the float in position against the push of waves or wind.

Select the flotation material from what is available locally. The material must be buoyant, and it should be inexpensive because you will have to replace it some day. Ten years is about the maximum life of most flotation materials.

One of the better materials for floating floats is foam plastic. It is not affected by anything likely to be found in or on the water except gasoline, which dissolves it. There are protective coatings on the market, however, which prevent this deterioration.

Empty 55-gallon drums have good buoyancy, but they last only a few years in salt water and corrode in fresh water if left in all year. Small balsa rafts also work well, but they are more expensive and not as readily available. Logs of most species absorb water too readily and become waterlogged after a few years. Treating logs with water repellent delays this absorption, however.

Build floats in sections not over 12′ long. Place some flotation material under the ends and continue to add more material until you achieve the proper buoyancy. But beware of too much buoyancy; it makes the float unstable. All flotation materials must be boxed in so that they won't pop out of position in rough weather.

Floats must be anchored loosely to pilings so they can rise and fall with changes in water level. You need fewer pilings than for piers, however, and you can stagger them. If the pilings lie outside the edges of the float, you can hold sections of the float in place with galvanized steel strapping, pipe, cables, or a wood frame (Fig. 18–4, top left and bottom). If you want the float to have a clean edge, stop decking just short at the corners of each section, frame an opening, and let the piling protrude through the opening (Fig. 18–4, top right). Bolt the sections of the float together so that the entire assembly moves as a unit, rather than as individual sections.

### Installing a Gangplank

The connection between a float and either the shore or a pier is moving constantly as long as there is any movement of the water. This situation calls for a gangplank. You build a gangplank like a section of float, except that the supporting frame is made of 2 × 4s laid flat.

The high end of the gangplank should be attached with hinges to the fixed pier or to the shore. At the lower end attach rollers; wheels from roller skates

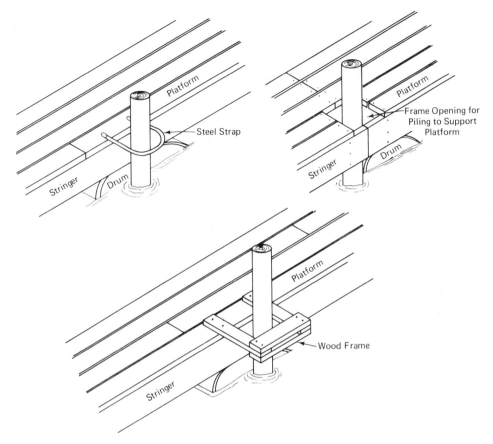

**Fig. 18-4.** Three ways of connecting floats loosely to pilings. Where the piling lies inside stringers (upper right), and therefore cuts into the walkway, the float should be another plank wider for safety.

work nicely. To prevent the rollers from wearing tracks in the wood platform on which they turn, cover the area with a metal plate. Both rollers and plate must be coated to prevent rusting.

## BUILDING A RAFT

A raft is nothing more than a section of a float, usually square in shape and at least 6' on a side. It should rest lower in the water than a float so that swimmers and divers can climb onto it easily. Metal handholds at the corners are useful for this purpose and also as a place to hang on while resting.

The edges of rafts should be carefully smoothed to remove all splinters. Anchor the raft to the bottom of the lake with a length of cable and heavy weights such as concrete blocks.

# TOOLS YOU WILL NEED

To build and anchor piers, floats, and rafts, you will need the following tools:

sledge
power saw
brushes (for preservative)
hammer
wrench
hacksaw
metal shears

# Estimating

Accurate estimating is a complex process that requires much experience. But if you have any flair for basic mathematics, you can handle all the estimating necessary for your vacation house.

Why is estimating necessary? For five reasons. First, a preliminary estimate gives you a good idea of whether the house you want to build is within your budget. Second, you need some sort of estimate before you can secure any financing. Third, an estimate helps you to gauge a little better whether bids from subcontractors are really accurate or out of line. Fourth, you need to calculate quantities of materials before you order, and estimating their costs is the next simple step beyond. And fifth, knowledge of estimating helps you to stay within your budget after construction begins.

## MAKING A PRELIMINARY ESTIMATE

To make an initial estimate of what any house will cost you, start with a set of working drawings. Then you need to find out the range of cost per square foot and cost per cubic foot in the area where you intend to build. And you should know what percentage of their costs local builders allocate to materials, labor, overhead, and profit.

The ideal sources for cost information are contractors themselves, but they aren't likely to give out that information willingly. Your next best bets are local building materials dealers, your source of financing, or your real estate agent. For relatively straightforward vacation housing, the cost per square foot should fall in the range between about $18 and $30. As a general rule, the more remote the site, the lower the cost per square foot. Costs per cubic foot should be in a range between $1.50 and $2.25.

Information on percentages may not be available at all, and you'll have to work with averages. You can generally use a figure of about 15% for profit. Overhead will vary from as little as 1% for the one-man contractor who operates out of his home up to 5% or 6% for the larger, more urban contractor. Labor will run 35% to 45%, with the percentage highest in more populous communities. The remaining 35% to 50% is for materials.

For purposes of discussion, assume that local costs are $20 per square foot and $1.75 per cubic foot, and that percentages are roughly 40% for materials, 40% for labor, 5% for overhead, and 15% for profit.

## Calculating Cost Per Square Foot

On the first-floor plan find the overall dimensions from outside of wall to outside of wall. Square footage is always calculated from overall dimensions. Calculate the square footage of living areas, including finished second floors, at full square footage. Calculate basements, garages, and structurally supported decks at half their square footage. Ignore crawl space and unfinished attics.

The overall dimensions of the plan in Fig. 19–1 are 32′ 0″ by 24′ 0″. The deck is 7′ 3″ wide across the entire front and 4′ 4″ on half the side. The house is built on a small basement and crawl space (Fig. 19–2), and ceilings follow the roof line.

Thus the square footage for costing purposes is

| | | | |
|---|---|---|---|
| House | $32 \times 24$ | = | 768 |
| Basement | $12\,2/3 \times 13\,1/3 \times 1/2$ | = | 85 |
| Decks | $36 \times 7\,1/4 \times 1/2 + 12 \times 4\,1/3 \times 1/2$ = | | 157 |
| Total square footage | | | 1,010 |

At $20 per square foot, the cost is roughly $20,200. That is accurate enough, but it is still a rough estimate.

## Calculating Cost Per Cubic Foot

The cost per cubic foot is more accurate, but harder to work out. You again will be working with overall dimensions, but now you must also know the heights involved, since cubage is length times width times height.

Heights are shown in the main sections in working drawings (Figs. 19–3 and 19–4). The bottom measuring point for a height is the top of a basement floor if there is a basement. It is average grade at the foundation wall under any other circumstances. The top measuring point is the midpoint of the rise of the roof.

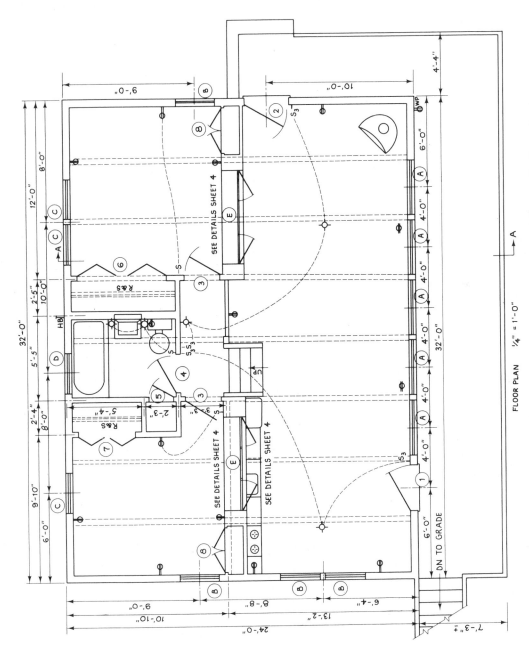

**Fig. 19-1.** This is the first-floor plan of the vacation house used frequently throughout this chapter as an example for methods of estimating various materials. The same plan also appeared in Chapter 5, in case it looks familiar.

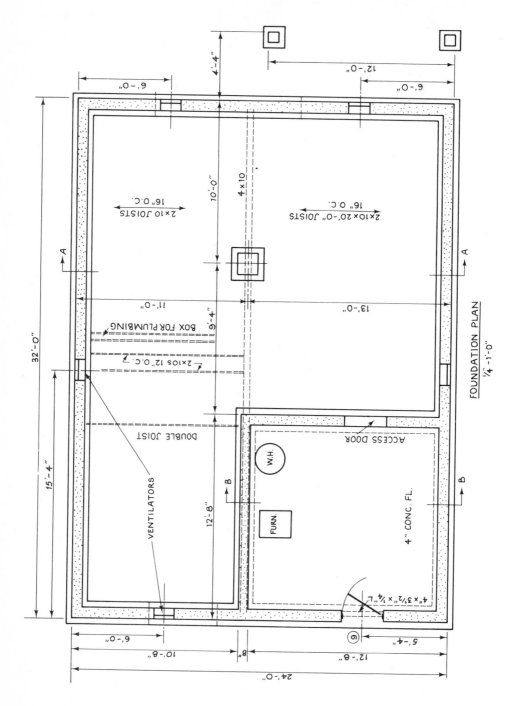

**Fig. 19-2.** Foundation plan of the vacation house used as an example.

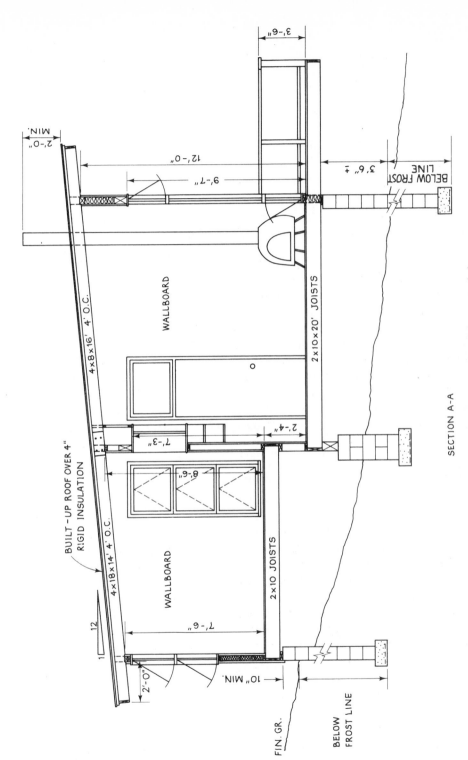

**Fig. 19-3.** Section through the crawl space of the example house.

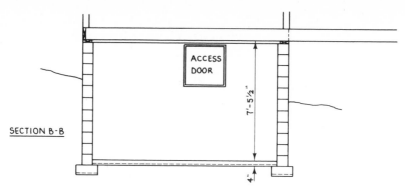

**Fig. 19-4.** Section through the basement area of the example house.

Because the house in Figs. 19-1 to 19-4 inclusive is a split level with a shed roof and built on a slope, you must calculate the two floor levels separately. At the upper or bedroom level, the length is 32′0″. The width is 10′10″ to the center line of the partition between levels, which is a good enough measuring point for preliminary cost estimating.

Four dimensions are included in the height calculation. The grade is 22″ below the floor line at the outside wall (10″ joist + 2″ sill + 10″ from top of foundation to grade). At the center wall the grade is 2′4″ lower still, or 50″ below the floor line. Therefore the average grade is half of 22″ + 50″, or 3′0″ below the floor line.

Minimum ceiling height is 7′6″, and the thickness of the roof structure is another 9″. Roof pitch is a low 1 in 12. Therefore in a run of 12′10″ (10′10″ of width + 2′0″ of overhang), the roof rises a little over 12″. The midpoint of this rise would then be 6″. Therefore, total height of the upper level of the house is

$$3′0″ + 7′6″ + 9″ + 6″ = 11′9″$$

Thus the cubic footage of the upper level is

$$32′0″ \times 10′10″ \times 11′9″ = 4{,}073 \text{ cu ft}$$

Because part of the lower level has a basement and part has a crawl space, you will have to calculate their cubages separately. Using the same process as for the upper level, you will find the cubage of the section over crawl space is its length (19′4″) times its width (13′2″) times its height. Average height of the floor level above grade is half of 22″ (at the inner wall) + 52″ (below the deck), or 3′1″. Minimum ceiling height of the lower level is 10′10″: 7′6″ + 12″ of rise + 2′4″ difference between floor levels. The midpoint of the rise is half the total rise over this section, or about 8″. Total height, then, is

$$3′1″ + 10′10″ + 9″ + 8″ = 15′4″$$

Thus the cubage of the section over crawl space is

$$19′4″ \times 13′2″ \times 15′4″ = 3{,}903 \text{ cu ft}$$

Similarly, the length of the section with basement is 12 ' 8 ", and the width is again 13 ' 2 ". The height is 8 ' 3 1/2 " (floor to floor) plus the same 10 ' 10 ", 9 ", and 8 " as in the other section—a total height of 20 ' 6 " rounded off for easier multiplication. Therefore the cubage of the section over crawl space is

$$12 ' 8 '' \times 13 ' 2 '' \times 20 ' 6 '' = 3,419 \text{ cu ft}$$

Although the deck is cantilevered, it requires more expensive materials than the rest of the house. So calculate its height at 1 ' 9 "—half the dimension from the bottom of the structure to the top of the rail. The area of the deck you know from previous calculations is 316 sq ft. Therefore the deck has a cubage of

$$1 ' 9 '' \times 316 \text{ sq ft} = 553 \text{ cu ft}$$

If you now add up the four cubages, you will find that the total for the whole house is 11,948 cu ft. At $1.75 per cubic foot, the estimate comes in at $20,909.

The costs you estimate on a square foot and cubic foot basis aren't likely to match exactly, but they should be close. Within 1% is good, within 3% is reasonable. If you get a greater disparity, go through your calculations again. Either you made an arithmetical error, or you received some inaccurate advice.

For estimating purposes always use the higher of the two figures as your cost estimate—say $21,000 in the example. This is the cost of having the house built for you. It does not include the cost of land. It includes both rough and finish grading around the foundation, but does not include other site clearing, extensive road work, nor correction of special site problems. It does not include the working costs of sinking a well, or installing a septic system, nor fees for an extension of power lines. These working costs might run another $2,000.

Of the new total of $23,000 plus land, suppose that the bids submitted by contractors for the work you want them to do come to $5,000. Of the remaining $18,000, 40%, or $7,200, is for materials. The only labor cost would be for someone you hire to help you. You pay yourself no profit. You don't pay overhead either, but you will have some overhead yourself, such as insurance during construction and losses from theft, so add in 5%, or $900, for overhead.

Adding the figures together—$5,000 for subcontracted work, $7,200 for materials, and $900 for overhead, you find that the cost of the vacation house comes in at $13,100, plus the cost of the site.

The estimates and calculations above are given solely as an illustration of the method you should follow to determine whether the vacation house project is within range of your bank account. You will certainly have other costs, and you should include them in your budget. You will probably need to buy or rent some additional tools. You will have the cost of transportation to and from the site, plus a lot of running around in the early stages of planning before construction even begins. It's better to estimate high than to estimate low and be unpleasantly surprised. Try to visualize the whole project, and you may think of some things that hadn't occurred to you before. For instance, how about budgeting for an occasional night's lodging on weekends of heavy physical labor, when a good bed and a hot shower can add 50% to your efficiency the next day?

# PREPARING TO ESTIMATE MATERIAL USAGE

The materials list that comes with purchased working drawings is an excellent starting point for estimating the quantities of the various materials you need. But it is only a starting point. You are asking for trouble if you accept the quantities listed as gospel. For one thing they are not and cannot be complete. They include basic structural materials, but not such equally important items as fasteners, paint, hardware, flashing, and finishing materials that are a matter of personal preference.

For another thing they may be inaccurate, in spite of careful work by estimators. Most materials lists carry a disclaimer that says that the source of plans cannot be held responsible for any errors. Take this disclaimer as fair warning, and make your own materials takeoff. If your estimate and the materials list agree on an item, you can feel safe. If there is a small difference, use whichever figure is higher. You will rarely add in things that aren't there, but it is easy to overlook something. If there is a big difference, go through your calculations again looking for errors. Then, again, use the higher figure.

## Making a Dimension Sheet

When you estimate materials, you will be using the same dimensions over and over again. There are too many to remember, however, and you can save a lot of time by committing key dimensions, perimeters, areas, and volumes to paper. Make up your own dimension sheet, using Fig. 19–5 as a guide. An 8 1/2-by-11 sheet of paper is big enough. If you must, use both sides. Adapt the dimension sheet to your particular house.

For example, under Overall Dimensions in Fig. 19–5 are lines for two heights—footing to ridge and grade to eave. With the house shown in Figs. 19–1 to 19–4 you need at least five heights: grade to eave at front, grade to eave at rear, footing to plate at front, footing to plate at rear, and footing to plate at center. By the time you finish reading this chapter, you should have a fair idea of what changes to make in the dimension sheet.

All the information you need for developing and filling in a dimension sheet appears in the working drawings.

## Units of Measure

In estimating, you should establish certain basic measurements first. They are linear feet for perimeters, square feet for areas, and cubic feet for volumes. From these stem the units of measure by which you order materials, and there are many. You are likely to order materials by each, sheets, sacks, rolls, bags, squares, board feet, gallons, and boxes. To determine the quantities per standard unit of measure, you convert basic measurements.

**Fig. 19-5.** A typical dimension sheet. You should devise your own to fit the house you plan to build.

```
┌─────────────────────────────────────────────────────────────────┐
│                      DIMENSION SHEET                              │
│                                                                   │
│ House_____    Date_____         │
├─────────────────────────────────────────────────────────────────┤
│       LINEAR FEET                          OVERALL DIMENSIONS     │
│                                                                   │
│ Main house:      L_____ W _____    Length          _____     │
│ Garage (att.):   L_____ W _____    Width           _____     │
│ Garage (det.):   L_____ W _____    Ht. (ftg. to ridge)  _____    │
│ Porch or patio:  L_____ W _____    Ht. (grade to eave)  _____    │
│ Breezeway:       L_____ W _____                                   │
│                                                                   │
│ Ceiling heights:  Basement _____ 1st Fl._____ 2nd Fl._____  │
│ Roof:  type_____ pitch _____ spans _____             │
│        type_____ pitch _____ spans _____             │
├─────────────────────────────────────────────────────────────────┤
│                       PERIMETERS                                  │
│                                                                   │
│ Foundation wall _____ No. piers _____      │
│ Exterior wall:  house _____ garage _____ porches_____ │
│ Roof:           house _____ garage _____ porches_____ │
├─────────────────────────────────────────────────────────────────┤
│                         AREAS                                     │
│                                                                   │
│                                                   Interior Walls  │
│        Floor   Fin. Clg.   Roof   Ext. Wall    Room  Area   Trim  │
│ Basement  ___    ___      ___     ___          ___   ___   ___    │
│ 1st fl.   ___    ___      ___     ___          ___   ___   ___    │
│ 2nd fl.   ___    ___      ___     ___          ___   ___   ___    │
│ Garage    ___    ___      ___     ___          ___   ___   ___    │
│ Porch     ___    ___      ___     ___          ___   ___   ___    │
│ Deck      ___    ___      ___     ___          ___   ___   ___    │
│           ___    ___      ___     ___          ___   ___   ___    │
│                           ___     ___          ___   ___   ___    │
│                                                ___   ___   ___    │
│ Area Totals                                    ___   ___   ___    │
│                                                ___   ___   ___    │
│ Floor:  concrete _____ wood _____ resil.____ ___   ___   ___    │
│         ceramic_____        _____            ___   ___   ___    │
│ Ceiling:  drywall_____ plywood_____ tile____                   │
│ Roof:     pitched_____ flat_____                               │
│                                                                   │
│ Ext. walls:  horiz. siding _____ vert. siding_____ plywood_____   │
│              shingles (         )_____ brick _____ stone _____     │
│ Int. walls:  drywall _____ plywood_____ hardboard_____         │
│              brick _____ stone _____ ceramic _____            │
├─────────────────────────────────────────────────────────────────┤
│                        VOLUMES                                    │
│                                                                   │
│ Main house_____ cu. ft.  Garage _____ cu. ft.  Deck _____cu. ft │
│ Basement_____ cu. ft.  Other _____cu. ft.         │
├─────────────────────────────────────────────────────────────────┤
│                         UNITS                                     │
│                                                                   │
│ Posts: length_____ size_____ Beams: length_____ size_____  │
│ Vents: foundation_____ soffit_____ gable_____ roof_____│
│ Shutters_____ Fireplaces _____ Mantels _____          │
│ Windows, wood _____ Screens _____ Storms _____              │
│ Windows, metal _____ Screens _____ Storms _____             │
│ Doors, exterior_____Screens _____ Storms _____          │
│ Doors, interior_____ Cased opgs. _____ Drawers _____       │
└─────────────────────────────────────────────────────────────────┘
```

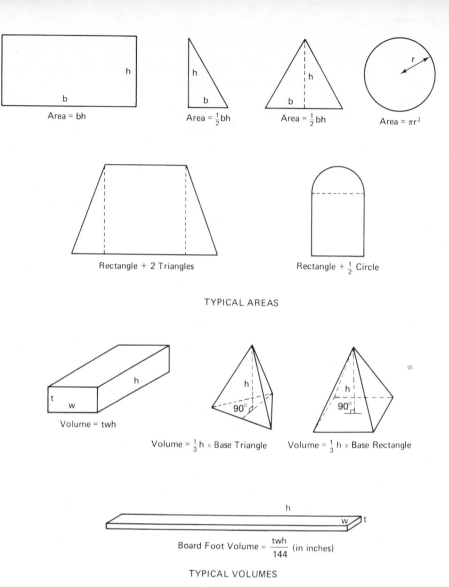

Area = bh

Area = $\frac{1}{2}$bh

Area = $\frac{1}{2}$bh

Area = $\pi r^2$

Rectangle + 2 Triangles

Rectangle + $\frac{1}{2}$ Circle

TYPICAL AREAS

Volume = twh

Volume = $\frac{1}{3}$ h × Base Triangle

Volume = $\frac{1}{3}$ h × Base Rectangle

Board Foot Volume = $\dfrac{twh}{144}$ (in inches)

TYPICAL VOLUMES

**Fig. 19-6.** Here are the basic formulae for calculating typical areas (top) and volumes (bottom).

Take some typical examples. You merely count to find the quantity of some units, such as 6′ 8″ by 2′ 6″ doors. You add the lengths of lines to find total linear feet, as for the amount of base molding required.

To find square footage, multiply two dimensions. Most areas, such as walls, are rectangular, and the area of a rectangle is its base (the longest dimension) times its height (the shortest dimension). The area of a triangle is 1/2 its base times its height, with the height being the length of a line between the base and the opposite point of the triangle, drawn perpendicular to the base. The area of a circle is pi ( $\pi = 3.14$) times the radius times the radius again. Figure 19-6 shows the formulae for calculating typical areas. You can divide almost any area, however odd its shape, into rectangles, triangles, and parts of a circle.

Finding volumes involves three dimensions. The only materials commonly measured in volumes in residential building are concrete, sand, gravel, and excavated earth, which are calculated by the cubic yard. A cubic yard is 27 cubic feet. Formulae for typical volumes are also shown in Fig. 19-6.

*Board feet* is a special designation for volume that applies only to lumber. Actually, a board foot is 1″ by 12″ by 12″. But 1 board foot amounts to 144 cubic inches of lumber regardless of the nominal dimensions of a particular stick of lumber. And you use nominal dimensions in figuring board feet, not actual dimensions.

To calculate the board footage of any piece of lumber, multiply the nominal thickness by the nominal width by the actual length *in inches,* and then divide by 144. For example, a 2 × 4 stud 8′ long contains $\dfrac{2 \times 4 \times 96}{144}$ or 5.33 *b.f.,*

the usual abbreviation for board feet. Tables I and II at the end of this chapter will help you with board footage.

## ESTIMATING FOUNDATIONS

When you calculate materials, it is better to estimate your requirements for each stage of construction, rather than by type of material or individual item. It's all too easy to miss an item unless you think through each stage step by step. The list of materials in Fig. 19-7 is a guide to what you are likely to need during the foundation stage.

**Fig. 19-7.** You are less likely to overlook a material if you make materials lists for each stage of construction. These are the materials that might be needed for the foundation.

MATERIALS REQUIRED FOR THE FOUNDATION

stakes
form boards
form oil
gravel (for concrete base)
sand
cement
reinforcing rods
polyethylene (for moisture barrier)
wire mesh (for slab reinforcement)
drain tiles
concrete blocks
mortar
ready-mix concrete
expansion strips
foundation vents
basement windows
basement doors
bricks (for chimney)
cleanout door and parts
flue tiles
steel angles
steel beams
sill mastic
sill bolts
exterior waterproofing
termite shield

## Forms

In the cost of footings you must include the cost of the concrete itself, plus the cost of forms and reinforcement. Refer to your dimension sheet to find the overall dimensions. Add 8″ to each dimension, because the footings extend beyond the overall dimensions. Round off each length to the next greater half foot to arrive at the perimeter of exterior forms. The perimeter of interior forms is 32″ less on each side.

With a 32′ by 24′ house on a level site, then, you have 116 linear feet of outside form and 104 linear feet of inside form. If you use 2 × 8s for forms, each linear foot contains 1.33 b.f. Therefore you need 220 times 1.33, or 294 b.f. of forms for footings. Add 5% for waste. Even though you may reuse the forms elsewhere, don't count on it in estimating. You can always return unused material in good condition.

Stakes are usually 1 × 4s, 17 1/2″ long so that they can be used for spacing forms. Each stake contains 1/2 b.f., and stakes are spaced about 4′ on centers. Divide the spacing into the perimeter (200 ÷ 4), and you get 55. Add 2 stakes— you need an extra stake at the last spacing of both forms—and you find that you need 28.5, or 29, b.f. of 1 × 4. As with form boards, consider stakes used up in the forming process.

## Footings

The concrete mix recommended for footings is 1: 2¾ :4 (see Chapter 6). Using this formula you need 0.17 sacks of cement, 0.52 cu ft of sand, and 0.72 cu ft of aggregate for every cubic foot of concrete. To find the total amount of concrete you need, multiply the dimensions of the footing in section by the perimeter of the house. But be careful. Some of these dimensions are in inches, some are in feet, and you want the result in cubic feet (if you mix your own) or cubic yards (if you buy ready-mix).

It's best to work with feet. Use 0.67′ and 1.33′ as the dimensions of the footing instead of 8″ and 16″. Then multiply by the perimeter of the house (112′ from the dimension sheet). This gives you an answer in cubic feet—0.67 × 1.33 × 112 = 100. Divide this answer by 27 to arrive at 3.7 cu yd of concrete.

If you order ready-mix concrete, this is the extent of your calculations. The plant operator will make a standard allowance for adjusting the individual quantities of ingredients. If you mix your own, however, you then apply the formula figures above. To mix 100 cu ft of concrete you'll need 17 sacks of cement, 52 cu ft of sand, and 72 cu ft of aggregate. Because sand and aggregate are sold by the cubic yard, you should order 2 and 3 cu yd, respectively.

These estimates are for perimeter footings only. If you have any footings under partitions, you must remember to add in their requirements, too.

### Reinforcement

Reinforcement comes by the pound. The standard reinforcement for footings is #4 bars, which weigh 2/3 of a pound per foot of length. Footings under foundation walls have three continuous bars, so the total reinforcement needed, in feet, is three times the perimeter of the house. Add in reinforcement under walls which are not counted in the perimeter. Footings under piers take about 9' of bar each—three 18" lengths in each direction that form a grid.

### Concrete Blocks

Determining the number of concrete blocks for a foundation wall is relatively easy. First find the height of the wall in the plans. From the dimensions sheet you know the perimeter of the wall. As there are three blocks in every 4' of perimeter, you multiply the perimeter by 3/4 and subtract 2 to find the number of blocks in each course. The reason for subtracting 2 is that you have a duplicate half-block at each corner.

If the height of the wall in inches is divisible by 8, such as 48", you need one course of 8" cap blocks and five courses of stretcher blocks. If the height is divisible by 4 but not by 8, such as 52", you should use 4" cap blocks and six courses of stretchers. Walls of any other heights should be lengthened to accommodate full-height courses plus a cap course.

From the total of stretcher blocks you must subtract a corner block at each corner in each course. Thus a foundation wall 52" high for a 32' by 24' house requires 82 cap blocks, 24 corner blocks, and 468 stretcher blocks.

### Mortar

Allow 4.25 cu ft of mortar for every 100 sq ft of block wall area or for every 110 blocks. In the foundation wall above, with its 574 blocks, you would need about 22 cu ft of mortar, of which 1/4 of the volume is cement. A sack of cement contains one cubic foot, so you would need 5 1/2 sacks of cement and 16 1/2 cu ft or 0.6 cu yds of sand.

## ESTIMATING FRAMING MATERIALS

With the materials for the foundation estimated, begin work next on framing materials. Let Fig. 19–8 guide you in estimating these requirements.

The lengths of individual studs, joists, and rafters that you will need for your house are fixed by the drawings. Some of the other items of lumber, such as sills, headers, sole plates, top plates, and doublers, are not. And by careful estimating you can often save some money.

**Fig. 19-8.** These are the materials you might need during the framing stage. Note that chimney materials are all included here, because chimney work, except for its footing, usually begins after the foundation is finished.

MATERIALS REQUIRED FOR FRAMING

wood posts
steel columns
steel girders
bolts
beams
ledgers
joists
joist hangers
headers (for floor openings)
bridging
subflooring
bottom plates
studs
headers (in wall openings)
window sills
cripples
top plates
diagonal bracing
firestops
blocking
rafter plates
rafters
ridgeboards
lookouts
headers (at roof openings)

collar beams
roof sheathing
wall sheathing
spikes
common nails
staples
ash dump
firebricks
firebrick mortar
damper

As an example, in the house in Fig. 19–1 you would need 32 ' of 2 × 6 sill for each of the two long walls. On the sides at the upper level the plates are 10 ' 6 " long. Why? The 10 ' 10 " dimension on the plan runs from the outside edge to the center line of the partition. You have to add 2 " at the center because the sills continue under the partition, but you must subtract 6 " at the outside wall because the sills don't overlap at the corner. Similarly, the sills at the lower level are 13 ' 0 " long; they also extend 4 " beyond the center line of the partition.

Lumber comes in even-foot lengths. So for side sills you are stuck with two 12 ' lengths and two 14 ' lengths, with some waste. These sill pieces must be costed at the length purchased, not the length used. For the longer walls a pair of 16 ' lengths fit nicely. But you could also use two 12 ' lengths and a half a 16-footer in each wall for sills.

Before you decide which to order, check your dealer's stock and current prices. Prices often vary from week to week. Sometimes a dealer is overstocked on a particular length, and he has it on sale at a bargain price. Costs for lumber are not constant per board foot, either. Four 16 ' lengths of 2 × 6 may cost the same, more, or less than one 16 ' length and four 12 ' lengths. It pays to shop before you order, and to know exactly what you can use so that you can adapt your purchases to the best buys of the same quality.

If you are framing on posts on an uneven site, determine the length of each post. Then count the piers to make sure you have counted all the posts. Add the total post requirements, and then see what lengths are available from which you can cut with minimum waste. Don't forget to allow 1/4 " for the thickness of each saw cut, however.

## Joists and Rafters

Framing plans usually give the size and spacing of joists and rafters, but seldom their lengths. The best way to make a materials takeoff of horizontal framing members is to determine the lengths of repetitive members and count them. Then work on the odd-length members individually as you would with posts.

The method for determining the length of a common rafter is covered in Chapter 10. You should work from plan dimensions to find joist lengths. Joists must bear at least 4″ on sills or girders or plates at each end. But they don't extend to the edge of the foundation, remember. They end 2 1/4″ away—the thickness of a header joist set back 3/4″ from the edge of the foundation.

In Fig. 19-2 the length of lower joists is specified because the exact width of the deck isn't important, and the length of the joist is. The length of upper joists is 10′ 10″ less 2 1/4″ at the outer foundation, plus 1/4″ at the partition (half the width of a stud less 1 1/2″ for the header there). The length needed, then, is 10′ 8″. Therefore your best bet is to order 12′ lengths, and use the cutoffs between the joists where they pass under the front wall. Each joist contains 16 board feet of lumber.

When you count joists in an uninterrupted floor at 16″ o.c., remember there are three joists in every 4′, plus one at the end of the floor. At the lower level of the house in Fig. 19-1, then, you need 25 2 × 10 joists 20′ long. Joist spacing is uniform throughout, since nothing goes through the floor anywhere.

When you count joists, always check out the exact location of the soil stack and the drain for the water closet. At the upper level in Fig. 19-1, for example, normal joist locations are 12′ 0″, 13′ 4″, 14′ 8″, and 16′ 0″ from the right hand wall. The center line of the soil stack is 14′ 5″, and the center line of the drain is usually 12″ from the *finished* surface of the wall behind it, or 15′ 8 1/4″. Ask your plumbing contractor how much space he needs on each side of these center lines. He will probably want at least 3″ of clearance so that he has some working room. If so, the joists at 14′ 8″ and 16′ 0″ are in the way of the stack. So you must add a joist and adjust the spacings as shown in Fig. 19-2.

## Studs

Counting studs is a little more difficult than counting joists. Work around the perimeter of the house first, and remember to count two full-length studs at each side of doors and windows. Next count the studs in partitions running the long dimension of the house, and then the studs in shorter cross partitions. To help you keep track, mark up one set of working drawings for your materials takeoff. Devise a color system to keep track of what you've counted and what you have yet to count—say green for horizontal structural members, red for vertical structural members, blue for short verticals, and yellow for trim.

When studs vary in length, as they do in the example house, list each length in the same way suggested for posts, and see what combinations you can make to save on lumber. Here the studs in the rear wall are 7′ 1 1/2″ long, and in the front wall they are 11 ' 7 1/2 ". In the center partition stud length is 8 ' 5 3/4 " by calculation. The common difference—the difference in length between adjoining studs in side walls—is about 1 1/2 ".

Therefore you could order 16 ' stud lengths for the side walls of the upper level and cut two studs from each length, like jack rafters. All side studs at the lower level are more than 10 ' long and less than 12 ', so you could cut all those studs from 12 ' lengths.

### Headers

To estimate the quantities of header lumber, make a list of door and window openings from the window and door schedules. Add 3 " to each rough opening width to find the exact length of header needed. Since headers are double members, multiply this length by two.

The listing below gives you the minimum total length of header material. Now study the list to determine how to save money by cutting with minimum waste. As an example, suppose that all window openings are 2 ' 6 ". Headers, then, are 2 ' 9 ". Allow 1/4 " for saw cuts. Assuming that you can buy header material in various lengths, look at the variation in waste:

| From | You Get | You Use | You Waste |
|------|---------|---------|-----------|
| 8 ' lengths | 2 pieces | 5 ' 6 1/4 " | 31.2% |
| 10 ' lengths | 3 pieces | 8 ' 3 1/2 " | 17.0% |
| 12 ' lengths | 4 pieces | 11 ' 3/4 " | 7.8% |
| 14 ' lengths | 5 pieces | 13 ' 10 " | 1.2% |
| 16 ' lengths | 5 pieces | 13 ' 10 " | 13.5% |

Obviously you can get the maximum usage out of 14 ' lengths. Use this same approach to calculate your needs for any material when lengths are variable.

### Miscellaneous Wood Parts

You aren't likely to make a mistake in figuring the lengths of plates or the quantities of joists or rafters. It's the accumulation of small pieces that is difficult to estimate and order correctly. You don't want to order more than you need just to be safe; that is expensive. On the other hand you don't want to run short of materials, particularly if your building supply dealer is an hour's round trip away from your site.

The best way to avoid a problem is to make up estimating sheets. You will need one for foundation materials, and probably two or three for lumber. Make one for windows and doors and their hardware, another for exterior finishing materials, and another for interior finishing materials. You will probably want a separate sheet for cabinets and shelves, and another for miscellaneous items—fasteners, sealants, and their like. In Figs. 19–6 to 19–9 inclusive are the types of items you will put on your lists. Use the lists as a means of checkoff when you estimate materials usage.

**Fig. 19-9.** These are typical materials that may be needed to finish the roof and exterior walls, fill openings, and seal the house against weather.

MATERIALS REQUIRED FOR ENCLOSING THE HOUSE

roofing paper (felt)
metal edging
roll roofing
roof shingles
roofing nails
roofing cement
siding
wood shingles
bricks
mortar
flashing
window frames
door frames (exterior)
wedges
thresholds
caulking
ceiling insulation
wall insulation
finishing nails
staples

Try to group materials on each sheet by supplier, and as far as possible list them in the order in which you expect to use them. Reserve the left-hand half of each sheet for a description of the material required. Divide the right-hand side into six to eight columns for keeping track of where the material goes, the total needed, and cost data.

The headings on these columns may vary somewhat from sheet to sheet. On lumber sheets, for instance, possible headings are floor, walls, roof, deck, total units, cost per unit, and total cost. Suppose the material for which you are making a takeoff is 2 × 4 and 2 × 6 lumber. You could have a dozen entries under each category.

Your sheets might look something like this:

| Item | F | W | R | D | Total Units | Cost/ Unit | Total Cost |
|---|---|---|---|---|---|---|---|
| 2 × 6 sills, 2 @ 14' | x | | | | 28 bf | .53 | $14.84 |
| 2 × 6 sills, 2 @ 12' | x | | | | 24 bf | .54 | 12.96 |
| 2 × 6 sills, 96 l.f. | x | | | | 96 bf | .35 | 33.60 |
| 2 × 6 bottom plate, 40 l.f. | | x | | | 40 bf | .35 | 14.00 |
| 2 × 6 top plate, 40 l.f. | | x | | | 40 bf | .35 | 14.00 |
| 2 × 6 doubler, 40 l.f. | | x | | | 40 bf | .35 | 14.00 |
| 2 × 6 studs, 6 @ 8' | | x | | | 48 bf | .35 | 16.80 |
| 2 × 6 cripples, 25 @ 1 1/3' | | x | | | 34 bf | .35 | 11.90 |
| 2 × 6 headers, 4 l.f. | | x | | | 4 bf | .35 | 1.40 |
| 2 × 6 splice plates, 4 l.f. | x | | | | 4 bf | .35 | 1.40 |
| 2 × 6 blocking, 8 l.f. | | x | | | 8 bf | .35 | 2.80 |
| 2 × 6 railing, redwood, 56 l.f. | | | | x | 56 bf | .72 | 40.32 |

By adding up the last column, you have the cost of the 2 × 6 lumber of all kinds that you need. You can estimate usage and costs for 2 × 4 lumber the same way:

| Item | F | W | R | D | Total Units | Cost/ Unit | Total Cost |
|------|---|---|---|---|-------------|-----------|-----------|
| 2 × 4 sole plates, 2 @ 14 ' | | x | | | 19 bf | .36 | $ 6.84 |
| 2 × 4 sole plates, 2 @ 12 ' | | x | | | 16 bf | .35 | 5.60 |
| 2 × 4 sole plates, 64 l.f. | | x | | | 43 bf | .33 | 14.19 |
| 2 × 4 sole plates, partitions, 58 l.f. | | x | | | 39 bf | .33 | 12.87 |
| 2 × 4 top plates, 198 l.f. | | x | | | 132 bf | .33 | 43.56 |
| 2 × 4 doubler, 198 l.f. | | x | | | 132 bf | .33 | 43.56 |
| 2 × 4 splice plates, 3 l.f. | | x | | | 2 bf | .25 | .50 |
| 2 × 4 blocking, 30 l.f. | | x | | | 20 bf | .25 | 5.00 |
| 2 × 4 cripples, 36 l.f. | | x | | | 24 bf | .25 | 6.00 |
| 2 × 4 headers, 43 l.f. | | x | | | 29 bf | .25 | 7.25 |
| 2 × 4 window sills, 76 l.f. | | x | | | 51 bf | .25 | 12.75 |
| 2 × 4 interior railing, #1 clear, 8 l.f. | | x | | | 6 bf | .66 | 3.96 |
| 2 × 4 deck and steps, redwood, 948 l.f. | | | | x | 632 bf | .70 | 442.40 |
| 2 × 4 lower railing, redwood, 56 l.f. | | | | x | 38 bf | .70 | 26.60 |

Another way of listing is to enter first all items that have a specific length, and then add the items of variable length. You can sometimes save money by buying lumber in random lengths as long as most of the individual lengths you need are less than 8 ' long. On the other hand sills, top plates, doublers, and railings should be in the longest lengths available for maximum strength.

## ESTIMATING SHEET MATERIALS

When you estimate quantities of plywood for subflooring, solid sheathing, and wallboard, assume that you will be covering all openings that aren't at least 4 ' wide. Certainly in estimating sheathing for the front wall of the house in Fig. 19–1, you would calculate full-length sheets 4 ' wide at the corners of the house and shorter 4 ' widths above the window wall. On the rear wall, however, the joint between 4 ' pieces falls directly below the pair of bedroom windows. It is possible to piece here, and you would save about 2/3 of a sheet by doing so. But unless you have a specific place to use the offal, you are better off estimating and ordering full sheets, and accepting a little waste.

On the subject of waste, you have already included it in such items as joists, rafters, subflooring, and sheathing. On items where the total quantity is made up of a number of pieces, such as cripples, you must add in waste. Add about 10% for scrap on lumber items, 15% on interior trim, and 5% on fasteners of all kinds.

### Roof Sheathing

When you calculate roof areas, use the information that you have already developed on your dimension sheet, and refer to Table III at the end of this chapter. The area of a shed or a flat roof is the total rafter length times the roof length. The area of a gable roof is the length of a common rafter times the length of the ridge times 2. The area of a hip roof is the rafter length times the overall length including overhangs times 2. The overall length of a hip roof is the length of the ridge plus twice the length of a common rafter.

If your roof has several hips and valleys, the best way to estimate solid sheathing, roofing paper, and roofing itself is to make a drawing to scale of each area of the roof, as if it were flat. Most cuts in sheathing will be at a 45° angle, and you can fit the offall from one course along the valley or hip of the next course above.

To estimate the board footage of board sheathing under wood shingles, begin by finding the area of each section of roof. Then let's say that you are spacing the sheathing boards at the relatively common 9″ on centers. If you use 1 × 4 boards, multiply the roof area times 1/2 and add 5% for waste. If you use 1 × 6 boards, multiply the roof area by 2/3 and add 5%. Your answers will be in square feet of coverage. To convert the square footage to board feet, divide your answer by 3 if you use 1 × 4 boards. Divide by 2 if you use 1 × 6 boards.

## ESTIMATING EXTERIOR MATERIALS

Making an accurate takeoff of material requirements for enclosing a house after it is framed and sheathed is more difficult than any previous estimating. The main difference is that most exterior materials have an overlap, and you must calculate the overlap carefully or your estimate will be woefully short of your actual requirements.

### Roofing

The area covered by roofing paper is the same as that for sheathing. But that's only a starting point. Each layer of roofing paper overlaps the layer below it. The overlap adds anywhere from 14% to 50% to the total amount of paper to be used, depending on the pitch of your roof. You'll find details under the section on sheathing in Chapter 10. In addition you must allow one extra square foot for every linear foot of eave and rake, and three square feet for every linear foot of ridge, hip, and valley.

Allow 10% waste for roofing paper and asphalt shingles. You order asphalt shingles by the square, which is 100 sq ft of coverage. You order wood shingles by the bundle, and a bundle covers about 25 sq ft of roof area. Allow 5% for waste, and estimate one extra bundle for every 25 linear feet of hip and ridge.

### Sheet Metal

One of the most difficult of all material to estimate accurately is flashing, because you use it in so many places in small pieces. Order it by the square foot, and cut each piece to size.

For flashing in valleys or where the roof meets a wall or chimney, allow 1 1/2 sq ft for every foot of valley or meeting point. For flashing around windows and exterior doors, allow 1/3 sq ft for every foot of jamb, and 1 sq ft for every foot of head or sill. If you install a termite shield between the foundation wall and sill, multiply the perimeter of the wall by 1 1/3 sq ft to calculate the total square footage you need. If any of your sheet metal requires jointing, don't forget to include flux and solder in your estimate and order.

### Wall Materials

To estimate the quantities of any exterior wall material, work from the areas in your dimension sheet. If you use sheet materials such as plywood, the chances are that each sheet will contain, not the 32 sq ft you have been working with for other plywood usage, but 36 or 40 sq ft, depending on length. Do not subtract for openings less than 4' wide, and don't plan to piece at openings unless the joints will be covered by battens.

In estimating siding or shingles, you do subtract for openings. Determine the square footage of wall to be covered, then increase the amount by the percentage of overlap. Say you are applying 8" siding with a 6 1/2" exposure. Only 84% of the siding will actually be exposed, so you must increase the quantity of siding you order by 16%. Then add another 5% for waste in cutting. Remember to include in the estimate the building paper behind the siding, and also the boards you will need at corners and at the water table. Follow these same procedures for wood shingles on walls, but you don't need to allow for waste.

To estimate brick usage, you must know the size of the bricks you intend to use and the thickness of mortar joints. If you lay standard bricks with a 3/8" mortar joint, allow 6 1/2 bricks for every square foot of veneer wall. The standard unit for a brick order is 1,000, but you can sometimes order in hundreds. Allow 12 1/2 cu ft of mortar for every thousand bricks laid up with a 3/8" mortar joint.

### Insulation

Blanket insulation comes packaged in rolls. The total length per roll depends on the R factor of the insulation, but 32′ and 56′ are standard. One roll of insulation 16″ wide will fill 75 sq ft between framing members, while a roll of 24″ insulation will fill 90 sq ft. To estimate the number of rolls you will need of each thickness and width, work from the areas in your dimension sheet.

### Fasteners

The number of fasteners you will use on your vacation house project depends partly on the size and quality of the lumber you build with, and partly on your talent with a hammer. You order by the pound; poundage is estimated on the basis of board feet or square feet of usage. At best the answer is a guess, but Table IV at the end of this chapter gives typical usages for a handy amateur.

## ESTIMATING YOUR TIME

Before continuing with estimates of interior materials, let's take a look at the time involved between the day you start to form for footings and the day your vacation house is completely enclosed and watertight. The working times that follow are based on the man-hours normally required by experienced workmen, adjusted upward for the amateur. They assume that you have normal manual dexterity with tools, good reasoning powers, the ability to organize the job at hand, and some experience in building things. Sound like you? If not, time yourself on the first few aspects of the work, check the times against the estimates that follow, and adjust future estimates accordingly.

### Forming For Footings

Unless you specify otherwise in your agreement with your excavating contractor, he will leave the excavation as square and level as he can get it with his equipment, and you must do the rest by hand. This work includes leveling the earth beneath footings, cleaning corners, and possibly cutting some banks, especially at corners. If you selected a good man and the weather hasn't disturbed his work, allow four man-hours for cleanup. If the site is not in good shape, you could have a couple of days of work here.

By having someone help you place forms, you can cut man-hours a good 25%. A two-man team can form a little more than one footing the first day and the other three footings the second day. This pace allows for a slow but accurate start, with much checking and rechecking, and an accelerated pace as the process becomes more routine. Allow at least one extra day if you need stepped footings. Figure that a row of piers takes the same time as one straight wall.

## Placing Footings

If you can arrange to order ready-mix concrete in small quantities as needed for footings, have a three-man crew on hand when the truck arrives. You won't be able to keep up with the pour with fewer people. You will have a couple of hours of frantic effort that gradually tapers off. In four hours the footings should be poured, reinforced, leveled, and protected, and your tools cleaned. Allow eight hours if you mix your own concrete. After the concrete has set, allow two man-hours for removing the forms and cleaning them for reuse.

## Building Foundation Walls

One man, working alone and mixing his own mortar, can lay about 75 concrete blocks the first day, and expect to increase the pace about 10% per day. His maximum pace will level off at about 100 blocks a day.

If you have another person to mix the mortar and keep you supplied, you can increase the numbers to 85 and 120. Laying 100 blocks a day is a good average for continuous work. When you work only on weekends, it is an excellent average.

## Framing a Floor

About the only way you can estimate the time needed to build wood structural systems is on a basis of man-hours per board foot of lumber. Allow one man-hour for each of these floor framing jobs:

> Setting posts—4 posts per hour
> Attaching sills—40 b.f.
> Setting header joists and edge joists—40 b.f.
> Building a girder—50 b.f.
> Positioning a girder—30 b.f. (two-man team)
> Setting floor joists—25 b.f. (working alone)
> Setting floor joists—60 b.f. (two-man team)
> Laying subflooring—100 sq ft
> Installing bridging—4 sets

## Framing Walls and Partitions

The various phases of wall construction, including cutting parts to length and nailing them into the wall or partition assembly, moves at a rate of about 30 board feet per man-hour. Therefore one man can build a straight, unbroken exterior wall one story high at a rate of about 6 linear feet per hour. Add an hour for every door opening, and 1 1/4 hours for each window opening. Partitions go a little faster because you work with shorter pieces.

These time estimates may seem slow to you, and they are. But they allow for the time lost in finding a piece of the right length to cut with minimum waste;

for locating the saw or hammer that you didn't leave in the usual place; for getting another pocketful of nails, for checking prints, for getting a drink, and all the myriad little things that add to actual working time.

## Framing a Roof

Roof construction goes more slowly than that of any other structural wood system, partly because the individual members are usually long and heavy, but also because you are no longer working from the safety of the ground or subfloor. Assuming that you can muster the help of two people until the roof structure is stable, and retain one helper thereafter, allow one man-hour for each of these tasks:

> Setting and attaching doublers—40 b.f.
> Setting ceiling joists—50 b.f. (two-man team)
> Cutting common rafters from the sample rafter—6
> Positioning the ridgeboard—25 b.f.
> Positioning common rafters—1 1/2 pairs
> Cutting and fitting hip, valley, and jack rafters—20 b.f.
> Installing collar beams—50 b.f.
> Installing roof sheathing—75 sq ft
> Installing roofing paper—100 sq ft
> Laying asphalt shingles—50 sq ft
> Laying wood shingles—30 sq ft
> Installing metal roofing—20 sq ft
> Fitting flashing—15 sq ft
> Installing ceiling insulation—55 sq ft

## Finishing Exterior Walls

Closing openings and applying finish exterior wall materials goes a little more quickly than work on the roof. The following jobs take about one man-hour each, and one man can do most of them alone:

> Installing sheathing—85 sq ft
> Attaching building paper—110 sq ft
> Fitting flashing—15 sq ft
> Installing a window in its frame (two-man job)
> Installing a door in its frame (two-man job)
> Attaching siding—40 sq ft
> Attaching shingles (any kind)—30 sq ft
> Laying bricks—10 sq ft
> Installing wall insulation—60 sq ft

The preceding estimates are to be used as guides only, so that you can begin to develop some sort of time schedule for the work you plan to do. They should serve their primary purpose well: to help you establish the dates on which you will need your subcontractors available to tie their work into yours. Once you have the house under roof and protected from the weather, the pace of work inside isn't as important.

## ESTIMATING INTERIOR MATERIALS

On your dimension sheet you have already worked out the areas of ceilings, walls, and floors. Estimating the materials for interior surfaces is primarily a matter of converting these areas to the size of materials you need for finishing. You then add in the materials for attachment.

### Plywood Panels

Order lengths of panels for ceilings that will give you the least waste. In a room 9 1/2 ' wide, use 10 '-long panels and cut them down, rather than 8 ' panels and short pieces at the edges. Aim at having the fewest possible feet of seam. Estimate any panel of less than half a full length as half a panel, and any cut panel of more than half a length as a full panel.

Order panels for walls long enough to cover from floor to ceiling. Assume in your estimating that all openings except sliding glass doors and banks of windows do not exist, and will be covered. Consider no panel as less than a full panel unless you know in advance where the offal will fit.

For example, a room 10 ' 6 " wide will require six panels to cover the two end walls. A room 10 ' 0 " wide, however, can be covered with only five panels, provided that studs are located in the right places for the split panel. All plywood panels for wall application can be ripped easily into 1/3, 1/2, and 2/3 widths. Grooved boards usually have grooves at these three points.

For attachment of plywood to either ceiling or walls, estimate fasteners at 2 nails per sq ft of area covered.

### Wallboard

With wallboard, as with plywood, order the longest lengths that will do the job or that you can handle. If you build your house with roof trusses, estimating is easy, because you can cover the entire ceiling without interruption or cutting at partitions. In other houses the 12 ' length is the most common for use on both ceilings and walls. Remember, however, that unless walls are more than 8 ' 1 1/2 " high, lay wallboard horizontally across studs, not vertically.

Wallboard comes in packages of two sheets, edge-wrapped and shipped with the finished surfaces face to face; therefore the minimum order of any length is two sheets. A 5% allowance for scrap is enough if you handle the panels carefully.

If you attach wallboard with annular ring nails, allow 1 lb for every 190 sq ft of wallboard. If you use screws, allow one screw for every square foot of board.

One gallon of ready-mix joint compound will finish about 200 sq ft of surface. A 60′ roll of tape is needed for every 180 sq ft of surface. A 250′ roll will suffice for 750 sq ft of wallboard.

### Ceiling Tiles

Work from the ceiling layout you made to calculate the board footage of furring strips. Count the strips, subtract one (you can rip the two end furring strips from a single 1 × 4), and multiply by their length. Then divide by 144.

To estimate 12″ square ceiling tiles, increase room measurements to the nearest foot and multiply width times length. A 1% scrap factor is ample if you cut accurately. For any other size of tile divide the area by the size of one tile in square feet—by 2 for 12″ by 24″ tiles, for example.

### Ceramic Tiles

You estimate the area of the field—the part of the wall to be covered with standard tiles—and add about 3% for breakage. Order trim pieces by the linear foot, with a 5% waste factor. To estimate tiles in sheets for use on either walls or floors, divide the area by 6.25 to estimate the number of sheets 30″ square. Be sure to include special pieces, such as soap dishes and towel bars, in your order.

### Mastic

The label on each can of mastic tells you approximately how many square feet of wall or floor area you can cover with that can's contents. Follow this manufacturer's estimate in making your calculations.

### Underlayment

Estimate underlayment in the same way that you estimate subflooring. Divide the floor area of each room by 32, and that gives you the number of 4′ by 8′ sheets you will need. Multiply the floor area by 5 to estimate the number of fasteners—whether you use nails or staples.

### Resilient Tiles

As you did when you calculated your ceiling tile requirements, increase the interior dimensions of each room to the nearest whole foot. Multiply the two figures, and add one tile for each foot or partial foot of width of each doorway; this applies to 12″ tiles. With 9″ tiles you increase room sizes to the nearest greater dimension divisible by 9″. Then multiply the resultant area by 1.75, and add a tile for each 9″ of door width.

There is no need to add a scrap factor if you are laying tiles at recommended temperature conditions. If you are laying tiles in a pattern, the only way to estimate is to work from an accurate floor layout, and count the pieces of each color. You will need the layout anyway as a guide to laying the floor.

## Linoleum and Carpeting

Linoleum comes in rolls 6 ' or 12 ' wide, and you can estimate usage by determining the total length you will need of either width. Unless the pattern must match at a doorway between two rooms being covered, run the linoleum the short dimension of rooms when both dimensions are less than 12 '. Run the pattern the long dimension of rooms when one dimension is less than 12 ' and one is more. Run the pattern the shorter dimension when both room dimensions are more than 12 '. In this way you have the least amount of scrap under most circumstances. Calculate carpeting by this same method.

Just to be sure of your estimate, take an extra moment to figure the number of feet of 12 '-wide linoleum or carpet you would need if you were to run the floor covering at 90°. After you have arrived at the linear footage you would need, multiply by 12 to get the area in square feet to be covered. Then divide by 9 to convert to square yards, since linoleum and carpeting are both sold by the square yard.

## Wood Flooring

You can estimate the amount of wood block flooring in the same way as you did for floor tiles. In addition to the flooring itself, you will need nails or adhesive for application and compounds for finishing, and you should probably allow for renting a sander.

Laying a wood floor of hardwood strips or softwood boards is not a job for amateurs. For that reason this book includes no instructions. If you are experienced and want to go ahead, however, you should know the formulae for determining usage.

With hardwood flooring, first find the area of the room. Then

- with 1 × 2 or 1 × 3 flooring, increase the area by 36%, or
- with 1 × 2 1/2 flooring, increase the area by 28%.

To the total add 2 sq ft for each door opening.

With softwood flooring you must first find the width of the room in feet, since this type of flooring is always laid the long dimension of a room. Then

- for 4 "-wide boards, divide the width by 3 and multiply by 11. Add 1 board if the room is more than 12 ' wide. Or
- for 6 "-wide boards, divide the width by 3 and multiply by 7. No adjustment is required for wide rooms.

Now multiply your answer by the length of the room, increased to the next full foot. Add 3 sq ft for each door opening.

## Decking

To find the total length of 2 × 4 decking required, first determine the width of the deck. Then multiply by 2.8, and adjust your answer to the nearest whole number. Multiply this result by the length of the deck to estimate the number of linear feet required. To adjust this answer to board feet, multiply by 2/3.

### Wood Stairways

There is no special formula for estimating stairway requirements. Go back to Chapter 12 for the basic information about lengths of stringers and dimensions of treads and risers.

Treads for finished stairways are milled to a thickness of a full inch, have a rounded nosing, and are notched to accept a riser. The depth of a tread is the run of the step plus the rounded projection, which is usually about 1".

Risers are usually made of 1" *S4S* stock (smooth four sides). The height of a riser is not as great as the rise of a step, and you must rabbet the upper edge to fit into a tread. The widths of treads and risers are equal to the distance between stringers.

### Trim

Any flat boards used for trim, such as fascias, are estimated on a board foot basis. Trim that has been shaped at the mill, which is called *millwork,* is estimated by the linear foot.

For windows you will need a length of stool, a shorter length of apron, and three pieces of casing. For double-hung windows you may also need three pieces of window stop.

For exterior doors you will need a threshold and three lengths of casing. A door stop and exterior trim may or may not be furnished with the frame. With sliding doors you must order trim for both sides. Interior doors require three pieces of casing on both sides, plus three pieces of door stop.

When you calculate the lengths of casing, remember that the lengths of jamb casing extend the width of a casing beyond the head of the door or window frame on both sides. Similarly, head casings extend two casing widths beyond the opening.

Estimate ceiling cove by finding the perimeter of the wall at the ceiling line. Estimate floor base and base shoe by taking the same perimeter and deducting the widths of door openings. Determine the requirements for corner moldings and any battens for seams on a room-by-room basis.

## ESTIMATING TIME FOR FINISHING

To apply plywood paneling to a ceiling, with two people working, allow one hour for every 100 sq ft of area. Wall application goes a little faster. Working alone, you can probably put up almost 100 sq ft yourself in an hour.

Wallboard application is slower because of the weight and attachment process. A two-man team of amateurs is making good time if they can hang 90 sq ft on a ceiling in an hour, and 125 sq ft on walls. Allow one man-hour for taping each 50 ft of joint, and another man-hour for the three-step process of finishing and sanding.

If you plan to install ceiling tiles, allow about one hour to put up nailing strips and establish chalk lines for every 35 sq ft of ceiling area. You can apply about 30 sq ft of square tiles in an hour, and about 50 sq ft of rectangular tiles.

Application of ceramic tiles goes slowly. If you set individual tiles in mastic, plan on completing no more then 8 sq ft per hour, including spreading the mastic, cutting tiles, grouting and finishing joints, and cleaning up. You can complete twice that area with tiles that come in sheets on backing. Setting tiles is a job that should not be hurried, however, so allow plenty of time for it.

To nail down underlayment, 100 sq ft per hour is a good pace. To apply adhesive to the underlayment and lay resilient tiles, linoleum, or wood blocks, allow another three man-hours to cover the same area. If you are experienced in laying wood strip flooring, allow one hour for every 20 sq ft of hardwood flooring or 40 sq ft of softwood flooring.

Allow a full day to build a rough stairway for every 8′ of rise. To build a straight, finished stairway inside the house is likely to be a full three-day project. To build any type of stairway, you will need help for the first half day. After that you can work well alone.

Trimming out rooms and openings takes longer than you might expect if you've never done that type of work before. To fit window frames in their openings, as estimated earlier in this chapter, takes about 1 1/4 hours per window. To fit trim and attach hardware takes another two hours. For each door, whether interior or exterior, allow five man-hours. These time estimates are based on two men working together during the fitting and hanging process, and one man working alone on trim. To assemble the window wall in the house shown in Fig. 19–1, it would take two men a full three days, including trimming. It takes as much time to install a fixed window as it does an operable sash.

Running trim—fascias, soffits, ceiling coves, corner trim, and bases—can all be cut, fitted, and fastened at a rate of about 15 linear feet per hour. That rate applies to each type of trim. In a room 9′ by 12′ with an 8′ ceiling, one door, and trim in the corners, you would have to fit 42′ of one-piece cove, 32′ of corner trim, and 39′ each of base and base shoe. That's a total of 152′ of trim, or one mighty long day's work.

## ESTIMATING CABINETS AND SHELVING

There is no accurate way to estimate the time it may take to build cabinets and finish closet interiors. As in applying ceramic tiles, you won't do a good job unless you work slowly and make sure every piece fits properly before you attach it. If you are very careful with your measurements, you can save some overall time by building the cabinets at home in sections and carrying·them to your vacation house on one of your trips. Build countertops on the job, however. You will have to test the fit often during construction.

For finished shelving you can buy *S4S* boards in widths up to 12″ (nominal) and in various lengths. For wider shelves you may be able to find edge-jointed boards up to 24″ wide. If not, use 1/2″ plywood and trim exposed edges. If you use plywood, the only way to estimate your needs is to list the sizes of the shelving and cabinet parts you will need. Then make a cutting layout (Fig. 19–10) to make the best possible use of the raw materials. Lay out the largest or longest pieces first, and then fill in with smaller pieces.

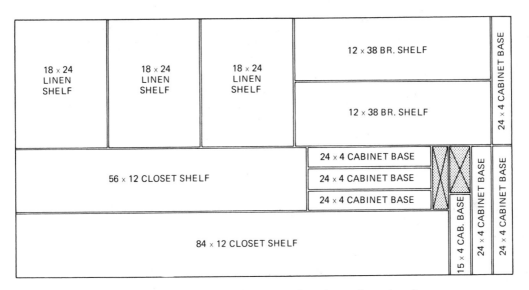

**Fig. 19-10.** When you must cut quite a few pieces of varying sizes for cabinets and shelves, make a cutting sheet like this for each type and thickness of material. The only waste here is in the two rectangles marked out with an X.

Attack the problem of cabinet parts in the same way. Aside from shelves and drawers, you will need stiles and rails, door and drawer fronts, toekicks, light framing lumber, cleats, sides, and backs. Use hardboard or 1/4″ plywood for backs and sides; clear boards for toekicks, stiles, and rails; and lower grade boards for cleats and framing. You can cut doors and drawer fronts out of plywood, but it is difficult to get smooth, good-looking edges. Edge-jointed boards are better, but more expensive. Table V at the end of this chapter will help you in estimating drawer materials.

Plastic laminate for countertops is manufactured wide enough for two 25″ widths per sheet. Here again, making an accurate layout of the countertop after base cabinets are set will help you order the length or lengths that will give you the least waste.

# ESTIMATING COATINGS

Almost any painter you talk to has his own method for estimating the number of gallons of paint or stain needed for a job. One simple and reasonably accurate way for estimating each coat on exterior materials is to determine the area to be coated and add 10% for the edges and ends of siding or shingles. The area covered by a gallon varies with the liquid and its formula, and is stated on the can's label. It ranges from about 300 sq ft for priming rough wood to 650 sq ft for a final coat on smooth wood (see Table VI).

To the wall area you must add an allowance for coating trim. For every linear foot of exterior trim less than 12″ wide, add 1 sq ft of surface per coat. On interior trim of all types allow another 1/2 sq ft of coating for every linear foot of molding.

To estimate the number of square feet to be covered at each door opening, add 2′ to the two dimensions of the door and multiply. A 3′ by 7′ door thus becomes a 5′ by 9′ door for painting purposes, with an area of 45 sq ft. Estimate coverage at windows the same way, but allow an extra 2 sq ft for each pane of glass. A 2′ 6″ by 4′ 0″ window with a single pane of glass, then, has an area of 29 sq ft for painting purposes.

# ESTIMATING FLAT CONCRETE WORK

You can estimate the volume of concrete needed for slabs, walks, and driveways in the same way you estimated concrete for footings. Wire mesh reinforcement comes in rolls 5′ wide, and the lengths must be overlapped no less than 6″. For a 20′ by 20′ parking pad, then, you would need 5 strips each 20′ long, or 100 linear feet of reinforcing mesh. Rolls are usually 150′ long.

As to labor, a dumped pile of gravel can be converted to a tamped concrete base at a rate of about 5 cu yds per day. To prepare a 6″ base for the parking pad above, you would use $\dfrac{20 \times 20 \times 1/2}{27}$, or about 7.4 cu yds of gravel. Therefore it would take you a day and a half working alone to do the job right.

Forming and other preparation takes two men about one hour for every 12 linear feet. Allow an hour for you and two helpers to mix, transport, level, and finish 50 sq ft of slab surface. With ready-mix concrete you can place and finish twice as much.

TABLE OF BOARD-FOOT CONTENT

**Length in Feet**

| Size In Inches | 8 | 10 | 12 | 14 | 16 | 18 | 20 | 22 | 24 |
|---|---|---|---|---|---|---|---|---|---|
| 1 × 2 | 1⅓ | 1⅔ | 2 | 2⅓ | 2⅔ | 3 | 3⅓ | 3⅔ | 4 |
| 1 × 3 | 2 | 2½ | 3 | 3½ | 4 | 4½ | 5 | 5½ | 6 |
| 1 × 4 | 2⅔ | 3⅓ | 4 | 4⅔ | 5⅓ | 6 | 6⅔ | 7⅓ | 8 |
| 1 × 5 | 3⅓ | 4⅙ | 5 | 5⅚ | 6⅔ | 7½ | 8⅓ | 9⅙ | 10 |
| 1 × 6 | 4 | 5 | 6 | 7 | 8 | 9 | 10 | 11 | 12 |
| 1 × 8 | 5⅓ | 6⅔ | 8 | 9⅓ | 10⅔ | 12 | 13⅓ | 14⅔ | 16 |
| 1 × 10 | 6⅔ | 8⅓ | 10 | 11⅔ | 13⅓ | 15 | 16⅔ | 18⅓ | 20 |
| 1 × 12 | 8 | 10 | 12 | 14 | 16 | 18 | 20 | 22 | 24 |
| 1 × 14 | 9⅓ | 11⅔ | 14 | 16⅓ | 18⅔ | 21 | 23⅓ | 25⅔ | 28 |
| 1 × 16 | 10⅔ | 13⅓ | 16 | 18⅔ | 21⅓ | 24 | 26⅔ | 29⅓ | 32 |
| 5/4 × 4 | 3⅓ | 4⅙ | 5 | 5⅚ | 6⅔ | 7½ | 8⅓ | 9⅙ | 10 |
| 5/4 × 6 | 5 | 6¼ | 7½ | 8¾ | 10 | 11¼ | 12½ | 13¾ | 15 |
| 5/4 × 8 | 6⅔ | 8⅓ | 10 | 11⅔ | 13⅓ | 15 | 16⅔ | 18⅓ | 20 |
| 5/4 × 10 | 8⅓ | 10⁵/₁₂ | 12½ | 14⁷/₁₂ | 16⅔ | 18¾ | 20⅚ | 22¹¹/₁₂ | 25 |
| 5/4 × 12 | 10 | 12½ | 15 | 17½ | 20 | 22½ | 25 | 27½ | 30 |
| 6/4 × 4 | 4 | 5 | 6 | 7 | 8 | 9 | 10 | 11 | 12 |
| 6/4 × 6 | 6 | 7½ | 9 | 10½ | 12 | 13½ | 15 | 16½ | 18 |
| 6/4 × 8 | 8 | 10 | 12 | 14 | 16 | 18 | 20 | 22 | 24 |
| 6/4 × 10 | 10 | 12½ | 15 | 17½ | 20 | 22½ | 25 | 27½ | 30 |
| 6/4 × 12 | 12 | 15 | 18 | 21 | 24 | 27 | 30 | 33 | 36 |
| 2 × 4 | 5⅓ | 6⅔ | 8 | 9⅓ | 10⅔ | 12 | 13⅓ | 14⅔ | 16 |
| 2 × 6 | 8 | 10 | 12 | 14 | 16 | 18 | 20 | 22 | 24 |
| 2 × 8 | 10⅔ | 13⅓ | 16 | 18⅔ | 21⅓ | 24 | 26⅔ | 29⅓ | 32 |
| 2 × 10 | 13⅓ | 16⅔ | 20 | 23⅓ | 26⅔ | 30 | 33⅓ | 36⅔ | 40 |
| 2 × 12 | 16 | 20 | 24 | 28 | 32 | 36 | 40 | 44 | 48 |
| 2 × 14 | 18⅔ | 23⅓ | 28 | 32⅔ | 37⅓ | 42 | 46⅔ | 51⅓ | 56 |

**Length in Feet**

| Size In Inches | 8 | 10 | 12 | 14 | 16 | 18 | 20 | 22 | 24 |
|---|---|---|---|---|---|---|---|---|---|
| 2 × 16 | 21⅓ | 26⅔ | 32 | 37⅓ | 42⅔ | 48 | 53⅓ | 58⅔ | 64 |
| 3 × 4 | 8 | 10 | 12 | 14 | 16 | 18 | 20 | 22 | 24 |
| 3 × 6 | 12 | 15 | 18 | 21 | 24 | 27 | 30 | 33 | 36 |
| 3 × 8 | 16 | 20 | 24 | 28 | 32 | 36 | 40 | 44 | 48 |
| 3 × 10 | 20 | 25 | 30 | 35 | 40 | 45 | 50 | 55 | 60 |
| 3 × 12 | 24 | 30 | 36 | 42 | 48 | 54 | 60 | 66 | 72 |
| 3 × 14 | 28 | 35 | 42 | 49 | 56 | 63 | 70 | 77 | 84 |
| 3 × 16 | 32 | 40 | 48 | 56 | 64 | 72 | 80 | 88 | 96 |
| 4 × 4 | 10⅔ | 13⅓ | 16 | 18⅔ | 21⅓ | 24 | 26⅔ | 29⅓ | 32 |
| 4 × 6 | 16 | 20 | 24 | 28 | 32 | 36 | 40 | 44 | 48 |
| 4 × 8 | 21⅓ | 26⅔ | 32 | 37⅓ | 42⅔ | 48 | 53⅓ | 58⅔ | 64 |
| 4 × 10 | 26⅔ | 33⅓ | 40 | 46⅔ | 53⅓ | 60 | 66⅔ | 73⅓ | 80 |
| 4 × 12 | 32 | 40 | 48 | 56 | 64 | 72 | 80 | 88 | 96 |
| 4 × 14 | 37⅓ | 46⅔ | 56 | 65⅓ | 74⅔ | 84 | 93⅓ | 102⅔ | 112 |
| 4 × 16 | 42⅔ | 53⅓ | 64 | 74⅔ | 85⅓ | 96 | 106⅔ | 117⅓ | 128 |
| 6 × 6 | 24 | 30 | 36 | 42 | 48 | 54 | 60 | 66 | 72 |
| 6 × 8 | 32 | 40 | 48 | 56 | 64 | 72 | 80 | 88 | 96 |
| 6 × 10 | 40 | 50 | 60 | 70 | 80 | 90 | 100 | 110 | 120 |
| 6 × 12 | 48 | 60 | 72 | 84 | 96 | 108 | 120 | 132 | 144 |
| 6 × 14 | 56 | 70 | 84 | 98 | 112 | 126 | 140 | 154 | 168 |
| 6 × 16 | 64 | 80 | 96 | 112 | 128 | 144 | 160 | 176 | 192 |
| 8 × 8 | 42⅔ | 53⅓ | 64 | 74⅔ | 85⅓ | 96 | 106⅔ | 117⅓ | 128 |
| 8 × 10 | 53⅓ | 66⅔ | 80 | 93⅓ | 106⅔ | 120 | 133⅓ | 146⅔ | 160 |
| 8 × 12 | 64 | 80 | 96 | 112 | 128 | 144 | 160 | 176 | 192 |

**TABLE I.** To determine the board footage of any wood member, find its nominal size in inches in the left-hand column and read across until you come to the length of your member in feet. The figure in the box is its square footage. Example: a 2 × 8 rafter 20′ long contains 26 2/3 b.f.

| CONVERTING LINEAR FEET TO BOARD FEET | |
|---|---|
| Size | Formula Used to Obtain Board Feet |
| 1" x 3" | Divide linear feet by 4 |
| 1" x 4" | Divide linear feet by 3 |
| 1" x 6" | Divide linear feet by 2 |
| 1" x 8" | Multiply linear feet by 2 and divide by 3 |
| 1" x 10" | Multiply linear feet by 10 and divide by 12 |
| 1" x 12" | Linear feet and board feet are the same |
| 2" x 3" | Divide linear feet by 2 |
| 2" x 4" | Multiply linear feet by 2 and divide by 3 |
| 2" x 6" | Linear and board feet are the same |
| 2" x 8" | Multiply linear feet by 4 and divide by 3 |
| 2" x 10" | Multiply linear feet by 10 and divide by 6 |
| 2" x 12" | Multiply linear feet by 2 |
| 3" x 8" | Multiply linear feet by 2 |
| 3" x 10" | Multiply linear feet by 10 and divide by 4 |
| 4" x 4" | Multiply linear feet by 4 and divide by 3 |
| 4" x 6" | Multiply linear feet by 2 |
| 4" x 8" | Multiply linear feet by 8 and divide by 3 |
| 4" x 10" | Multiply linear feet by 10 and divide by 3 |
| 4" x 12" | Multiply linear feet by 4 |
| 8" x 8" | Multiply linear feet by 16 and divide by 3 |
| 10" x 10" | Multiply linear feet by 100 and divide by 12 |
| 12" x 12" | Multiply linear feet by 12 |

**TABLE II.** If you know the size of the wood members, and the total length needed of that size, use the formula in the right-hand column to determine board footage. This table is useful when you have a lot of short pieces, say of 2 × 4s, and you need to estimate cumulative usage.

TABLE OF ROOF AREA FACTORS
(For Computing Roof Areas
From Working Drawings)

| Rise | Factor | Rise | Factor |
|---|---|---|---|
| 3" | 1.031 | 8" | 1.202 |
| $3\frac{1}{2}$" | 1.042 | $8\frac{1}{2}$" | 1.225 |
| 4" | 1.054 | 9" | 1.250 |
| $4\frac{1}{2}$" | 1.068 | $9\frac{1}{2}$" | 1.275 |
| 5" | 1.083 | 10" | 1.302 |
| $5\frac{1}{2}$" | 1.100 | $10\frac{1}{2}$" | 1.329 |
| 6" | 1.118 | 11" | 1.357 |
| $6\frac{1}{2}$" | 1.137 | $11\frac{1}{2}$" | 1.385 |
| 7" | 1.158 | 12" | 1.414 |
| $7\frac{1}{2}$" | 1.179 | | |

**TABLE III.** You can use this roof area table in two ways. If you know the pitch of a roof and its run, you can find the length of a common rafter. Say the pitch is 3 1/2 in 12, and the run is 15. Use 1.042 as a factor times the run, and rafter length is 15.63'. You can use the same principle for estimating quantities of roofing sheathing and shingles.

TABLE IV. Nail usage will vary from one carpenter to the next, but the figures shown here are good averages for a handy amateur. M in the description stands for 1,000, and C stands for 100.

| TYPES AND QUANTITIES OF NAILS FOR WOOD FRAMING | | | |
|---|---|---|---|
| Job and Material Description | | Nail Size | No. Lbs. |
| Joists and rafters — 2″ x 6″ | per M bd. ft. | 16d com. | 7.0 |
| Joists and rafters — 2″ x 8″ | per M bd. ft. | 16d com. | 5.2 |
| Joists — 2″ x 10″ | per M bd. ft. | 16d com. | 4.3 |
| Joists — 2″ x 12″ | per M bd. ft. | 16d com. | 3.5 |
| Studding — 2″ x 4″ | per M bd. ft. | 16d com. | 10.0 |
| Bridging — 1″ x 3″ | per 20 sets | 6d com. | 1.0 |
| Sheathing — 1″ x 4″ | per 20 sets | 8d com. | 30.0 |
| Sheathing — 1″ x 6″ | per 20 sets | 8d com. | 25.0 |
| Subflooring — 3/4″ plywood | per C sq. ft. | 8d com. | 2.5 |
| Sheathing — 3/4″ plywood | per C sq. ft. | 8d com. | 2.6 |

| DRAWER SIZES | | | LUMBER FOOTAGE |
|---|---|---|---|
| Width | Run | Depth | Board Feet |
| 12″ | 24″ | 11″ | 8 |
| 15″ | 24″ | 3½″ | 5 |
| | | 4½″ | 6 |
| | | 5½″ | 7 |
| | | 7¼″ | 8 |
| | | 9″ | 9 |
| | | 11″ | 10 |
| 18″ | 18″ | 3½″ | 5 |
| | | 4½″ | 5 |
| | | 5½″ | 6 |
| | | 7¼″ | 7 |
| | | 9″ | 8 |
| | | 11″ | 9 |
| 24″ | 24″ | 3½″ | 7 |
| | | 4½″ | 8 |
| | | 5½″ | 8 |
| | | 7¼″ | 10 |
| | | 9″ | 11 |
| | | 11″ | 12 |
| 36″ | 24″ | 5½″ | 11 |
| | | 7¼″ | 13 |
| | | 9″ | 15 |
| | | 11″ | 16 |
| 36″ | 36″ | 7¼″ | 17 |

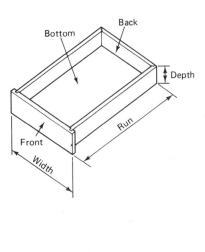

TABLE V. Although you can build drawers out of plywood, hardboard, and lumber, the best and most durable drawers are built of 1″ lumber stock. This table shows how to calculate board footage per drawer. For example, a drawer 15″ wide, with a run of 24″ and a depth of 5 1/2″, contains 7 board feet of 1″ lumber, including the drawer bottom.

| APPROXIMATE COVERAGES ON VARIOUS SURFACES | | LABOR REQUIREMENTS FOR VARIOUS TYPES OF WORK | |
|---|---|---|---|
| Surfaced to be Covered | Covering Capacity | Painting—Type of Work | Hours per 100 sq. ft. |
| Prime coat — smooth wood or wallboard | 400 to 450 sq. ft. per gal. | Priming wallboard or woodwork | ½ hr. |
| Prime coat — rough wood or brick | 300 to 400 sq. ft. per gal. | 2nd and 3rd coats, each coat | ½ hr. |
| | | Filling nail holes and sanding trim | 1½ hrs. |
| Second and third coats | 550 to 650 sq. ft. per gal. | Priming trim | 1 hr. |
| Wood stains | 400 to 500 sq. ft. per gal. | 2nd and 3rd coats, each coat | ½ hr. |
| Wood fillers | 300 to 330 sq. ft. per gal. | Staining, varnishing, or enameling trim | 1 hr. |
| Shellac and varnish | 550 to 650 sq. ft. per gal. | Filling hardwood floors | ¾ hr. |
| Shingles — dip stained | 350 to 400 shingles per gal. | Varnishing floors, each coat | ½ hr. |

**TABLE VI.** These two tables combined will help you estimate how much paint you will need to finish various surfaces, and how long it takes the average painter to do the job.

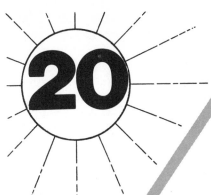

# Protecting

# Your Investment

Although the main reason you build a vacation house is for the pleasure and relaxation it brings you, it is nevertheless an investment. And, like any other investment, you must protect it. You need to be prepared in case of fire. You need insurance coverage. You need to protect the house through a planned closing and opening procedure at the end and beginning of the vacation season. And you need to follow a program of regular maintenance.

## PREVENTING FIRES

The first and most important step in fire protection is prevention. If you do your own electrical wiring, have the building inspector or a local electrician check your work before it is hidden behind finished wall and ceiling materials. If you hire an electrical contractor, get from him the wiring load on each circuit in the fuse box or breaker panel. Write down—or better still, memorize—what outlets and appliances are on which circuit. And stay within load limits! The most common cause of fires is overloaded electrical circuits.

If you burn gas for cooking or heating, study the diagrams provided by the manufacturer of each appliance. The owner's manual or instruction sheet tells you clearly how to operate the equipment, how to maintain it, and what to do in an emergency. Everyone in your family who uses gas-fired equipment should know the rules for using that equipment.

Have an adequate supply of ashtrays where they are likely to be needed. Even if you don't smoke, some of your guests will. Set out the type of ashtray that has grooves sloping inward, so that lighted cigarettes won't fall out. Even better is the type with metal grips to hold lighted cigarettes while the smoker's hands are busy at something else. When the cigarette burns down to the metal, the metal absorbs the heat and the cigarette goes out. Store matches and all types of lighters high above the reach of small children.

When you burn anything in a fireplace, either stay in the room and keep an eye on the fire, or use a screen that will contain sparks and hot ashes within the confines of the hearth. Use a fireplace only as a fireplace, never as an incinerator. Flaming papers and hot ashes may rise up the chimney and start a fire outdoors.

Find out before you move in what local ordinances govern the burning or disposal of trash. If outdoor burning is permitted, use an incinerator approved by the local fire department. Even if their approval isn't required, this is a good public relations gesture if you ever do need their help in a hurry. Burn only with the lid on or the door closed. Set the incinerator in an area you have cleared 10 ' in every direction, including upward.

If you build in a part of the country where brush and grass fires are common in the dry season, clear a fire break to stop the spread of someone else's fire before it reaches your house and any other buildings. The ground doesn't have to be bare. Several varieties of low-growing plants resist fire, particularly if you keep them properly irrigated. Ask the local nurseryman what he recommends for your particular site and circumstances.

## FIGHTING FIRES

In established vacation communities there is often a well-organized fire department, usually manned by volunteers. In season, volunteers are plentiful and service is good. Out of season, when a fire is likely to be well under way before it is discovered, the service may not be adequate.

If you build in a protected fire district, invite the fire chief to visit you so that he knows the lay of the land. By becoming familiar with your particular site and conditions, he can be ready to move quickly in an emergency, and know in advance what to expect. He can recommend the auxiliary water supply you should have for adequate protection.

The fire chief will make sure that you have your name and address, or some sort of identification, at the entrance to your driveway or access road. He will test your road to see whether he can get in and out with his equipment. He will want to know the source of water, if any, and the amount of flow.

Most wells and springs provide only enough water for an auxiliary supply, and not enough to fight a fire. Even water mains in many established but unincorporated communities are often inadequate for fire fighting. If the cost of adequate protection is too great for you to finance alone, investigate the possibility of cooperative action on a central supply with nearby neighbors.

## BUYING INSURANCE

The most important insurance protection you can have is against fire from any cause, including lightning. The rates vary considerably from one location to another. Each fire protection system is rated, and its rating determines the basic cost of fire insurance. The rating is predicated on the community's or area's fire alarm system, the size and capacity of fire-fighting equipment, the department's permanent and volunteer manpower, and the availability of water in unincorporated areas.

Another factor in rate variation is type of construction. A frame house costs more to insure than a masonry house. A house built on piers usually costs more to insure than one on a continuous foundation. The resistance to flame spread of the surface materials inside the house also has a bearing on your insurance rate.

A simple fire insurance policy is relatively inexpensive. A little more expensive, but a better policy, is fire and extended coverage. This type of policy insures you against loss from fire. It also covers you against direct loss from weather—wind, hail, snow, sleet, and ice. It further covers you against indirect loss from weather—broken glass, fallen limbs, blowing sand, and freezeups.

You can buy an even more comprehensive policy that insures you against vandalism and malicious mischief. The more limited fire and extended coverage policy is usually available with or without a $50 or $100 deductible clause. The comprehensive policy is available only with deductibles.

It pays to shop around for insurance. The chances are, however, that your best bet will be with the company that insures your house back home. Often the least expensive way to insure your vacation house is with an endorsement on your regular home insurance policy. The lower rates also apply to an extension of your home personal liability policy if it is separate. Liability coverage is well worth the cost, especially if you expect to have frequent guests.

## USING YOUR HOME FOR THE FIRST TIME

When you move into a new home built by a contractor, there is a specific date of first use. By that time you should have checked out all systems for proper operation, before you release the contractor from further obligation.

When you build your own home, that "first use" goes on over a period of time as work is completed. As each phase of your work was finished, you should have already checked out the operation of the fireplace, the chimney and other exhaust systems, the power supply system, the fuel system for any central heat, and the septic system.

If you are getting your water from a well, you have one other major check remaining: to disinfect the water system. No matter how carefully a well is drilled, it is still necessary to disinfect the system to kill any bacteria resulting from construction.

The procedure has five simple steps:

1. Into the well pour a gallon of chlorine bleach or its equivalent strength in calcium chloride tablets.

2. Connect a hose to the pump, and let the water run until you smell chlorine.

3. With the hose, flush the well casing and wash off the well cap. Disconnect the hose.

4. Open every water tap in the house one by one until you smell chlorine. Then close each tap. While the chlorine is in the water system, do not use any water.

5. After 12 hours have passed, open all taps and let the water run until the smell of chlorine is gone. Your water supply is now safe to use.

## CLOSING THE HOUSE AT THE END OF THE SEASON

The only way to protect your vacation house in the off season is to close it up tight. There are three basic rules for closing a house for the winter or any long period of time:

1. Completely shut down all utilities.

2. Leave nothing around to attract invaders, whether they are four-legged, two-legged, crawling, or winged.

3. If you must leave anything attractive, make it as inaccessible as possible.

There is no special order of procedure for closing a house. Developing a check list of what has to be done, however, makes the task a lot easier and more thorough. List the steps at the left of the sheet, then add columns in which you place a check every time you leave the house for a prolonged time. Here are the important items that should be on your check list.

### Outdoors

Leave nothing loose. If it isn't anchored down or built in, store it. Pull rafts and floats out of the water, and store them where they won't be touched by high water or thieves. Bring all outdoor furniture into the house. Empty the incinerator into a trash bag, and store the incinerator out of sight.

Climb onto the roof and cover all flues against entry by birds. Some sizes of cans will fit tightly over vents and flues. As an alternative, you can wire-tie aluminum foil as a cap. A termite shield is a good deterrent to rodents interested in eating their way into the house.

Remove screens from windows and doors. Covering windows with plastic affords some protection, but wood covers are better protection against wind and robbery. Build covers of plywood reinforced with wood or metal to prevent warping. Fit them tightly into window openings, and hold them in place near the corners with thumb latches.

As a final exterior step, coat all hardware with a light film of grease to prevent rusting.

### Indoors

Remove all food. If you plan to use the house on weekends, and want to leave some supplies behind, store them in a metal-lined box or in canisters with screw tops. The containers must be sealed tightly to protect their contents against both rodents and mildew.

Clean out the refrigerator, wash it thoroughly inside, and leave the door ajar for air circulation. Scrub the range to remove all accumulations of grease. Rodents love it. If you have a range hood, remove and wash the filter, and clean the inside of the hood at the same time. Store candles and soaps in metal containers with lids. Do not leave cereals; weevils will get into them in spite of almost any precaution. Either pour out all liquids or take them with you.

Empty and wash out drawers and cabinets. Leave doors and drawers ajar to permit air circulation. Store bedding in a metal-lined chest, or enclose it in moisture-proof plastic bags. Roll up rugs and store them across chairs above floor level to prevent mildew. Close draperies if you don't protect windows with wood covers. Otherwise, close them only part way so that air can circulate around them.

Shut the fireplace damper, and close foundation vents. Then wax and polish floors to protect them against moisture.

### Utilities

Shut off a municipal water supply at the main valve. If your water system has a drain valve (and it is worth installing), open the valve and give the system time to drain completely. If you have no drain valve, shut off the water and open every faucet to let the water drain out of the pipes.

Flush all toilets, and pour a little antifreeze into the bowls. Pour antifreeze also into each drain to prevent water from freezing in the traps and bursting them.

Drain the water heater, any water softener, and any water-connected appliances, such as the icemaking attachment to a refrigerator.

To close down a well-water supply system, begin by disconnecting the pump. This allows the system to drain. Then, as with a city water system, open all taps, flush toilets, add antifreeze, and drain appliances.

Unless you want to keep some heat in the house during short absences, such as between weekends, turn the thermostat all the way down. If you burn LP gas, close the valves at all appliances, plus the main valve at the tank. If you burn natural gas, shut down all appliances to pilot light operation, according to instructions provided by the appliance manufacturer. If you have any doubts about what to do, talk with your gas supplier, or ask him to shut down the system for you.

Shut off electricity at the service entrance panel, either by throwing the main breaker or disconnecting the main fuse. If you must maintain power to some appliance during a short absence, throw breakers or disconnect fuses for all circuits not in use. Then unplug all lamps and other appliances on the remaining live circuit.

Be sure to cut off all delivery and pick-up services, such as newspaper, mail, and garbage.

## OPENING UP AT THE START OF THE SEASON

It takes almost as long to open up a vacation house as it does to close one down, but the work seems to go much more quickly. The first step, which is easy to forget, is to bring a rag with you to wipe off the grease on the door knob, so that you don't get everything else you touch greasy.

If you are like most owners of vacation houses, you and your family will get the itch to open up the house on the first nice weekend of spring. At that time the house will be much cooler inside than the air outside. So the first few procedures are to open up draperies, remove window covers, uncover flues and vent pipes, and get some heat in the place. If you start a fire in the fireplace, remember to open the damper. Build a hot fire of crumpled paper to move the stack of cold air out of the chimney. Otherwise a log fire will smoke badly until the flue begins to draw properly.

If you have a warm-air heating system, turn on the furnace for a little while even if you don't need the heat. The circulation of warm air will remove moisture and dust that have accumulated in ducts.

You open up a house in approximately the reverse order of closing. Get all utilities in operation first before you begin unpacking. To activate a gas system, open the main valve while all the other valves at individual appliances remain closed. Then light appliances one at a time to make sure that gas is reaching them properly. Natural gas has an odor, and LP gas has an odorizer added so that you can smell gas if you have a leak. Never use an open flame to test for a leak. If you suspect a problem at a connection, mix a solution of soapy water and coat the connection. Wherever there is a leak, the gas will blow bubbles in the soapy water.

Unless something abnormal has happened in your absence, such as high water that might have affected the purity of your well water, you should not have to disinfect the system again. Let the water run for a minute or so at each tap, however, to wash out rust and residue until the water is clear and cold.

# MAINTAINING YOUR VACATION HOUSE

The opening-up weekend is the ideal time to run a maintenance check. Begin with the furnace. Clean the blower and squirrel-cage cover. If they become clogged with dirt or lint, the blower motor can burn out. Change the air filter, or wash it with a mild detergent and water. Oil the blower according to the manufacturer's instructions. Too much oil is as bad as too little. Check gas orifices for signs of pitting. Replace all worn parts promptly.

If you have an electric water heater, be sure to let the tank fill with water before you turn on the power. Otherwise you may burn out the heating element.

After you have opened the main water valve, go over the entire piping system for signs of leaks. Ruptured pipes and traps must be replaced. Most small leaks can be stopped with a joint-sealing compound.

While you are on the roof removing flue caps, walk lightly over the entire surface. Look for damage from fallen branches, cracks in shingles, and turned-up corners. Unless the air and roof are warm, delay repairs. By trying to repair a roof in cool weather, you may make the problem worse instead of better.

Make shingle repairs with roofing cement and a putty knife. To seal down raised corners, place a dab of cement on the underside of the shingle, and press down firmly to spread the cement. To close cracks, seal the exposed side of the shingle with a narrow line of cement, and then coat the underside with a wider band of cement to prevent the crack from spreading.

Remove the season's accumulation of twigs, leaves, and pine needles from gutters. Then run a good stream of water from a hose down the gutters to check for leaks, and to blow clear all downspouts. To close leaking cracks at joints in the gutters you can use either roofing cement or putty.

As you clean off the grease from exposed hardware on doors and windows, check their operation. Tighten screws that may have worked loose. Reset loose hinge pins and, with a little oil or powdered graphite, lubricate all working parts. Examine the caulking around door and window frames, and recaulk wherever you find pockets or even hairline cracks.

Scan exterior walls carefully for loose nails, signs of rust or staining, or cracks. Reset or replace loose nails, fill holes and cracks with wood putty, and seal nailheads against bleeding.

With well-chosen and properly applied exterior materials you won't have much maintenance for the first five years or so. But by catching incipient problems before they develop into larger ones, you prevent a buildup of maintenance work that can kill most of one year's vacation.

Interior care of a vacation house is no different than maintenance of a year-round house. If you selected materials for durability and ease of maintenance, a good cleaning and waxing on a regular basis is all that is normally needed. Let the old saying, brought up to date, be your guide: a gram of prevention is worth a kilogram of cure.

Have fun!

# Index